ELEMENTS

OF

MORAL PHILOSOPHY;

ANALYTICAL,

SYNTHETICAL, AND PRACTICAL.

BY

HUBBARD WINSLOW,

AUTHOR OF INTELLECTUAL PHILOSOPHY.

NEW YORK:
D. APPLETON AND COMPANY.
LONDON: 16 LITTLE BRITAIN.
1856.

PREFACE.

THE cause of morals has its stronghold in man's innate consciousness of responsibility. Mammon is enshrined in his lust of gain, power in his pride of dominion, fame in his thirst of applause, and pleasure in his sensual desire; hence the dependence of all these is capricious, and their rewards are at the best transient; while morality reposes, with calm and eternal assurance, in his imperishable conviction that he is responsible for his conduct. Against this conviction infidelity arrays its arguments, and vice hurls its scorn in vain.

Morality, as a *science*, is so implicated with psychology, that it cannot be erected symmetrical and entire without its aid; but as a *practice*, it can rise without that aid even to its culmen. No systematic psychology is taught in the Bible, yet the highest practical morality is taught there. Metaphysics and logic are also of service in the erection and defence of its outposts, especially "when Greek meets Greek;" but, unless obedient to the high behests of consciousness, they become little else than troublesome cobwebs. The feeble and the unwary are frequently caught in their meshes, but the snare is at length broken and the victims escape.

It seems to have been a prevailing error of the theorizing moralist, that, instead of taking his stand-point directly and centrally in man's consciousness of freedom and accountability, and making metaphysics and logic subservient to him in that position, he has first entrenched himself behind metaphysical speculations and logical deductions, and then called upon consciousness to yield to their requirements. He has thus given the dominion to the wrong master; he has placed his cause in the wrong hands. In the gossamery subtleties of speculative and transcendental metaphysics, the learned Brahmans of India excel all other philosophers; they even out-German the Germans. Yet we find little in Brahminical lore that is truthful and actual; little that renders man really wiser and better.

The general nature of the present work may be hence anticipated by the reader. It is throughout a direct and confiding appeal to his conscious sense of accountability. It presents to him no wire-drawn arguments, no metaphysical subtleties, and no complicated deductions of logic. Its proofs are mostly *statements* of undeniable truths, sometimes attended with illustration, and confidently submitted to his practical judgment and conscience.

It is because the central law of conviction and belief is essentially the same in all minds, and because all men are endowed with a consciousness of moral obligation, that the Bible, although written at different periods and in every variety of composition and style, is reasonably addressed to all classes alike ; that it has demonstrated its power to withstand every assault, and with firm and yet firmer voice, as time rolls along, continues to challenge the undoubting homage of the world. As the present volume is restricted within the legitimate limits of moral science, it does not profess to teach religion ; yet whatever philosophy it teaches, if true, must *harmonize* with religious truth. If, then, our philosophy shall be found at variance with the Bible, or shall tend to mystify and enfeeble its plain and nervous demands upon every heart and conscience, it will deservedly come to naught, with all other "philosophy falsely so called."

It will be the author's humble endeavor to disintegrate and define the materials for the work in hand, to eliminate the principles by which to arrange them, and to reconstruct them in a system of scientific and practical morality, without embarrassing the reader with conflicting theories and speculations, but by a direct "manifestation of the truth, commending" it "to every man's conscience in the sight of God." The apostles commended themselves to the consciences of men, not less by the directness of their appeals than by the purity of their lives.

This volume was promised by the writer, some years since, in the preface of his Intellectual Philosophy. Contrary to his intention, that volume has passed through several editions without its promised accompaniment.

The delay has been occasioned by his ill health and absence in Europe, and his desire to make the book as worthy of the public as possible. So grave and difficult a work could not be safely hurried. Great consideration was due to the many able writers upon this subject. No pains have been spared to examine them in their own languages, at least upon all doubtful or critical points, and to give due weight to their various reasonings and opinions.

Having thus bestowed upon the work much careful thought and research, more than is obvious to persons not conversant with studies of this nature, the author now respectfully submits it to teachers, students, and all thoughtful inquirers after truth and duty, with the hope that it may meet their approbation, and may contribute something towards assisting the reader to understand and to fulfil his responsible mission.

That the young reader especially, whose life is still mostly in prospect, whether hastening to the calls of business and of domestic care, or aspiring to the higher walks of literature and of the learned professions, may not, by a perversion or neglect of his powers and opportunities, allow that existence to sink into an essentially grovelling and worthless affair, which he ought to make sublime and glorious, is the earnest desire and prayer of his very sincere friend,

THE AUTHOR.

CONTENTS.

PART III.

MORAL ACTION.

PART IV.

PRINCIPLES.

I. NATURAL PRINCIPLES OF MORALITY.

II. REVEALED PRINCIPLES OF MORALITY.

PART V.

THE CODE OF DUTIES.

INTRODUCTION.

Between most of the learned books of moral philosophy and the popular mind there is a great chasm. The same is true of the searching reviews of them in the Quarterlies and Monthlies. Instructive and interesting to those conversant with philosophical speculations, to all others they are in a great measure unintelligible. This volume is not designed to take the place of any of these, but to assist the student to understand them, and to benefit the general reader.

Although the writer has carefully examined the most important works accessible upon this subject, and has endeavored to secure all available advantage from them, he has yet ventured upon a plan of analysis and arrangement, mostly original. His object has been to avoid giving undue prominence to disputed points, which are often really least important, and to present the entire subject, with its just proportions, in a clearly practical light, and as related to Christianity, in a way to bring it within the apprehension of the attentive popular reader, as well as the student. He has, with the same view, written in a simple but free style, sometimes expanding and repeating the thoughts and placing them in various lights, for their greater elucidation and enforcement.

But it is hoped the reader will not identify simplicity of

language with shallowness of thought. Few tasks are easier, on subjects like the one in hand, than that of introducing strange words, learned quotations, and mysterious arguments; thus challenging a claim to erudition and to depth of thought, while confounding the student with the jargon of the schools.

The physician's learned and mysterious prescription becomes a very obvious affair, when put in plain language. It respects perhaps a common herb in your yard or garret, whose properties your grandmother knew before the learned doctor was born. This however does not alter the nature or diminish the value of the remedy. So it is with philosophy. The chasm between the learned and the ignorant is often more in the language than in the thought.

On some important points the writer's views will be seen to differ from those of authors, whose opinions it may seem presumptuous to question. But he could conscientiously do no less than frankly express his own views, giving his reasons for them, and leaving the candid reader to judge of their correctness. The particular points referred to, have respect to the precise nature and functions of the rational motive powers, especially the conscience; the origin and quality of certain malevolent affections and desires; the source of the moral quality of actions; the first ideas or principles of morality; and the groundwork and limits of human accountability. On all these points profound and earnest inquiries have been often raised, and to these the reader's careful attention is particularly solicited.

Our general subject is divided into Five Parts. In the First, we distinguish between the intellective and the motive powers, and between human actions as natural or moral. In the Second, we examine the nature and functions of the rational motive powers. In the Third, we distinguish between moral actions as right or wrong. In the Fourth, we investigate the principles of morality. In the Fifth, we expound the code of human duties.

The two leading schools of philosophy are the transcendental and the phenomenal. Of the former are Leibnitz, Kant, Schelling, Fichte, Hegel, Cousin, and most of the other Continental writers, together with Cudworth, Coleridge, Morelle and others in England and in America. Of the latter are most of the English and Scotch philosophers, of whom Sir William Hamilton is perhaps at present the most able champion.

The former school speculate ontologically upon the absolute and the infinite, regarding all inquiry respecting the mere phenomenal as "dirt philosophy." They distinguish between the reason and the understanding, *Vernumft und Verstand*, considering the former that sublime faculty by which we transcend the phenomenal universe, and directly possess unconditioned and absolute ideas; and regarding the latter faculty as that by which, through the bodily senses and a discursive process, we obtain those ideas which are conditioned in nature. The "reason" is considered generic to the race, the "image of God" in man, and that by virtue of which man sees truths to some extent as God does, and is therefore a revelation to himself. Hence this philosophy is primarily and intensely subjective, and hence the tendency of all its advocates, from Leibnitz to Carlyle, to exalt human reason above divine revelation and to substitute man-worship for God-worship.

The latter school maintain, that it is only by the study of the phenomenal universe, aided by express revelation from God, that we obtain any just and positive ideas of what transcends it. They consider reason, as understood by the other school, an intuitive faculty, but suppose that our intuitive ideas, like all others, are not innate but acquired, and are first apprehended not in the abstract but in the concrete. Through the study of the phenomenal we ascend with conditioned and positive ideas to the limits of human knowledge, whence we look off upon the illimitable and awful unknown, learning thence only our ignorance.

God himself is transcendent, absolute, infinite; seen only by the eye of faith; known only as the I AM, whom no mortal can know, excepting in his works. He is above the phenomenal universe and gives rise to it. Whatever be the powers of the "reason" in man, they are not infinite; hence no human reason can comprehend God; for the finite cannot comprehend the infinite. By studying his two great revelations, his works and his word, we are enabled to know something of him, enough for our present mode of being; but "who by searching can find out God?"

If we are liable to be unduly fascinated with the bold and splendid speculations of the Continental philosophers, we may be equally liable to do them injustice. Our language, our institutions, our intellectual training and habits of thinking, are so unlike theirs, that we often find ourselves compelled to be in just doubt whether we apprehend their real meaning. To quote and comment upon detached portions of their writings, without a more prolonged and earnest study of them, in their own language and under their own teaching, than is often given, amounts to little else than a pedantic show of learning, unjust to them, and profitless to the reader. But after making due allowance for these causes and for national prejudice, we are constrained to think, that with all their subtlety of intellect and brilliancy of imagination, they do not appear to best advantage in mental science.

For clearness, precision, and beauty of language; for exact analyses in the physical sciences; for minuteness and correctness of detail in natural history; for every form of sensuous and social culture that directly tends to embellish life; the French are unrivalled. While for richness, freedom, and pathos of language; for patient plodding in study, and bold daring in speculation; for abounding and successful endeavors in the great field of hermeneutics; and for the heaven-winged poetry of fearless and glowing imagination; the Germans are pre-eminent.

But for thorough practical common sense in the great business of life; for the successful investigation of the principles which underlie all science; for severe and exacting logic, as applied to solving the problem of human destiny; for apprehending the true nature and end of all governments, especially of that which respects man as an accountable and immortal being; we fall back upon the strong, clear, Anglo-Saxon intellect as the most reliable.

Although the author has endeavored to render the subject as

plain as possible, readers must not presume that any effort of his can exonerate *them* from the necessity of earnest and patient thought. Every person must "*think* on these things," if he would understand them. And they are truly *worthy* of his most laborious thought. "Happy is the man that findeth *wisdom*; the merchandise of it is better than the merchandise of silver, and the gain thereof than fine gold. She is more precious than rubies, and all the things thou canst desire are not to be compared with her." This "wisdom" of such priceless value, is the practical knowledge of the truths and duties herein discussed.

The public mind is so preoccupied with more exciting and fascinating topics, that it is with no expectation of temporal gain that the writer adventures before the public upon a subject like this. But if any thing is successfully done towards promoting an interest in this kind of study, towards making plain the path of duty, towards guiding and encouraging fellow beings to secure the great object of life, it will be remembered with inexpressible gratitude when all earthly considerations shall have passed away.

It is greatly to be desired that the reading public have their attention directed more than it is to studies of this nature; and especially that educational institutions give them more prominence. The thought of the age is projected outward. Natural sciences, practical arts, languages, history, with works of imagination, are the absorbing subjects. These are important. They elevate and refine humanity, but they cannot save it.

If *duty* is neglected, *all is lost!* However great and splendid his other attainments, without the "wisdom" to which we have referred, man is in a perilled and miserable condition. It is only as he obtains this wisdom, and sacredly holds it as the treasure of his heart, that his present existence is rendered safe and happy, and that he can see his way clearly onward into the everlasting ages.

MORAL PHILOSOPHY.

Moral Philosophy is the science which treats of our responsibilities and duties. It investigates the principles of morality, as they exist of necessity, or in the nature of things; and also as they are involved in positive institutions claiming to be obligatory.

It neither assumes nor ignores the truth of any particular religion. It subjects religious claims to the same ordeal to which it does all others. It is, hence, the rational pioneer to an enlightened religious faith. It goes everywhere with the inquiry, What is morally right?

Not that we must be philosophical before we can be religious. A devout spirit is the duty of even the most untaught, and is an important aid in all inquiries after truth and duty. We must not wait until we can philosophize upon food before we eat; some experience of effects must precede searching inquiry into causes. Neither should we wait to learn all the grounds and reasons of duty, before doing what we already know to be right.

Christianity, although proved to be divine, does not make us accountable beings. It assumes that we *are* such; that is, it assumes what philosophy teaches. It builds upon necessary and fundamental truths. Our obligations are enhanced by it; but they originate in our moral constitution, as related to essential and everlasting laws.

Moral Philosophy investigates, also, the springs of human conduct; distinguishes between actions as natural or moral, and between moral actions as right or wrong; and subjects all its teachings to an order or nexus, so as to embrace them in a harmonious system.

Our subject is naturally divided into Five Parts. We are to examine

I.—The Natural Motive Powers.
II.—The Rational Motive Powers.
III.—Moral Action.
IV.—The Ppinciples of Morality.
V.—The Code of Duties.

PART I.

THE NATURAL MOTIVE POWERS.

CHAPTER I.

THE MENTAL POWERS AND EXERCISES DISTINGUISHED.

THE mental faculties are divisible into two generic classes: the *intellective* and the *motive*. The former are the *knowing* faculties; or those by direct virtue of which we *know*.* The latter are the *moving* faculties; or those by direct virtue of which we *act*. The philosophical refinement which would merge these two classes into one, and consider a feeling only a vivid idea, is beyond our comprehension, and is so much aside from the practical judgment of mankind as to be of no importance in this connection.

Both of these classes of mental powers, however, are active; but their activities are of different kinds. The activity of the former is *speculative*; finding its end in

* The terms *intellective* and *intellect* are used in this work to denote *all* the knowing powers both of reason and sense.

knowledge. The activity of the latter is *practical;* finding its end in action. An examination of the former belongs to Intellectual Philosophy; that of the latter, to Moral Philosophy.

As all responsible action is directly predicable of the latter, they are often called *moral* powers. But they have also important functions which involve no moral quality. Dugald Stewart calls them *active* powers. But the powers of intellect, as we have said, are also active, although in a different way.

THE TERMS POWER AND FACULTY.

We use the terms *power* and *faculty* as synonymous, and, in accordance with established usage, to indicate what is strictly a *state* or *exercise* of mind, as well as a constitutional ability. A desire or volition is a power, because in virtue of it we are induced to act. In the same view we also call it a motive. But the power to desire or to choose, sustains, of course, some relation of cause to the desire or choice, and lies back of it in the mental constitution. The terms in question are applied to both, but the reader will easily see by the connection to which they refer.

VARIOUS TERMS APPLIED TO THE MOTIVE POWERS.

The motive powers are variously named, according to the particular relations or functions contemplated.

When viewed as making us recipients of impressions, they are called *susceptibilities;* from the Latin *suscipio*, to receive. When regarded as rendering us propense, or inclined to certain actions, they are called *propensities;* from the Latin *propendo*, to incline.

When considered as urgently inciting us to act, they are termed *impulses;* from the latin *impello*, to impel.

In their more common states, they are simply termed *motives;* from the Latin *moveo*, to move.

Considered in the mere relation of moving powers analogous to those of nature, they are called the mind's *dynamics;* from the Greek δυναμις, power.

Viewed in all their relations, both to the individual himself and to others, as the centre and source of good and evil, they are in the Bible termed *the heart;* * a word of Saxon origin and familiar to all.

For the sake of convenience and for the want of a better term, we designate all this class of faculties by the general name Motive Powers. We are obliged to borrow terms from nature; but it must be clearly understood that we are not passively moved by these powers, as effects are produced by causes in nature. The mental dynamics are not of this kind. It is the *man* that wills, moves, acts; these powers do not of themselves will him, move him, act him. They are merely the subjective motives, with regard to which *he* acts. Thus when we say that a man's desire of office moves him to seek it, we only mean that it is from a regard to this desire that *he* moves to seek the office. Not any or all of his motives, but the man himself, desiring, willing, acting, is the efficient and responsible agent. The motive is the man's and not the man the motive's.

THE MOTIVE POWERS OF TWO KINDS.

Our motive powers, like the intellective, are of two kinds, those which the brute creation share with us, in some humble degree, and those which are possessed exclu-

* See Matt. 15: 9.

sively by accountable beings. The former are Appetite, Affection, Desire, Emotion, Volition. These we denominate the *natural* motive powers.

The latter are Conscience, Taste, Rational Will. We here distinguish will from mere brute volition, *brutum arbitrium;* the former being in the service of reason and therefore rational, while the latter is controlled by mere instinct. These we denominate the *rational* motive powers.

GENERAL USE OF THE MOTIVE POWERS.

We can imagine a being possessing all of the intellective without any of the motive powers: although we have no belief that such a being ever existed. Such a being would be incapable of moral and religious character, and even of affections or emotions of any kind. Possessing only cold and dry intellect, he would resemble the ice-ribbed regions of the poles, glittering with moonbeams but frozen and cheerless.

We are therefore indebted to the faculties which we are now to examine for all that makes creation to us beautiful, grand, charming; for all that renders the bounties of Providence desirable; for all that sustains the toils and relieves the burdens of life; for all that is precious in the tender sympathies and warm charities of society; and most of all, for the distinguishing honor of sustaining moral and religious character, and the exalted and everlasting happiness of loving God. Such is the importance of those faculties, which we now propose to examine.

WHICH CLASS OF FACULTIES ACT FIRST.

The intellective and the motive powers are intimately united and mutually dependent. Other things equal, the more earnest our affections, desires, emotions, the more vivid are our perceptions; and, on the other hand, the clearer our perceptions, the more intense are our feelings. But it has been debated which act first, the intellective or the motive powers. Dugald Stewart thinks the latter. "Our active propensities," he says, "are the motives which induce us to exert our intellectual powers, and our intellectual powers are the instruments by which we attain the ends recommended to us by our active propensities."

This is true, but not the whole truth. In all cases of *sensational* activity, that is, of mental action through the senses, the *motive* powers act first. In all other cases, the *intellective* powers act first. For instance, appetite may excite desire, which puts thought at work to gratify it. In this case a *motive* power takes the lead. On the other hand, the intuitive perception of a truth or falsehood may excite a corresponding emotion. In this case the *intellect* is first to act.

Thus an act of the intellect is often the means of exciting propensities, which subsequently re-act through the instrumentality of the intellect to obtain their ends. But it is not the same intellectual faculty, which is employed in these two cases. In the first instance, it is the power of *intuition;* in the second, the power of *contriving*, or adapting means to ends. This last is a combination of primitive faculties. We are hence morally bound to take heed how we employ the intellect, not only as an instrument to secure ends already desired but as a means of exciting the desires themselves. This is true of other powers besides that of intuition, and especially of imagination.

The direct object of intellectual activity is knowledge. Knowledge excites the motive powers, and these incite us to action. The object of that kind of intellectual activity

2

called imagining, is a substitute for knowledge. That is, it substitutes a fancied object for a reality. It is therefore adapted, like knowledge, to move the feelings; and is often even more effectual to excite desires and emotions than reality itself. Hence the person who would keep his heart pure must have special care of his imagination.

THE ACTION OF THE MOTIVE POWERS NATURAL OR MORAL.

Having distinguished the motive from the intellec tive powers, we are next to discriminate between those acts or states of the motive powers which are purely natural, and those which involve moral quality. But we must first define what we mean by natural and by moral action.

By *natural* action, we do not mean that the action itself is not beautiful, amiable, desirable, nor that it does not imply wise design and moral excellence in the responsible author of it. It *does* imply these in the highest degree. We see them in the instincts of the bee, and of all animals. We see them also in those *human* instincts, those purely constitutional activities of our nature, which are directly due to the creating and guiding power of God. When we say they are natural, characterless, &c., we only mean that they imply no moral worthiness in the man, any more than the amiable instincts of the animal imply moral worthiness in the animal. The man's conscience, his regard to duty, does not enter into them at all, any more than it does into the beatings of his pulse.

By *moral* action, we mean that for which the man himself, as a moral agent, is personally responsible. It is action which, if by him conscientiously conformed to the rule of right, attaches to *him* character of moral excellence; but if otherwise, it attaches to him guilt. Every specific moral state or action is thus right or wrong, the responsible author of it being the agent himself.

When our affections, desires, emotions, volitions, are simple spontaneous outbursts, such as mere nature designs and prompts, they are as characterless as nature herself. They are sometimes called human instincts. They incite us to preserve and defend our lives, to foster and protect our offspring, to relieve misery, to provide for our natural wants. To do otherwise is *un*natural. When the person keeps them in obedience to enlightened conscience, having thus faithful regard to duty, they are morally right. When he allows them to violate the laws of conscience, they are morally wrong. They are then wrong as being wrongly motived, indulged to excess, or directed to unworthy and forbidden objects.

Applying the above rule, we find a large class of humane, lovely, beautiful feelings and actions, on which we are prone to pride ourselves, which are the pure gifts of God in nature, as truly so as the instincts of the mere animal. They evince a fine nature as made and endued by God, but attach no more moral worthiness to the responsible man than does the color of his skin. They are strictly God's creative work, acting itself out, so to speak, in the nature which he has given.

ILLUSTRATIONS OF THE ABOVE DISTINCTIONS.

The mere constitutional desire of *esteem* has no moral quality. It is as natural and useful to the mind as breathing is to the body; the one implies no more moral character than the other. But when this desire is directed to unworthy ends, or is excessively earnest for human applause, it subverts right principle and is morally wrong.

The constitutional desire of *power* is in itself innocent,

and subserves important uses. But let it be wrongly directed, or become a ruling passion, overriding justice and benevolence, and it is highly criminal. It is the main motive of demagogues and tyrants.

Let us now reverse these cases. The desire of esteem, rightly directed, exerts a most elevating and ennobling influence upon the character. When supremely directed to the Supreme Being, it becomes one of the loftiest elements of virtue and piety. None have a brighter record on high, than they who "seek the honor that cometh from God only."

The desire of power, often so dreadful when perverted, when wisely directed to benevolent ends, imparts strength and greatness to character, and often renders its subjects illustrious benefactors of mankind. To desire power and influence for the sake of being largely beneficial, and to retain the purity of the desire and the sincerity of the motive unto the end, through a life of distinguished public success, is to form a character like that of the illustrious Washington.

The *natural affections* are not only innocent, but they are so essential to us that without them man is a monster. The mother's love for her infant child, is an original and pure instinct. Rightly controlled, it becomes one of the most beautiful elements of character. What more pleasing than the sight of the affectionate mother, watching with solicitous and untiring devotion over her helpless child? Who can contemplate her self-forgetting in devotion to the object of her love, enduring his waywardness, forgiving his faults, relieving his pains, enjoying his pleasures; pouring incessantly into his opening soul the warm current of her sympathies and the mature wisdom of her counsels, and following him with her untiring prayers, as he advances from childhood, and finally goes forth to battle with the temptations and trials of life, without feeling that the true mother's heart is the noblest of heaven's gifts?

But let that affection become by excess an idolatrous fondness; let it induce her to look not only with endurance but with complacence upon her child's faults; let it so contract her heart that it shall retain no adequate affection for any child but her own; let it be allowed to supplant the higher affection due to God, and thus induce her to murmur against him, if he removes the idol; it then becomes morally wrong. Allowed to reign in the heart, it will ultimately displace all its finest sensibilities and subvert every principle of morality and religion. Every natural affection, however lovely and important, when allowed to become idolatrous, selfish, exclusive, tends to the same disastrous result.

Hence Jesus Christ said, "He that loveth father or mother more than me, is not worthy of me, and he that loveth son or daughter more than me, is not worthy of me."

Now let that mother, instead of giving her supreme affection to her child, give it to God. Chastened, reverent, devout, modified to the nature of its object, let it ascend in holy devotion to Him who alone has the right to claim it, and to whom alone she has a right to give it. Her parental affection thus falls into its appropriate sphere and assumes the right character. She does not love her child the less, because she loves God more than him, but her maternal love is now a morally regulated and Christian affection.

This is not an affection which looks complacently upon and defends her child's faults. Although sincere and ardent, it is still discriminating. Neither is it an affection that closes the fountain of her heart against others.

On the contrary, it opens and enlarges it for all the human race. Nor yet does it resist the will of God, conflict with his laws and providence, and obstinately insist upon its own ends. Cheerfully recognizing that higher claim, resigned even in the removal of its dearest earthly object, it says, "The Lord gave and the Lord hath taken away, and blessed be the name of the Lord." This is true moral excellence; it is sublimely beautiful.

What we have said of the desires and affections, is equally true of *all* the primitive motive powers. Characterless in themselves, they are morally right or wrong, according as they are kept in obedience to the law of moral rectitude, or are allowed to transgress it. Hence a man may be, to a great extent, naturally amiable and lovely, while he is morally perverse and wicked. He may have fine natural endowments of soul as well as of body, rich impulses, genial feelings, glowing and humane affections, and yet live without God in the world. He may be a practical atheist. But if the will of God is our supreme law of moral right, as we shall hereafter show it to be; if we ought supremely to regard his pleasure, and to devote all our powers to his service; then, the man who withholds this homage from God, however fine his natural endowments, is wrong in the capital respect, the very respect in which he is personally and most of all responsible. He does not do as he *ought* to do, even in the highest and most important relation of his being. The duty that comprehends all other duties he ignores and disowns. He is thus, as an accountable being, radically and utterly in fault.

An additional fact must here be introduced, as an element essential to every philosophical system true to humanity, which is, that man is a morally *fallen* being, disinclined to do the will of God. Thus morally perverse and guilty, he is dependent upon a dispensation of grace. A true and complete system of moral philosophy must therefore show both what man is, and what, through the grace of the gospel, he may and should become. The principles of morality are thus both natural and revealed.

CHAPTER II.

NATURAL APPETITE.

The appetites are those propensities of our nature whose object is to supply our bodily wastes and to perpetuate our race. Of these we have two, adapted severally to each of the above ends. One of them is active from infancy; the other is developed later in life. Both are, however, alike provided for in the original constitution.

Some authors reckon *three* appetites, considering the appetite of thirst distinct from that of hunger. This results from their confounding appetite with the *desires* to which it gives rise, when excited. The propensity to supply the bodily wastes perpetually exists in the constitution as a part of it, while the desires which it occasions do *not* perpetually exist; their existence depending upon the particular bodily and mental states. In certain states of the body, the propensity to supply its wants occasions desire for liquid, in other states for solid substance. The particular desires of appetite are numerous, but the propensity to supply the wants, whatever they may be, is ever one and the same.

The above distinction between appetite and desire is

important. Appetite itself is natural and innocent, but the desires to which it gives rise may be virtuous or vicious, according as we direct them to lawful or unlawful indulgences. This remark is equally applicable to both of the natural appetites, and to their desires.

THE APPETITES NECESSARY.

It might seem that reason and experience are sufficient to direct us to the means necessary for the preservation of our lives and the perpetuity of our race, and that consequently the appetites are superfluous. Why then are they implanted in our nature, since they so often enslave and torment us? Is it not unworthy of rational beings to be actuated by such inferior principles? We despise the man who is controlled by his appetites; why then were they not left entirely out of his constitution, that all his actions might be directed by the loftier dictates of reason and conscience? Some light may be thrown upon this question by the following considerations.

THE APPETITES ARE PROMPTERS.

Without the promptings of appetite, the vigilance of the rational powers and the lessons of experience would often fail to remind us of the means necessary to the important ends which they contemplate. When intensely occupied, for instance, or absorbed in some favorite object, or when in circumstances unfavorable for procuring the means of subsistence, without the urgent promptings of appetite, men would often perish for want of nourishment. The appetites, therefore, in their natural and healthy condition, are invaluable monitors. Without them, despite of their rational powers, the human race would have long since ceased from the earth.

FURTHER USE OF THE APPETITES.

Controlled by virtuous principle, the appetites not only admonish us *when* to indulge, but they serve to *regulate* the indulgence. They indicate the quantity, as well as the time. Indeed, the instinct of healthy appetite subserves much the same purpose for supplying the system with nourishment, which that of breathing does for supplying the lungs with air. They do not supersede the necessity of rational and moral control, but they greatly relieve it. "Suppose, for example, that the appetite of hunger had been no part of our constitution; reason and experience might have satisfied us of the necessity of food to our preservation; but how should we have been able, without an implanted principle, to ascertain, according to the varying state of our animal economy, the proper reasons for eating, or the quantity of food that is salutary to the body?" *

THE APPETITES CONTRIBUTE TO ENJOYMENT.

But the appetites have a higher end than mere physical necessity. They were designed to promote our happiness. Indeed our enjoyment is provided for in *all* providential arrangements; and is never sacrificed but by some misdoing of ours, or for purposes of moral discipline having a higher good in prospect.

Without appetite, even the taking of our needful food would be a matter of sober and grudging necessity. The plain substantial luxury, so welcome to the laborer when returning from the toils of the day, the savory viands and delicious fruits upon the rich man's table, even the crys-

* Stewart, p. 10.

tal water that sparkles so temptingly in the temperate man's cup, would all cease alike to have any attraction, or to afford any pleasure. We should eat and drink by rule, and from mere motives of necessity. What a cold, mercenary, calculating business, would eating and drinking be! It would not be easy to calculate the amount of enjoyment, individual, domestic, social, which would be taken from the world, by the annihilation of the appetites.

MORAL AND RELIGIOUS USES OF THE APPETITES.

The appetites serve to *discipline* us. If they tempt us to vice, they also afford us opportunity to test and strengthen virtuous principle. "Blessed is the man that *endureth* temptation; for when he is *tried* he shall receive a crown of life." It is not he who has nothing in his nature or circumstances to try his virtue, but he only who is capable of being tempted and who *overcomes* the temptation, that is worthy to inherit the promised crown. It seems to have been by appetite, unlawfully indulged, that our progenitors *fell* from innocence. An opportunity is afforded, by rightly controlling this and other propensities, to rise from the servile bondage of the flesh to regained dominion more glorious than was lost.

The appetites also serve to awaken our *gratitude* to God, for his constant care and numerous gifts. They occasion wants in our nature, produced by the same gracious Being who provides for them; the necessity and the provision for it being always so adjusted to each other as to yield us repeated enjoyment, make us feel our dependence, and thus awaken our gratitude. "Give us this day our daily bread," is a prayer suggested by the demands of appetite; and every answer to it is a fresh appeal to the grateful homage of the heart.

Whenever the devout man sits down to his repast, the blessing of a healthy appetite brought into connection with the means of supplying its demands, naturally lifts his soul to God; and, in imitation of the Saviour's example, he offers to him his tribute of thanks. Thus appetite, rightly used, becomes an important means of rendering the heart grateful and devout. The true Christian "eats and drinks to the glory of God." *

ERRORS RESPECTING APPETITE.

There are two opposite errors, to which men incline, respecting the appetites; that of undue denial, and that of undue indulgence. The former is undoubtedly the safer; but we should avoid the errors on both sides.

UNDUE DENIAL.—Observing the evils of undue indulgence, some have concluded that the hand of an iron mastery should be laid upon the appetites; that they should be reduced to the lowest possible extremity; that all the happiness they proffer should be eschewed; and that the very essence of virtue consists in a state of entire indifference to their demands.

This is *Asceticism.* It is of heathen origin. Its views of morality and religion are severe and unnatural. It entirely mistakes the Creator's design; or, if it sees it in part, does not apprehend its entireness, beauty, and beneficence. Applied to religion and guiding the conscience, it has led to deeds of cruel penance, to macerations of the body, to celibacy, and even to the entire destruction of faculties implanted in our nature for the most important ends. Such is the wisdom of heathenism, or of man in the absence of Christianity, when attempting to regulate the

* 1 Cor. 10: 31.

appetites. And even Christians themselves, like some of the Jews in the time of Christ, have not always kept their morality and religious devotion entirely free of the ascetic element.

UNDUE INDULGENCE.—This is the more dangerous error. Perceiving that the appetites were evidently designed to contribute to our enjoyment, and not considering the importance of keeping them in due subjection, many allow them to gain the mastery. Men thus become abject slaves to them. They are what the Scriptures denominate "lovers of pleasures." The pleasures of sense, no longer subordinate and incidental, become to them the supreme and ultimate object. They tease and stimulate the appetites to the highest pitch of excitement, and then give to them the reins of free indulgence.

This is *Epicurianism.* It is so called from a noted heathen philosopher, who was reputed to teach, what he never did teach in so gross a sense, that pleasure is the chief end of man. Not only morality and religion, but even the decencies of social and domestic life are by it sometimes sacrificed to a mad devotion to "the lusts of the flesh." It defeats its own end. Its race is short; it usually has more of pain than of substantial pleasure, even while it lasts; and it terminates in hopeless ruin.

But while the theoretical error may draw many into the bondage of appetite, it is not true that all who come into this bondage theoretically embrace the error. Men become the slaves of lust by errors of practice more than by errors of speculation. So dominant do unduly indulged appetites often become, that their unhappy slaves groan under the bondage while freely admitting the claims of virtue, and even eloquent in its praise. The most lucid arguments and touching appeals in favor of temperance and chastity, have fallen from the lips of intemperate and licentious men. In the bitterness of his spirit, the wretched victim of lust is often constrained to say,

> "I know the right, and I approve it too,
> Condemn the wrong, and yet the wrong pursue."

RELATION OF APPETITE TO PLEASURE.

Pleasure is an object, but not the chief and ultimate object, for which the appetites were given us. The question here arises whether it is right to indulge the appetites *merely* for the pleasure thus obtained. In answer to this, it is evident that he acts an irrational part, and therefore morally wrong, who allows present indulgence at the expense of greater enjoyment in the future. He who eagerly snatches a few transient pleasures, at the loss of great and permanent future good, acts a brutish part, and thus offends against the high dictates of wisdom and morality. A rational being is bound to *act* as such; and rationality enjoins forethought.

There is not so much as an *apology* for this impatience to indulge, even with those who regard happiness as the end; for Providence has so ordered events that the virtuous control of appetite secures the highest present satisfaction, as well as future reward. Hence all vicious indulgence is as truly a mistake, as an immorality; it is as unwise, as it is wrong. If the present year, or even the present month, were the whole of a man's existence, the balance of enjoyment would still be on the side of virtue.

But the mere question of enjoyment is not the main one here. Morality takes a higher view. While virtue bestows present as well as future happiness, it must be conceded that she demands self-denial; and sometimes

Pitanga, which a short distance below the station expands into a large pond. At the head of this pond I found a gentleman with six men washing for diamonds. An excavation several yards square had been made in the flat alluvial ground. The lowest stratum seen was a stiff blue clay, called by the miners *pizarra*, over this was a sheet of a few inches in thickness of *cascalho*, or gravel composed principally of quartz and fragments of the different rocks of the neighborhood, this cascalho being mixed with a mottled reddish clay. This was the stratum from which the diamonds were washed. Over the cascalho was a thin stratum of clay. The washers were seated on benches level with the water of a little pond; a portion of the gravel was thrown into a large shallow wooden pan, water was mixed with it, and the pan with its contents was whirled about on the surface of the pond, the muddy water being allowed to escape until only the gravel and sand remained. This was now placed in a sort of sieve, the bottom of which was made of copper, pierced with round holes about an inch in diameter, which allowed all the little pebbles and sand to pass through. Not long since, at one of the Brazilian diamond washings, a diamond too large to pass through the openings of the sieve was found in the heap of coarse refuse. It had been picked up by a child as a plaything. After washing, the pebbles are picked out, when the overseer, looking carefully over the sand, selects the diamonds with ease, should there be any; but during the weeks which they washed at Pitanga only five minute stones had been found. A few years ago quite extensive washings were carried on beside the river nearer the station, and a large number of fine stones were discovered; but the owner of the land has put a stop to further operations. On the west side

A very interesting section occurs in a cut about a mile and a half below Matta station. The gravel sheet here is very thick, — ten feet, more or less,* — and is irregularly and obliquely stratified, and mixed with layers of sand, as if the whole had been laid down by a current coming from the north. The sheet is very irregular, and varies much in thickness.

Matta station, and the village of Matta de São João, are situated on a plain, formed by the widening of the valley which the railroad follows. The tertiary hills still border it, and these are, in some cases, much denuded.

Above Matta, at the cutting at the fazenda of Coronel Sipuda, there is a decayed, fine-grained sandstone or arenaceous shale seen, probably cretaceous, and thence on to Pitanga station, rocks of the same general character. Just below the station at Pitanga I made the following section.

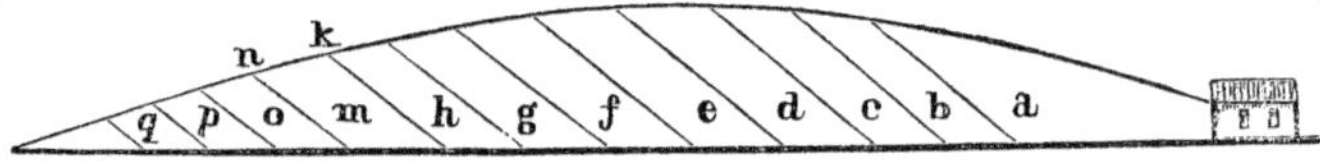

a. Sandstone.

b. Shale, slightly arenaceous.

c. Shale; very argillaceous, and so soft as to be easily moulded by the hand. Decomposed, it is of a gray or light slate-color, with bright red patches. It contains apparently the same Estherian found at Pojuca tunnel, to be presently described.

d and *e*. Shale decomposing yellow and red.

f. Sandstone; soft and ochre yellow.

g. Shale decomposed to a pink and white clay.

h. Sandstone.

k. Layer of concretionary iron-stone a foot or two in thickness. The surface is very irregular, and some of the projecting knobs have a sort of septaria structure.

m. White sandstone.

n. Layer of iron-stone.

o. White tabatinga, with red iron-stone nodules.

p. Decomposed shale.

q. Sandstone (soft). The dip is exaggerated in this section.

The railroad here skirts a flat along which flows the Rio

* I have omitted to note it exactly.

self-denial very severe and protracted. And when the question lies between indulgence and virtue, between pleasure and morality, the decision in favor of the latter does not admit of a question, even though it be at the sacrifice of a right eye.

There are two kinds of pleasure, which here conflict: that of indulged appetite, and that of obeyed conscience; and however great the former, that of the latter is sure to be greater. And so also there are two kinds of conflicting *pain;* and however great the pain of denying appetite, that of disobeying conscience will surely transcend it. And to this we must add, that even if we take no higher ground than respect to mere physical enjoyment, the loss of it from vices of appetite is ordinarily, within no distant period, more than an offset to the pleasure. These reasons are conclusive, why the appetites should never be used as means of pleasure, excepting as they are controlled by strict and unbending virtue. But when indulgence and virtue clearly coincide, self-denial ceases to be either virtuous or wise.

ILLUSTRATION OF THE ABOVE.

If we have the choice of two kinds of food equally at our command and conducive to health, the only difference being that our appetite craves the one rather than the other, our appetite is then the only providential indication to guide us. Indeed, what a healthy appetite best relishes, is usually best for us. Nor can one person decide here for another; for as Providence has afforded a variety of provisions, so he has constituted various appetites with reference to them.

Moreover, the appetites were clearly designed to be indulged, subject to the laws of strict virtue, with direct reference to the satisfaction which they afford. They were designed, as we have said, to minister to our enjoyment; and happiness is both a good in itself, and a means to permanent moral benefit. It is not less essential than suffering, as an element of moral discipline; and God has dispensed his bounties with reference to this law of our nature. We are so constituted, that the absence of all pleasure on the one hand, as well as the absence of all pain on the other, would be fatal to our moral discipline.

DESIGN OF PROVIDENTIAL GIFTS.

Why has the Creator spread such a world of beauty around us, in the varied and beautiful landscape; in the rich hues of the opening flowers and the richer tints of the ripening fruits; in the gorgeous splendors of the western sky, when the sun is sinking to rest beneath a canopy of sapphire and of gold; in all the forms of grace and grandeur, which open to our view in ceaseless variety, by day and by night; but to afford us enjoyment through the sense of sight, and thereby raise our hearts to him in grateful homage? And why has he filled the air with music, and provided for our producing it by artificial means, adapting the laws of melody and harmony to our enjoyment through the sense of hearing?

And are not his provisions and designs the same, in respect to the sense of appetite? There is but one answer. If there is no merit in shutting our eyes against the gifts addressed to the sense of sight, or our ears against the gifts addressed to the sense of hearing, there can be none in rejecting the gifts addressed to the sense of appetite. All of the senses sustain to us the same relation; they are all equally designed to afford us enjoyment; and they are all to be governed by the same rules of virtue.

SELF-DENIAL FOR BENEVOLENT ENDS.

When benevolence induces a person to forego gratifications of appetite for the sake of doing good to his fellow-beings, the virtue of self-denial rests upon higher ground than that of mere secular morality. When a man denies himself luxuries, or in any way restricts personal indulgences, for the sake of saving the cost of them to supply the wants of the destitute, or to afford relief to the suffering, or to send the Gospel to the heathen, he adopts the Christian principle.

Nor does he herein act the ascetic, aspiring to be righteous overmuch; for he would gratefully enjoy the luxury and bestow the favor too, if he could; but seeing he cannot do both, his benevolent heart prompts him nobly to relinquish personal gratification, for the sake of affording greater and more important good to others. This is the self-sacrificing spirit of Christianity.

THE BEST MEANS OF GOVERNING THE APPETITES.

It is not the highest order of morality, that does little else than maintain severe and scrupulous exactness in regard to the appetites. Not that they should ever be ungoverned, or ever allowed to transgress in the least particular; but to be ever inquiring to what extent they may be indulged, and how they may be kept in due subjection, tends to debase the mind, and to displace nobler motives of action.

Indeed such a course sometimes tends, by a natural law, to render the appetites more ungovernable. When the conscience is duly enlightened, and the aspirations of the soul are pure and elevated, the lower propensities naturally fall into their proper place. Hence the best of all directions for governing the appetites, is, to have some worthy and absorbing object in view, and to be diligently engaged in pursuing it.

The truly noble man governs his appetites almost unconsciously. Like dutiful children, they render him cheerful obedience. Not clamorous for their rights, they never set up the standard of rebellion. Rightly trained from infancy, submission has become their habit. As they never solicit undue indulgence, it is never needful to lay upon them any painful restraint. To "keep under the body and bring it into subjection," is no arduous task.

Such a man lives, not by a rule of mechanical exactness, or of pedantic and self-conscious accuracy, but by the lofty impulse of a divine heroism. High aims and high endeavors, conscientiously pursued, place him above the reach of temptations addressed to his lower propensities. Such is the high-souled man. But he whose moral history is made up of attempts nicely to define the exact limit of virtuous indulgence and to keep precisely within it, lives at a mean rate, and can never in this way reach a point of excellence worth naming.

CHAPTER III.

MORBID APPETITES.

Two causes operate to impart *morbid* or *diseased* action to the appetites. In the first place, the *organs* of the sense of appetite may be in a diseased or abnormal condition. When the organs of the sense of *sight* are diseased, its *vision* is unnatural; so when the organs of the sense of *appetite* are diseased, its *cravings* are unnatural.

In the second place, appetite may be disordered by *excessive* and *repeated indulgence*, by which a bad *habit* is formed. There are then both the disease of the organ and the power of the evil habit to be overcome, before healthy appetite can be restored. The influence of the two is reciprocal; repetition increases the disease, and the disease instigates repetition.

Dugald Stewart calls them *acquired* appetites. "Besides our natural appetites," he says, "we have many *acquired* ones. Such are our appetites for tobacco, for opium, and other intoxicating drugs. In general, every thing that stimulates the nervous system produces a subsequent languor, which gives rise to a repetition." * He

* Active and Moral Powers, p. 12.

here confounds appetite itself with the *cravings* to which it gives rise. When the appetite, designed to suggest the *appropriate* nourishing stimulant, becomes perverted or morbid, it produces unnatural cravings for *hurtful* stimulants, such as alcohol, opium, tobacco, and highly seasoned dishes.

APPETITE DISEASED BY NATURE.

It may be a question how far appetite is ever *originally diseased*. It seems to be a law of nature, that the peculiarities of parents, both physical and mental, descend in some measure to their posterity. This law extends to diseases. The morbid states as well as the constitutional peculiarities of parents, become to some extent the inheritance of their children. The vices of sensuality and their sad effects, are propagated by blood scarcely less than by example. This appears to be one of the ways in which God "visits the iniquities of the fathers upon their children, unto the third and fourth generation." This fact should be an effectual inducement to all who would not entail calamities upon their offspring, to avoid every kind of vicious indulgence.

APPETITE DISEASED IN INFANCY.

While vitiosity of appetite may be to some extent inherited, it is doubtless more due to the nursing and the habits of infancy. The seeds of intemperance may be implanted in children long before they arrive at years of discretion. Intoxicating drinks taken by the mother and retaken by the infant at the breast, cordials administered as a beverage or an anodyne, may implant the germs of morbid appetite, which future years will serve only to mature. Appetite thus depraved operates through the subsequent periods of childhood, producing various cravings for injurious indulgences, which nothing but the most determined self-denial can resist; and which, alas, are too often allowed to destroy their victims.

There is then a serious responsibility upon all who have infancy and childhood in charge, to practise great caution in forming the appetite. No propensity of our nature is more easily affected at an early age, for good or for evil, than this. Physicians have mostly ceased to encourage nursing mothers to take intoxicating drinks, and to countenance the frequent administering of drugs and cordials to children. Pure air, simple diet, invigorating exercise, and cheerful society, are the natural means of fostering healthy appetite.

APPETITE VITIATED IN YOUTH.

Whatever may be the depravity of appetite obtained by inheritance, or in the period of infancy, it cannot annul the subsequent obligation of the individual to control it. If a youth finds himself the unhappy victim of morbid appetites, urging him to vicious indulgences, he should put in requisition the greater self-denial and the more determined efforts to be virtuous. He should take counsel of reason, not of appetite; he should listen to the voice of God and of conscience, cautiously shun temptations, and address himself with unflinching determination to his duty. And for encouragement he should consider that the greater the struggle, the more glorious the victory, and the richer the reward.

The appetites are not often so depraved at birth, or in infancy, as to render it very difficult for a virtuous will to control them. The severest trials which men realize from them, are of their own procuring. It is during the period of youth, between the ages of ten and twenty-five, when passion is ardent, reason immature, and habit in the process of formation, that persons are most liable to render their desire for pleasure strong by indulgence, and thus to fall victims to its demands. Since many descend to ruin in this way, it may not be amiss, for a warning to the young, to indicate the leading steps in the process.

1. *Inordinate desire for present pleasure.*—Since indulgence affords present enjoyment, it makes the youth of strong desires and little forethought its easy victim. He has as yet tasted only the sweet, none of the bitterness, of vice. Hence, regardless of the counsels of parents and teachers, of the commands of God, and of the admonitions of conscience, he gives himself up to pleasure. At length the abused appetites, as if in retaliation for this unlawful use of them, assume the reins and hurry their victim into still bolder and more desperate steps towards ruin.

2. *The influence of bad example.*—Having entered upon this course, he finds companions to keep him in countenance, and help him along in it. Associated with those more advanced than himself in vice, he finds his progress greatly facilitated. The tendency to imitate is perhaps never stronger with those who have deviated from the path of virtue, than when vicious indulgence is the object.

Indeed the mutual influence of pleasure-seeking companions in confirming each other's vices, is almost irresistible. "The companion of fools *shall be destroyed.*" The only possible hope for one thus ensnared, is in the dissolution of the companionship; an event which he is usually slow to desire.

3. *False association of ideas.*—The youth supposed is yet more encouraged in his course, by associating indulgence with *high life and independence.* He knows sons of rich and distinguished parents, moving with honor in

fashionable circles, who practise unblushingly the vices to which he is inclined. Not regarding true excellence as independent of external condition not having learned to associate virtue with honor, and vice with disgrace, under all circumstances; the free indulgence of appetite becomes with him a matter of *ambition*, as well as of pleasure.

He scorns to be numbered with the stupid slaves of superstition, or with the humble poor who cannot *afford* to indulge; he aspires to freedom, and to an honorable rank. Thus becoming one of those "who *glory* in their shame," his pride and appetite unite their forces to destroy him.

4. *A vicious imagination.*—His imagination having become perversely active, fills his mind with corrupting images. It vividly mirrors to him "the wine when it is red, when it giveth its color in the cup, when it moveth itself aright," and the numerous accompanying objects which minister to depraved appetites. Objects, thus furnished by the imagination, have frequently as much power to excite the cravings of appetite, as those actually present. In some cases they have even more. Thus one of the finest of the mental faculties, given to elevate and enrich the soul, becomes by perversion a fatal instrument for its destruction.

5. *Utter recklessness of the future.*—The frenzied appetites at length render their victim desperate. There is now scarcely a risk which he will not encounter, nor terror which he will not brave, for the sake of their indulgence. His ruin has thus approached the point of completion. His remaining days upon earth will probably be few; but whether few or many, they will never be to him again as they have been.

That glorious sun will never again shine upon his head

with golden beams, as in the days of his innocence and hope; the sweet music of nature, that once came to his bounding and joyous spirit like angel-voices, is turned into the deep and hollow wail of a ruined life; all creation, once green, bright, and charming, looks faded, withered, repulsive; and often, under a painful conviction of his ruin and the pangs of remorse, he almost sighs for the dreaded grave to bury him for ever from the world and from himself. If in Paris, his presence in a den of gamblers may be suddenly missed, and the morning may find his remains at the foot of the Triumphal Arch, or floating in the Seine.

6. *The closing scene.*—But if he lives in America, and has received Christian instruction, he will not probably terminate his days by suicide. A lingering probation of misery awaits him. The appetites which once afforded him pleasure, now exhausted of their resources, refuse to do so any longer; and he is thus left both to the painful chidings of conscience, and to the cruel mercy of those long-cherished and remorseless cravings, that can never be satisfied.

Nothing short of one of those rare miracles of mercy, which Heaven in the stupendous reaches of its grace sometimes deigns, can avail to rescue him, and to turn him, through agonies of repentance and of struggle, into the long forsaken paths of virtue. Few indeed, in this stage of vice, are ever reclaimed. Nearly all die as they have lived, leaving the hearts of surviving friends to weep bitter tears, and the loving breezes of heaven vainly to sigh over their dishonored graves.

THE REVERSE OF THE ABOVE PROCESS.

Every youth, however morbid his early or acquired appetites, may, by commencing early, entirely reverse the above process. His moral salvation is yet, under God, in his own keeping. He may become a virtuous, high-minded, and happy man, reigning as a king over all his house. But in order to this, he must enter *at once* upon a persistent conflict. He must adopt and firmly maintain the rule of him who said, "*I keep under my body and bring it into subjection.*" He must now, henceforth, and for ever, count all pleasures valueless, which are obtained at the expense of virtue.

He must disconnect all vicious indulgences from the fascinations and allurements with which they are too often connected. He must never associate them with respectability and greatness, however arrayed with splendor, or commended by wealth and fashion; he must practically esteem them as mean and disgraceful as they are morally wrong and wicked. The principle of *self-respect* will thus arm him against them.

He must check the wanderings of *imagination*, guide but not cool its burning energies, and bid it rise to objects pure and ennobling. Whether it be a novel, a picture, a song, a theatrical exhibition, or even a fact of history or personal knowledge, that would defile his thoughts, and excite vicious cravings of appetite, he must turn away from it, and for ever shun it, as he would a pestilence that walketh in darkness.

He must also shun all bad company. Until his vicious habits have become thoroughly subdued, and virtuous habits firmly established, vicious companions will present temptations formidable for him to withstand. He must, therefore, resolutely cut himself entirely off from all "fellowship with the unfruitful works of darkness," from all communion with those who are pursuing "the lusts of the flesh," and throw himself heartily into the society and sympathies of the strictly virtuous. "He that walketh

3

with wise men shall be wise, but the companion of fools shall be destroyed."

But he must not think to govern his appetites by making war on nature, acting the ascetic, and denying himself *innocent* amusements and *wholesome* pleasures. There are such, and all youth must have them. If they do not, restrained nature will react, will demand her rights; and, if she cannot have them in one form, she will have them in another. If she is denied them in innocence, she will have them in guilt

Let the youth supposed, then, cultivate and indulge the pleasures of his higher nature. Let him add to his diligence in business the culture of literature, of taste, of poetry, of music, of refined social recreations and amusements; let him feast his imagination and elevate his desires, by communing with the beauties of nature and the triumphs of art. Thus, taking hold upon the higher pleasures of his rational soul, he will naturally leave the inferior pleasures of appetite to fall into their appropriate place of subordination.

Above all, conscious of his weakness and guilt, he must throw himself upon the strength and grace of God; and he must set an infinite value upon those virtuous principles and high endeavors, which, superior to present indulgence, and patient of all needful self-denial, can afford to wait long and toil hard, in expectation of glorious reward in the future. Persisting in this course, an approving conscience will sustain him; he will teach his appetites obedience; he will feel the delightful assurance that he is gaining the victory and rising in character. He will soon find the wise and virtuous gathering about him and becoming his personal friends. He will at last have the unspeakable satisfaction of respecting himself, as a man of conscious virtue, and of receiving the growing confidence and esteem of mankind.

As in the previous chapter we endeavored to show how the *natural* appetites should be *controlled;* so in this we have endeavored to show how the *morbid* appetites should be *restored.* The youth who would do well for himself, is earnestly requested to examine the directions, and to apply them as his case may demand.

CHAPTER IV.

NATURAL AFFECTION.

Affection is the feeling usually termed *love* and *hatred.* It is attended with more or less emotion, and when the emotional element is intense it becomes a passion. Hence we say a person is passionately in love. The passion may be great, and yet be attended with little or no benevolence towards its object. This is a very impure affection, and sometimes degenerates to mere lust. And so also the passion of anger, which is a feeling of excited hostility, may become less and less rational, and thus pass into a blind frenzy. But the simple affection itself, as a primitive faculty, is to be distinguished from these passionate excitements.

DISTINCTION BETWEEN AFFECTION AND DESIRE.

Affection has respect to *persons;* desire, to whatever respects their enjoyment, or their suffering. We love or hate the man; we desire his good or harm. We love our children; we desire their happiness. Religious men love God, they desire to promote his glory. Thus the object of affection is living beings; the object of desire is inanimate things.

There is an affection, also, which we bestow upon the brute creation, but it is of a different kind from that which we bestow upon rational beings. We justly consider a person wanting in some important qualities of heart, who manifests no love towards animals. A man may truly love his faithful dog, although the affection is unlike that which he has for his child. The girl may love her playful kitten, but not as she does her little brother.

Men sometimes speak of loving certain kinds of food and drink. But we have not an *affection* for them; it is a *desire* or *relish*. We also speak of loving our homes, firesides, the graves of friends; of loving scenes of rural quiet, groves, mountains, sequestered valleys. So far as real affection is concerned, and not merely impassioned desire and sentiment, our feeling here results from associating these objects with living beings.

The sacred writers sometimes employ the same term, comprehensively, to designate both affection and desire. "Love not the world, nor the things that are in the world." "Set your affection on things above." Men also speak, in popular language, of loving money and applause. Strictly speaking, however, it is not an *affection* which they have for these things; it is a covetous and vain *desire*.

Affection, as we have seen, is not merely a feeling of love; it includes the opposite, *hatred*. Whether the malevolent affection is a part of our original constitution, or a result of the apostasy, love turned to hate, is a fair question, which we may consider hereafter. And here again it is restricted to conscious beings. We may hate a fellow-being; we may also, in an inferior sense, hate certain animals, as a toad or a snake, but we cannot properly be said to hate an inanimate object. It does not appear that the woman hated the serpent, before the fall; on the contrary, she seems to have loved it too confidingly; but the fall put enmity between them, and turned the love to hatred.

Brutes have natural affection, but not moral. Having no rational nature, no conscience, their affections can never be regulated by moral principle, and must therefore remain mere instincts.

The most important of the natural affections are the following:

1. Parental Affection.
2. Filial Affection.
3. Fraternal Affection.
4. Conjugal Affection.
5. Social Affection.

We shall examine them in the above order.

I. PARENTAL AFFECTION.

Parental affection is the *love of parents towards their offspring.* It is not restricted to our race; we share it with brutes. It does not spring from the relation itself, but from the knowledge or belief that it exists. An animal loves and nourishes the young of another as fondly as her own, if she receives the charge under circumstances to conceal the imposition. The same is true of the human affection. Let a new-born infant be presented to a mother, in case her own is dead; let her from the first suppose that infant to be her own offspring; and she will have for it the genuine mother's affection.

Hence the idea entertained by some of a certain discriminating feeling, leading parents to recognize and love their own offspring independently of the admonition of the senses, is a pure chimera. We trace the parental affection to its source, when we say, the parent is so constituted that the moment she sees in the infant child her own or her *supposed* offspring, a peculiar feeling towards it springs up in her heart. This feeling is parental love; and it is as spontaneous as the desire for food, or the flow of the blood.

Parental Love Modified by Circumstances.—Thus commences the parental affection. It is born into the world under the same providence that gives birth to the infant, that it may embrace the helpless stranger, and care for its wants. But let that infant die, or be for ever separated from its parents, and the intensity of the affection will gradually diminish. This is a merciful provision.

On the other hand, let the infant grow up under the fostering care of the parent, and every day will entwine new chords of love around the parent's heart. Every smile and every tear, every joy and every pain, of the cherished and dependent child, augments the parental love. This, again, is a kind provision; since every additional care and anxiety for the child, demands a fresh supply of love to sustain it.

Design of Parental Affection.—1. It is the first obvious design of this affection to secure the *requisite attention* of parents to their offspring. In the case of the brute, it is the *only* means of securing it. Without this, all the offspring of brutes which are dependent on parental care, would be left to perish.

A sense of duty should indeed induce parents to take care of their children; but it would not do to depend upon this motive alone. In multitudes it is nearly or quite wanting; and in all, at some periods of life, it is too feeble and inconstant to insure the result. Without the promptings of parental love to supply its place, or to attend it, multitudes of infant children, which are now cared for, would undoubtedly be abandoned to suffering and death.

2. This affection seems to have been designed to ren-

der parents *happy* in their duties to their offspring. What a burden would be imposed upon the mother, if all her care and watchfulness were from a mere sense of duty! With what languid step and heavy heart would the toil-worn father go to his daily task, to earn bread for his dependent family, if he did not love them. The thought of taking the dear little ones on his knee at evening, reconciles him to the labors of the day.

As the mother has usually more to do with the children than the father has; as it is especially *her* suffering and patience that are taxed; so to her is given the larger portion of parental love. Indeed, the heart of the affectionate mother has been well called "the masterpiece of nature's works." There is perhaps no other form in which humanity appears so lovely, or "presents so fair a copy of the divine image after which it was made."

It is often truly said, that parents love their children more than children do their parents. Here again is a gracious adaptation of means to ends. Parents have ordinarily more to *do* for their children, than children for their parents. The providing, the care, the anxiety, the patience, the sacrifice of health, and sometimes of life itself, are all mostly on the parent's side. Hence the parent naturally *requires* the greater share of love.

3. This affection is designed to subserve important *moral* and *religious* ends. It imparts earnestness and perseverance to the efforts of parents, to train up their children in the way they should go. Thus nature prompts the parent to do what duty demands. How many sons have been rescued from destruction by the promptings of maternal love. There is, perhaps, no principle of our nature, with which Christianity more gracefully blends, or which it more charmingly adorns, than parental love.

II. FILIAL AFFECTION.

Filial affection is the *love of children towards their parents.* This, as well as the preceding, springs not from the relation itself, but from the knowledge of it, or belief that it exists. The child that has always supposed his nurse to be his own mother, has towards her all the natural love of an own child. The same is true of his relation to the supposed father. If only the longing to sustain the relation expressed by the word *own*, as related to the parent, is gratified, the filial affection springs into life.

How the filial affection is developed.—Although filial love is as truly instinctive as parental, it is not so soon developed. As it does not depend upon the relation itself, but upon the child's knowledge of it, it cannot of course be exercised until the child is old enough to comprehend the relation. But filial love, in its early stages, has more of passion and less of benevolence than parental love has. Hence the child loves his mother, who smiles upon him and gives him kisses and sweetmeats, more than he loves his father who toils for his bread. As he grows older, and better appreciates the father's labors, he divides his affections more equally ; but the early cares and caresses of the fond mother have so preoccupied his heart, that he seldom fails to give her his warmest affection through life.

It is often said that daughters love their fathers more than they do their mothers, and that sons love their mothers more than they do their fathers. If this be so, it may be owing to the tendencies of the sexes to love each other ; the more delicate qualities of the one and the stern qualities of the other awakening a reciprocity of interest ; and perhaps, also, to the fact, that the father has the principal government of the sons, and the mother of the daughters, each thereby in a measure thwarting the inclinations with which natural affection is intimately blended. For although an ungoverned child does not truly love, the child is very apt to give the greater share of affection to that one of the parents, from whom the least restraint and punishment directly come.

Design of filial affection.—Filial affection was designed to secure the needful *submission* of children to their parents. Unless the offspring of brutes had some attachment to their parents, they would die of exposure and starvation. It is essential to their preservation, that they should be subject to guardianship. The same is true of children. Incapable of taking care of themselves, in the exercise of their own will, they must be subject to the will of their parents. Filial affection tends to secure this subjection.

The same affection also makes the child *happy* in this subjection. Obedience is not cordial without it. The child is cheerful and glad to obey his parents, only as he loves them. Without love, like the prisoner in chains, he submits only from necessity.

This affection is also designed to subserve *moral* and *religious* ends. Many a parent has been saved from vice and ruin through efforts prompted by filial love. Such is the reciprocity of effort for each other's welfare, induced by the mutual love of parents and children, that morality and religion have ever looked to it with special and availing hope.

III. FRATERNAL AFFECTION.

Fraternal affection is the love which exists *between children of the same family.* It originates, like the preceding, with the knowledge of the relation. A peculiar affection is enkindled by the knowledge of an *own* brother or sister; and, unless destroyed by some untoward event, it is as lasting as life.

This affection does not seem to exist in the brute creation, excepting as it is occasioned by the offspring of the same parent being associated together. Their affections are merely *social*, because their knowledge does not embrace the nature of the fraternal relation.

Design of fraternal affection.—As children of the same family have an interest especially common; as they commence existence in the same nursery, gather in the same domestic circle, sit around the same table, share in the same inheritance, participate in the same joys and afflictions; it was needful that they should have an affection especially adapted to this relation.

Fraternal love was designed to render brothers and sisters happy, earnest, faithful in devotion to each other's welfare and to the common interests of the household. When this love is true and constant, it presents one of the most lovely scenes on earth.

What more pleasing than to see the elder sister extending an almost maternal care over her younger brothers? Or the brother tenderly watchful of the character, the wants, the happiness, of his sisters? What sight better calculated to impress convictions of the wisdom and goodness of the Creator in implanting these affections, than that of a family whose members thus seem to seek each other's welfare as sincerely as they do their own!

Fraternal affection has often less of passion and more of benevolence than conjugal. Unless some alienating circumstances interpose, it commonly lasts through life, and induces brothers and sisters to make sacrifices for each other's good, which they will make for no other human beings, excepting those of their own families. It is thus one of the strongest as well as most lovely of the natural affections. Solomon has even honored it so highly as to make it inferior only to the highest and best of all affections. "There is a friend that sticketh closer than a brother."

IV. CONJUGAL AFFECTION.

Conjugal affection is *the love that exists between husband and wife.* It differs in the order of development from fraternal and filial love. Instead of *springing* from the perceived relation of the parties, it *gives rise* to it. They do not love each other because they are married, but they were married because they loved.

Another peculiarity of this affection is, that it exists only *between the sexes.* It is therefore apt to have, especially in its earliest stages, more of passion and less of benevolence than the love of kindred. But after the parties have become legally united, so that each is felt to be rightfully and for ever the other's *own*, a new desire is gratified, a new element is added to the affection; and from this time it has all the qualities of conjugal love. It gradually becomes more chastened, pure, benevolent; it becomes stronger and steadier; and is finally the most dominant and enduring natural affection of the human heart.

Although provision is made for conjugal love, in the physical and mental constitution, it is optional with us whether to avail ourselves of this provision. Many live and die apparently satisfied, without ever tasting the sweets of conjugal love. But as provision was made for it in our nature, it is clear that Providence designed it, and that to be married, at a suitable age, is the most natural and the happiest state of man.

Design of conjugal affection.—The objects contemplated by conjugal affection, are, the continuance of the species; the united care and training of offspring; the mutual happiness of the parties in each other, and in their children; and, generally, all the benefits of the do mestic constitution. It was not good that man should be alone, hence, the Creator made an "help-meet for" him; but had he only made the help-meet, without making provision in the nature of each party for the conjugal *affection*, the relation would have been a task instead of a pleasure.

Were it made the *duty* of parties to unite in marriage, without conjugal love, that duty would be seldom undertaken and poorly executed. Conjugal love heightens every enjoyment, lightens every burden, divides every care, relieves all anxieties, sweetens afflictions, and strews all along life's toilsome and rugged path the flowers and fruits of primeval paradise.

Hence the design of the marriage *covenant*. This covenant, provided for in the constitution of the sexes, was instituted in paradise by God himself. To it are due all the inestimable blessings of domestic life; and, indirectly, of all those social and civil relations which elevate and adorn the human race.

Thus all the family affections combine to form, protect, and bless the domestic institution; the most important institution upon earth, and that on which all others depend. Nothing can be imagined more worthy of Him who made and blessed it, nothing can be more fruitful of good to mankind, than the family in which all the parental, filial, conjugal, and fraternal affections are fully developed, and are in healthy and harmonious play. Such a family, itself happy, is both the germ and the emblem of a happy civil community, a happy state, a happy nation. Thus all our hopes, for our country and for the world, revert to the family, and depend upon the domestic affections.

V. SOCIAL AFFECTION.

This affection differs from those which we have examined in being *less specific.* Love for more distant kindred, for members of the same society, for townsmen, for countrymen, is naturally less intense than that which we have for our family relatives, but is not wholly different. We love our cousins, partly because we feel that some of our family blood flows in their veins. There is in it something of the *fraternal* feeling. For a similar reason we love persons of our *race* more than those of another. We love Americans and Englishmen more than Indians and Hottentots, because they are naturally nearer to us. More of their blood flows in our veins.

Exceptions to the above rule occur only when affection takes an eccentric and unnatural direction. For this reason, people of the same race incline to intermarry and to form nations. And hence marriages between individuals of nations very unlike each other, as between an Englishman and a Chinese, are clearly contrary to the design of Providence. We feel an instinctive repugnance to all such unnatural alliances.

On the other hand, near relatives, however sincere and intense their mutual love, do not naturally have for each other a conjugal affection. Intermarriage between them is also further interdicted by the fact, that it tends to the destruction of both mind and body, and thus to the ultimate extinction of the race. Hence the true conjugal affection exists between parties of the same or similar nations, and of similar taste and culture, but of different family connections.

The affection which results merely from being of the same society, town, or country, is easily accounted for.

Intercourse and identity of interests naturally tend to beget mutual affection. They produce similarity of views, tastes, principles, habits; they introduce men to that intimate acquaintance with each other's private life, from which affection mostly originates. Our conscious love is mostly restricted to those with whom we have, by personal intercourse or by other means, a somewhat intimate knowledge. Hence the affection between members of the same literary, secular, or religious society. They have common views and instincts, and they often meet together under circumstances favorable to excite friendly feelings.

We may not be conscious of any peculiar affection for the people of our own town, state, or nation, whilst we are in the midst of them, but after having passed some time in a strange land, we greet one of them as a brother. Persons who scarcely cared to speak with each other in their native place, on meeting in distant lands, can hardly express their mutual satisfaction.

Affection for our country, or patriotism.—The particular affection which we have for the people of our own country, together with the special interest we take in its soil, its institutions, its struggles, its conquests, its fortunes, is termed *patriotism.* Imagination and association have much agency in producing this affection.

Patriotism is usually truer and more intense in small than in large countries, and in countries rough and barren than in those smoother and more fertile. The reason, in the former case, is, that the people are brought nearer together; that their interests are more strictly one; and that, in their relative feebleness as a nation, they are more dependent upon each other. In the latter case, the common struggles and mutual sympathy of the people, in the peculiar exposures and hardships of their condition, as in the case of the Swiss, the Highlanders of Scotland, and the Laplanders, tend to endear them to each other.

When, however, a nation becomes very large and powerful, so as to hold a proud rank among other nations, as was the case with the Roman empire, and is now the case with the British empire, and with the United States, there is an appeal to the national love of glory, which operates powerfully upon the people to attach them to their country and to its institutions.

GENERAL REMARKS UPON THE AFFECTIONS.

We have thus noticed the leading affections which are strictly *natural*, and the purposes for which they were designed. Had they been wanting, our race would have long since ceased from the earth, or would have continued only to perpetuate its wretchedness. As they are excellent in their nature, and perfectly adapted to their end, they reflect honor upon their Creator, but imply no praiseworthiness in us. They are *his* doing; not ours. But while the mere presence of them implies in us no moral worthiness, their absence or abuse implies guilty violence done to our nature, and usually results from a profligate life. He that is "without natural affection," is in the Bible ranked among the vilest of men.

It should also be observed, that as God has *commanded* us to exercise these affections, while it is an immorality and a sin to withhold or pervert them, to exercise them in the spirit of obedience to the divine will, is both a moral and a religious act. On the right use of them our character eminently depends. Some of the purest joys of life on earth, and most seraphic joys of eternal life in heaven, spring from obedient and holy affection.

CHAPTER V.

NATURAL DESIRE.

Some authors confound desire with appetite. What Whewell terms "bodily desire" is *occasioned* by appetite, but the cause and the effect should not be identified. Appetite, as we have seen, is a permanent principle of our nature, but we desire food or drink only when appetite is excited by a state of hunger or thirst. And, as to all other desires, they may exist in every state of the physical system. A man desires food only when he is hungry; but he as much desires fame, wealth, power, knowledge, after his hunger is satisfied, as he did before. Hence, neither class of desires should be identified with appetite.

Desire differs from emotion, in the following particulars. First, emotion has reference to the past, as well as to the future: desire has respect only to the future. Hence Thomas Brown calls desire "prospective emotion." But the emotion attending desire is not the desire itself. Secondly, desire is less fluctuating than emotion. While emotion rises and falls, like the sea-tides, desire moves steadily onward, like the river, to its object. Emotion is more immediately dependent than purely mental desire upon exciting causes. We hence speak of the cause of emotion and of the origin of desire. Thirdly, emotion may exist in reference to objects of aversion, hatred, disgust; but desire always implies the wishing or longing for its object.

The most important of the natural desires are the following:

1. Desire of Life.
2. Desire of Happiness.
3. Desire of Society.
4. Desire of Knowledge.
5. Desire of Esteem.
6. Desire of Owning.
7. Desire of Power.*

DESIRE OF LIFE.

A desire to live for ever is natural to all human beings. Agonizing or protracted disease, repeated disappointments, the pangs of remorse, sometimes overcome it; but no other desire so long and so resolutely resists their attacks. It is the last to die out of the heart. "All that a man hath will he give for his life." When we hear a man say, his existence has become such a burden that he has no longer any desire for life, our sympathy is excited for him, as one on whom crime or misfortune has laid its heaviest hand.

Some suppose that the desire of life results from a consideration of the good connected with it. But the fact

* Reid reckons *three* primitive desires, that of Power, of Knowledge, and of Esteem. Vol. IV., p. 76. Stewart makes *five*, adding to the above, Desire of Society and of Superiority. Whewell also has five, but substitutes Desire of Safety, and of Having, for Stewart's Desire of Knowledge and of Power. Vol. I. p. 42.

that men cling tenaciously to it, sometimes even in the entire absence of all present or prospective good, and in despite of the most appalling evils, justifies the conclusion that they have a strong inborn desire of life for its own sake.

The most important of the purposes which it seems designed to subserve are the three following.

1. *It was designed to protect life.*—By connecting the desire of life with our existence, the Creator has given a guardian angel to protect us. Without this, how feebly should we endure our trials; how often should we be fatally tempted to throw life away! Sustained by this, man often submits to protracted pains of hunger, to agonizing operations upon his body, and to endless varieties of intense mental suffering. It serves to render him patient, enduring, victorious.

There is, indeed, a higher motive, a sense of duty, that should induce us to prize and protect life; but this does not operate in all, nor in any at so early a period, or with such unfailing constancy, as the case requires. Here, as in many other instances, natural instinct serves as a substitute or an aid to moral principle, in securing our welfare.

2. *This desire contributes to our enjoyment.*—Coöperating with the sense of duty, it makes it our *pleasure* to cherish and protect life. If parents had no desire for the continuance of their offspring, if all labors and sufferings for them were prompted only by a sense of duty, the happiness of the parental relation would be immeasurably diminished. For the same reason, if we had no natural desire of our own life, if all we do and suffer to protect it were from a mere feeling of obligation, much of the service that we now enjoy would become an irksome and painful burden.

3. *This desire has a moral and religious end.*—It has been already said, that the desire in question combines with the feeling of duty in enabling us to struggle with trials. It thus helps us to gain a victory on the side of virtue. Nor is this all. The same desire of life, projecting itself into eternity, predisposes us to welcome that Gospel which brings life and immortality to light. One of the strongest holds which Christianity has upon us, is found in our desire to live for ever.

The desire of life moves us also to *gratitude.* In granting us from day to day what we ever desire, our Creator makes constant demands upon our grateful acknowledgments; a debt which we should never be slow to pay. And when he lifts the gate of the tomb, and points us to an endless life beyond it, language is too feeble to express the gratitude we owe.

The Christian is reconciled to the dissolution of the body, not because life is to him a burden, but because he has faith in Him who said, "He that believeth in me shall never die." Never is his desire of life more real and intense, than at the moment when he is about to die.

DESIRE OF HAPPINESS.

Some have considered this the *only* primitive desire, laying the foundation for all the others. Thus they suppose the desire of life, of society, of knowledge, &c., only secondary to that of happiness, the former being valued only as means to the latter. This view, advocated by Hume, Hobbes, and others, is sometimes called the *selfish* scheme, because it makes all human desires and actions spring from motives of personal happiness. It is a sufficient refutation of this view, that the primitive desires seek their ends, irrespective of consequences. This may at first seem a begging of the question. There can be no doubt that the desire of happiness is all-pervading. It commences with our rational existence, operates at all times, and modifies all our actions. We cannot annihilate it, if we would. It is probably the most constant and powerful natural motive of which we are the subjects.

It does not follow, however, that we desire nothing but from a mere regard to happiness. Instead of saying that we desire life, society, knowledge, esteem, only for the happiness they afford, we ought rather to say, that they afford us happiness because we have an instinctive desire for them. We should find little enjoyment in society, if we had not a social nature. Thus our desire of happiness harmonizes with our other instincts, as well as with our moral nature.

But while some have supposed that all our other desires, even those of a religious nature, spring from the desire of happiness, it has been maintained, on the other hand, that this motive ought to have *no* place. The notion of a disinterested benevolence has even been pressed so far, as to denounce every desire, affection, and act, not disconnected from all motives of personal happiness. This again is making war upon the wisdom of the Creator. Such a notion, seriously entertained, puts conscientiously religious persons upon the rack of self-torture, to divest themselves of a portion of their mental constitution; thus introducing discouragement and gloom into the soul, in place of repentance and hope; or, what is scarcely less to be deprecated, mocks them with the vain presumption, fatal to all genuine humility, that they have at last made the more than angelic attainment. He who imagines himself entirely indifferent to his own happiness, is either deceived or insane.

DESIRE OF SOCIETY.

Man is by nature a *social* being. Indeed the disposition to associate and share each other's pursuits and enjoyments, seems to pervade all living creatures. The domestic fowls about our dwellings, the sheep and cattle in our pastures, the wild deers and buffaloes in the forest, the birds of the air, the fishes of the sea, all manifest the same propensity.

Something analogous to this seems to pervade even the inanimate creation. All atoms and all portions of matter tend to unite. The stars of heaven move in clusters; no one of them wanders in space alone. Each has a mission for others, as well as for itself.

So strong is the disposition in creatures to associate, that, when deprived of society from their own species, they seek it in others; even those whom they naturally hate. Thus sheep and dogs, horses and oxen, cats and birds, for want of companions of their own species, have sometimes formed earnest attachments with each other.

For the same reason, men in solitude have sometimes become intensely attached to the most hateful creatures. "The Count de Lauzun was confined for nine years in the castle of Pignerol, in a small room, where no light could enter but from a chink in the roof. In this solitude he attached himself to a spider, and continued for some time to amuse himself with attempting to tame it, with catching flies for its support, and with superintending the progress of the webs. The jailer discovered his amusement, and killed the spider; and the Count used afterwards to declare, that the pang he felt on the occasion, could be compared only to that of a mother for the loss of a child." *

* Stewart's Active and Moral Powers, p. 25.

The helplessness of infants forbids in them so early a development of the social principle, as is seen in animals, but they manifest it by indubitable signs, as soon as they are capable. "Attend to the eyes, the features, and the gestures of a child on the breast, when another child is presented to it; both instantly, previous to the possibility of instruction or habit, exhibit the most indubitable expression of joy. Their eyes sparkle, and their features and gestures demonstrate, in the most unequivocal manner, a mutual attachment." *

This desire was evidently intended to render beings subservient to each other's wants, and happy in each other's society. If they were compelled to associate merely for mutual protection and sustenance, society would be a burden to be endured rather than a luxury to be enjoyed.

The social principle extends to religious as well as secular interests, uniting man with man in the bonds of a common faith. All religious bodies depend upon this principle, both for their origin and continuance. But for this, each individual would only worship his God alone. There would be no churches, no common altars, no social heaven. The same social instinct which unites us in the humbler affairs of time, which makes families, neighborhoods, nations, unites us also in the higher interests of religion, and finally brings human and angelic beings together, in fulness of sympathy and mutual joy, around the throne of heaven.

DESIRE OF KNOWLEDGE.

The human mind is naturally *inquisitive*. It desires to *know*. One of the first manifested propensities of the

* Smillie's Phil. Chap. XI.

little child is, to become acquainted with every object about him. He is not yet old enough to ask questions, but his actions indicate to every observer that a thousand questions are struggling in his mind. What is this? What is that? say his little glancing eyes and busy hands.

The first acts of infancy are engaged in experimenting with the senses upon the outer world. The infant has every thing to learn. He does not at first know how to interpret his own sensations and perceptions. Whether the object before him is at a distance, or in contact with the eye, whether it is yielding or resistant, substance or shadow, reality or phantom, he has yet to learn. The inborn principle of curiosity sets him earnestly and successfully upon this work.

Hence the eagerness with which children handle every thing in their way, their attempts to thrust their fingers into the flame of a candle, and their readiness to take up a shadow. The interest they realize in correcting their errors and gaining new ideas, urges them on, in subsequent life, to higher attainments; to the investigation of mathematical truths, historical facts, and all the phenomena of nature.

Nor is the desire of knowledge restricted to obvious and useful facts. It soon begins to search out latent causes. It explores not only the needful, but the curious. Even when one has no reason to suppose the desired knowledge will be of any practical utility, he still pursues it. When a physician has lost a patient by an internal cause that has baffled the diagnosis of the profession, he desires a post-mortem examination, scarcely less to gratify his curiosity than to guide his future practice. The astronomer eyes the heavens for months, with intense gaze, to descry the feeble twinkling of some star, the knowledge of which can add nothing to the comforts of life.

If any suppose that thirst for applause occasions all this, the answer readily is, that were it not for the principle of curiosity in man, ambition could not find in the popular response any reward for its services. Such is our desire of knowledge, that we both seek it ourselves, and bestow the meed of honor upon those who successfully seek it for us.

This desire was intended both to stimulate us in the pursuit of knowledge, and to render us happy in obtaining and possessing it. It thus sustains to the mind a relation like that which appetite does to the body. Knowledge is the mind's appropriate food. But without the desire for it, all study would be mere "weariness of the flesh," toil and drudgery, without any rewarding satisfaction.

Incited and nerved by this desire, the human mind has surmounted immeasurable difficulties; it has scaled more than Alpine summits. Urged onward by the same indomitable principle, it is laying this entire world under contribution; and it is encouraged in its career, with the sublime hope of another and a boundless one to explore beyond the present

DESIRE OF ESTEEM.

No human being is entirely indifferent to the opinions of others respecting him. Indeed man was made to find much of his enjoyment in the approving smiles of his fellow-beings. We are so constituted, that the approbation or disapprobation of those especially whom we love, is cordial or wormwood to our spirits.

We may contend against the desire of esteem, we may call it by hard names; we may imagine it vanquished; still it clings to us, as undying and active as the soul itself. It is the Creator's own work within us; why then should we condemn or disown it? Milton calls it an "infirmity," but the "infirmity of a noble mind." Some have endeavored to prove, from a mistaken idea of something wrong in this principle, that it is no part of our constitution. They maintain that "the esteem of our fellow-creatures is at first desired on account of its apprehended utility, and that it comes in time to be pursued as an ultimate end, without any reference on our part to the advantages it bestows." To this notion it has been justly replied, "As the object of hunger is not happiness, but food; as the object of curiosity is not happiness, but knowledge, so the object of this principle of action is not happiness, but the esteem and respect of other men." *

The desire of esteem is not confined to the present; it projects itself into the future. We desire to be held in honor by our fellow-beings after we are laid in the grave, scarcely less than while living among them. The numerous monuments of war, of genius, of art, of literature, which ambition has erected to perpetuate the fame of its subjects after they have passed away, are all witnesses of the activity of this principle.

The question is often asked, Why should we desire the esteem of others, after it can no longer be of any advantage to us? The answer is, We desire it in future, for the same reason that we desire it in the present, not for its advantages, but for itself.

Some attempt to resolve this desire into an illusion of the imagination, produced by habit. They suppose that habit has taught men to imagine themselves present, enjoying a reputation among their fellow-beings after they are dead. "Men please themselves," says Wollaston, "with notions of immortality, and fancy a perpetuity of fame secured to themselves by books and testimonies of

* Stewart, p. 29.

historians; but, alas! it is a stupid delusion when they imagine themselves present and enjoying that fame or the reading of their story after their death.

And beside, in reality, the man is not even known the more to posterity, because his name is transmitted to them. *He* doth not live, because his *name* does. When it is said, Julius Cæsar conquered Gaul, beat Pompey, and changed the Roman Commonwealth into a monarchy, it is the same thing as to say, The conqueror of Pompey was Cæsar; that is, Cæsar and the conqueror of Pompey are the same thing, and Cæsar is as much known by the one designation as by the other. The amount, then, is only this, that the conqueror of Pompey conquered Pompey; or, rather, since Pompey is now as little known as Cæsar, *somebody* conquered *somebody*. Such a poor business is this boasted immortality; and such as has been described, is the thing called glory among us." *

Now the obvious truth here, as in all other instances, is, that the instinct of our nature is in beautiful harmony with God's moral government and our immortality. We were made both to find happiness in the esteem of good beings and also to exist for ever. The two facts are not to be disconnected. When, therefore, we desire to be "had in *everlasting* remembrance," and pursue the right course to be thus remembered, we are fulfilling our true destiny.

The most important purposes of the desire in question are the three following:

1. It was designed to induce us to *merit* esteem. It is thus a powerful motive to virtuous action. When a youth has learned to say, he "don't care" for the opinions of others, he is not far from ruin.

* Quoted by Stéwart, p. 28.

If any suppose that the desire of esteem, as a motive to virtue, would naturally make us endeavor to appear better than we really are, it is sufficient to reply, that Providence has so constituted us, that we cannot really *enjoy* esteem, unless conscious that we *deserve* it.

2. This desire was intended to render us *happy* in the favor of others. It furnishes an important part of the good man's motive and reward. It makes him welcome with delight every approving smile, and thus leads him on to higher merit and a still richer inheritance. The most enviable person on earth, so far as this life is concerned, is he who truly desires and fully receives the approbation of all good men. No gold nor glory compares with this. Who would not have the reward of Washington, rather than the wealth of Crœsus, or the wreath of Cæsar?

3. This desire was given us to subserve *religion*. Supremely directed to the Supreme Being, it becomes a religious principle of high order, and fosters every pious sentiment. Much as the Christian may value the esteem of his fellow-beings, he values the approbation of God immeasurably more. Whenever, therefore, a conflict arises between the two, the instinct of his nature, under guidance of Christian principle, prompts him to seek the "honor that comes from God only." He is thus sure of ultimately securing the esteem of *all* good beings.

DESIRE OF OWNING.

This is called by Whewell the desire of *having*. But the entire idea is not thus expressed. We may *have* what is not our *own*. He however explains himself to intend, at least in part, what we mean by the word own. "But the desire to possess such objects, as it exists in man, goes beyond the measure of their obvious use. He considers them as connected with himself in a permanent and exclusive manner, and looks upon them as *his*, as his *own*. The things which he thus looks upon as his own, he is disturbed at the prospect of losing, and is angry at any one who attempts to take them from him. Nor can he be at ease in his thoughts, or act steadily and tranquilly, except he be allowed to possess in quiet and security what he thus has as his. He needs to hold it as his *property*." *

But it would not be correct to speak of a man's holding his wife, or his child, as his "*property;*" yet they are his *own*.

Some writers do not consider the desire of owning original in our nature, but resolvable into other and more simple principles. Thus Stewart says, "The idea of power is, partly at least, the foundation of our *attachment to property*. It is not enough for us to have the *use* of an object. We desire to have it completely at our own disposal, without being responsible to any person whatever for the purposes to which we may choose to turn it."

Doubtless the desire of power, as it exists in mature life, is partly the foundation of attachment to property; but the child wants more than the entire *use* of an object; he wants to feel that it is his *own*. "There is an unspeakable pleasure," says Addison, "in calling any thing one's *own*. A freehold, though it be but in ice and snow, will make the owner pleased in the possession and stout in the defence of it."

To have the *disposal* of an object, is not the same thing as to have it as one's *own*. The child has not the disposal of his parent, yet the parent is his own. Neither has the parent the absolute disposal of his child; yet the child is his own. Suppose an *adopted* child, over which the pa-

* Vol. I. p. 45.

rent is made by law to have as full control as over his own child; is it precisely the same thing, either to parent or child, as though the child were really his own? In that little word *own* there is a charm, springing from an instinct of our nature, of which none are ever fully divested.

It will hence be seen, that while some writers have failed to recognize this instinct, others have failed to give a definition sufficiently generic to convey the entire idea of it. A man's house, farm, wife, children, are all his own; but only the first two are his property. Wives generally call their husbands their own; but they do not often lay claim to them as their property; nor are they often so fortunate as to be able to say, We have them "completely at our own *disposal*," however much they may desire it.

The two following seem to be the most important ends for which this desire was given us.

1. It seems to have been intended to nourish the *domestic affections*. By it the bonds of conjugal, fraternal, filial, and paternal love, are greatly strengthened. When the happy suitor can look upon the object of his affections as truly his own, he realizes peculiar emotions of delight, which increase his love for the person. When he looks upon the smiling infant in its mother's arms as his own, he realizes an additional satisfaction.

It is not because he has the entire control of these objects of his love, or that he anticipates some advantage from them, that his pleasure is by them augmented; it is because they are his *own*. Along with this gratified desire springs a new affection, and thus peculiar pleasures and affections pervade all the relations of domestic life. The reason why none but husbands and wives have the entire conjugal affection, and none but parents the entire parental affection, seems to be, that none but they realize the gratification, in these particulars, of the desire now contemplated.

2. This desire combines with others, especially with that of power, to produce the *desire of property*. It thus becomes an element of one of the main springs of human action. That the desire of property may be excessive, that it may degenerate into avarice, is no proof that it is not, when rightly controlled and directed, of great value. Annihilate it, and the wheels of enterprise would soon move sluggishly around; civilized nations would soon fall from their eminence to the abject condition of those savage hordes, with whom industry has no motive, because property has no protection.

DESIRE OF POWER.

We mean by power the *ability to produce results*. Its greatness is measured by the results it can accomplish. Man delights in the consciousness of being able to surmount difficulties, and secure brilliant results. It is not merely the object gained, that gives him pleasure; it is the consciousness of being *able* to gain it. Men desire success for its own sake.

"When we are led to consider ourselves as the authors of any effect, we feel a sensible pride or exaltation in the consciousness of *power*, and the pleasure is in general proportioned to the greatness of the effect, compared with the smallness of our exertions. The pastimes of the boy are almost without exception such as suggest to him the idea of *power*. When he throws a stone or shoots an arrow, he is pleased in the being able to produce an effect at a distance from him; and, while he measures with his eye the amplitude or range of his missile weapon, contemplates with satisfaction the extent to which his power has reached. It is on a similar principle that he loves to bring his strength into comparison with that of his fellows, and to enjoy the consciousness of superior prowess." *

The desire of power includes that of *liberty*. The power to do as we please, implies also the *liberty* to do so. We may have the liberty without the power, but we cannot have the power without the liberty. The one is generic to the other. But the desire of each is equally extensive. Every human being wishes to be free. He is naturally impatient of any bond upon either his soul or body. He desires freely to use his limbs and members, his intellect, his will, his entire being.

No constitutional desire is more marked and more obviously universal than this. The infant manifests it at the earliest period of activity, and the weight of fourscore years does not avail to repress it. Nor does the highest attainment in moral excellence abate it. The purest and most angelic being, as well as the humblest, desires to be at liberty to use all his faculties as he pleases, responsible only to his conscience and his God. This is true liberty, and this is power.

This principle of our nature was obviously designed to be an important stimulus to virtuous and noble endeavor. Without it, man's right arm would be crippled. Had the child no natural desire of power, he would probably end his days nearly as powerless as he commenced them. It co-operates with the desire of knowledge. The mastery of languages, sciences, arts, the command of logic, poetry, eloquence, insight into the springs of action, and the connection of causes and results, afforded by philosophical analysis and patient abstraction, all afford stirring induce-

* Stewart, p. 41.

ments to effort by appealing to this desire. Lord Bacon is said to have originated the maxim that knowledge is power, but long before his day mankind knew that knowledge was powerful, and ignorance weak.

The same principle is active in urging men to high attainments in moral excellence. If knowledge is power, no less truly is excellence of character. If we desire the former to augment our influence over fellow-beings, why not for the same reason desire the latter? We may have indeed another motive, of a moral kind, to urge us to this; but here again, as in instances previously noticed, a *natural* motive coöperates with a *moral* one, to induce us to aim at the highest possible attainment in excellence, with a view to accomplishing the greatest good to mankind.

CONCLUDING REMARKS ON THE DESIRES.

We have thus enumerated *seven* primitive desires. It may seem unaccountable that they are so few. A young lady on being asked how many original desires there are in the human mind, replied, that she should think there are about a thousand! She doubtless spoke out of the fulness of her own heart.

But we must consider that our list enumerates merely the *primary* desires. These are only the *elements* from which all other desires are formed. The whole world is made from a few simple elements. Out of nine digits we form combinations reaching to infinity. As there is no measurable limit to the numbers into which the nine digits may be wrought, so there is none to the secondary desires of the human heart. Their name is *legion*, for they are many.

It is very important to remark, that we learn the *designs* of the Creator respecting us by our *constitution*, not by our character. The former is *his* work; the latter is ours. Let us then look attentively at these constitutional desires, to learn from them his will. The reader is requested to recall each of them, as related to the following particulars.

We learn from them, that our Creator would have us prize the being he has given us; that he would have us value happiness, and pursue the course tending to perpetuate and exalt it; that he designed us to live in society, and to find enjoyment in the reciprocity of sympathy and affection; that he made us to aspire after knowledge, and to cherish the expectation of endless progression in it; that we ought so to conduct as to merit and ultimately receive the esteem of all wise and good beings; that we were designed, without any sacrifice of general benevolence, to sustain to certain objects a relation which renders them peculiarly our own, such as accords with the tenderest affections and most personal wants of our nature; and finally, that it was the divine intention that we should improve all our faculties with a view to the highest practicable attainment, in physical, intellectual, and moral power.

Who that examines the primitive desires of his nature, as implanted by the hand that made him, can fail to see that these are truly the benign and glorious designs of his Creator concerning him; and who, that studies the Bible, can fail to see that precisely the same designs are revealed there? How clearly does the light of philosophy blend with that of divine revelation. How certainly does a correct analysis of the human mind point us to the revealed will of God, as coincident, in all points, with that indicated in our constitution.

CHAPTER VI.

NATURAL EMOTION.

We have a great variety of transient feeling termed *emotion.* It is more or less associated with affection and desire, but may exist without them. We may have an emotion in reference to an object towards which we have neither love nor hatred, desire nor aversion. All such emotion, as well as that involved in natural affection and desire, is purely natural.

An emotion takes its particular type and name from its outward or *objective cause.* When occasioned by the perception of a beautiful object, it is called an emotion of beauty; when by a sublime object, an emotion of sublimity; when by a terrific object, an emotion of terror; when by a ludicrous object, an emotion of the ludicrous. The specific susceptibility to these various emotions differs much with different individuals; and indeed in the same person the emotions gradually merge together, so that no exact line can at last be traced between them. In their extremes they are very dissimilar, but as they approach each other they assimilate, and finally become apparently the same.

ILLUSTRATIONS OF THE VARIOUS EMOTIONS.

Emotion of beauty.—As one goes out into the country on a bright June morning, looks upon the green hills, the winding streams, the rich foliage, the fields of springing grain, the happy flocks and herds feeding in the pastures; as his grateful lungs inhale the balmy air and his ears drink in its melodies, a feeling of fresh delight comes over him. He perhaps left his house feeling dull and depressed, but now he is alive with pleasure. He is realizing an emotion of *beauty*. This emotion has various degrees of intensity, but it is always *pleasing*.

Emotion of sublimity.—As the person supposed continues on his way, a cloud arises. It increases in size and blackness, and at length spans the heavens. Its deep broad folds sweep majestically along the horizon; the forked lightnings begin to play, and the thunders to roll in its dark bosom.

His emotion has now changed. Before, it was comparatively mild, gentle, tranquil; now it has become strong, earnest, intense. This is an emotion of *sublimity*. It is pleasing, but not as purely so as the emotion of beauty; it has in it an element of the awful.

Emotion of terror.—The above person turns to escape the approaching tempest, but it is too late. The lightnings, which before played sublimely in the distance, now hurl their fiery bolts around him. The mingled rain and hail pour in torrents; the hurricane sweeps furiously along, prostrating trees and buildings; nature seems to be frantic, and her enraged elements threaten universal destruction.

The emotion of the person supposed has now undergone another change. It has become still more intense.

It is violent, spasmodic, and perhaps uncontrollable. Instead of being simply pleasing, as at first; or pleasing with a dash of pathos approaching the awful, as in the second instance, it is decidedly and wholly painful. This is an emotion of *terror*.

Emotion of the ludicrous.—The tempest at last subsides, and nature is again tranquil. All the sublime and terrible emotions of our friend have ceased, and he is returning composedly to his dwelling. But just as he is entering the town, he sees a young dandy, fresh from the toilet and dressed in his finest, making his first adventure out since the storm, and tripping gaily across the way. Stepping incautiously upon a slippery place, the unfortunate dandy loses his perpendicular, and goes headlong, with all his finery, into the mire.

Our friend may indeed realize some feeling of pity for the unfortunate youth, but as no injury is done to his person, the predominant emotion is of another kind. He is instinctively convulsed with laughter. This emotion is rather pleasing, but very unlike that of beauty. This is an emotion of the *ludicrous*. It is much like the excitement which one feels on beholding the ludicrous capers of a buffoon, but is modified by the fact that the feat of the dandy was undesigned and unfortunate, while that of the buffoon is designed and fortunate.

Emotions of surprise and wonder.—The man supposed at length returns to his dwelling. On entering it he finds there a former neighbor, whom he has not seen for many years, and whom he supposed was long since lost at sea. He at first scarcely credits his own eyes; but after a full survey of the person before him, and on hearing his voice, all his doubts are removed. It is indeed no other than his veritable friend and neighbor, whom he had supposed dead. His feeling is now quite changed from what it was when he entered the house. He is realizing an emotion of *surprise.*

After reflecting a few moments, he begins to agitate in his mind the question how his friend escaped the wreck, and by what means he has safely returned. His emotion thus gradually subsides into that of *wonder.* Less violent than at first, it assumes a composed and deliberate type.

Simultaneous emotions.—It is not necessary to take all the *time* supposed above, to bring before the mind the various exciting causes of emotion. The powers of conception and imagination may array them in very rapid succession. By the aid of these alone, while sitting solitary in his own apartment, a person may pass almost unconsciously from one emotion to another, and may sometimes become the subject of them all apparently at the same time. Thus the mind seems to resemble an organ or a violin, vibrating at the same time under various impressions and giving out discordant notes.

This is realized most vividly when one is listening to an oratorio, or attending a theatrical entertainment, or reading a highly wrought story, in which variously exciting scenes are mingled together. The mind is then sometimes almost tortured with conflicting emotions. Tears and smiles, agonizing terror, and convulsive laughter, the sublime and the ridiculous, seem to keep company in the soul, and to play together upon the accommodating countenance.

Conflicting emotions.—Although these emotions may seem to be simultaneous, they are not strictly so. Two conflicting feelings cannot possess the mind at the same instant. To suppose the heart joyful and sorrowful, pleased and displeased, angry and complacent, at the same identical moment, is much the same as to suppose a body at the same time hot and cold, fluid and solid. But the alternations between these mental states may be imperceptibly rapid. Generally, however, they are not so rapid as to elude our notice. The pantomime that would successfully play upon our passions, must regard this law of mental operation, and not attempt to excite two conflicting emotions at the same time, nor to pass us suddenly from the one to the other.

Thought is quicker than emotion. It usually takes a perceptible time to make the transition from sadness to joy, and from the calm emotion of beauty to one of sublimity or terror, although there may be but a step between them. It is only under intense pressure, or some undue excitement, that very rapid alternations of emotion are realized. They are mostly undesirable. They often injure the sensibilities. Under their repeated influence, the mind sometimes loses its balance, and tends to insanity, in which state they culminate in their wildest forms.

OBJECTIVE CAUSES OF THE VARIOUS EMOTIONS.

Of beauty.—We have already alluded to the objective causes of emotion, in defining the emotion itself. But they must be more fully noticed. We shall find that the world without us is an exact counterpart to the world within us; the adaptation of the one to the other being a striking illustration of the wisdom and goodness of God. If there was no error in the construction of the universe, there was none in the constitution of the human mind, on the supposition that the one was made for the other; for their mutual adaptation is perfect.

As the emotion of beauty is healthful and may be continually repeated with advantage to the mind, the Creator has provided largely for its habitual exercise. He has richly supplied it with daily food. All creation is replete with objective beauty. There is beauty of form, beauty of color, beauty of proportion, beauty of fitness, beauty of sound, beauty of motion, and beauty of all these combined. The changing seasons, as the year rolls round, bring with them almost every imaginable form of beauty.

The human figure and countenance are beautiful; so are the forms and movements of the animal tribes. What more graceful than the horse or the doe, bounding over the fields, leaping the hedges, and darting through the opening forests? All the birds of the air are beautiful in their plumage, their motions, and their music. Scarcely less beautiful are the finny tribes, sporting in the waters. All flowers are beautiful. So are the green fields, the bending corn, and the branching trees waving in the zephyrs.

Every hue of solar light is beautiful, whether painted upon a flower, or upon an evening cloud, or a glorious heaven-spanning rainbow. The entire firmament, by day and by night, is a vast dome of ever-varying beauties; while the earth beneath, as if vying with the heavens above, is also enameled all over with living beauty. And the works of art, responsive to those of nature, copy her fine pictures with exquisite skill, and sometimes almost transcend the original.

Human hands rear imposing forms of architectural beauty around us; adorn them and their occupants with beauties of the finest mould and finish, in which are blended all the colors of nature and of art; furnish them with breathing canvas and speaking marble; and then, with curious instruments of their own framing, catch and combine all the tones and voices of the living creation, and pour them in endless varieties of enchanting music upon our delighted ears. Thus, through both the senses of sight and of hearing, beauty is pouring from without upon the mind. The emotions thus awakened are almost as perpetual as our being, are never violent but always agreeable, and are therefore exhaustless sources of pleasure.

Of grandeur and sublimity.—Emotions of grandeur are pleasing, but they are so earnest and impressive that they soon exhaust the mind. The author, whose pages are crowded with passages of grandeur, intensely pleases us for a time; but we are soon exhausted, and seek relief in more quiet beauties. Natural scenery whose features are strikingly grand, like those of the Alps, produces a similar effect; and we are at length glad to emerge from it into scenes of more tranquil delight. When we contemplate the vast rolling ocean, or the lofty azure vault of heaven, or the clear evening sky bespangled with stars, our first emotion is that of grandeur, mingled with that of beauty; and as the former gradually subsides, the calmer emotion of beauty takes the entire possession.

The emotion of sublimity, together with its cause, is much the same as that of grandeur; but the latter has more respect to what is mighty, vast, boundless; the former, to what is lofty, incomprehensible and approaching the terrible. Grandeur is a term of greatness, sublimity of loftiness. The wide expanse is grand, the dizzy height sublime. Hence an object may have the attribute of grandeur without that of sublimity. A huge column is grand, but not always sublime. A kite, darting upwards into the clouds, is sometimes sublime, but not grand.

When we look upon the fire-sped car, dashing furiously along on its iron path, or gaze upon the stupendous cataract of Niagara, or upon the wide, pathless ocean, we have an emotion of grandeur. But when we look upward to the summit of Mont Blanc, resting as a stupendous silvery dome in mid-heaven; or when we contemplate eternity; or when we see a dark cloud rolling portentously up the skies and shooting down its lightnings; we have an emotion of sublimity. These, also, like emotions of grandeur, are too powerful to be long endured. They are of a pleasing nature, but the pleasure is sometimes closely allied to pain. Beauty, grandeur, and sublimity are, however, frequently all combined in the same object.

Of awe.—The emotion of awe is in many respects like the foregoing, but it has some peculiarities. There is in it much of dread, reverence, and astonishment.

We are awed at Jehovah's exhibitions of sovereignty, justice, and majesty. When we contemplate a pestilence, sweeping over the land, and hurrying thousands to eternity; or an earthquake, or volcano, engulfing and burying up whole cities; or a storm of fire reducing Sodom and Gomorrah, with all their inhabitants, to ashes; or a deluge of water, burying the whole world in a common grave; we then have an emotion of *awe.*

In scarcely less degree, although from humbler causes, we realize a similar emotion, when we read an account of a shipwreck, or of the burning of a steamboat, or of a railroad catastrophe, by which many of our fellow-beings have been suddenly destroyed. We are awe-struck by such providential events.

But it is not essential to this emotion that there should be the destruction or even endangering of life. We may "stand in awe" before exhibitions of Jehovah's power, when they contemplate our welfare, as well as when they are made in judgment, or to accomplish ends of justice. The children of Israel had emotions of awe beneath the burnings and quakings of Sinai, not because life was thereby sacrificed or endangered; nor yet so much because they regarded those events as judgments, or as ministers of justice, as because they saw in them indications of their great Jehovah's presence and majesty.

Of terror.—The emotion of terror is obvious and well defined. Every person has experienced it, and knows exactly what it is. Yet some have identified it with sublimity, or have at least supposed them complements to each other. They are frequently united, but are still essentially distinct. The one often exists in full force without the other.

The soaring of the eagle is sublime, but not terrible. On the other hand, a poisonous reptile, a mad dog, a stinging insect, has no sublimity, but it is terrible. While a thunder-storm is often both terrible and sublime. In general, we have emotions of terror from whatever endangers our personal safety. As such emotions are wholly painful, we incline to shun their causes as much as possible.

Of the ludicrous and the ridiculous.—As there is in us a constitutional susceptibility to an emotion of the ludicrous, so there are causes without to excite it. Nature exhibits some curious freaks. The monkey performs laughable tricks, and some other irrational creatures make similar appeals to our sense of the ludicrous.

But it is in the conduct of the human species, that we find most of that which excites the emotions in question. Many persons seem intent to render themselves ludicrous, and even ridiculous, in the eyes of their fellow-beings. An emotion of the ridiculous differs from that of the ludicrous, as it is associated with a feeling of contempt. It is not merely the harlequin, who cuts his capers for a reward, nor the comedian, whose *business* it is to make men laugh, to whom we now refer.

Nor need we repair to the great watering-places, and

other resorts of fashionable folly, where it would seem to be the main object of some to appear ridiculous, to find exciting causes for this emotion. On every side we may witness those irrational displays of pride and vanity, which can hardly fail to provoke contempt.

The struggles of the poor in aping the rich, and of the rich in outdoing each other's follies; the tenacity with which the fashionable world often hug the very chains which they affect to despise; the gilded miseries of high life, writhing beneath a smiling mask, received in eager barter for a good conscience and a contented mind; the shallow tricks of brainless ambition to conceal its ignorance and shine in borrowed splendors; all these things are ridiculous enough, and have furnished lawful matter for the pen of the satirist in every age.

But there is a brighter side to this picture, and one which greatly redeems humanity from the opprobrium under which the above views would place it. If humanity exhibits much that is contemptible, it also exhibits much to be admired. Its noble self-sacrifices; its deeds of chivalrous valor; its triumphs of genius and art; its patient endurings and determined endeavors in well-doing; its free surrender of life itself upon the battle-field for its country, or at the stake for its conscience; these are deeds which make humanity cease to appear contemptible, and which summon all our most vivid emotions of beauty, sublimity and grandeur.

CONCLUDING REMARKS ON NATURAL EMOTIONS.

The brute creation have many of the emotions which we have described, but the absence of a rational nature restricts them to such as are *merely* animal. They have, in some sense, emotions of delight, of pain, of fear, of surprise, but those occasioned by causes strictly rational, æsthetical, and moral, are without their province.

The reader will now carefully notice the distinction between *emotion*, and the other mental states and exercises which we have examined.

Appetite occasions *desire*, the gratification of which is *attended* with an emotion of pleasure, and the refusal of which, with an emotion of pain. We thus see that the emotion is not the same thing as either the appetite or the desire.

If our affection for a friend is severely simple and benevolent, it may be attended with little emotion, and is then usually a very sincere and pure affection. If it is attended with excess of emotion, it becomes a passion, and is then often less pure and reliable. There is then in it less of principle and more of excitement.

And since affection is exercised only towards conscious beings, every emotion occasioned by inanimate objects, or mere exciting events, has no relation to affection, and is therefore either a *mere* emotion, or an attendant on some desire.

Emotion is thus an accompaniment of the other mental states and exercises, serving to invigorate and enrich them, and is much the same as is understood by the common word *spirit*. A man of lively spirits is one favored with a large endowment of the emotional element. He is easy to kindle, and may be equally so to burn out. His emotion may also be deep and calm; but when it is so, it is by virtue of the depth and steadiness of the affection or desire to which it pertains. Hence a man of little real affection and of feeble principle, may be on fire with emotion to day, and a spiritless corpse to-morrow.

Still, we must not fail to see that the susceptibility to

emotion is a very important element of the mind, not only as related to the objects of this world, to which we have referred, but also to those of a higher world; having much to do with religious devotion, and often imparting wings to the spirit, with which it soars to mingle its raptures with the angels around God's throne.

CHAPTER VII.

NATURAL VOLITION.

The feelings which we have thus far considered move us to act, and volition is the executive motive power which determines our conduct. The former are the breezes which fill the sails of the ship: the latter is the helm by which reason guides it.

Thus, appetite occasions hankering for food; volition decides to gratify or to refuse it.

Affection loves a friend or hates an enemy; volition determines to embrace or to shun him.

Desire longs for wealth, fame, indulgence; volition chooses or refuses to pursue it.

When volition merely executes an original impulse or pure instinct, it has no moral quality. Such are the volitions of the brute creation. We have many such in common with them.

In this view, writers have distinguished between *volition* and *will;* regarding the former as executing the mere impulses of nature, and the latter as related to reason and conscience. The acts of the former are then strictly instinctive; while those of the latter are rational and responsible. This distinction has been made by some German philosophers.

But so far as the *power* of volition is concerned, it is a distinction without a difference. In both cases it is the power to will or choose; nothing more nor less. In the one case it is a power to choose in view of rational motives; in the other, from the mere impulses of instinct.

Let us now proceed to indicate those volitions which are strictly natural.

We begin with those which execute the demands of *appetite.* When reason and conscience are developed, they should take these demands in charge, at least so far as not to allow them to transgress the rules of temperance and chastity; but in the absence or the partial development of reason and conscience, the cravings of appetite are the only or the principal motives to prompt and to regulate the volitions to gratify it. Such are the volitions of infants and of all animals to take their food.

The same is true of volitions prompted by mere *natural affection.* We have seen that the parental, filial, fraternal, conjugal, and social affections, are all a part of our nature. Hence the simple volitions employed in their service, and with exclusive reference to their appropriate ends, are as destitute of moral quality as the affections which they subserve. Such are volitions to care for and caress our children, to dwell with our parents, to befriend our brothers and sisters, to live with our companions, to reciprocate social civilities and friendships. However valuable and excellent these volitions, they imply nothing praiseworthy in us, but only in the Being who made us. God is the author of them, in the same sense that he is of those volitions of the brute which make it care for its young.

The same is true of volitions to execute the *natural de-*

sires. These are the desire of life, of happiness, of society, of knowledge, of esteem, of owning, and of power. So far as volitions are engaged only by these in seeking their appropriate ends, they are as characterless on our part as the desires themselves. Such are our primitive volitions to protect life, to secure happiness, to cultivate society, to pursue knowledge, to secure esteem, to have our own, and to possess power. To choose this is *natural.* It requires no conscience and no regard to what is right. While, therefore, as in the former case, such volitions imply no moral merit in us, but only in Him who made us, it is unnatural and wrong in us to withhold them.

The same again is true of volitions prompted by *natural emotions.* We have emotions of beauty, of sublimity, of terror, &c., which induce volitions with direct reference to their ends. We instinctively prefer the beautiful, reject the ugly, and flee the terrible. The man who does not will to avoid a rattlesnake, to save himself from drowning, or to clear the track of an approaching car, is untrue to his nature. As in the cases above, there may be nothing in these volitions of a moral quality; nothing done from a regard to duty; but to do *otherwise* would be rebellion against nature, and therefore against God.

Many of our volitions are prompted only *in part* by natural impulses. Motives of a moral quality are often associated with them, and thus give the choice a mixed character. Our volitions may thus rise above or sink below the quality of mere naturalness, according as our natural impulses are associated with motives morally right or wrong.

The mother, for example, instinctively loves her child. That love may blend with a feeling of *duty*, and thus receive a moral element. A man has a natural desire for life. This may be associated with a feeling of moral obligation to cherish and protect it. A man naturally desires happiness and dreads misery. These feelings may combine with the dictates of conscience, to induce him to pursue a course which will save him from the one, and secure to him the other.

We here see the perfect adaptation of our constitution to the high moral and religious purpose which it contemplates. We see, demonstrably, that man was made for an end for which the animal was not made. The animal and the man, for important reasons, begin and move on together, so far as the earthly and the spiritual, the temporal and the eternal, can be united; but with the natural impulses of man, may be associated the motives of morality and the higher motives of religion; and all, blending harmoniously together, conspire to the same glorious end, the highest perfection and eternal happiness of his being.

AGENCY OF VOLITION ON THE BODY.

Let it be remembered that when we speak of the agency of volition, we mean the agency which the being himself exerts by means of willing. All the direct executive power which a person has over his body, he exerts by his will. Here is a large class of volitions purely natural.

It is no part of our present object to explain the mysterious connection between the will and the muscles, or to show how the one moves the other. We are here concerned only with the fact.

Now the tongue is silent. The person wills to speak, and instantly it obeys. Now the eye is shut. The person wills to see, and quick as thought the eyelids open.

His hand is holding a pen in the act of writing. A friend enters the room and he wills to embrace him. In a moment the pen is dropped, and his hand grasps that of his friend.

He is sitting in his study, absorbed with thought. It occurs to him that the mail has arrived, by which he expects a letter. He wills to go for it, and is immediately on the way. But while on the way, he thinks of a letter left in his study, which must now be mailed. He wills to return for it. Forthwith the body turns upon its heel, and is on the way back to the study.

Such is the power of volition on the body. It lifts it up from the recumbent state, and pulls, turns, and twists it, at pleasure, in every imaginable direction. The stately step of the chieftain, the graceful movements of the lady in the drawing-room, the antics of the school-boy, the capers of the clown, are all due to the same subtle and mighty agency of the will.

And this voluntary control over the body is shared with man by the brute creation. The movements of every reptile, and of every beast upon the earth, of all the fishes that sport in the waters, of all the birds that cut the air, are due to this same mysterious agency.

As all such volitions accomplish their ends in the movements they respect, they are as natural as the impulses which prompt them. In brutes they *must* be *purely* natural; for brutes have no moral nature. But the impulses which prompt them in man, may be associated with those having moral quality.

It is *natural* for a man to choose to rise up and exert himself, when he has reposed long enough. He may also choose to do so from a sense of *duty*. It is *natural* for the hungry and thirsty man, as it is for the brute, to choose to eat and drink; but the man may *also* "eat or drink," as the brute cannot, "to the glory of God." Thus while the brute accomplishes its mission by obeying only

its natural impulses, man does not accomplish his, but by obeying also the dictates of his rational nature.

MOVEMENTS PARTLY INVOLUNTARY.

The movements of the bodily members are involuntary, semi-voluntary, and voluntary. The *involuntary* movements are, the beating of the heart, the flowing of the blood, and the action of the secretory organs. Over these our volition has no direct control. Our life would be a laborious business indeed, if we were obliged to attend unremittingly, by day and by night, to these movements.

The semi-voluntary movements are, those of the lungs, eyes, and some other organs. Over these we have a partial voluntary control. Did these depend wholly upon the activity of the will, we could not be relieved from attending to them so as to sleep at night; and the perpetual service demanded would be a burden by day.

On the other hand, if we had *no* voluntary control over them, we should suffer great inconvenience. If we could not regulate our own breath, nor open and shut our eyes at pleasure, both our comfort and safety would be taken from us. We cannot, therefore, fail to see the divine wisdom of this arrangement.

The movements which are *wholly* voluntary, are those of the limbs and external members, and of the body as a whole. Thus volition is man's natural and sole power, with which to direct and manage his physical system. External force and the influence of disease apart, he moves his body as he wills.

AGENCY OF VOLITION OVER THE INTELLECTIVE POWERS.

Although we are passive in sensations, volition is concerned in occasioning them. If food is in a person's mouth, he experiences from it an involuntary sensation; but volition placed the food there. If we visit a theatrical entertainment, we realize from it a variety of sensations, which put the intellect in action, but we are voluntary in going there. Thus many of our sensations, and of course the intellectual activity resulting from them, come of our will.

Those powers of mind which the brute creation share in part with us, are so dependent upon the will, that unless we exert its vigilance to elevate and guide their operations, they will never rise much above their corresponding powers in the mere animal. Hence a most important part of education consists in bringing them under a steady and determined voluntary control.

And even those higher faculties which so distinguish us from brutes, are true and faithful to their objects only as a true and faithful will makes them so. The judgment itself, which we are prone to think under the sublime sway of pure evidence, is sometimes sadly controlled by a perverse will. And imagination also, the bird of angel-wing, which outspeeds the lightning, and has more than magic power to create airy worlds in the twinkling of an eye, can do little else than flutter, until the will bids her go.

Thus dependent upon man's voluntary agency, are the movements of his physical and of his intellectual powers. He uses his body and his intellect, mostly, as he *wills* to do. A large proportion of the volitions concerned in these movements, as we have seen, are merely natural.

Those of them which have moral quality, or for which we are morally responsible, will be indicated in a subsequent part of the volume.

PART II.

THE RATIONAL MOTIVE POWERS.

CHAPTER I.

CONSCIENCE.

MAN alone of all creatures upon earth is capable of *moral* action. He alone realizes what is indicated by the word *ought.* The brute is moved by instinctive appetites, affections, desires, emotions, and so also is man, to a certain extent. Man thus puts forth many characterless actions, as we have seen, in common with the irrational creation; but he is also the subject of a *higher* motive, a regard to *duty*, which imparts moral quality to his actions.

We hence view the same act very differently, as performed by a brute, or by a human being. If the poor brute kills her young, we *pity* her; but if the mother, favored with enlightened reason, kills hers, we *blame* her. We never speak of the *duty* of the brute. We never say it *ought* to do so and so; but we say this emphatically of all rational beings.

Terms indicating duty are found in all languages, proving the universality of the idea itself and the importance attached to it. Thus the feeling of moral obligation is coextensive with our race. All rational beings *know*, as soon as reason operates, that there is a right and a wrong in human action, and that they ought to refrain from the one and do the other.

The intellect is concerned in *ascertaining* duty; the susceptibility of conscience, true to its demand, is concerned in securing *obedience* to it. The intellect takes the lead. The senses act first, giving to the mind its first *individual* ideas, and arousing it to general activity. The power of purely intuitive, as well as sentient perception, is thus excited.*

What we call *intuition*, is included in what some German philosophers call the *pure reason*, (Ger. *Rein Vernumft*, Gr. λόγος, Lat. *ratio*, Fr. *raison*,) and is possessed by rational beings only, none of the brute creation having any part in it. Jacobi and others term it *rational* intuition, (*rationale Anschauung*.) It is by this that we obtain our first *general* ideas, through which we systematize individual ideas furnished by the senses, and comprehend their philo-

* For the sake of brevity and convenience, I use the term *perception* to indicate both rational and sentient cognizance, although it is usually restricted in philosophy to the latter. Several of the German philosophers, Fichte, Schelling, and others, employ intuition to designate the cognition of the absolute, as opposed to the conception of it. While others, such as Leibnitz, Jacobi, Descartes, and Locke, denote by it the power of immediately apprehending the relations of subject and predicate in what are called self-evident propositions. But Sir William Hamilton applies the term intuitive in a wider sense, as related to all direct knowledges, whether sentient or strictly rational. To avoid these ambiguities and save repetition, I shall throughout use the term perception to denote man's ability to cognize or know, or the act or result of cognizing, both as a rational and a sentient being. Whether the mind comes into possession of its knowledge by pure intuition, or by sensation, or by argument and reflection, is all the same in a moral view.

sophical relations. The truths thus obtained are called *first principles.* Known intuitively, they require no proof. They are often termed *axioms.*

First principles are mathematical, metaphysical, or moral; but they are all apprehended by the same rational faculty. It is always the same reason or intuition, although directed to different kinds of truth. In neither case does reason *feel* the truth, for its office is simply knowing, not feeling. The feeling is furnished by another faculty.

The power of mental feeling, like that of perception, is suited to its various objects. Thus the human soul is endowed with various susceptibilities, adapted to its various cognitions. The cognition of a mathematical, or of a metaphysical, or of an æsthetical, or of a moral truth, appeals to our susceptibility to that particular kind of truth, and excites one or another feeling according to the nature of the truth perceived.

We have previously noticed the mutual relations of the intellective and the motive powers, and have said that, other things equal, the clearer the perception the more vivid will be the feeling, and the keener and more delicate the feeling, the clearer will be the perception. The relation of the susceptibility of *conscience* to the perception of *moral* truth, is like that of the susceptibility of *taste* to the perception of *æsthetical* truth. Conscience quickens the rational spirit to discern between right and wrong, as the sensibility of taste quickens it to discern between beauty and deformity.

Our only intuitive perceptions with which the susceptibility of conscience is associated, are those which relate to *moral* truths. Other feelings attend other perceptions; here is the exclusive dominion of conscience. It must also be remembered that intuition, when directed to *moral* truths, as well as when directed to others, is severely restricted to first principles. Beyond these, therefore, the admonitions of conscience will naturally differ, according as minds are differently taught.

Intuition or unaided reason alone cannot inform us respecting particular duties, nor the moral quality of specific actions. It cannot inform us, for instance, whether infanticide and parricide are right; whether a man ought to have many wives, or only one, or indeed whether the marriage covenant should exist at all; whether any day of the week, or any portion of time whatever, should be kept as especially sacred; whether we ought to worship one God, or a plurality of gods; whether we should conduct with reference to an interest beyond the grave, or solely with reference to an interest in this life; whether we should practise penance for our misdeeds, and inflict sufferings and perhaps death upon our persons; whether we should support parental and civil government, or whether all government is oppression; whether disputes should be settled by duelling, &c., &c.

All such questions, important and eminently practical as they are, involving morality in the most vital points, are yet not to be decided by the unaided glances of reason. Indeed the fact that they *are* questions, throws them at once out of the pale of intuition; for respecting what we learn by intuition no question can be raised.

Here then we see the need of instruction in morals and religion, as well as in other departments of knowledge. All the specific truths of moral science are to be learned by a process of education, as truly as are all the specific truths of *natural* science. We can no more be sound and well furnished moralists without education, than we can be sound and well furnished mathematicians without it. In each case, we start with only first principles. Upon these we must erect the superstructure, by applying to them, in scientific arrangements, their numerous subordinate specific truths. This is work for education. Hence the necessity for suitable schools, books, teaching, parental guidance, preaching, correct example, good laws, and just government, rightly to enlighten and form the conscience of the rising race.

We have only to look where these are not enjoyed, to see little else than conscience misguided and morals prostrated. Let us then divest ourselves of all fanatical conceits respecting the "inward light," the "sufficient guide," the "divinity in man," the "sovereign arbiter;" these are pleasant rhetorical flourishes, but they do not answer the purpose where scientific truth and not poetry is the object.

DEFINITION OF CONSCIENCE.

Conscience, as mentioned in the Bible and generally understood, is not a *single* primitive faculty. It includes both the power of *perception*, and a susceptibility to a peculiar *feeling*. But the power of perception is always the same, to whatever truths it may be directed. To suppose that a man has two perceiving faculties, one for one kind of truth, and another for another kind, is as preposterous as to suppose that he is two persons. He is both a rational and a sentient being, and hence he perceives in various *ways*, intuitively and through the senses, but his *power* to perceive is ever one and the same. The activity of his cognitive or discerning power is always assumed, when we speak of the operations of conscience. He may know without feeling, but he cannot feel without knowing. We know that we feel, and we feel that we know. By one act of consciousness, we know our feeling and we feel our knowledge. Thus every legitimate operation of conscience involves two psychological elements, the cognitive and the motive, affirmed in one and the same deliverance of the personal consciousness.

But while all the susceptibilities of the soul are dependent upon the intellect, there is one only, which, as united and coöperating with it, constitutes the distinguishing and sublime faculty of conscience. It is this which we are now to examine.

The Latin word *conscientia*, and the Greek *συνειδησις*, used in the Bible, denote an inward susceptibility to or realization of the mind's perceptions. Thus a man's intellect *perceives* the beauty of an object, and his susceptibility to the beautiful makes him *realize* it. He thus not only *knows* it, but he *feels* it. The former is *speculative* knowledge; the latter is *experimental*. As both of these mental acts respect the same objective fact, the former is the *scientia* of it, the latter the *conscientia* of it. The one confirms the other.

Precisely thus a man's intellect *perceives*, and his conscience makes him *feel*, that is, it makes him *experimentally* know, the distinction between right and wrong. We have other specific terms by which to indicate the other susceptibilities, but the most emphatic was employed by the sacred writers, and by the ancients generally, to indicate the most characteristic and important of them all.

CONSCIENCE, then, including the power of perception, is man's SUSCEPTIBILITY TO MORAL DISTINCTIONS. It is a faculty implanted in our mental constitution expressly to make us *feel* the distinction between moral truth and falsehood, and between right and wrong action, and thus to incite us to duty. It was not designed to go *before* reason, or to act independently of it, to teach us what *is* true and right, but to be always strictly in its service.

Until the mind is instructed in specific truths and duties, the admonitions of conscience are reliable only within the limits of intuitive truths or first principles. Beyond these, its impulses are blind and fanatical. It must be kept strictly in school to reason, as taught by God and by experience; for it belongs to our impulsive nature, and we were made to be guided by enlightened reason, and not by blind impulse.

That which *distinguishes* the susceptibility of conscience from all other susceptibilities, is its exclusive interest in what pertains to the person's *own* conduct as *morally right or wrong.* It has nothing to do with the actions of others, nor yet those of one's self, except as they are related to his *personal duty.* In addition to this, the feeling of obligation, and the feeling of pleasure and of pain, which it imparts, are *unlike any other.* No other feeling is like that of moral obligation; no other *pain* is like that which arises from a consciousness of having *done wrong;* no other *pleasure* is like that which arises from a consciousness of having *done right.* It is not a difference in mere *degree,* but in *kind.* Our appeal here is to every man's experience.

CONSCIENCE HAS THREE FUNCTIONS.

Considered as a motive power, conscience is both passive and active; a susceptibility and an impulse. Besides prompting the rational spirit to *discern* between right and wrong, it has *three functions,* or, in other words, there are three ways in which it incites us to *do* right. It makes us feel that we *ought* to do so; it affords us a feeling of self-approval, when we *have* done so; it inflicts upon us a painful feeling of self-reproach, when we have *not* done so.

The first feeling is *prospective.* It is one that we have in view of something *to be* done. The last two are *retrospective.* They are feelings which we realize in view of something which we *have* done. The present moment is but a point; hence, all actions upon which we deliberate, must precede or follow the deliberation. These three functions of conscience require particular explanation.

FIRST FUNCTION OF CONSCIENCE.

Conscience makes us feel that we *ought to do what we believe to be right.* In the same connection we may say, that it makes us feel that we ought *not* to do what we believe to be *wrong.* Both amount to the same thing; for, failing to do right, is doing wrong.

A boy sees tempting fruit in a neighbor's garden. He knows that it would be wrong to steal it. Now, whether we say, his conscience admonishes him that it is right to let it alone, or that it is wrong to steal it, our meaning is of course the same.

On returning from the bank, a man finds that the teller has accidentally counted to him a ten dollar note too much. We mean the same, whether we say, his conscience reminds him that he ought to return it, or, that it would be wrong not to do so.

Suppose a man's mind enlightened by Christianity respecting the being and perfections of God. He then perceives it to be right for him to render to that glorious Being his supreme homage. He perceives it to be wrong not to do so. This perception is attended with an admonition of conscience, a feeling of obligation. If the conscience is in a normal condition, the intensity of its admonition, that is, the vividness of the feeling of obligation, will be in proportion to the clearness and fulness of the perception.

But men may have "their conscience seared with a hot iron,"* while their intellective faculty is in good

* 1 Tim. 4 : 2.

condition, and their *perception* of truth and duty is clear. They may perceive with great distinctness what they *ought* to do; and yet through defect of conscience, from its being in a seared or torpid state, they may be entirely indifferent about *doing* it.

The case here is the same; whether our views of duty are intuitive, or are obtained by an educational process. In either case, the perception of what is right may be as bright as a sunbeam, while the conscience may be as unfeeling in regard to it as marble.

But if conscience is tender and quick, the perception of a duty to be performed instantly excites the feeling of obligation; this feeling tends to render the perception more distinct; thus, a reciprocity of action, and an intimate alliance is established between them. A good man's susceptibility to obligation, and his perception of truth and duty, are ever harmoniously one in their object and action. This is doubtless the reason why popular writers have often so confounded the intellective and the motive in conscience, as to consider them psychologically one and the same primitive faculty, which they have called a moral sense.

SECOND FUNCTION OF CONSCIENCE.

The second function of conscience is, to afford us a *delightful feeling of self-approval when we have done what we believe to be right.* This feeling is especially vivid, after a successful encounter with a strong and dangerous temptation to do wrong. When a severe struggle has been had, and a triumph has been won on the side of virtue, the feeling of satisfaction is peculiarly rich and delightful.

It is needless to attempt to analyze or to define this feeling. To know it, we must experience it. It was evidently designed to be a token of approbation from the Being who made us; a present reward of virtue, or rather, a foretaste of the richer reward awaiting it hereafter. It is a kind of first fruit of goodness. It was meant to encourage us to *persevere* in the conflict with temptation, and thus to strengthen and establish every right principle. It is not a feeling of vain exultation. It is humble and grateful, but joyous and inspiring. The joy of Cæsar, when marching in triumph up the Appian Way, is not to be compared with it.

But it is not merely the thrill of pleasure imparted by conscience after signal victories over temptation, that we should notice. The calm and settled peace, the prevailing satisfaction, resulting from a good conscience faithfully obeyed, is a perpetual feast, a daily and hourly luxury, which none but the upright in heart can realize. Deprived of conscience, even if capable of rational conduct, man would be for ever deprived of this angelic luxury.

THIRD FUNCTION OF CONSCIENCE.

The third function of conscience is, *to inflict upon us a peculiar painful feeling, when we have done what we believe to be wrong.* When the conscience is not seared, reflecting upon wrong conduct of which we have been guilty, is invariably attended with this feeling. It is termed *remorse.* It is designed, in part, as a present punishment for misdoing, or rather as an admonition of its guilt, and of the fearful ultimate consequences to which it tends. It is thus evidently meant to warn us against *repeating* the act.

It is useless to attempt a definition of remorse. Dictionaries define it, the keen pain or anguish excited by a sense of guilt. But as we have keen pain and anguish from other sources, this definition only refers us to its cause; thus leaving every person to learn, from his own experience, what the pain and anguish actually are.

The rebuke of offended conscience is not like grief, sorrow, repentance; it is not like the pain of bereavements, loss, or disappointment; neither is it mere regret, nor a sense of danger. Some of these feelings, especially the last two, usually accompany it, but they may exist without it. As it cannot be defined, like every other primitive feeling, it can be known only as it is experienced.

Even the little child who disobeys his mother, or does other things which he knows to be wrong, has the painful feeling of a disturbed conscience. The young man rightly taught at home, who, when removed from parental watchfulness, begins to venture upon vicious indulgences, sometimes passes many a sleepless night in painful reflections upon his conduct.

It is important to observe, that the retributions of conscience are by no means always immediately consequent upon wrong doing. They are sometimes delayed, especially in the case of hardened transgressors, for months and for years.

The law of the operation of conscience seems to be this. In the early stages of transgression, its rebukes are prompt and earnest; but if these are disregarded, its sensibility gradually becomes less active, and, like the deep fires of a volcano when crusted over at the top, prepare for a tremendous outburst at a future time.

Thus the libertine, the thief, the defrauder, the murderer, has sometimes gone on for a series of years, realizing, especially during the latter part of his career, but feeble, if any, compunctions of conscience.

He is thus greatly emboldened in crime. "Because sentence against an evil work is not executed *speedily*, *therefore* the heart of the sons of men is fully set in them to do evil." *

Retribution at length overtakes the guilty man. Perhaps the civil arm arrests him, and places him in circumstances to reflect upon his ways. His feelings are at first mostly those of regret and chagrin. But conscience is at length aroused. His *guilt* now stares him in the face, and darts its fiery stings into his inmost spirit. *Remorse*, relentless and agonizing, makes him its prey, and drags him to the gates of despair.

Let no one, then, who offends his conscience, hope to escape its retributions. They may be slow, but they are sure; and when they come, they will be all the more severe for the delay; for they will find greatly enhanced guilt. Sooner or later, they will certainly overtake him, and they will be in proportion to his crimes. But there will not have been made an even barter of pleasure for pain. Far, very far from it. All the pleasures of vice will prove at last to have been as nothing, compared with those merciless and bitter pangs, which an avenging and relentless conscience will justly inflict.

Such are the threefold functions of conscience, in accomplishing the great moral end for which it was given us. It is to our moral and religious interests what the desire of life is to our existence. The former would induce us to prize and protect character, as the latter would to prize and protect life. It is an original faculty. This susceptibility, as truly as the discerning intellect, with all its fearful power to bless and to torment us, is a part of our mental constitution, and, like the soul itself, imperishable. It is doubtless one of the mightiest agents created by God, by which "he will render to every man according to his deeds."

* Eccl. 8: 11.

As conscience includes the rational power to discern, with the susceptibility to feel our moral obligations, we are to regard its enlightened decisions as the will of God. The rule of duty thus enjoined, or what is called the law of conscience, is what we understand by the law of God written in the hearts of men. "For when the Gentiles, which have not the law, do by nature the things contained in the law, these, having not the law, are a law unto themselves; which show the work of the law written in their hearts, their conscience also bearing witness, and their thoughts the meanwhile accusing or else excusing one another." *

* Rom. 2: 14–16.

CHAPTER II.

VARIOUS VIEWS OF CONSCIENCE.

HAVING in the previous chapter stated what we believe to be the true nature and functions of conscience, it is due to the subject to say that other views have been advocated. It is our present object to examine them. Those deserving of particular notice may be reduced to two, that which regards conscience as a moral *judgment*, and that which regards it as a moral *sense*. The undefined notions of an "inward light" and of a "divinity within," are too vague and mystical to be seriously noticed; for they amount to little else than rhetorical flourishes.

CONSCIENCE NOT A MORAL JUDGMENT.

Some have supposed conscience nothing more than judgment applied to moral subjects. They hence call it the *moral* judgment. They appeal to its decisions on moral subjects, as we appeal to the decisions of the natural judgment on other subjects. In this view, it is to decide upon questions of right and wrong, just as the natural judgment is to decide upon questions of law, upon evidence in courts, upon the quality of merchandise, or upon the prospects of the market. Considering the influence of passion and prejudice upon judgment, this view puts all morality out upon a shoreless sea, to be tossed about for ever by the caprices of wind and tide.

But conscience is not mere judgment, as we have seen in the previous chapter, for it includes a *susceptibility;* and this susceptibility is peculiar, and belongs exclusively to conscience. Moreover, the intellective powers are not altered by the nature of their subjects. The powers of perception, of memory, of judgment, are the same, whether employed upon natural or upon moral subjects. To maintain, then, that conscience is only the judgment applied to moral subjects, is to resolve it into another faculty, and thus virtually annihilate it.

CONSCIENCE NOT A MORAL SENSE.

Some authors have considered conscience a literal moral *sense*, sustaining the same relation to moral facts or truths which the other senses do to those of nature, and also imparting appropriate feelings respecting them. It will be observed, that in this view conscience is a *perceiving* faculty, *distinct* from that with which we perceive natural truths; and that it also performs two distinct offices, offices belonging to two different powers of mind, that of *perception* and that of *feeling*. This must certainly be a very strange faculty, an anomaly in the mental constitution.

The importance of the subject, and the deference due to those who have advocated this view, make it our duty to give it a careful examination.

To make our discussion as concise as possible, instead of quoting from various books, we will refer to such only as are in the hands of our readers generally, and are inferior to none in claims to our attention. They clearly represent the views of the class.

"By conscience, or the moral sense, is meant that faculty by which we discern the moral quality of actions, and by which we are capable of certain affections in respect to this quality." * * * "We do not say, that all men discern this quality with equal accuracy, any more than that they all see with equal distinctness: but we say that all men perceive it in some actions; and that there is a multitude of cases in which their perceptions of it will be found universally to agree." *

It is here asserted, that conscience is a "moral sense;" that faculty by which men "discern the moral quality of actions;" and that "there is a multitude of cases in which their perceptions of it will be found universally to agree." But then there is another multitude of cases, in which they do *not* agree; and who shall decide which is right?

It is claimed that conscience is a "moral sense," sustaining the same relation to facts in morals that the other senses do to facts in nature. But is it so? Let us look critically at this point.

The sense of sight is our sole and undisputed teacher in respect to colors. From its decisions there is no appeal. The same is true of the sense of smell, in relation to odors; of the sense of taste, in relation to flavors; of the sense of hearing, in relation to sounds; of the sense of touch, in relation to resistant bodies. Each sense is supreme umpire in its dominion. No instruction, no laws, no change of country or society, no religion, no amount of knowledge from other sources, can affect its decisions. They are absolutely fixed and reliable.

* Wayland's Moral Science, p. 49.

If then conscience were a sense, like the above, by which to discern the moral quality of actions, its decisions, like those of the above senses, would also be absolutely fixed and reliable. As there is no appeal from the sense of sight in relation to colors, no appeal from the sense of taste in relation to flavors, so there could be no appeal from the sense of conscience in relation to morals. To suppose instruction to avail to correct the errors of the sense of conscience in regard to moral actions, would be as preposterous as to suppose it to avail to correct the errors of the sense of sight in regard to colors, or the errors of the sense of smell in regard to odors.

Men *must* then infallibly agree respecting the decisions of this moral sense, not only in "a multitude of cases," but in *all* cases where moral action is the object. Do not men of all nations, all religions, all kinds and degrees of learning, agree as to *all* things decided by the senses? They do. Why? Because the senses were *given* to teach us in regard to these things; and they accomplish their mission. But *do* men agree thus in regard to the moral quality of actions? Far from it. The Christian's conscience stings him with remorse, for doing what the pagan approves; and the pagan's conscience stings *him* with remorse, for doing what the Christian approves. Their consciences are essentially the same, but their views of right and wrong, owing to difference of education, are widely different. Education, however, does not thus affect the decisions rendered by the senses.

It may be said, the pagan's conscience is "defiled." This is no doubt sadly true; but it does not meet the difficulty. So the pagan may say, the Christian's conscience is defiled; and who shall decide between them? Who ever heard of a pagan's *senses* discerning things so differently from those of the Christian? No difference of education nor of character can alter the decisions of the senses, in reference to their several appropriate objects. The pagan's sense of sight reveals to him *all* colors, his sense of taste reveals to him *all* flavors, just as the Christian's do to him.

The reason, then, why men differ respecting the moral qualities of actions, is perfectly obvious. A man in one nation justifies idolatry, polygamy, infanticide, and a man in another nation condemns them, not because conscience is not the same faculty in all, but because *it is not a distinct discerning sense, and cannot teach us as the senses do*, and because these men have been differently taught.

There is evil in ascribing too much to conscience, as well as too little. By assigning to it duties which it was not intended to perform, and to which it is inadequate, we make men sceptical, on the one hand, because they see that it does not do what is ascribed to it; or fanatical, on the other, because they mistake for its sacred admonitions the blind promptings of a perverse and obstinate self-will. Few men betray a depravity more offensive and hopeless, than those laboring under such unhappy delusions.

PLAUSIBLE ANSWER TO THE ABOVE.

But it is said by the advocates of the moral sense scheme, that the senses teach us only in appropriate circumstances. The sense of sight, for instance, does not discern colors in the absence of light. So of conscience. In order to discern moral qualities, it must have moral light. Hence the fact that the benighted heathen do not clearly discern moral qualities, only proves that they are in comparative moral darkness.*

This analogy is plausible, but not just. It fails in the material point. So far as their *intuitive* perceptions go,

* See Stewart, p. 122.

the untaught heathen apprehend moral truths as Christians do. Having no written law, they are a law unto themselves. "Axioms in mathematics, principles in philosophy, rights in morals, are the same to all minds, when seen in the same grounds." * But what is thus known in morals, like a mathematical axiom, by pure intuition, does not of course depend upon the affirmation of a "sense." The power to discern is, however, always one and the same, whether directed to physical, mathematical, or moral truths.†

We therefore proceed to notice what we learn through the medium and testimony of *sense*. And here it matters not whether it be what is termed an outer or an inner sense; since all the senses sustain the same relation to the perceiving mind, and are subject to the same essential law. They are all the mind's teachers, and they teach it by sensation.

In the light of day, all men of sound organs perceive colors alike. They also perceive alike by all their other senses, when the senses are directed to their appropriate objects. It is not true that their perceptions agree only "in a multitude of cases." They so entirely agree, in *all* cases, that the several kinds of knowledge taught us by the several senses are reduced to exact systems, and are registered in books of science among the most indisputable facts. If any one of a man's senses seems to teach him

* Hickok's Moral Science, p. 55.

† "We have not one faculty by which we discern physical truths, and another by which we judge of mathematical theories, and another for matters of taste, but all these are the one and the same understanding, exercised on different subjects. Accordingly, when moral qualities are the objects of our contemplation, it is not a different faculty from the reason or understanding which thinks and judges, but the same exercised on other subjects; and the only difference is in the objects."—ALEXANDER'S *Outlines of Moral Science*, p. 14.

6

otherwise, he is regarded as having a disordered intellect, or a diseased organ, and so his case has no effect upon the general conclusions of mankind.

But it is quite otherwise with conscience. There is not only a Pagan conscience, a Mahommedan conscience, and a Christian conscience, but even the Christian conscience decides very differently in different men. Under the same Christian light, one man condemns slavery, while another approves it; one man condemns oath-taking, while another approves it; one man condemns all wars, while another justifies those of self-defence; one man condemns capital punishments, while another upholds them; and so it goes. Yet all these men are, in the judgment of true charity, alike conscientious in their views.

We hence see that while the senses, in their several appropriate spheres, are infallible teachers and guides, conscience, apart from the light of reason and instruction, is no guide at all. If it were a moral *sense*, designed to *teach* us moral truths, as the other senses teach us other truths, we should be obliged to admit an utter failure in this part of our mental constitution. But we are driven to no such conclusion. We believe that the varying decisions of the so-called moral sense, are mere acts of *judgment* in cases of ethical casuistry. The judgment may be affected by prejudice, interest, education, idiosyncrasy; but these cannot affect the decisions rendered by the senses.

IMPORTANCE OF THE ABOVE DISTINCTION.

The distinction between these two views of conscience is of great practical importance. According to the view which we have advocated, conscience was not designed to go before and teach us, as the senses do, but must itself be taught. As a susceptibility, it is entirely dependent upon the perceptions of the intellect; as a discerning faculty, it is that intellect itself, and is subject to all the necessities of intellectual discipline and culture. It is ignorant or enlightened, erring or true, according to its education. Taking this view, an accountable being commences his moral career with the first lesson of true wisdom; the lesson of humility. He takes the submissive attitude of a pupil.

The intuitions of his unaided reason only reveal to him his ignorance, and the first principles of his duty. He sees that he has every thing to learn. He turns the eye of his mind in all directions, seeking light. Thus docile and expectant, he receives instruction from the light of nature, from providential events, from the admonitions of wise and good men, from the experience of past ages, and above all, from the Word of God. All these conspire to render his perceptions of truth and duty clear, accurate, and comprehensive, and the sensibility of his conscience discriminating, just, and effective. He is thus forming a character of enlightened and high excellence.

According to the other view, the whole course is theoretically reversed. Conscience is a literal moral sense. It is a distinct discerning faculty, given to teach us moral truths, as the other senses teach us other truths. It has the same right to decide for us, independently of instruction, upon the quality of actions, as the natural taste has to decide upon the quality of flavors. It is as much to be trusted to discern the moral hues of an action, as is the sense of sight to discern the colors of the rainbow.

In vain then do you reason and expostulate with it. It is a sense, a seer, a guide; its office is to *teach*, not to *be taught*. Approach not the man of conscience, who practically entertains this view, to teach him his duty. He knows it already, better than you do. He is too wise to be taught by God or man. He has the light within him. He will defy your reasoning and hurl your arguments to the wind.

The effects of this view of conscience are by no means chargeable upon its worthy advocates; but we are bound to assert, what we have all been painfully compelled to notice, that it tends to make men conceited, malapert, opinionated, and self-willed. It thus helps to people the ranks of fanatical delusion, and is disastrous to the welfare of sound morality and of pure Scriptural piety.

RELATION OF CONSCIENCE TO REASON.

"Before you resolve upon an action," says the distinguished author cited above, "or a course of action, cultivate the habit of deciding upon its moral character. Let the first question always be, "Is this action right?" Sound advice. But the writer adds, "For this purpose, that is, to decide whether an action is right, God gave you this faculty (conscience). If you do not use it, you are false to yourself, and inexcusable before God. We despise a man who never uses his reason, and scorn him as a fool. Is he not much more to be despised, who neglects to use a faculty of so much higher authority than reason?" *

It is here asserted, first, that God gave us the conscience for "deciding" upon the moral quality of actions; and secondly, that it has "much higher authority than reason." The decisions of conscience are here considered distinct from those of reason, and of "much higher authority."

The first of the above positions we have virtually examined. The second is a legitimate inference from it. If conscience is strictly a sense, sustaining to moral truths

* Moral Science, p. 80.

the same relation which the other senses do to other truths, then, of course, its province is to teach reason, as the other senses do, and not to be taught by it. It is of "much higher authority than reason." It is reason's schoolmaster. Conscience must never go to school to reason, but reason must go to school to conscience, as it does to the other senses.

If conscience is above reason, then, instead of acting at all times as *reasonable* beings, men are to be guided by what they may chance to suppose an imperative of conscience, which is *above* the jurisdiction of reason. They are to consider conscience "of so much higher authority than reason," that it may decide for itself, and have its own way, in defiance of reason's dictates.

Such a view must of course tend to make those who act upon it CONSCIENTIOUSLY UNREASONABLE. They may be good men in their way; they may even be martyrs to what they honestly suppose to be the dictates of their consciences. They may be deserving of much credit, at least in their own eyes; for the fault may lie in their head, rather than in their heart. They may have been badly taught. But after all, the fewer we have of such men, the better it is for the welfare of society.

And such men, too, may be very *bad, conscientiously* bad. "Men have often committed," says Whewell, "thefts, frauds, impositions, homicides, thinking their actions right; though they were such as all moralists would condemn as wrong. Such men act according to their consciences. Were they therefore justified?"

"To allege that an act is according to my conscience; meaning thereby that I act according to a rule which is already fixed and settled in my mind, so that I will no longer examine whether the rule be right, is to reject the real signification of moral rules. It is the conduct of a person who pursues a wrong road to the place he aims at, and refuses to have it proved that the road is wrong."

"It has been said, that, if I *talk* of my humility, I lose it; something of the same kind may be said of conscience." *

"If the moral judgments of the mind were from a faculty distinct from the understanding," says Dr. Alexander, "and often differing from it, the harmony of the mental operations would be destroyed. While reason led to one conclusion, conscience might dictate the contrary. And upon this theory, conscience must always be correct, unless the faculty be morbid."

"The conclusion therefore is, that conscience is not a distinct faculty from reason, so far as it consists in a judgment of the quality of moral acts. Reason or understanding is the genus: the judgments of conscience are the species. Reason has relation to all intelligible subjects; the moral faculty is conversant about moral qualities alone." †

CONSCIENCE ALWAYS TO BE OBEYED.

To the question, Ought we always to obey the dictates of conscience? there can be but one answer. We ought. To do otherwise is an immorality. A man can never innocently offend his conscience. But suppose his conscience decides one way and his reason another. Must he act unreasonably? Certainly he must, if conscience is "*above* reason." He ought certainly to obey the highest authority. But this is a dilemma for those who advocate the view to which we have objected. According to the view which we have advocated, the case is *impossible*. For, according to our view, reason is itself a part of con-

* Vol. I., p. 265. † Outlines, p. 43.

science, and is always to be its guide. REASON IS THE EYE OF CONSCIENCE.

The *impulse* or *feeling* of conscience is always in favor of duty. It urges a man to do only what he supposes to be right; it rebukes him for doing only what he supposes to be wrong. Under its influence, therefore, a man always intends to do right. And as the moral quality of an action essentially depends upon the intention, no man conducts morally right when he disregards his conscience. If the impulse of conscience is not in the right direction, the fault is not in the impulse, any more than the fault is in the steam, if the ship which it impels goes the wrong way.

But suppose a man meaning to do right, does wrong. Where is the blame? Not in the man for his impulse of conscience, which was towards duty, whatever the duty might be; nor yet in the man for his intention to do right, in obeying his conscience; but in the man for not having duly *enlightened* his conscience, or for allowing passion or prejudice to blind him.

Such was the fault of Paul when he was opposing Christianity. He tells us that he "verily thought" he was doing right, but confesses that he did wrong. He was true to the impulse of his conscience, but he allowed prejudice to blind his mind. When a man does what is wrong through *inevitable* ignorance, it is not a fault of heart, but of circumstance; not a crime, but a misfortune. But in most cases of misdoing through ignorance, men *are* blameworthy; for they might have known better. They should have better enlightened their consciences. It is usually because men are too indolent to inform themselves, or are selfish and obstinate, that they mistake their duty.

The terms *moral sense* and *sense of duty*, must then be understood to mean the *sensibility* of the conscience to what is supposed to be right. When we speak of a sense of shame or a sense of honor, we do not mean that man has a particular *sense* to *discern* what is shameful or a particular sense to discern what is honorable; we mean only to indicate his sensibility to what he perceives or supposes to be shameful or honorable.

No sooner do we suppose *another* perceiving faculty, which is moral instead of rational, than we perpetrate the philosophical blunder of hypothesizing a superfluous faculty, and also open the way to fanatical conceits and delusions. A true moral perception is never an irrational perception. Indeed, strictly speaking, the mere power or act of perception is *never itself* moral, and we justly term it so only in a figurative sense, when directed to moral ends; as we say that a sword is valiant, when it is valiantly used.

Extensive practical evils often come of fundamental errors in speculation. Multitudes are misled, but they do not see what has misled them. The better class realize the misgivings of common sense, which prevent them from going far astray; but others are less fortunate. The evils resulting from those views of conscience which make every man a revelation to himself, which embolden him to disregard teaching from without, especially that of the Bible, thus tending to subvert true faith and loyalty, are too well known to all who are conversant with the strange history of humanity.

CHAPTER III.

DIRECTIONS FOR THE CULTURE OF CONSCIENCE.

From the views which we have taken of conscience, it is evidently susceptible of indefinite improvement. This respects the clearness, steadiness, and fulness of the light to guide it, and the delicacy, uniformity, and promptness of its susceptibility. What we would say on this subject may be briefly included in the following directions.

1. Spare no pains to *enlighten the mind respecting duty.*—We need to inform ourselves in regard to truth in morals and religion, as well as other subjects. We must employ the same powers, with equal diligence, to know what to believe and how to conduct in matters of *duty*, as we must to understand mathematics, history, geography, or any other branch of study. Hence earnestness to *know* the truth, and diligence to apprehend it, are themselves no mean virtues. "If thou criest after knowledge, and liftest up thy voice for understanding; if thou seekest her as silver, and searchest for her as for hid treasure; then shalt thou find the knowledge of God."

When men seek half as earnestly to know their duty, as most do for golden treasures; when they are as anxious for the wisdom that is from above, as they are to know how to be rich, or to gratify "the lusts of the flesh;" when the buyers and sellers are as zealous to know whether the Bible is the word of God, sent to teach them their duty, and if it is, what it teaches, as they are to know the prices of the markets, and the chances for profitable trades and investments; their consciences will be full of light, and the straight and narrow path of duty will be as bright before them as noonday.

2. To be successful seekers of duty we *must have singleness of purpose*.—Not only must we bring the same intellectual powers to bear upon moral as upon other subjects, but we have here especial need to bring a truly candid and honest heart. Motives of interest, pride, prejudice, party spirit, if allowed to influence, may sway the judgment, and thus mislead the conscience. Men thus become conscientiously obstinate in error. Careful self-examination should exclude all such motives, and hold the mind true to the single purpose of knowing and doing what is *right*. "If thine eye be single, thy whole body shall be full of light."

3. Great care should be taken *not to mistake other impulses for that of conscience*.—Even though a man have honest intention, he may mistake for the dictate of conscience a less worthy impulse. A feeling of mere *desire* or *passion* may be regarded as a *conscientious* motive. Some men practically place their conscience in the *stomach;* others in the *gall* or *spleen*. A splenetic conscience is no uncommon phenomenon. Others place it in the *ilium*. They are prone to think they do *well* to be angry. In fits of anger, they feel for the time that they *ought* to take vengeance; or at least that it is *right* to do so. Under almost any passion, they justify themselves in doing what the law of God condemns; and even

what *they* condemn, in their more sober and reflecting moods.

Hence the important rule, not to decide and act under strong excitements of passion. In the storm and the whirlwind, the still small voice of conscience is not heard. Other impulses overmaster it, and even claim to be conscience itself. Satan is thus transformed into an angel of light. In seasons of calm reflection, and in the light of all available truth, let the single inquiry be, *Is this action right?* Have I reason to think that I shall review it with satisfaction in after life, in the hour of death, at the bar of God, through eternal ages?

Acting thus as a *rational* being, and in full view of his responsibility, the man who is true to his conscience will ask himself, Is it my *duty* to do this act? If on the whole it appears to be so, the impulse of a faithful conscience will be to *do* it. If it appears otherwise, the impulse of that conscience will be *not* to do it. Nor can this admonition, under these circumstances, be easily mistaken. It is a peculiar, firm, distinct utterance; there is no passion and nothing of the animal in it; it is as if an angel spoke from a shining cloud, "THIS IS THE WAY, WALK YE IN IT."

4. *No violence must ever be done to conscientious scruples.*—As the impulse of conscience depends upon light in the intellect, its admonitions may not be distinct for the want of more light. The mind in this state is said to be laboring under *scruples* of conscience. These scruples should not be trifled with, neither by the person who harbors them, nor by those who would guide him in duty. So long as they remain, be they reasonable or not, they are laws to the subject of them. No person should be regarded with more tenderness and respect than he, for he furnishes the best evidence of being truly conscientious.

When a person has any doubt of the rightfulness of an act, he should keep upon the safe side by avoiding it. But in such a case, if he gives careful and dispassioned attention to his conscience, he will usually discover an inclination to the one side or the other; for the impulse of conscience is never self-balanced. It may be balanced against *other* impulses; but when other impulses are in abeyance, it moves decidedly towards what on the whole seems the least doubtful course.

This impulse must be obeyed. A person acting thus may have future cause to regret that his conscience had not been better enlightened, but he can never feel remorse for having obeyed its dictates.

5. *Conscience should be obeyed promptly.*—By delaying present duty, its admonitions are often weakened, and the danger increased of losing sight of the duty altogether. Resisting its admonitions tends to stifle them, and thus to bring men into the condition of those "having their consciences seared with a hot iron." Such persons are in a most hopeless state. Better to have been left in ignorance of duty than thus to have seared the conscience by resisting convictions. "For it had been better for them not to have known the way of righteousness, than, after they have known it, to turn from the holy commandment delivered unto them." *

But by rendering prompt and cordial obedience to the behests of conscience, we quicken and exalt its power over the soul. Its impulses are also *purer* when promptly obeyed, than when time has allowed other motives to mix with them. A man is prompted, for instance, by a pure conviction of duty, to do an immediate act of justice to his neighbor. He resists the conviction for several

* 2 Pet. 2: 21.

days, till at length motives of interest, fear of detection, dread of the shame of exposure, come in and mingle with the motive of duty to induce him to perform the act. Had he done it at first, the act would have been from a pure motive. He would have been in that act strictly *conscientious;* but now other motives have interposed and injured its moral purity. Prompt obedience to the voice of duty is thus essential to purity of motive.

6. Obedience must also be *determined and persistent.*—When the convictions of duty are clear, they must be obeyed at all pains and hazards. It is sometimes the least of the duty to be prompt; the main struggle may come afterwards. To persevere is often more than to begin. The noblest virtue and richest rewards come of long and arduous conflict. Many a witness for the truth who seemed to begin well, has faltered at the sight of the stake. "He that *endureth unto the end*, the same shall be saved."

The triumphs and rewards of a good conscience will surely come at last. With this assurance every person must be well armed, who would succeed in a world like this in the great battle of righteousness. This is his "shield of faith, and helmet of salvation." Chains may bind the limbs, but they cannot bind the conscience. Prisons of stone and iron may hold the body for long and painful years in darkness, but they cannot shut out the light of truth from the truth-loving soul; they cannot destroy the peace of the dutiful spirit. Burning fagots may torture the nerves and reduce flesh and bones to ashes; but they cannot disturb the good man's inward repose, nor arrest his sublime progress to honor and glory and immortality.

7. *We should faithfully review the past.*—If we would not be self-deceived, we must often survey our course and

critically examine our motives. We can usually sit in judgment upon deeds after they have been done, more impartially than before. We are then freer from the excitement and passion incident to *expected* action, and can scrutinize what we have done at leisure. It was for this reason that a man was led to remark, that he had an accusation against his conscience, because it did not always *warn* him against *doing* wrong, but was sure to *condemn* him after he had *done* so.

Had he listened more attentively to it, he would have heard its warning voice; but having failed in that duty, he should take warning for the future. This part of self-examination is of the highest importance. Without it, no man knows "what manner of spirit" he is of. He is out upon the wide sea of life's events, at the mercy of every gale, knowing neither his position nor direction.

Many have occasion to mourn the neglect of this duty, when it is too late. They have allowed themselves to be driven along by the excitements of gain, of pleasure, of ambition, for perhaps a series of years, impelled by motives and doing acts which their consciences, had they soberly reflected, would have utterly condemned. But they did *not* reflect; therefore, the wrongfulness of their course did not impress them.

The time has at length fled, and can never be recalled. The thought of this sometimes darts upon them as an arrow from the skies; they pause for a moment and think of redeeming the past; but again their panting spirits are upon the fast trodden way, heedless as ever of conscience, and all the more impatient for having been molested by it.

But this cannot last always. Age or affliction at length brings them to a stand. They are *compelled* to pause; to survey the past; to see that they have lost their golden opportunity *for ever!* That priceless treasure, a pure and upright character, they have fatally sacrificed, and with it all that imparts value to their existence. They may have gained their objects, but in so doing they have bartered away the pearl of infinite and enduring value for a few bursting bubbles.

All youth should be warned by such examples to enter upon life's perilous course with frequent, thorough, impartial surveys of what they have done, the motives which have impelled them, and the end towards which they are tending.

8. In view of misdeeds and failures in duty, *we should repent and reform.*—All persons, on faithfully reviewing the past, find much in their conduct and motives to lament. But if they are early in the review, there is hope of amendment. They should not be discouraged, but humbled; they should not yield to despair, but nerve themselves to a better fight. They should sincerely *repent,* seek pardon and strength from on high, and strive to do well in future. There is for such a gracious provision. "He will not break the bruised reed."

Repentance does not of itself remove the evil of misdoing, but there can be no remedy without it. In the mere light of morality, it is an eternal loss to have done wrong; but having done so, the best possible thing that remains, is, to strive to regain, by timely repentance, the path of duty. Of the remedial dispensation, we are to speak in the proper place. All we need to say here, is, that they who *do* repent sincerely, and strive in earnest to do their duty in future, will find their approving consciences uniting with the sympathies of all good beings to speed them in the right way.

9. We should always be *grateful for success.*—It is as much a duty to be grateful for success as to be penitent for failures. If a man has been enabled to resist temptation, and to pursue a straight path of duty; or if he has succeed-

ed to regain the path when he had lost it, he has cause indeed for unspeakable gratitude. If he is truly grateful, he will be equally *humble;* for the graces of gratitude and of humility are indissolubly united. Duly exercised, they will nourish every other grace, and will impart strength, steadiness, firmness, to all future good endeavors.

Thus an approving conscience and a grateful heart, become at once a present reward and a pledge of future success. Under their benign influence, men "go from strength to strength." The aspirations of just desire and the joys of approving conscience, are as eagle-wings, bearing them steadfastly upward to their glorious inheritance. They "shall renew their strength; they shall mount up with wings as eagles; they shall run and not be weary; they shall walk and not faint."

And there is no halting in this sublime career. There is no end to the culture and improvement of conscience, as there is no reaching ultimately the heights of moral excellence. Far above our feeble thoughts they rise, above the stars, and into the third heavens of eternal purity and bliss. Higher and yet higher, is ever the good man's motto.

"We never can have done all that is in our power, in this respect. It never can be consistent with our duty, to despair of enlightening and instructing our conscience beyond what we have yet done. Our standard of virtue is not high enough, if we think it need to be made no higher. Virtue has never so completely taken possession of a man, but that she may possess him still more completely; and therefore any conception of virtue, which we look upon as perfect, must on that very account be imperfect. Conscience is never fully formed, but always in the course of formation." *

* Whewell, Vol. I., p. 263.

And indeed, in every view of it, conscience is the most august and fearful faculty of the human soul. It is this, more than all others, that distinguishes us from the brute creation. On our conduct in relation to it depends all that is excellent in character, and all that we must ultimately enjoy or suffer, as long as we exist. It is in our power to make it our most precious and abiding bosom friend, our most terrible and relentless foe.

Including the highest of the intellective and of the impulsive powers, and combining them in one great end of securing man's highest excellence of character, its authority over all the other faculties is supreme, and should never be resisted for a moment. All other impulses; all appetites, emotions, desires, affections, volitions; must stand in awe of it, and be for ever subject to its righteous demands. Duly enlightened, it is the voice of God in the soul.

CHAPTER IV.

TASTE.

The next rational susceptibility of our nature to be noticed, for the sake of a better name, we call *Taste.* We were made not only to *do the right*, but to *enjoy the beautiful.* Indeed the right itself is beautiful. We were made to appreciate and enjoy beauty of character, as well as to practise it. In this view there is a very close affinity between the moral and the esthetical susceptibilities, and some writers have even considered them one and the same. But we shall find them to be distinct faculties.

As conscience is a rational susceptibility to right and wrong, taste is a rational susceptibility to beauty and deformity. But it is not merely the beauty or deformity of moral action, to which taste is related. It sweeps the entire range of the natural, the intellectual, and the moral world, and lays them all under contribution.

We use the term *beauty*, also, in this connection, in its broadest sense, as comprehending *all* that to which man is related as an *esthetical* being. In this broad sense, sublimity, grandeur, majesty, are beautiful; so also are order, fitness, proportion; so are melody and harmony: so are the doctrines of exact science; and so are all the laws of nature, as well as the eternal lessons of truth and righteousness.

Taste, as well as conscience, has the motive element, but it moves us very differently. Conscience incites us to *do* the *right;* taste, to *admire* the *beautiful.* Conscience moves us to *act*, in view of *duty;* taste moves us to *exclaim*, How *beautiful!* Conscience finds its end in the *right done;* taste finds its end in the *beautiful enjoyed.* Hence the feeling of taste, in distinction from that of conscience, is by some called, like that of complacent affection, *sentiment.*

The power of cognition sustains precisely the same relation to the susceptibility of taste, which it does to that of conscience. Without it neither of these susceptibilities could be excited; and in each case the quality and direction of the motive force depend much upon the accuracy and clearness of the perception. For this reason the conscience of a Christian condemns many acts which that of the savage approves, and the taste of a Christian is disgusted with many things which the savage regards as beautiful. The difference is principally owing to *education*, leading them to *view* things differently.

So distinct are the susceptibilities of conscience and taste, that we can conceive of an accountable being entirely *destitute* of the latter. But he would be angular and stiff; unlike the rounded and beautiful universe in which he exists. With conscience and will in perfect play, he would do exactly what he *ought*, and no more. Conscience would impel him to duty; preeisely that he would do, and there his lesson would end. He would be like a man composed of only bones, sinews, and tendons. At the bidding of his will, all the parts would swing and play round in their joints and sockets, just as they *ought;*

but the absence of flesh and color would make him an unsightly object.

We occasionally see men somewhat after this fashion; and while we do homage to their severe morality, we feel that there is in them an awful void of that which renders humanity genial and lovely. It seems to have been no part of the Creator's plan to make man such a being; he therefore inserted in his constitution the principle of taste. But the difference between men respecting it, as in the case of conscience, is more due to culture than to constitution. All men have both conscience and taste as original parts of their nature; and the difference between the taste of the rude savage and that of the refined Christian, is not greater than the difference between their consciences.

None will pretend that the *morality* of our puritan ancestors was not of a high order. But it was of the severe stamp. There was more of *conscience* than of *taste* in it. They feared God; they reverenced law; they were ever true to the stern behests of conscience. They strenuously endeavored to do their duty, as accountable beings; but they were not wholly true to themselves, as esthetical beings. Their style of dress and of speech, their mode of constructing churches, their music, their abjuration or neglect of the fine arts, are sufficient proof of this. The difference between them and their descendants, in this particular, is clearly owing to difference of culture.

CONSCIENCE AND TASTE COMBINED.

Here then we have the two rational impulses, that of conscience and that of taste, side by side, in the rational soul; the first *indispensable* to a moral being, the second *desirable.* Without the first, a being is not *accountable;*

without the second, he is not *beautiful.* The first is the husband, commanding and firm; the second is the wife, engaging and lovely. These twain hath God joined together in the soul, to exalt it in excellence and beauty; and what God hath thus joined together, let not man put asunder.

In the nature of God himself, we speak it reverently, these two principles seem to unite. In all his doings, he evidently regards the laws of taste, as well as of justice. He has not only placed the rational universe under righteous moral law, but he has made all things beautiful.

From the humblest flower that opens its modest eye in the valley, to the sparkling glories of an evening sky; and from the feeblest hues that play upon the dew-drop, to the gorgeous splendors of the rainbow; there is beauty in every trace.

All animal creation, from the microscopic reptile and insect, up to the lord of creation, is beautifully made. The universe is one vast gallery of fine arts, in which the sentiment of taste may luxuriate and grow for ever, and be never nearer exhausting its treasures than at first. How clearly then is taste an element of the divine nature, as it is of ours, made in its likeness.

COMPARATIVE IMPORTANCE OF CONSCIENCE AND TASTE.

If the question be asked, Which is the more important to be cultivated, conscience or taste? the answer must be in favor of conscience. A man of bad conscience is guilty and dangerous; a man of bad taste is vulgar and disgusting. A man may be right in part, with a bad taste; but he cannot be right at all, with a bad conscience. Both in morals and in religion, the culture of mere taste may so supersede that of conscience, as to produce disastrous results upon the character.

This is strikingly seen in some parts of continental Europe. Taste is there exalted to a passion. Its impulse sways the soul, and its gratification is meat and drink. The fine arts are more studied than the Ten Commandments, and to offend taste is a greater crime than to break God's law. To be immoral is no crime, but to be vulgar is horrible. The most fervent devotions of the soul are paid in the picture-gallery; and even the temple of God is scarcely a place for worship, unless richly adorned by the fine arts.

When taste thus usurps the place of conscience, and as it were, absorbs and controls its impulses, it often leads to the worst of consequences; it even countenances shameless immodesty, and arrays vice itself with charms.

But after all, this is no reason why we should neglect to cultivate it. The fault is not in cultivating the taste, but in neglecting to cultivate the conscience. Let those to whom we above referred cultivate the conscience, according to its relative importance, with as much zeal as they do the taste, and they would become splendid specimens of humanity. Had Raphael been *morally* what he was *esthetically*, he would have been almost divine.

It is then the duty of every person to be first of all morally upright, and *also* to cultivate and exalt his taste as much as possible. He may thus present to God and man a character complete in all its parts; full, rounded, beautiful, having the grace and finish of a living form, and fraught with delicate and genial impulse.

THE PRINCIPLES OF BEAUTY SUBJECTIVE.

We have seen that man is constitutionally esthetical as well as moral; designed to commune with the beautiful as well as the just. We have also seen that the taste should be cultivated, and is susceptible of indefinite improvement. Are we then to infer that there is no inherent *standard* of beauty in the mind? No more than we are to infer that there is none of morality. The mind is so constituted that it intuitively perceives the first principles of beauty, just as it does the first principles of duty. These principles are woven into the very texture of the mind; they are wrought into it by the finger of God as a "living sentiment;" and it needs only to be aroused to consciousness to recognize them.

Why do the beauties of the landscape so delight even the untaught savage? Why has music the power to hold him entranced and spell-bound? Why do the well executed works of sculpture and painting kindle in him such pleasing emotions. He may not discern in them all the fine touches obvious to more cultivated minds; still he feels the difference between a rude and a finished work. He realizes the beautiful far beyond his power to explain.

And why does all nature, in her endless variety and profusion of forms and colors, find in him such quick and glad response? Just because both the mind within and the world without, are everywhere alike constructed with reference to the essential principles of beauty; and hence, when they are brought in contact, there is in the living spirit a vivid recognition of this fact. Emotions of delight are then kindled in the spirit, as when one recognizes the glowing features of a dear friend.

EVERY PERSON HAS HIS OWN IDEAL OF BEAUTY.

Thus every person may apprehend the first principles of beauty, and these are essentially the same in all. But there are endless degrees of culture. Nature herself is an educator; the rudest savage is in her school, and has received some of her teaching. And with these endless degrees of culture, from that of the most abject savage to that of the most refined and accomplished scholar, are corresponding ideals of the standard or highest type of beauty. The standard rises in every mind in the degree of its culture, and hence every mind has its own standard.

Every person then carries in his own mind his ideal of beauty. He arraigns all nature and all art before his sovereign tribunal. His conscience is not surer nor quicker to approve or to condemn, than his taste is. His taste, like his conscience, is improved by culture, and thus, like it, may approve to-day what it will hereafter condemn; still, he has his present ideal, such as it is, and that of no other man will answer for him. It is in vain that others assure him a thing is beautiful. Unless it suits his own ideal, to *him* it is not beautiful. He may as well attempt to use another man's conscience, as another man's taste.

But the ideal of a man of culture will always be in advance of his power to execute, and perhaps of that of any other man. The living spirit is quicker to conceive than the hand is to accomplish. Hence an artist is ever pursuing his ideal, and never reaches it. Sometimes he seems to himself farther from it at the end, than at the beginning. The reason is, that by his culture his ideal keeps rising, and often outstrips his growing skill. It is said that Raphael destroyed some of his finest pictures, because they fell so far below his mark. The most beautiful pictures were never yet painted; the most enchanting music was never sung. They have existed only in the minds of the artists.

"The rational spirit can itself create its own pure forms, which shall express the living emotion more full and perfect than can be embodied in any media of nature or of art; and thus the cultivated genius has his own absolute ideal beauty, as the highest and purest conception of the living sentiment in any particular case; and this he makes his ultimate criterion to judge of any representation in nature or art, and becomes the critic, measuring and estimating every actual form of beauty that he finds, and pronouncing it fine or faulty in proportion as it squares with his own absolute ideal." *

TASTE INDEPENDENT OF THE OUTER WORLD.

It follows from what we have seen, that the soul of man may enjoy an independence of all nature and of all art in respect to the pleasures of taste. It deigns to be moved by them, as external and occasional causes; but it can be moved without them, by virtue of its powers of conception and imagination. In the absence of the present world, it can create worlds for itself. It can realize more glorious forms, more beautiful and enchanting scenes, than were ever addressed to mortal eyes; more enrapturing music, than ever fell from mortal lips. These material organs are too gross and feeble to convey to the mind any thing fully adequate to its high ideals of beauty.

Hence Milton, wholly blind, and Bethoven, wholly deaf, enjoyed visions and music more glorious than ever reached them through the organs of sense; and Tenant, with all the organs of sense entirely suspended, enjoyed

* Hickok's Moral Science, p. 33.

sights, and sounds, and society, and employments, akin to those of heaven, if not indeed those of heaven itself. These facts, evincing the soul's capacity for enjoyment independently of the body and of the material creation, when its powers are in the exalted service of perfected conscience and taste, afford us some conception of the reality and value of its active existence beyond the grave.

DESIGN OF TASTE.

The design of this faculty has been partly anticipated. Without it man would be incomplete. The brute, by the absence of reason and conscience, is put in relation only to the lower world of the senses. For this it is complete without taste. But man, by the possession of reason and conscience, is put in relation to the higher world of spiritual excellence and of essential and divine beauty. For this he is incomplete without the susceptibility in question.

Taste, as well as conscience, punishes and rewards; the latter by a feeling of approbation or of disapprobation, the former by a feeling of satisfaction or disgust. Each of these faculties enhances our enjoyment or our suffering, according as we are true or false to its behests. Thus the man of elevated taste and pure conscience, is brought into delightful relation with all the works and laws of Jehovah.

While the profound sciences and the rich endowments of art open to him their exhaustless treasures of beauty, the entire face of nature, in all its changing aspects, is to his eye traced with the delicate pencillings of the divine hand. He feels the genial and glowing impulse of beauty excited, not only by the more obvious and exciting scenes furnished by revolving scenes, by rich and varied landscapes, by gorgeous evening skies, but by the less observed and less exciting objects ever at hand.

When the "king of day" goes to rest beneath curtains of gold, fringed with diamond lustre, *all* men feel the impulse and exclaim, How beautiful! But the person of true culture does not depend upon these rare exhibitions alone for the gratifications of taste; he finds them in every blade of grass, in the structure of every leaf, in the insect's wing, in the spider's web. Like the bee, he gathers honey from every flower, and extracts it from even the humblest sources.

The design of this faculty in a strictly *moral* view cannot be mistaken. Vice is truly an offence against taste, as well as against morality. Whatever is morally wrong is in bad taste. All decent men admit this of low vices. They justly esteem them vulgar. The same is strictly true of *all* immoralities. They are all in bad taste. Had this fact been universally regarded, the world would have been spared many of those vices which have disgraced the fine arts. But let us not despair of the time, when a thoroughly correct and chastening taste will unite with conscience in the universal condemnation of vice.

Not less intimate is the alliance of taste with *religion.* Christianity is as beautiful as it is good. It appeals to the taste as well as to the conscience, and is equally adapted to elevate and perfect both. Its divine mission to the soul of man will not be completed, until he is perfectly qualified to glorify and enjoy God in *all* his works and ways.

The teachings of the Bible and the worship which it enjoins, are sublimely beautiful, and can be *fully* appreciated and enjoyed only by the man of true taste. The description of heaven itself; the walls of jasper, the gates of pearl, the streets of gold; the harps, the crowns, the robes, and the eternal anthems of music; all show, however figuratively interpreted, that the pleasures of refined and perfected taste enter largely into the rewards of the heavenly state.

THE CULTURE OF TASTE.

We have seen that taste, as well as conscience, needs to be *educated.*

1. It must be *enlightened.* As its susceptibility depends upon the mind's perception of things, its impulses will be rude or refined, according as the intellect is ill or well informed. There is probably a difference between the original susceptibilities of men, but the main difference is made by culture. The fault in the taste of a savage is more in the intellect than in the feeling. He is by no means wanting in taste; he is delighted with his beads, and paint, and feathers; but his taste needs culture.

We must then enlighten our taste by studying books and models of beauty, just as we would enlighten our conscience by studying the Bible and models of Christian character. If one would improve his taste in literature, he must read the best standard writers; if in the fine arts, he must study the best models; if in dress and equipage, he must have a critical eye to those approved by competent judges; if for architecture and gardening, he must carefully notice their best specimens; if for the beauties of nature, he must not only be true to his original perceptions, but must add to these a careful study of her endless forms and features of beauty. He must also mingle with cultivated and refined society, and catch its living spirit and manners, just as he must mingle with enlightened and pure Christian society, to improve his conscience and elevate the tone of his morality and religion.

It may be objected that taste thus formed is *conventional.* So far as it is so, it ceases to be taste, and degenerates to *fashion.* A style of dress or equipage, for example, may be fashionable, but in bad taste. So may a style of literature, or of building, or even of manners. The folly and impudence of fashion may for a time override the principles of taste, just as vice may override those of morality. But fashion is mutable, while the principles of taste, like those of morals, are unchanging; and to these all judgment must ultimately appeal.

It requires but a measured degree of discrimination to distinguish between taste and fashion. There is a fitness, an ease, a naturalness, and hence a peculiar charm in whatever is in accordance with the essential principles of taste, which commends it irresistibly to the human mind.

2. The taste must be *exercised.* To do this may be thought out of the power of most persons. It may be supposed that they have not the means of indulging it. But true taste may be exercised with the humblest means. Indeed it is sometimes even more demanded and more exhibited in the use of small means than of large. There is here an important distinction between taste and fashion. Taste may shine in acknowledged poverty; fashion must always ape the rich. Taste walks erect and independently; fashion goes crouching and clinging at the skirts of wealth. The poor man can be as tasteful as the millionnaire.

Taste does not need to rustle in silks, or glitter with diamonds, or dwell in palaces. The poor peasant girl, with her simple and tidy dress of the cheapest fabrics, may exercise as true taste as the daughter of the rich, with her laces and ribbons. The log cabin may be made to exhibit as true taste, in the circumstances, as the proudest mansion of the metropolis.

The directions for the culture of taste are then summarily these: always have an eye to whatever is truly beautiful in nature and art, and always endeavor, as means and circumstances permit, to repeat and enjoy it.

CONCLUDING REMARKS.

It may be thought that in a treatise of morals, what we have said upon taste is out of place. But it is a question whether this element has not been either too much neglected, or put in a false relation. If it has any thing distinguishing, it pertains to our susceptibilities, and belongs to moral rather than intellectual philosophy. We might indeed have an esthetical philosophy, but it would be incomplete without the moral, as the moral would be incomplete without the esthetical.

They who attempt to ignore or to repress the principle of taste in their nature, and to conduct *only* with reference to that of a severe and exacting morality, feel a want which they cannot innocently supply. A part of their nature is unprovided for. Their morality teaches them that the pleasures of taste are doubtful, and lead to vice, and they suppose that to deny them is a part of the self-denial enjoined by Christianity.

But it is not a legitimate indulgence of a constitutional principle of our nature, that Christianity would have us deny. It is a *perversion* of it. And they who attempt to practise an unnatural and undemanded self-denial, are apt to become ascetic and gloomy, and thus to impair their usefulness, and even their health. While others, less conscientious, or less firmly fortified in the principles of morality, for the want of the rational and pure pleasures of taste, falter in their course, and sink into gross and forbidden indulgence of the appetites.

Let taste, then, be allowed its due place in the ethical system; let its relations to conscience and to duty be well defined; and we shall have no occasion to make war either upon conscience, on the one side, or upon a rational demand of our nature, on the other. "Happy is he that condemneth not himself in that thing which he alloweth," and happy also is he that *wisely alloweth* what *nature demands*, that so he allow *not* what *morality condemns.*

Still it must never be forgotten that the pleasures of taste, however exalted and refined, as truly as those of sensuality, may be immoral and wicked; and that they always are so, when they conflict with the demands of that law, which requires us to make it the supreme object and end of life to glorify and enjoy God, by securing the highest moral and spiritual well-being of ourselves and of mankind.

CHAPTER V.

WILL.

We have already noticed the distinction between the power of mere instinctive volition, as it exists in the animal nature, and the rational will. It is the latter, the power of responsible choice, that we now propose to examine. With this view, we must be allowed here to trench a little upon the limits of psychology.

It must be remembered that what we call *powers* of mind, are only man's ability for certain kinds of mental action. This term variously qualified indicates, in systematic order, various attributes of one and the same person. To say that a man has the powers of perception, imagination, memory, is only saying that he can perceive, imagine, remember. So also to say that he has the powers of affection, desire, will, is only saying that he can love, desire, choose.

This seems indeed too obvious to need to be said; and yet serious difficulties, especially in relation to the will, have often arisen from considering the several mental faculties as agents, in some sense independent of, or actually controlling, the one responsible man. They are indeed agents or instruments, but they are agents of the *person*, to whom God has given them, to be *used* by him as an accountable being.

Now all the world well knows what is meant by *choosing*. The act cannot be explained, just because it is a simple one and *needs* no explanation. And when we say that man is endowed with *will*, we only say that he *can choose*; thus asserting a fact of which every person is conscious, and which therefore requires no further proof. No philosophy can go behind this fact; for the fact is ultimate, and philosophy cannot go beyond what is ultimate.

To speak of free will, is tautology; to speak of enslaved will, is a solecism. Man *can* choose, or he *cannot*. If he can, he has the power which we call *will*; if he cannot, he has no such power. We are now speaking of constitutional ability. Inclination or predisposition to right or wrong *use* of the will, is another matter, and will be considered when we treat of *moral* states and actions.

In the action of the will, a convenient distinction is made between choice and volition. The word *choice* expresses a *determination* or *purpose* of mind, with reference to a certain act or course of action. It may be strictly immanent, and may repose fully formed in the mind for months and years. Thus a man determines to-day to go to Europe next year. *Volition* expresses the *nisus*, or direct *exertion* of the will, to carry the purpose into effect. In both choice and volition, the man is equally free and responsible, but he is not responsible for the *success* or *failure* of the volition, for of this he has not the control. Hence all the *morality* of the act obtains before that point is reached.

"I can absolutely make the *nisus* to move my hand, but the nisus will be followed by the motion only on condition that no antagonistic physical cause overcomes the mechanical force of the hand. If the hand is bound with a cord, or manacled, I am not free to move the hand, although I am still free to make the *nisus* or *volition*." * The *morality* of the act must therefore terminate with the volition, precisely where the *liberty* terminates. The choice may long precede the volition, as we have said, or they may be co-instantaneous, but they are always equally free acts of the same will and the same responsible person.

A man may purpose to-day to murder a person to-morrow, whom he is expecting then to meet; and thus the guilty murderer at heart, may exist twenty-four hours, before the volition is made that strikes the fatal blow; or his victim may be present, and the volition to strike may instantly follow the purpose; but both the purpose and the volition have each a moral quality; for which the man is responsible. If he *freely arrests* his murderous purpose, and does not strike the fatal blow, he is less guilty than if he *adds* to that purpose the final volition that consummates his crime. In the latter case he is guilty for the purpose, and he is guilty also for the *volition* that wields the blow; but whether the blow is *effectual* or not, does not affect his guilt.

All this, the truth of which we cannot fail to see, is predicated of the fact that the man is not the instrument of his will, but that his will is the instrument of the man; which will he is free to use, and is justly held responsible for the way in which he employs it.

"To talk of liberty," says President Edwards, "or the contrary, as belonging to the very *will itself*, is not to speak good sense. For the will itself is not an agent that has a will; the power of choosing, itself, has not a power of choosing. That which has the power of volition is the

* The Doctrine of the Will, by Henry P. Tappan, p. 95.

man, or the soul, and not the power of volition itself. To be free is the property of an agent who is possessed of powers and faculties, as much as to be cunning, valiant, bountiful, or zealous. But these qualities are the properties of *persons*, and not the properties of properties." *

IN WHAT SENSE ACTS OF THE WILL ARE CAUSED.

The necessitarian scheme has most of its support from arguments founded on the laws of cause and effect in the natural world. It is a law of nature, that any body at rest will continue at rest until acted upon by something called a *cause*. Thus every movement in nature is, in some sense, an effect of a preceding one, and that of another preceding it, until we reach the Supreme Being, who alone acts of himself. Now the human *will* has been by some philosophers placed in this chain of cause and effect. Our volitions have been supposed to be caused by something without our control, acting upon the will, as the turning of the wind-mill is caused by the wind. This is fatality.

We say in reply, that we do not deny the all-pervading law of cause and effect, but maintain that it operates in the material world conformably to the nature of matter, and in the mental world conformably to the nature of mind. Now man is a rational, spiritual being, made in the image of his Maker; and, like him, is capable of free and responsible action. Like God himself, he can *begin*, *originate*, a series of actions; and, so far as the actions are in his own mind, he can *arrest*, *terminate*, a series which he has begun. He can *begin* to do good or evil; he can *cease* from so doing. This is implied in the very idea of a responsible will.

The *fact* is certain; so rendered by three invincible

* Works, vol. II.

proofs, human consciousness, the Bible, and the clearest deductions of reason; but the *modus* of the fact transcends our present powers. Here a true, honest philosophy only looks, admires, and confesses her ignorance.

"*How* the will can possibly be free, must remain to us, under the present limitation of our faculties, wholly incomprehensible. We are unable to conceive an absolute commencement. Nay, were we even to admit as true what we cannot think as possible, still the doctrine of a motiveless volition would be only casualism; and the free acts of an indifferent, are, morally and rationally, as worthless as the pre-ordered passions of a determined will. How, therefore, I repeat, moral liberty is possible in man or God, we are utterly unable speculatively to understand. But practically the *fact*, that we are free, is given to us in the consciousness of an uncompromising law of duty, and in the consciousness of our moral accountability; and this *fact* of liberty cannot be redargued on the ground that it is incomprehensible, for the philosophy of the conditioned proves, against the understanding, that things there are, which *may*, nay *must* be true, of which the understanding is wholly unable to construe to itself the possibility." *

Because man wills *freely*, it does not follow that he wills *without motives*. It is not to be supposed that God wills without motives; no more does man. Yet who will say, that because God wills in view of motives to create a world, he is therefore not *free* in creating? † Is it not

* Hamilton's Phil. of the Conditioned, p. 509.

† The author is aware that some *have* said it. They have denied the essential freedom of God himself, and asserted that his creative and other acts are *necessary*. But they have done so in obedience to a presupposed *theory*, to which every thing must yield, rather than from the spontaneous dictates of the primal and unbiassed judgment. Cousin and others have asserted the necessity, on the ground that God's distinguishing characteristic is that of an absolute creative force, which must necessarily pass into activity. "The subjec-

his glory that all his actions are transcendently free, and at the same time from the best of motives? Why then should it be supposed that *man*, just because he acts from motives, acts of necessity? The truth is exactly the *reverse* of this. It is only as a being acts from motives, that his actions are free. Action *not* directed by intelligent motive, is *necessary* action; like that of a brute obeying its instinct, or that of a cloud moved by the wind.

OCCASIONAL AND EFFICIENT CAUSES.

As these terms have extensive currency, we must explain and use them. The *occasional* cause, in moral science, is the *motive* from which the man wills; the *efficient* cause is the *man himself.* The term occasional cause is not a happy one,for it is often understood to imply necessity. The truth is, the fact which it indicates is not really a *cause* of volition. For to say that a man is by it *induced* to will, is only saying that in view of it he is *willing* to will; which is only saying that he *wills.* Thus all we can make of it, is, that in view of the fact the man

tion of the Deity to a necessity, a necessity of self-manifestation identical with the creation of the universe, is contradictory of the fundamental postulates of a divine nature. On this theory, God is not distinct from the world; the creature is a modification of the creator."—HAMILTON *on the Conditional, p.* 480.

Whilst others, from adopting a metaphysical error, and mistaking the essential nature of *moral* action, have predicated a necessity of the divine goodness, as *compelling* choice from the highest motives. The assertion is suicidal; for in the very act of *asserting* the excellence of God, they *deny* his excellence, by denying his freedom. The *moral* quality of any act depends essentially upon its being a *free* act. See Cousin, Cours d' Hist. de la Philosophie Morale, Hume's Treatise on Human Nature, Cudworth's Intel. Sys., Coleridge's Aids to Reflection, Edwards on the Will, Day on the Will, Tappan on the Will, and others of a similar class, in which the reader will find both sides ingeniously and sometimes ably discussed. Above all, see Hamilton's Phil. of the Conditional, a thesaurus of great and mighty erudition, collated and applied as a Scotch intellect knows how to do it.

freely wills. If the fact or motive had no existence, not only would the man not will freely, but he would not will at all.

Neither is the *efficient* cause of human choice and volition, the same as an efficient cause in nature. In the natural world, the efficient cause of all phenomena is either God himself, or some power lodged by Him in the antecedents. But in the case of human choices and volitions, the immediate cause, by the supposition, is not God; nor is it a power, like that supposed in nature, lodged in the antecedents. For the supposed power in nature, or what some philosophers call a natural cause, is *always* active and effective. This is a first law of physics. Nothing short of a miracle can suspend the operation of a cause in nature. Its operation, miracle apart, is made necessary and constant, by the direct power of God. But man, like the Being in whose likeness he was made, while he has at all times the *power* to will, is not *constantly willing.*

"Let it be borne in mind, then, that there is more than one process in the universe. Some things are produced, it is most true, by the prior action of other things; and herein we behold the relation of cause and effect, properly so called; but it does not follow that all things are embraced in this one relation. This appears to be so only to the mind of the necessitarian; from which one fixed idea has shut out the light of observation. He no longer sees the rich variety, the boundless diversity, there is in the works of God. All things and all modes and all processes of the awe-inspiring universe, are made to conform to the narrow methods of his own mind. Look where he will, he sees not the free and flowing outlines of nature's true lineaments; he every where beholds the image of one fixed idea in his mind, projected outwardly upon the universe of God; behind which the true secrets and operations of nature are concealed from his vision. Even when he contemplates that living source of action, that bubbling fountain of volitions, the immortal mind of man itself, he only beholds a *thing*, which is made to act by the action of something else upon it; just as a body is made to move by the action of force upon it. His philosophy is, therefore, an essentially shallow and superficial philosophy." *

HOW THE WILL IS DETERMINED.

The great question respecting the freedom of the will, on which Jonathan Edwards and others have largely written, turns on the way or means by which human volitions are determined. For, merely attempting to prove that the will is free, is only attempting to prove that the will is a will; or, in other words, a power of willing. This would be gravely attempting to prove, that what is, is. The mind of that great man was engaged in no such idle play, as some have vainly imagined. But there is sometimes in his reasoning a confusion of terms, from his using the same term in different senses; which he might have avoided by always referring the influence of motives to the agent himself, instead of his will.

On this point Stuart has justly remarked: "Instead of speaking, according to the common phraseology, of the influence of motives on the *will*, it would be much more correct to speak of the influence of motives on the *agent*. We are apt to forget what *the will is*, and to consider it as something inanimate and passive, the state of which can be altered only by the action of some external cause. The habitual use of the metaphorical word *motives*, to denote the intentions or purposes, which accompany our voluntary actions, or, in other words, the *ends* which we

* Bledsoe's Examination, p. 54.

have in view in the exercise of power intrusted to us, has a strong tendency to confirm us in this error, by leading us to assimilate in infancy the *volition* of a mind to the *motion* of a body, and the circumstances which give rise to this volition to the *vis motrix* by which the motion is produced."*

OBJECTIVE AND SUBJECTIVE MOTIVES.

The occasional causes, so called, or, more properly, motives, which influence us in our choices and volitions, are of two kinds, objective and subjective. The objective motive is the object chosen, or the object without our mind, in view of which we choose. The subjective motive is the feeling, or state of mind, which prompts us to choose. Thus, a man is induced to go to California in pursuit of gold. His objective motive in going is *money;* his subjective motive is the *desire* for the money. These two motives are correlative. The one is of no avail without the other. The gold would be no motive, without the desire for it; and the desire would be no motive, without the prospect of the gold.

A man submits to a painful operation to save his life. The objective motive is his *life;* the subjective motive is his *desire* to live. The prospect of saving his life would be no motive for submitting to the operation, if he were not desirous of living.

A man leaves his business, and performs a long journey, to be united in marriage with the object of his affection. His objective motive for the journey is the *person* whom he loves; his subjective motive is his *love* for her. The object of his love would be no motive for the journey, if there were no prospect of obtaining her;

* Phil., p. 25.

and the prospect of obtaining her would be no motive, if he did not love her.

Thus the Creator has made the world without us to correspond to the world within us. Rational acts of will are in view of objective motives, and these motives are relevant to the subjective motives or feelings of the mind. There is then a regular law of action in the mental as well as in the material universe.

But motives do not *control* the will, according to the law of cause and effect in the natural world. The law is as *regular* in the one case as in the other, but it is not the *same*. In the one case, it is the law of *passive matter;* in the other, of *active spirit*. In the one case, there is no reason to perceive, and no will to choose; in the other case, there are both of these.

When a live spark is thrown upon a trail of dry gunpowder communicating with a magazine, an explosion *must* follow, by an irresistible law of nature. There is no reason in the spark to foresee the disastrous effects, and no will to resist the explosion. But in the mind of him who threw the spark, there *was* reason to foresee the effect, and will by which he could decide against the act. His motives for firing the magazine may have been powerful; they may have been, so to speak, almost omnipotent; but *omnipotent* they *could not* be, unless the will ceased to be will, at least in respect to that act.

Thus every rational being has the responsible control of his own will. To say that he has this, is only saying that he wills for himself, and not another for him. He also wills, not by blind impulse, as effects take place in the natural world, but as an intelligent being, ever bound to act in view of his responsibilities and duties. Hence, to will *freely*, is by no means the same thing as to will *capriciously*. The laws of the moral world are as certain and uniform as those of the natural. Responsible choice always implies intelligent design, having reference to that correlativeness of motives, which is as steady and uniform as the course of nature. Without such design, a man's volitions imply in him no more character than the pulsations of the heart or the sports of the breezes.

III.

DISTINCTION BETWEEN THE WILL AND THE AFFECTIONS.

Some distinguished authors have considered the affections and the will, one and the same faculty. Thus Edwards says, "The affections are no other than the more vigorous and sensible exercises of the inclination and will. The will and the affections of the soul are not two faculties; the affections are not essentially distinct from the will, nor do they differ from the mere *actings* of the will and inclination, but only in the liveliness and sensibility of the exercise."*

But this celebrated author was not here attempting a minute psychological analysis. He was considering the soul with simple reference to a point of religious doctrine, under two general divisions, understanding and will; thus merging all the intellective faculties into the former, and all the motive into the latter.

"In the general division of our faculties into understanding and will," says Reid, "our passions, appetites, and affections, are comprehended under the will; and so it is made to signify not only our determination to act or not to act, but every motive or incitement to action. It is this, probably, that has led some philosophers to represent desire, aversion, hope, fear, joy, sorrow, all our appetites, passions, and affections, as different modifications of the will; which, I think, tends to confound things which are very different."†

* Works vol. V., p. 10.

† Vol. IV., p. 6.

Indeed Edwards himself finds it necessary sometimes to make the distinction. He calls the affections "immanent," the will "manent." "The former," he says, "remain in the mind without any immediate relation to any thing to be brought to pass in action; the latter respect something to be done."

THE WILL AND THE AFFECTIONS HAVE DIFFERENT OBJECTS.

The affections have *beings* for their object, the will has relations, duties, interests. We love friends; we choose their society. A woman loves a child; she chooses to adopt it. A man loves a person; he chooses her as his wife. The people of a parish love the man, whom they choose as their pastor. Thus the will sustains to the affections, in this particular, the same relation which the desires do. Both the desires and the will have *things* for their object, while the affections repose only in *living beings.*

The will can resist the affections and desires.—Instead of being the same with the will, the affections and desires are only motives of action, which the responsible person may or may not adopt. He is at liberty to determine to indulge or to refuse them.

First, the will can resist the *affections.* We have seen that the *affections* have respect only to their specific object; whilst a man may *choose*, with reference to all the *circumstances*, within the range of his mental vision. Hence the saying, "Love is blind." It regards only its particular object. When we see a person congenial to us, our affections flow spontaneously towards that person, without regard to circumstances or results. But, guided by an enlarged view and a sense of duty, we may refuse an improper indulgence of the affections. We may not be able to exterminate the affection; it may be a part of our nature; but we can resist it, so far as to refrain from any wrong executive choice to which it may prompt us.

Secondly, the will can resist the *desires.* Whatever be a man's desires, he may always see reasons enough for controlling them as he ought; motives enough, if he duly regards them, for choosing the path of duty. But if he will not consider, and will heed neither the voice of prudence nor the admonitions of conscience, he must then, of course, be a creature of *mere impulse;* a *thing*, to be moved only as the machine carries him.

What we have here said of the affections and desires, is equally true of all the subordinate impulses. The will, as an executive faculty, is alike distinct from them all, and the responsible man is bound to employ it in the way most effectual to their due control and direction. The conflict may sometimes be severe, especially with a disordered appetite; but no demand of appetite, of passion, of affection, or of desire, can ever be so urgent, as to exonerate him from the duty of bringing them all into subjection to the laws of morality.

PART III.

MORAL ACTION.

CHAPTER I.

MORALLY RIGHT AFFECTION.

While natural affection is a mere spontaneous outburst of the heart, the work of the Creator in us, moral affection is in the keeping and service of conscience and the responsible will. When a person becomes practically conscientious in the exercise of affection, controlling it with a regard to duty, the affection is not only amiable, but *morally right.* It is not only what the mere animal naturally *does* exercise, but what a rational and accountable being *ought* to exercise.

Not only do natural affections thus become invested with moral quality, but entirely new affections may be called into existence.

Moral affection is a *complex* feeling. That we may

understand its various modifications due to different beings, we must analyze it.

It includes,

1. A *perception* of something pleasing in its object.
2. A cordial *affection* for him.
3. An agreeable *emotion* towards him, attending the affection.
4. A benevolent *desire* for his welfare.

If only the first three conspire, the affection may be mere *natural* love; but they are *all* united in the affection termed *moral* love.

For reasons that will appear, these elements must not be confounded. The perceptive part belongs to the intellect. The affection and the emotion coexist, but are not the same thing. A person may, at one time, have very lively emotion, accompanying feeble affection; at another time, he may have very deep and strong affection, attended with little emotion.

Emotion springs into life quickly; affection is the growth of time. With young lovers, *emotion* predominates; after they have been long and happily united, *affection* predominates. At first, they love more *ardently;* in subsequent years, more *affectionately*. The same law holds in all other affections. The young Christian has usually more vivid *emotion*, than he has after years of religious experience; but his pious *affection* may be continually growing deeper and stronger.

Moral affection is a steady *principle* of the heart, under control of the enlightened conscience. The emotion attending it does not depend merely upon the clearness of the perception, or the strength of the affection, but upon various exciting causes in the object and in circumstances. It is affected by age, by the state of health, by the weather, by the concurrence of pleasing or of disagreeable events.

The desire for the welfare of those we love, is a still more distinct element. We may most earnestly desire the welfare of a person, whose character is such that we can have little complacency in him. Indeed we may be able to find nothing in him to engage our interest, but the fact that he is a human being. Besides, as has been shown in a previous chapter, affection and desire respect different objects; the former having beings for its object; the latter, things. We love the person; we desire his welfare.

The above analysis will enable us to understand the various *modifications* of love. When the first element predominates, attended with little feeling, the love is very intelligent and discriminating. When the second element is decisive and strong, the love is characterized by sincerity and earnestness. When the third element is excessive, the love becomes a weak fondness, and sometimes a blind passion. If it is unaccompanied by the last element, it degenerates to mere lust. This is the name for selfish passion. If the fourth element predominates, with very little of the second and third, the love is chiefly benevolence, or good will. If accompanied with corresponding conduct, it rises to the virtue of beneficence.

It will be seen, also, that love indicating the same moral excellence, is of various modifications according to the nature of the beings we love, and according to our relations with them. The love of a parent for a child, is not like the love of a child for the parent. Conjugal love differs from either. Still unlike all the others is true love to God.

ONLY LOVE IS A RIGHT AFFECTION.

Love and hatred are opposed to each other; the former being the morally *right* and the latter the morally *wrong* affection. We shall in the next chapter see reasons for concluding that hatred is *never* right. We are now concerned with its opposite, love. It is right to love *all* beings, not excepting our enemies, or even the worst of men. But the love should correspond to its object. The proofs that love is always the right affection are the following:

1. Love is *instinctive* to the human mind. The disposition is strictly natural. It is the work of God in us; the normal state of affection. We were *made* to love. Children love before they hate; and except as they are perverse they do not hate at all, unless some unfriendly being comes in their way. Whether they *ought* then to hate, we are not now to inquire; for our only point here is to show that they are naturally inclined to love. It is only necessary to be with a child for a short time, exhibiting no unfriendliness, to secure his love. Indeed we are so constituted that we *must* love, or be miserable. But we have no such necessity to hate. This proves that we were made to love.

2. The loving affection is a *happy* one. It is always a source of enjoyment. "The sentiment of love is in itself agreeable to the person who feels it. It soothes and composes the breast, seems to favor the vital motions, and to promote the healthful state of the human constitution; and it is rendered still more delightful by the consciousness of the gratitude and satisfaction which it must excite in him who is the object of it. Their mutual regard renders them happy in one another, and sympathy, with this mutual regard, makes them agreeable to every other person."* If then the Being who made us wills our happiness, love is the right affection.

* Smith's Theory of Moral Sentiment, p. 80.

3. *Conscience* approves of the benevolent affection. Men never feel condemned for loving their fellow-beings, even their enemies. They often feel condemned for hating, but never for loving; unless the love is an impure affection. On the contrary, every man is conscious of a feeling of self-approbation, when he returns love for hatred and good for evil.

4. The believer in Christianity finds conclusive proof of the same, in its teachings. "Love all men." "Love your enemies." "Render not evil for evil." "If ye love your friends only, what thank have ye?" "Let us love one another; for love is of God." Indeed this affection is the crowning excellence of God himself. "God is love." To love all beings, the evil as well as the good, enemies as well as friends, is, according to Christianity, to be like our Father in heaven.

Having thus shown that love is always the right affection, we shall for the present leave the proof that the opposite, hatred, is always wrong, and proceed to explain the various *modifications* of love due to *different beings.*

THE AFFECTION DUE TO GOD.

It does not belong to our present task to adduce the formal proofs of the Divine existence, but for the present assuming that there *is* a God, such as Christianity reveals, we are to indicate the affection due to Him. We see in Him all that is worthy to receive our highest and most absolute homage. We have revealed to our faith an infinite Being, perfect and glorious in all his attributes. His love, his pity, his forbearance, his compassion, his justice, all absolutely infinite and unchanging, are under the guidance of an all-embracing and unerring wisdom. He is a Being of spotless purity, of transcendent holiness, of boundless benevolence.

He lives and reigns to do good. He sits upon the throne of the universe, not as an arbitrary monarch, not to subserve selfish ends, but to protect the sacred interests of righteousness and sustain its everlasting laws. He is hence just such a Being as all upright creatures would choose for their moral guardian and ruler.

But while he thus reigns in infinite and unbending righteousness, while justice and judgment are the habitation of his throne, he has yet an eye to pity every sorrow, and a heart to feel for every woe. The sublime and awful glory of his holiness, is equalled only by the tenderness of his pity and the gentleness of his compassion. Not a sparrow falls to the ground without his notice, and his tender mercies are over all his works.

That Being is our own God. He is the Maker of our frame and the Father of our spirit. He made us in his own likeness, to love and enjoy him for ever. To him we are indebted, not only for our existence, but for all that makes our existence a blessing. All that is desirable in the life that now is, and all that may be hopeful in the life to come, we owe to him.

He is not far off, like some earthly monarch, that we cannot approach him. He is ever with us. In him we live and move and have our being. We realize his power and goodness in every beating pulse, in every breath that is dealt out to us, in all the warm currents of life and joy that flow through our frames.

Although he is "the great and dreadful God," yet he condescends, in his Spirit and with his Word, to dwell in every one of us, to enlighten our consciences, to guide our steps, to warn us against every wrong way; to uphold our steps, to bear our burdens, to comfort our afflictions, to pity our sorrows, and cheer us with the hope of immortal life.

He is also perpetually round about us and communing with us, in his works and providential dealings. The heavens declare his glory, and the well-ordered seasons ever speak of him; seed-time and harvest, day and night, summer and winter, are all eloquent of his praise; all lands and seas are full of the riches of his goodness; every sunbeam and every breeze comes to us laden with his love.

Now the question is, What is the affection due to such a Being? All must see, that it should be supreme, reverential, filial, grateful, constant, and commanding. This need not be argued; it is only necessary to explain these qualities, and every conscience will approve of them.

1. Supreme. By this is meant, that we should love God more than any other being. He should be the first great object of our affection; we should have no other gods before him. There is more *in* him to love, than in any other being, or in all others combined. He is *worthy* of our supreme love; no other being is. Then the *relations* he sustains to us, as our Creator, our Heavenly Father, our Upholder and Moral Guardian, our Redeemer and our final Judge, all proclaim that to him alone our highest homage is and must be for ever due.

2. Reverential. To exercise towards this great and glorious Being the same fond and familiar affection which we may towards a fellow-creature, would be impious and profane. Such homage as this, we should not dare to render even to an *earthly* monarch. Our affection for God should be deep, strong, calm, earnest; the cordial surrender of the entire soul in supreme homage to him; but it should be ever characterized with the profoundest humility, awe, and reverence. Hence familiar epithets, such as *dear* God, should be publicly used with caution, if we would not offend the proprieties of religion and of good taste.

3. Filial. Still our affection for God should partake much of the *filial* quality. He is more than merely our Creator and Benefactor; he is our *Heavenly Father.* As he has for us, although in a higher and purer sense, the feelings of an earthly parent for his offspring, so we should exercise towards him the feelings of *confiding and devoted children.* Our love to God should be complacent and emotional, trustful and gladsome, as well as affectionate and devout. It should lead us to delight in him, so that we should esteem every other pleasurable emotion of small value, compared with that of beholding his face in beauty.

4. Grateful. We sustain to God the relation of *dependent* and *helpless* beings to an infinite Benefactor. We ought, therefore, to love him not only for what he is, and for what he has done, but for what he has done *for us.* Nor is this, as some have supposed, a selfish affection, if we also truly love God for what he is. It modifies and enhances that love. It is a feeling of obligation, blending with the feeling of love, and inciting the soul to a higher reach of affection. It leads us to inquire what *returns* we should make for these stupendous gifts. Its language is, "What shall I render to the Lord for all his benefits toward me? I will take the cup of salvation and call upon the name of the Lord; I will pay my vows now in the presence of all his people." This is any thing but a selfish homage.

5. Constant. From the nature of the human mind its emotions must vary, and even its affections cannot be always the same. Yet there is an affection, which is like the great and deep river, ever flowing in the same direction and into the same sea, although not always equally full and rapid. Such is the affection due to God. Himself ever the same, he is ever equally worthy of our supreme love.

No good reason can exist why we should love him less to-day than at any previous time; on the contrary, as our knowledge of him increases, and we have an ever-growing experience of his benefits, our constant love should be constantly increasing; like the river receiving tributaries, and thus perpetually enlarging, through its entire long way to the ocean.

To vary our illustration, true love to God is like that mysterious power which holds the planets in firm allegiance to the sun. In some parts of their orbits they are nearer to the sun, and move faster than at others; but their hold upon the glorious object of their devotion is never relaxed for a moment. Such should be the constancy of our love to God.

6. Commanding. A mere immanent affection, which loses itself in pleasant meditations and rapturous excitements, without inducing conformity of life to the divine law, is not the love due to our Heavenly Father. The right affection is *commanding;* and its commands are obeyed. It bids its subject *do* God's will; and he *does* it. It thus rules the heart and conduct.

It calls into steady and effective action the fourth element of moral love, the *desire;* it thus becomes a benevolent *principle*, lasting as existence. Emotion may rise and fall, but the affection abides in the heart; the principle of allegiance, the supreme desire and purpose to please God, is ever there. "This is the love of God, that ye keep his commandments." Thus the evidence of true love to God must be found in a course of life essentially conformed to the divine law.

Such is the affection *due* to God. It is as truly a *moral* as a *religious* affection. We clearly see, in the light of pure morality, that it is such an affection as we *ought* to render him. However right with his fellow-beings, in the view of a mere secular morality, no man is morally right with God, unless he renders to him the homage which we have described.

RIGHT DOMESTIC AFFECTIONS.

Under this general head we include conjugal, parental, filial, and fraternal affections. They all have their springs in nature, but they should be regulated by moral principle. Unless they are so, beautiful as they are by nature, they may become by perversion instruments of evil. They are all to be kept in subordination to the higher affection due to God. He who loves even father or mother more than God, is guilty of a moral wrong in respect to the most important of all relations.

1. Conjugal Affection. The affection subordinate only to the love due to God, is that which belongs to the *conjugal union.* The parties united in marriage are bound to love each other more than any other human being. Before this union existed, the filial affection claimed supremacy; now the conjugal supersedes it. "For this cause shall a man leave his father and mother, and be joined unto his wife, and they twain shall be one flesh."

Conjugal love should fully embrace all the elements of moral affection. The love which nature furnished; which was in the hearts of the parties before they were united and which led to the union, must now be taken into the custody of conscience, to be controlled, nourished, perfected, by moral principle. With the deep and growing affection must continue the complacent delight, which will ever make the parties happy in each other, and these must be attended with such benevolent desires for each other's welfare, as shall prompt every needful effort and sacrifice to promote it.

Thus the affection, which was at first, perhaps, little else than a complacent fondness, gradually grows to a full-orbed and shining love; in the warmth and the light of which the happy pair move on together in life's journey, mutually blessing and blessed.

Parental Affection. Next to the affection which parents owe to each other, is that due to their *offspring*. To aid and prompt them in this duty, the Creator has kindly implanted a natural affection; and it is their duty so to cherish and direct it, as to secure the best welfare of their child. It is not the love of mere fondness, which is demanded. This will blind them to their child's faults, and render them too indulgent.

Parental affection should be characterized by deep, steady, patient benevolence; otherwise the complacent emotion, with which the fond parent contemplates his children, may render him a most unfaithful guardian. It should be a sympathetic, enduring, and conscientious love, which is not blind to their faults, but forbearing; which firmly denies them what is wrong or injurious; which chastises, if need be, but not in anger; which encourages every virtuous endeavor; which anticipates every want; which seeks to guide, cheer, educate, and train up to a virtuous and elevated life, the precious beings intrusted to its care.

Filial Affection. The affection of the child for his parents, should have much resemblance to that which we owe to God. It is the love of a young, inexperienced, dependent being, for those to whom, under God, he owes his existence, and on whom he is dependent for support and guidance. Hence his love should be confiding and grateful, respectful and obedient. As parental love seeks to benefit the child, so filial love should seek to please the parent.

Filial affection is not supplanted by marriage. Another affection supervenes, to which it is relatively subordinate, but it should be absolutely as strong as before. The parent who gives a dutiful child in marriage, does not lose that child, but gains another.

The true filial affection seeks to repay the debt incurred in childhood; to do for the parent in age and feebleness, what the parent did for the child in infancy and helplessness; it honors the parent's gray hairs, supports his feeble steps, smooths the furrows ploughed in his face by care and time; it watches tenderly around his sick bed, pours its soothing voice into his dying ear; and it never forgets to drop tears, fresh and warm from the heart, over his grave.

FRATERNAL AFFECTION. The natural affection of the children of the same family for each other, important as it is, proves to be entirely inadequate to secure the welfare of the household, unless it is sustained and wielded by an enlightened conscience. Brothers and sisters cannot be too early and earnestly taught, that it is their duty to love each other, and to do all in their power to promote each other's present and prospective welfare.

The family is the smallest and most compact of all communities; hence the interests of its members are very closely interwoven. There is no avoiding collision, irritation, contention, but by that deep and steady affection which duty enjoins, and which makes every member as desirous of another's welfare as his own. Children trained to this principle, through the whole period of their minority, will not fail to make good members of that larger community, for which they are destined in future life.

RIGHT SOCIAL AFFECTION.

The modifications of affection due to our neighbors, and to our fellow-beings generally, depend upon various circumstances. We cannot love all alike. We naturally feel the most affection for those with whom we have been most associated. This is well. But we are not required to love even those with the same affection.

There is a congeniality of tastes, temperaments, pursuits, which inclines us to love some more than others, and thus leads to what are called *special* friendships. These are not only natural, but morally right, so long as they do not become exclusive. So soon as they are allowed to narrow the soul and shut off the affection that is due to others, they become selfish and pernicious. We may love our particular friends as much as we please, if we still love all our fellow-beings as we ought.

It was evidently intended that these particular friendships should exist. The foundation for them is laid in the diversity of tastes and callings; and it would be impossible to bestow those special attentions upon all, which are necessary to keep alive a particular friendship and to gratify its wants. Hence all have the right to select their intimate friends, with whom they visit and exchange hospitalities, and to whom they intrust their most sacred sympathies; and none may complain of this, or indulge jealousy and envy, since the same privilege is freely granted to all.

It is thus that the pure and refined virtues of social friendship, so productive of human happiness, are fostered and protected. When friends thus love one another "with pure hearts fervently," when they heartily reciprocate each other's feelings and seek each other's welfare, and when they consecrate their mutual love to the will and service of God, they may hope to perpetuate their friendship and minister to each other's joy in a future state of being. This is the true idea of a Christian church, anticipating upon earth the full fruition of heaven.

RIGHT AFFECTION TOWARDS BAD MEN.

We cannot feel towards bad men the same affection which we do towards good men. True love is and ought to be discriminating. It must see *reasons* for loving; and if it sees *any* in a bad man, it certainly sees *more* in a good man. Hence the affection must be different.

The only question is, ought we to love bad men at all? They may not be *worthy* of our love, in point of character; but it does not follow that we should not love them. If our Heavenly Father loved none but those who are worthy of his love, it is to be feared that few of us would have a place in his heart. Is there not something, even in the very worst man, that is a reason why we should love him? There may not be in his character, but is there not in his humanity? He is our brother, fallen and wretched, but still our brother. Then should not our hearts yearn towards him?

He was made in the likeness of God, as a rational being. He is the same being still. The divine image is still there; marred and defaced, but not annihilated. The glorious moral likeness to God has departed, but something of the primitive humanity remains. And is not *that* interesting to us? The divine mind so regards it, and so must we, if we would be the children of God. Yes, there *is* something in the man, however bad he may be, because he *is* a man, that calls for our affection.

We may abhor his character; we may be disgusted with his vices; but we should cherish the kindred regard for the *man*. This affection should be pitiful and benevolent, leading us to do all in our power to reclaim and save him. If we turn from him with a frowning and pharisaical spirit; if we utterly despise him, and cast him out of our sympathies to perish in his guilt; we are false to ourselves, and false to our brother. So did not Jesus Christ; and are not his spirit and life the perfection of all morality?

RIGHT AFFECTION TOWARDS OUR ENEMIES.

We now come to perhaps the most trying of all the duties of morality. Ought we to love our enemies? Some have boldly asserted that this is *impossible*, and have on this ground challenged the precepts of Christianity. That it is very difficult, we admit; but it is not impossible, for it has been done. Not only did Jesus Christ do it, but many thousands have imbibed his benignant spirit, and experienced the divine luxury of doing the same, in some humble measure. It implies self-denial, which is always hard to practise; yet often a duty on which life itself depends.

Heathen philosophers might pronounce it impossible, and expunge it from their moral code; but we, who may have the spirit and teachings of Christ to guide us, have no apology for so doing. Without this grace from on high, we might never aspire to this highest of moral virtues; but with it, we should at least make the attempt.

Suppose, then, a man to be our bitter and avowed enemy, and that too when we have done him no harm. He is wholly in fault, and we are entirely innocent. We thus assume the strongest imaginable case. We certainly cannot feel complacent towards his conduct; but he is still a man, a fellow-being; unreasonable, perverse, criminal, but still our brother. We should then separate the conduct from the man, think of him as God made him, and we may still find something to love. In the *man*, apart from his conduct, there is something that should engage the affection of every rational being. It is im possible, we grant, to love him as we do a friend; but there is a *benevolent* affection which we should not withhold, even from an enemy.

We are greatly aided in this duty, by considering how Christ loved *us*, even while we were "yet enemies." He had never done us any harm; we were entirely in fault; and yet so great was his love for us, that he laid down his life to save us. And despite of all our multiplied offences against him, he still loves us with the tenderness of a brother.

We owe a duty here to *ourselves*, as well as to our enemy. By cherishing hatred and revenge, we injure our own character. By cherishing a forgiving spirit, by seeking to bring him to repentance, and to promote his welfare, we nourish in our own hearts the purest and noblest feelings; while, at the same time, we take the most effectual means to convince him of his fault, to disarm his enmity, to reform his conduct, and to make him our friend.

And this is our *duty*. If we are utterly disinclined to do it, except as we receive the proffered grace of Christianity, then we should accept that grace. Whether Christianity is proved to be from heaven or not, if she disposes us to do what is *right*, we should accept the precious boon. No man's conscience ever condemned him for accepting that grace, which inclines him to love his enemies and to seek their welfare. And we should add, no man who has done so, has ever failed to become thereby a better and a happier man.

PHILANTHROPY.

Philanthropy, as the name imports, is the benevolent affection embracing all mankind. In this sense, every man is bound to be a philanthropist. Nor may his love for the human race exhaust itself in mere sentiment. It should be active and self-sacrificing, commanding our earnest endeavors to relieve the sufferings and improve the condition of our less favored fellow-beings.

Christianity is eminently a philanthropic system. It seeks to render all men wise and happy. Every true Christian is both in theory and in practice a philanthropist. But as the powers of man are limited, and his first duties are naturally to himself, his family, his neighborhood, and his country, it may be only his good will and fervent prayer, that he can bestow upon large portions of mankind.

It is not, however, a disposition of general good will to men, attended with scattered and miscellaneous efforts for their welfare, that gives to a man sufficient notoriety to mark him as a philanthropist. The man to whom the public award this name, concentrates his efforts upon some great benevolent enterprise. To this he devotes his talents and his substance. He thus, like Howard, or Wilberforce, makes his mark upon the world, and proves the sincerity and earnestness of his benevolence. His philanthropy may have an eminently Christian type, like that of the faithful missionary, devoting talents, property, and life itself, to spreading the Gospel among the nations.

CHAPTER II.

MORALLY WRONG AFFECTION.

WE have seen, in the previous chapter, that true *love*, or the benevolent affection, is always morally *right*. We are now to see that its opposite, *hatred*, or the malevolent affection, is always morally *wrong*. As the present writer is constrained to take a somewhat different view upon this subject from many others, and among them distinguished classical authors, it is due both to the subject and to them to examine it with care.

My opinion is that *every* malevolent affection has moral quality, that it is of man and not of God, and is morally wrong. I do not believe that it exists in God; that it existed in man when created in God's likeness; that it existed in the heart of Jesus Christ; or that it ever *ought* to exist in the heart of any human being.

VIEWS OF REID AND OTHERS.

We will here quote from only two or three of the more distinguished books used in educational institutions and regarded as standard authorities. "Are there in the constitution of man," says Reid, "any affections that may be called *malevolent?* What are they? and what is their use and end? To me there seem to be two, which we may call by that name. They are *emulation* and *resentment.* These I take to be parts of the human constitution, given us by our Maker for good ends; and, when properly directed and regulated, of excellent use."*

Stewart adopts nearly the same view, classing emulation among the desires. "It may be doubted," he says, "if there be any principle of this kind (malevolent) implanted by nature in the mind, excepting the principle of *resentment;* the others being ingrafted on this stock by our erroneous opinions of criminal habits."† Most writers have taken a similar view; some of them giving a much wider range to the malevolent affection.

The principle of *emulation* we shall consider under the head of *Desire.* We are now to examine the principle of *resentment.* The writers quoted above, and others, as we shall see hereafter, have argued in favor of this as a constitutional principle in man, from the fact that *brutes* manifest it.‡ It is said to be their defence. And so also they manifest *other* dispositions, which are proper and useful in *irrational* creatures, but which in *rational* beings must be condemned; for rational beings have other and higher means of defence and protection.

Who would infer that because certain animals practise a kind of instinctive deceit, and others get angry and fight and kill, that man was made to do the same? It is not wrong in brutes to resent injuries, for this is their only means of defence; but it by no means follows that it is not wrong in *man* to do so, who was made in the image of his Maker.

* Works, vol. IV., p. 110. † Active and Moral Powers, p. 86.

‡ See Reid's Works, vol. IV., p. 118. Also, Whewell's Elements, vol. I. p. 50.

Adam Smith contends for the principle of resentment in the following language: "A person becomes contemptible, who tamely sits still, and submits to insults, without attempting either to repel or to revenge them. We cannot enter into his indifference and insensibility. We call his behavior mean-spiritedness, and are as really provoked by it, as by the insolence of his adversary. Even the mob are enraged to see any man submit patiently to affronts and ill usage. They desire to see this insolence resented, and resented by the person who suffers from it. They cry to him with fury to defend, or to revenge himself. If his indignation rises at last, they heartily applaud, and sympathize with it. It enlivens their own indignation against his enemy, whom they rejoice to see him attack in turn, and they are as really gratified by his revenge, provided it is not immoderate, as if the injury had been done to themselves."*

There is some truth in the above remarks, but it is presented in such a form and connection as to encourage, in my opinion, feelings and conduct at variance with the sound principles of morality. The remarks do indeed express a very common *fact*, but an appeal to the desire, sympathy, and gratified revenge, of "the *mob*," to settle a grave and momentous question of moral right, is not in very good keeping with the subject. Arguments from this source would prove fatal to all moral truth and duty.

To the believer in Christianity, any refutation of the above sentiments would seem to be superfluous. They harmonize very imperfectly with the life and teachings of Him, "who, when he was reviled, reviled not again, when he suffered, he threatened not, but committed himself to

* Theory of Moral Sentiment, p. 25.

Him that judgeth righteously." Jesus Christ never indulged the spirit of resentment, and expressly forbade it in others. His language is too explicit to be mistaken. "Love your enemies; do good to them which hate you; bless them that curse you, and pray for them which despitefully use you. And unto him that smiteth thee on the one cheek, offer also the other."

Every thing like that resentment which, it is said, "we like to see," and which is claimed as a "purely constitutional principle," is absolutely condemned by the language, as it was also by the life, of Jesus Christ. The consistent believer in Christianity is therefore compelled to think that, however plausible the speculations of these writers, there is yet some serious error in them.

It is with the view of detecting this error, if it exists, that we proceed with our inquiry. We are bound, as philosophers, to settle the question, not by an exclusive appeal to the precepts of Christianity, whose authority may be by some questioned, but upon its own merits. It should not be forgotten, however, that every principle of morality, as it is found to harmonize with Christianity, not only adds new lustre to the evidence of Christianity as a revelation from God, but receives from it greatly augmented force and authority.

We may come at the merits of the question by putting it in two forms. Do we *need* any such principle as resentment? And have we positive proof that such a principle *exists*, as a part of our mental constitution? The former question anticipates the latter; for if it should be evident that we do not need the element in question, the presumption would be that it was not originally implanted in us. But this is only presumption, and each question must be examined by itself.

RESENTMENT UNNECESSARY.

We must distinguish between *resentment* and *self-defence*. The principle of self-defence is instinctive and highly important. It is a moral duty to obey this instinct, and defend ourselves from harm. But this we may do without any malevolence towards the aggressor.

To seek to defend ourselves from harm, is one thing; to seek, with malevolent intent, to injure him who has harmed us, is quite another. The former is self-defence; the latter is resentment. The former we believe to be morally right; the latter, morally wrong.

If a man attacks our person or our character, we have a right to do all that is necessary to defend ourselves from injury. If the result is fatal to his life or reputation, the fault is not ours. If we did right, we did not injure him with a spirit of resentment, but of pure self-defence. We only did what our safety and the common welfare demanded. No resentment, retaliation, or revenge, was in our heart; on the contrary, it was in our heart to pity and to pray for him. While seeking to protect ourselves, we desired him no evil; but we wished him to see the wrongfulness of his way, and to forsake it.

This is true self-defence. It is instinctive, moral, and Christian. That is, in so doing, we are, in both a moral and a Christian view, true to a primitive instinct of our nature. But when we allow the spirit of *malicious resentment* to supervene, we are false to that instinct, and charge to its account what is really a part of our moral perverseness.

But ought not the guilty to be punished? Perhaps so; but the injured one is not ordinarily the proper person to do it. Much less ought he to do it from a principle of resentment. As a man is a partial judge of his own wrongs, civil government has taken the business of redressing them out of his hands, and placed it in the hands of an impartial tribunal.

The *divine* government, also, to rebuke the fell spirit of resentment, has placed it, for final decision, in the sole charge of the Judge of all. "Avenge not yourselves, but rather give place unto wrath; for it is written, Vengeance is mine, I will repay, saith the Lord. Therefore, if thine enemy hunger, feed him; if he thirst, give him drink."

We infer, therefore, that the principle of resentment is not needed in our mental constitution; since all the purposes of self-defence, of punishment, and of the protection of the public welfare, can be better secured by other means.

RESENTMENT NOT ORIGINAL.

If we do not need this principle, the presumption is that the Creator has not implanted it. Still the point is not to be decided *a priori;* it is a question of fact. The simple question is, on a careful analysis of the mental constitution, do we find in it any form of the malevolent element? *Any principle, whose obvious design was to lead us to desire and to attempt the injury of our fellow-beings?* This is the plain question.

It proves nothing, to say, with the authors above cited and others, that brutes manifest the disposition to injure their enemies; that many of our fellow-beings manifest the same, and "we are pleased to see them do so;" all this only proves that many rational beings are so false to their noble nature as to act like irrational brutes, and "we are *pleased*" with such conduct. But who are the "*we?*" Not *all* men, certainly; for there are not a few, who regard such conduct in a very different light.

The question is not, what irrational brutes were made to do, nor yet, what men actually do, but what *we* were *made* to do.

INSTINCTIVE RESENTMENT. Bishop Butler has made a distinction, which others have adopted, between what he calls instinctive and deliberate resentment. But his instinctive *resentment*, when examined, turns out to be nothing more than the mere instinct of self-defence. Sudden emergencies sometimes occur, in which we have no time to deliberate; we must then act instinctively and instantaneously. There is not necessarily any malicious feeling in this, any more than there is in suddenly shutting the eyelids to keep out a mote. Whereas the wish to injure another must necessarily be, to some extent, intentional and deliberate.

"The final cause (design) of instinctive resentment," says Stewart, "was plainly to defend us against sudden violence, when reason would come too late to our assistance, by rousing the powers both of mind and body to instant and vigorous exertion. A number of our other instincts are perfectly analogous to this. Such, for example, is the instinctive effort we make to recover ourselves when we are in danger of losing our balance, and the instinctive despatch with which we shut the eyelids when an object is made to pass rapidly before the face. In general it will be found, that, as nature has taken upon herself the care of our preservation during the infancy of our reason, so in every case in which our existence is threatened by dangers, against which reason is unable to supply a remedy with sufficient promptitude, she continues this guardian care through the whole of life."*

Now this is precisely what we mean by the instinct

* Active and Moral Powers, p. 89.

of self-preservation, or self-defence, which we shall consider under its proper head. No man ever doubted the reality and importance of this instinct.

DELIBERATE RESENTMENT. "The final cause (design) of this species of resentment," continues the above author, "is analogous to that of the other: to serve as a check on those men whose violent or malignant passions might lead them to disturb the happiness of their fellow-creatures."

But if the affection is *deliberate*, it is not *instinctive*, and is hence of a moral nature. Deliberate resentment, then, must be one of these two things; either deliberate self-defence, not involving any malevolence, and therefore morally right; or deliberate retaliation, involving malevolence, and therefore morally wrong.

The same writer adds: "In order to secure still more effectually so very important an end, we are so formed that the injustice offered to *others*, as well as to ourselves, awakens our resentment against the aggressor, and prompts us to take part in the redress of their grievances. In this case, the emotion we feel is more properly denoted in our language by the word *indignation;* but, as Butler has remarked, our principle of action is in both cases fundamentally the same: an aversion, or displeasure at injustice and cruelty, which interests us in the punishment of those by whom they have been exhibited."

"Resentment, therefore, when restrained within due bounds, seems to be rather a sentiment of hatred against vice than an affection of ill-will against any of our fellow-creatures; and, on this account, I am somewhat doubtful, notwithstanding the apology I have already made for the title of this section, whether I have not followed Dr. Reid too closely in characterizing resentment, considered as an original part of the constitution of man, by the epithet of *malevolent*." "After all, however, that I have advanced in justification of this part of the human constitution, I must acknowledge that there is no principle of action which requires more pains, even in the best minds, to restrain it within the bounds of moderation."*

It will be observed that the above writer here virtually concedes nearly all that we have claimed. The principle for which he contends, instead of implying any ill will or malevolence, which can be properly exercised only against *beings*, is merely "a sentiment of hatred (aversion) against vice;" which is a virtuous moral feeling. To be heartily opposed to all wrong-doing, and conscientiously to throw our entire sympathy in favor of law and of the injured, is more than a mere instinctive impulse; it is a high moral virtue.

That there is, *in fact*, much of retaliation, with its kindred affections, in the human character, is too evident; but that such feelings are original elements of the mental constitution, has never been shown. On the contrary, they can be fully accounted for in other ways. They are a part of our *moral perverseness*, condemned by the law of God and by every enlightened conscience.

Malevolence of every kind is always attended with pain; a circumstance, doubtless, intended to guard us against it; as the smart of a wound was designed to warn us against cutting our own flesh.

After descanting upon the pure happiness arising from *love*, Adam Smith remarks, "It is quite otherwise with hatred and resentment. Too violent a propensity to these detestable passions, renders a person the object of universal dread and abhorrence, who, like a wild beast, ought, we think, to be hunted out of all civil society."†

* Active and Moral Powers, p. 90. † Theory of Moral Sentiments.

We could not desire stronger language than this against malevolent affections. It is no part of our task to attempt to reconcile it with what the same writer has said in other places; it is sufficient to ask, who does not see the absurdity of speaking of "*too* violent a propensity to *detestable passions?*" If these passions are "detestable," as they truly are, there should be *no* propensity to them. Any propensity to a detestable passion is morally wrong. Hence the Creator, as a pure and good being, could not have implanted it in our constitution. Its origin must be human, not divine.

With this view the teachings of Christianity perfectly accord. They condemn every degree and form of malevolent affection. But are we to suppose that the Creator has implanted a principle in our nature, which may never be called into action? This cannot be admitted. We must then conclude, that the malevolent principle is no part of our mental constitution. We have an instinct, or purely natural propensity, to love; but none, to hate. To love, is consonant with pure nature, and is therefore morally right; to hate, is against that nature, and is therefore morally wrong.

It is said that David hated the wicked. Even if he did, it does not follow that we ought to do so. His conduct is not in all cases an example for us. His language is indeed very strong. "Do not I hate them, O Lord, that hate thee, and am not I grieved with those that rise up against thee? I hate them with perfect hatred; I count them mine enemies." But it seems evident, on comparing these and similar expressions with his general teachings and life, that the hatred of which he speaks, did not include the malevolent affection; but was merely an earnest exercise of the feeling of sympathy with his God, in defending the cause of righteousness. That his pious zeal was ever adulterated with a mixture of malevolence, we have no proof; but even if it was, this does not make it right.

Those sacred scriptures which speak of God as hating the wicked, as being angry with them, &c., are not to be understood as implying any *malevolent* affection. They are bold expressions indicating his righteous abhorrence of wicked conduct, and his inflexible purpose, as the Moral Guardian of mankind, to sustain his laws. No student in oriental literature can be at a loss how to understand them.

CONCLUDING REMARKS.

We conclude, then, that the principle of malevolence is no part of our mental constitution. As it is always right to love, so it is always wrong to hate. If this be so, then the demand of pure morality is here in perfect harmony with that of Christianity. The law of morality requires us to love, and never to hate; and Christ has taught us that *love is the fulfilling of the law*. To fulfil the great law of our being, then, it is only needful to love; no hating whatever is needful.

Christianity does not teach us to love our friends and hate our enemies. It does not inculcate "resentment," with the caution "to restrain it within due limits." It takes entirely different ground. It commands us to love *all* beings, at *all* times, and under *all* circumstances. No provocation, however severe, can make it morally right for one rational being to hate another.

What we have said of this particular form of malevolent feeling, is true of *all* its forms. They are all equally condemned, both by the principles of pure morality and the positive precepts of Christianity. Envy, hatred, revenge, &c., are all modifications of the malevolent affection; none of them belonged to man in innocence; they are no part of his constitution; they pertain to him only as a being fallen and perverse.

To save us from even an apology for personal resentment as a means of self-defence, the government of God, and, by his authority, human government, take the punishment of our offenders out of our own hands; thus absolving us from the necessity, under which irrational brutes exist, of retaliating our own wrongs. Our defence is placed in the hands of a higher and an impartial tribunal. Thus, knowing that if our cause is just our defence is ultimately sure; that if an earthly tribunal fails to do us justice, a higher tribunal will not fail to do it; while we abhor the conduct of our guilty foe, we may still extend to him our benevolent compassion, and seek his repentance and salvation. This only is true Christianity; and this only is sound morality.

It is not to be disputed that this is a hard and unpopular doctrine. It is not the current doctrine of writers upon this subject; not the doctrine generally taught in the schools; and certainly not the doctrine upon which most men practise. Teachers of morals have here too often taken the wrong stand-point; they have deduced principles and duties from what man *is*, as a fallen being, rather than from what he *was*, as created by God. They have hence found it difficult to make their morality tally with the revealed law of God and the plain teachings of Christianity.

But the time is not to be despaired of, when a higher and purer philosophy will prevail. Just in the degree that men see the divine beauty, and feel the benign influence of Christianity, they will better understand themselves and their duties. By the regenerating grace of the the gospel, which alone is adequate to the effect, the bitter root of hatred, in all its malignant forms, will be utterly destroyed. Its very remains, infected as they all are, with the poison of the serpent's tooth, shall be cast forth from the heart of man and eternally abandoned; while *love*, which alone *fulfils the law*, the law of the soul's necessities, the law of conscience, and the law of God, shall have the entire soul, to flourish there undisputed, unrivalled, and forever.

CHAPTER III.

MORALLY RIGHT DESIRE.

WHILE natural desire is purely constitutional, like the instinct of the brute, moral desire is a cherished principle of action, such as enlightened conscience approves or condemns. In this chapter we are to consider those desires which are *morally right.*

It will simplify our subject to include them in two generic classes; those which relate to our *own* welfare, and those which relate to the welfare of *others.*

DESIRES FOR OUR OWN WELFARE.

As these desires have their natural origin in self-love, we must distinguish between this and selfishness.

Self-love is that principle in man which leads him to seek what he judges to be for his good. It does not conflict with the interests of others. It is entirely consistent with the desire for their welfare. It even blends with that desire, and increases its strength and activity. Only he who properly regards his own welfare, truly regards that of others.

Selfishness is a term of *opposition.* It is the setting of one's own interest against that of others. Thus the selfish boy at play consults his own wishes, regardless of the feelings of his companions; the selfish man in business consults his own gains, regardless of the losses he may bring upon others; the selfish politician consults his ambitious schemes, regardless of the public good. Hence selfish desire is always wrong.

Regard to our own welfare includes the desires of moral worthiness, intellectual attainments, health and vigor, and circumstantial advantages.

DESIRE OF MORAL WORTHINESS.—Perhaps no person is so thoroughly depraved, as not to have *some* desire for moral worthiness. Even if there were no other motive, the value of a good character and the influence which it confers, would naturally prompt him to desire it. Men perpetrate immoralities, not because they desire to be immoral, but for some imagined pleasure, or advantage from them.

Men steal, not for the sake of being thieves, but for the property stolen. They lie, not for the sake of being liars, but for the supposed advantage of the falsehood. They intoxicate, not for the sake of being drunkards, but for the pleasure of intoxication. In every such instance, they would usually be glad to separate the two, and to have the latter without the former. It is not until one has reached the most desperate stage of depravity, that he desires to be vicious for its own sake.

But men *do* desire moral worthiness *for its own sake.* They desire not only to *appear* to be honest, just, temperate, pure, courageous, magnanimous, but actually *to be* so. This is a morally right desire. In accordance with the manifest design of our being, it must ever be approved by an enlightened conscience.

The germ of this desire is natural, or at least rational.

If men do not attain to moral worthiness, it is not because they have not some desire, as rational beings, for such a character, but because they have a stronger desire for the pleasures of vice. They would be glad to have both, but they cannot; hence there is a conflict of desires, in which the evil prevails. Often does the vicious man sigh, in the bitterness of his spirit, to see himself thus taking leave of virtue and sinking into merciless and degrading bondage.

But let him give to the desire of moral worth the *ascendancy;* let it be made to control every vicious inclination; and it becomes itself a moral excellence of high order. He who turns a deaf ear to all allurements of pleasure, gain, ambition, indolence, which conflict with his desire for personal worthiness of character, is a noble specimen of humanity.

This desire is an essential element of Christian character, but does not of itself *constitute* that character. A man may have it without being a Christian, but he cannot be a Christian without it. Christianity, heartily embraced, elevates its aim and directs its efforts. When a man not only cherishes the effectual desire to practise all the virtues of morality, but also to devote them in supreme homage to God, he is more than merely moral; he is also Christian.

Ever conscious of being far below his standard, his desire is continually reaching higher and higher. He aspires to clearer and more enlarged views of truth and duty; to greater purity of heart and consistency of life; to more energy and constancy of purpose; to more patience and perseverance in difficulties: to all the virtues which perfect and adorn renovated humanity. Such a man is embraced in the beatitude of Christ: "*Blessed are they that hunger and thirst after righteousness; for they shall be filled.*"

Desire of Intellectual Attainments.—The germ of this desire, also, is found in our rational nature. The principle of curiosity, or desire of knowledge, is natural to all men. But along with this desire, the conscientious man cherishes the feeling that he *ought* to cultivate his intellect, and to make the most he can of the talents with which he has been intrusted. He feels it to be as truly his *duty* to elevate his intellectual as his moral nature.

This motive, like all other moral motives, operates as a *regulator* of the natural desires. Under its guidance, the student at school or college does not merely gratify his curiosity, by studying what he pleases, or by miscellaneous reading, as his fancy may suggest; but he gives himself conscientiously to the task of mastering his lessons, with a view to the highest ultimate intellectual advantage.

It is well to feel the promptings of the constitutional desire for knowledge; as all do, more or less. Without this, the duty of study would be as onerous a task as to eat without appetite. It is well, in a higher sense, to have this desire directed by a principle, which sacrifices present gratification, if need be, for the sake of securing the best mental discipline.

The student is bound to seek the highest mental culture in his power, and he can do this only upon principle. The false notion frequently obtains among his companions, that he is of course influenced by selfish ambition; and so they shelter their indolence, or find an apology for spending their time in light reading, by claiming for themselves more honorable motives. But as every student is morally bound to do his best in mental culture, he who is striving to do so *may be* doing right, to say the least, while they who neglect to do so, are *certainly doing wrong*. If the former may be in fault, for not improving his talent from the best of motives, the latter are certainly so, for keeping it "laid up in a napkin."

Desire of Health and Vigor.—If a person may desire moral worthiness and intellectual attainments as objects in themselves good, he may for the same reason desire health and vigor. The latter may be an inferior good; still it is a *real* one, and as such may be rightly sought. Indeed a man cannot secure his highest moral worthiness, unless he properly regards his health; for to do this is one of his moral duties.

There is also a law running through life and determining all results, that by aiming at the highest end we secure all subordinate good in that direction. Thus a conscientious regard to the highest moral worthiness, moulding the character to its standard, induces that industry which tends to the highest culture; and these united, so elevate and enlighten the mind, as to give it wholesome dominion over the lower nature. They induce those habits of temperance, prudence, and self-denial, which promote general health and vigor.

Desire of Circumstantial Advantages.—This is a cherished desire for all those possessions and relations which contribute to our personal welfare. When is this desire morally right? We lay down this rule: Whatever real good a man can secure to himself without wrong to others, it is right for him to desire. "Men shall praise thee, when thou doest well for thyself."

This is right, not only in the negative sense, as that which a man *may* do, but in the positive sense, as that which he *ought* to do. Every man ought to do well for himself. He is in circumstances of dependence. He needs clothing, house, food, books, instruction, and numerous other things essential to his comfort and welfare. It is his duty to provide them for himself, as far as possible, and not to impose his burden upon others. "Every man shall bear his own burden." He also needs social, friendly, and domestic relations, and the various comforts and attractions of home; some of which are too dear to be purchased by money, but yet come of faithful endeavors to do well for himself.

It hence becomes his duty, early in life, to set a value upon these things, and to regard them practically as objects of desire. It is a spurious morality, and a false view of religion, that would affect to discard them. They have their place; they were designed to be, under well-defined limits, objects of desire and wholesome stimulants of enterprise. Without the desire for them, man becomes stupid, indolent, sottish, more brutish than human.

Let us instance the desire of *property*, so often perverted that it has been called "the root of all evil." And yet, when rightly controlled, a root also of all blessings. It would be difficult to conceive of the wretched condition of our race, if this desire had no existence.

When a man desires and accumulates property in a way not injurious to others, he does well not only for himself, but for them. He is a benefactor to his town, to his country, to mankind. He is adding to the general stock of human comfort. A wealthy man, who obtains his wealth honestly and uses it rightly, is a great blessing to the community.

So long, therefore, as a man desires to obtain property by means strictly honest, and with a view to the right use of it, his desire is morally right, unless it is allowed to displace the desire of things more important. It is, then, not so much the presence of this desire, as the absence of another, for which the man is in fault.

There *are* things more to be desired than wealth. An

upright character, a cultivated mind, good health, an amiable temper, a peaceful and contented spirit, and, above all, a saving interest in religion, are of immeasurably more value; and he who allows the desire of wealth to supplant a due regard to these, ceases to "do well for himself."

Precisely the same rule applies to the desire of office, of power, of rank, of title, of domestic connections, and of all the circumstantial possessions or relations, which may contribute to one's advantage. Some men desire one or more of these before wealth; others give to wealth the preference. It is well for society that this diversity of desires exists. If all men rushed in one direction, they would crowd and jostle each other; none could be accommodated. But as their desires diverge and scatter in various directions, there is room for all to act, and motive and reward for all their activity. Thus society, in its endless callings, may move harmoniously on; and every man, in doing well for himself, may do well for his neighbor also.

DESIRE FOR THE WELFARE OF OTHERS.

A desire for the welfare of others is the benevolent element of love. It may exist towards those for whom we have little complacency. It may for this reason be the more benevolent. To persist in seeking the welfare of those who do us injury, or whose conduct we cannot approve, evinces more benevolence than to do the same for those whom we complacently love. To do good to our enemies, is more benevolent than to do good to our friends.

The law of morality demands that we desire the welfare of *all* men. That we ought to desire the welfare of our friends, and indeed of all who have never injured us, has seldom been questioned. But that we are bound to desire the welfare of our *enemies*, is a position which men have been slow to admit. The philosophies of pagan antiquity did not admit it; and even the writings of the Old Testament are, perhaps, somewhat ambiguous upon this subject.

It was left for Christianity clearly and boldly to assert the duty of doing good to our enemies. "Love your enemies, bless them that curse you; *do good* to them that hate you, and pray for them which despitefully use you and persecute you; that ye may be the children of your Father which is in heaven; for he maketh his sun to rise on the evil and on the good, and sendeth rain on the just and on the unjust."

Infidel writers have scouted this precept. They have assailed it with jest and ridicule, pronouncing it impossible for one to love his enemies; or, with any other than hypocritical pretension, to *do good* to those that *hate* him. This is bold assertion, often uttered in high places as well as low, and too generally sustained by human conduct. Let us calmly consider it.

The sacred writers often use the term *love*, as Christ here does, to indicate benevolent desire for their welfare. When he says, "Love your enemies," he means that we should desire and seek their good. This is evident from his own explanation. "Bless them that curse you; *do good* to them that hate you.

It is impossible for an upright being to have complacency towards wrong conduct, or to feel the same glow of genial affection towards an enemy as towards a friend. Jesus Christ did not. But if we cannot love a bad man as we do a good man, and if we cannot love an enemy as we do a friend, we may still love him as a *fellow-being*, and may sincerely desire and seek his welfare. So did

Jesus Christ. And many others, imbibing his spirit, have done the same.

In seasons of calm reflection, when malevolent passion is at rest, a good man will reason thus: "It is true that my enemy has injured me, and a selfish desire would prompt me to injure him in return. But ought I to indulge such a desire? He is related to *others*, who must also suffer by his injury, but who are innocent of any offence against me. Is it just in me to make *them* suffer, for what *he* has done? Moreover, of what advantage could his injury be to me? It could only nourish a selfish and revengeful feeling. If I seek his harm, his prosperity will give me only pain, while his injury will only feed a passion which I ought not to indulge. Let me then seek his welfare, that so I 'be not overcome of evil, but overcome evil with good.'"

Such reasoning his conscience will surely approve. He will feel that he *ought* to yield to it; he will feel condemned, if he does not. His conscience will never rebuke him, but will for ever commend him, for seeking the welfare of even his guiltiest foes. It may be hard to do it—a struggle of conscience against urgent wrong desire; but if he succeeds to "crucify the old man," his reward will be in proportion to his victory. Every enlightened conscience accords the declaration of Christ, that thus loving our enemies and doing good to them that injure us, is a grace which makes us emphatically worthy to be called the children of our Father who is in heaven.

But it may be said, that if our enemy has done wrong, he ought to be punished. Then let the *law* punish him. Perhaps that is the best thing that can be done for him. It may bring him to his senses, and make him a reasonable and a better man. It is with this view that God chastises. Let the chastisement be just, let it proceed from a regard to the public good and a reasonable self-defence, let it at the same time never lose sight of the ultimate good of the offender, and it is morally right.

If the benevolent desire exists only in that feeble and equivocal state, in which it makes its subject barely willing to confer favors, provided no sacrifice is demanded, it is hardly to be commended. But when it is that positive and operative principle, which leads to the sacrifice of ease, property, friendship, and, if need be, of life itself, it becomes the sublimest of virtues.

And even if it is a *misguided* benevolence, unless tempered with fanaticism, it is a noble virtue of heart still. It sometimes indicates a more intense benevolence, to persevere, with an amiable temper, in a course of self-sacrifice which the judgment of those around us condemns, than to do the same, sustained by their approval.

It is well for mankind that their desires of *doing* good, as well as of obtaining it, move in various directions. Every part of the field of benevolence is thus supplied with laborers, instead of all men being crowded into the same portion. Early association, education, or the influence of example, may conspire with original temperament, to turn one man's particular attention to the cause of temperance; another's to the relief of the poor; another's to the wants of the sailor; another's to moral reform; another's to the cause of the slave; another's to the welfare of prisoners; another's to the endowment of institutions of learning; another's to the spread of Christianity.

When a man fixes his desire on any one object, to the *exclusion* of all others, or practically disregards all interests not directly connected with his favorite object, he is called a man of *one idea.* His desire may be pure; but as his views are limited, his judgment is partial.

Benevolent desire does not of itself constitute Christian character. Indeed cases may exist, in which a misguided desire to do good may conflict with the express commands of Christ. But when it is guided and animated by a supreme regard to the will of God, it shines as one of the brightest stars in the constellation of Christian graces. In illustration of this, John Howard, laboring in the dungeons of civilized Europe, and Henry Martyn, laboring in the darker dungeons of pagan Asia, are brilliant examples.

CHAPTER IV.

MORALLY WRONG DESIRE.

Such desires as are condemned by the united voice of mankind need no comment. It is only those on which questions have been raised, that we are to examine. These are the desires of retaliation, covetousness, pleasure, and emulation.

The Desire of Retaliation.—The desire to retaliate and revenge our wrongs, has been partially considered in the previous chapter; as the spirit of retaliation is a compound of malevolent affection and malevolent desire. Some have considered the desire to retaliate constitutional; while others, especially some Greek and Roman moralists, have even exalted it to the rank of a moral virtue. Thus Cicero says, in his De Officiis, "It is equally base to be excelled by a friend in returning favors, and by an enemy in retaliating wrongs."

Retaliation is a perversion of the principle of self-defence. The instinctive desire of life, happiness, esteem, possession, &c., naturally prompts one to defend himself, whenever these interests are invaded. But brutes, in self-defence, resort to retaliation and revenge; and sometimes men, more brutish than human, do the same.

Self-defence is not only natural, but it is a duty. Every man is bound to be firm, courageous, resolute, in protecting the blessings which heaven has given him. They are his; he is their natural guardian; and he ought to take due care of them. The doctrine of non-resistance is the opposite to that of retaliation; and, like most other extremes, is unnatural and chimerical. To act upon it, is to expose one's self and all committed to his guardianship to every furious passion of lust, envy, or covetousness, which may come in his way. He ought to consider that he is not in a world of harmless beings, however harmless *he* may be, and that the duty is hence laid upon him to "beware of men."

But here we are asked, did not Christ teach, "Unto him that smiteth thee on the one cheek, offer also the other; and him that taketh away thy cloak, forbid not to take thy coat also?" But the connection in which he said this makes it evident, that he intended only to caution his disciples against the spirit of retaliation, and to enjoin the discretion demanded by their critical circumstances. This is evident from the fact that he warned them to beware of men, that is, to be on guard against their evil machinations; and that on one occasion he said, "He that hath no sword, let him sell his garment and buy one."

To expect a miracle, or any special interposition of Providence, to protect us, while we neglect the appropriate means of defence, is neither morality nor religion, but fanaticism. We should therefore clearly distinguish self-defence from retaliation. The former seeks *protection;* the latter seeks *revenge.* The former would only save ourselves and ours from harm; the latter would inflict harm upon others. A humane and upright man aims to protect himself and his, with as little harm as possible to others, and never with a feeling of revenge.

Even if there were no other reason why we should not avenge ourselves, a very conclusive one is the fact that we are partial and passionate judges of our own wrongs, and are therefore disqualified to avenge them justly. To attempt it, is to challenge the prerogative of God.

What is thus condemned by morality, is also condemned by the most unequivocal teachings of Christianity. "Recompense to no man evil for evil. Avenge not yourselves, but rather give place unto wrath; for it is written, Vengeance is mine, I will repay, saith the Lord. Therefore, if thine enemy hunger, feed him; if he thirst, give him drink; for in so doing thou shalt heap coals of fire on his head. Be not overcome of evil, but overcome evil with good."

THE DESIRE TERMED COVETOUSNESS.—The desire which we denominate *covetousness* is universally reprobated. Both pagan and Christian moralists have ever agreed in denouncing it as a detestable vice. We do not therefore need to spend time in proving it to be so. Our object is rather to ascertain precisely what it *is*. We wish to distinguish it clearly from desires that are *lawful* and *right*, with which it is often in a measure confounded. Such are desires for education and other personal accomplishments, for honorable connections, for elevated society, for rank and office, for reputation and influence, for health and beauty. Of the same class are desires for houses, lands, equipage, furniture, dress, and, in general, every species of property. All these things are *desirable*.

Now if these things are worthy to be desired, there must be such a thing as right desire for them. There is also its opposite, *wrong* desire for them; and it is this which we are now to examine. The question is, when is desire for these things *covetous?* It is so, when it would appropriate what belongs to others; when it is excessive;

when it regards the means as an end; and when it contemplates bad ends.

1. The desire is covetous *when it would appropriate another's.* A cherished wish to appropriate to one's self what belongs to a fellow-being, is selfish and unjust. It is a desire in *opposition* to another's welfare, and a disposition to deprive him of his own. Allowed to rule the spirit, it makes a man virtually a thief and a robber. Indeed there is scarcely a crime into which, when intensely excited, it has not actually plunged its victims. Frauds, thefts, murders, arsons, have come of it.

But the mischief done to the hearts of those in which it dwells, is greater than that done to society. In most cases it is restrained by law and public opinion, so as only to prey in secret upon its unhappy victim. It then makes desperate war on conscience, becomes prolific of other evil desires, and, if long and freely indulged, proves fatal to peace and to all virtue.

2. This desire is covetous *when it is excessive.* The desire of worthy things may become unduly strong, and thus subvert other and more important principles. The rule is, never to allow it to supersede a regard to the highest moral excellence. So long as one practically values moral purity before all these things, his desire for them is in due subjection. A faithful regard to the admonitions of enlightened conscience, will not fail to guide him aright.

But let the desire supersede this regard, and it becomes highly pernicious. It darkens the understanding, warps the judgment, narrows the soul, and endangers every virtuous feeling. It becomes more dangerous when directed to some things than when directed to others, but in every case it is evil. Even the desire for intellectual attainments, which is perhaps as little liable as any to be excessive, may be allowed so to subvert the higher regard due to moral worthiness, as to prove fatal to the brightest hopes. Its victim may be deluded into the most pernicious sophistries, and be left to fall into the gloom of even atheism itself. The exaltation of the intellect, without the heart, never lifts the soul to God.

The desire of *beauty*, in itself innocent, may be allowed to turn one's attention so much to personal appearance as to induce light-mindedness. The desire of *esteem*, may lead to vanity. The desire of *rank* and *office*, may become a burning ambition. The desire of *equipage*, *furniture*, *dress*, *servants*, *display*, may obtain such mastery, as to turn all noble thoughts and benevolent aims out of the mind.

3. The desire is covetous *when it regards the means as an end*. Most of these things have no *intrinsic* worth, as personal excellence has; they are valuable only for the purposes they serve. Thus rank and office, dress and furniture, have no value, except as they afford us means of personal improvement and comfort, and of conferring benefits upon others. Hence when one loses sight of their *use*, and desires them for their *own sake*, he is covetous and vain.

We have some consideration for the man who desires money, even excessively, in view of the advantage it affords; but when he comes to desire it for its own sake, we cannot help regarding him as a contemptible miser. There are such men. In their absorbing pursuit of the means, they lose sight of the end, and finally sacrifice ease, comfort, domestic enjoyment, health, usefulness, character, and even life itself, to the mere purpose of hoarding.

4. The desire is covetous *when it has respects to bad ends*. The covetous desire assumes perhaps its most ma-

lignant type, when it seeks these things with deliberate reference to bad purposes. Here the objective motive determines the character of the subjective.

Under the restrictions above given, to desire property, for the benefits which it affords to its possessor, and enables him to confer upon others; to desire education, for its intrinsic value and for the sake of being useful; to desire dress and furniture, for the sake of maintaining an appearance suitable to one's position; to desire books, journeying, recreation, with a view to the true object of the highest culture; is morally right.

But to desire property, as a means to indulge the lusts of sensuality; to desire office and power, in order to lord it over others; to desire personal beauty and accomplishments, to gratify vanity; to desire fine houses, dress, furniture, equipage, to challenge the homage and provoke the envy of neighbors; is criminal and base.

The Desire of Pleasure.—The desire of pleasure is innate, and is hence unlawful only when misdirected. That the pleasures of morality and religion may always be sought, will not be denied. The question is, Are there *other* pleasures, of an inferior kind, which we may rightly desire; and, if there are such, how may we distinguish them?

That there are such, is evident both from the wants of our nature and the provisions made for them. We were not constituted to depend *merely* upon the pleasures of moral worthiness and a good conscience. There must be pleasures superadded to these, or most men would be too miserable to become morally better.

And even the Christian, who has drunk most deeply into the pure pleasures of religion, must often fall back upon those which the world proffers; or he inclines to become ascetic and unamiable. We cannot be angels here. We are human beings, after all that morality and religion can make us. There *are* pleasures adapted to our lower natures; and he who would so divest himself of humanity as not to *need* them, would be neither a man nor an angel.

The pleasures to which we refer are those only which interfere with no duty, and are favorable to health, cheerfulness, mental growth, long life, and usefulness. They are suited to the various periods of life, from childhood to the grave. They are the pleasures of innocent sports and amusements; of rational and refined social intercourse; of muscular activity and mental diversion; of journeying and witnessing new objects; of contemplating the beautiful and sublime in nature and art; of learning and communicating the current news; of reading and music; in short, of all those agreeable recreations, which tend to make us cheerful and happy.

But no sooner do men transgress the above limits, than they enter upon forbidden ground. Hence morality condemns the desire of the sensualist, the rake, the tippler, the glutton, the libertine; of him who seeks such amusements as cock-fighting, gambling, attending impure exhibitions, and reading vicious novels; of those who covet the pleasures of pride and vanity; and even of those who pursue pleasures innocent in themselves, to the neglect or detriment of duty.

After all, perhaps no question in philosophy is left in more uncertainty, than that which respects the *precise limit* of lawful and unlawful indulgencies. Hence good men, both moralists and Christians, differ as to what pleasures are strictly innocent. This uncertainty is a part of our discipline. If all the forbidden and allowed pleasures were so exactly specified as to admit of no question, to say nothing of the monstrous book necessary to record them, our discipline would become more mechanical than moral.

Scarcely any disposition is more unamiable than that which is ever looking with jealous eye upon the pleasures of others. If we see our fellow-beings pursuing pleasures manifestly vicious, we should do what we lawfully can to restrain them. If they indulge in amusements which we disapprove, but which they judge to be right, unless we can convert them to our views, or they can convert us to theirs, we should amicably agree to differ. To be severe towards our own pleasures, and liberal towards those of others, is a virtue of no mean value.

THE DESIRE TERMED EMULATION.—The term emulation is susceptible of two meanings. It may indicate an aspiration to make the highest *absolute* attainment. In this sense, it is not a term of opposition. It indicates a person's desire to make the most of his talents and opportunities. He may wish to do this himself, and with equal sincerity may desire that all others should do the same. This is not a mere constitutional desire. It is obedience to a duty.

But this is not the sense in which those philosophers use the term, to whose views we object. They indicate by it the desire of *rivalry*, and have claimed that this desire is a part of our original nature.

As this is a very important point, and we are constrained to differ upon it from eminent authorities, let us examine it with care.

"Emulation," says Butler, "is merely the *desire of superiority over others*, with whom we compare ourselves. To desire the attainment of this superiority by the particular means of others being brought down below our own level, is the distinct notion of *envy*. From whence it is easy to see, that the real end which the natural passion, emulation, and which the unlawful one, envy, aims at, is exactly the same; and, consequently, that to do mischief is not the end of envy, but merely the means it makes use of to attain its end." *

"By emulation," says Reid, "I mean a *desire of superiority to our rivals* in any pursuit, accompanied with an *uneasiness at being surpassed.* Human life has justly been compared to a race. The prize is superiority in one kind or another. But the species or forms, if I may use the expression, of superiority among men, are infinitely diversified. Emulation has a manifest tendency to improvement. Without it, life would stagnate, and the discoveries of art and genius would be at a stand. This principle produces a constant fermentation in society, by which, though dregs may be produced, the better part is exalted and purified to a perfection which it could not otherwise attain."

"He who runs a race *feels uneasiness at seeing another outstrip him.* This is uncorrupted nature, and the *work of God within him.* But this uneasiness may produce either of two very different effects. It may incite him to make more vigorous exertions, and to strain every nerve to *get before his rival. This is fair and honest emulation.* This is the effect it is intended to produce. But if he has not fairness and candor of heart, he will look with an evil eye on his competitor, and will endeavor to trip him, or to throw a stumbling-block in his way. This is pure envy, the most malignant passion that can lodge in the human heart; which devours, as its natural food, the fame and the happiness of those who are most deserving of our esteem." †

I have italicised the lines which most distinctly in-

* Sermon I. on Human Nature. † Vol. IV., p. 113.

dicate the meaning attached to emulation, and have quoted the entire passage, to show the reasoning and explanations of the distinguished authors respecting it. It is hence clear that the emulation which they advocate, as a native and innocent principle, is the desire which parties feel, struggling as *rivals* in the same pursuit *to excel each other.*

More recent writers have adopted the same view, apparently without pausing to question its soundness. Thus Whewell says, "The *desire of superiority* may be placed among the *elementary desires;* since it is seen to exist as an instinct in many of the bolder animals, manifesting itself in the exertions which they make in their conflicts with one another." *

The above distinction between emulation and envy is obvious, but not to the purpose. Envy is a repining at another's prosperity. It may be accompanied with an effort to depreciate him, or it may not. Envy often *leads* to slander, and to putting a "stumbling-block" in the rival's way, but it may truly exist in the mind without making any such demonstration.

Envy has really nothing more to do with the *means* of getting above a rival, or of getting the rival down, than emulation has. Emulation desires to excel a rival; envy repines at not succeeding. Envy is very apt, indeed, to vent itself in ill-natured remarks and unfair actions, in order to put the rival down, but it may decidedly exist in the heart without doing any such thing.

As all agree to denounce *envy*, our only inquiry respects *emulation*, as here explained. The question is, whether it is a principle *implanted by the Creator*, or whether it has a *moral* quality, not to be approved. Observe that this is no part of the desire of power and influence over

* Elements of Morality, Vol. I. p. 50.

our fellow-beings, with a view of being useful to them; it is entirely another thing. Its direct and commanding object is *superiority over rivals.* To this single idea of it our minds must be strictly confined; as this is the precise idea of those to whose views we are compelled to object.

The argument that emulation is to "be placed among the elementary desires, since it exists as an instinct in many of the bolder animals," proves quite too much, if it proves any thing. Brute instincts, especially in the bolder and more ferocious animals, lead to many dispositions and actions which must be condemned in man. They instinctively contend, quarrel, and kill each other. They exhibit all the retaliating and revengeful passions.

In the absence of a rational and moral nature, this is all their defence. As they have no other means of self-protection, we only call them *unamiable* or *ugly*, even when they manifest dispositions for which a rational being would deserve the gallows. Whatever they may do, they do nothing morally wrong, for the plain reason that they *cannot.* All their actions are within the sphere of nature.

We have another serious difficulty with the above views. Can a man desire to hold the rank of superiority to his rival, without desiring his rival to hold the rank of inferiority to himself? Does not the one imply the other? But it is said, he may wish himself up, without wishing his rival down. No. We are not now speaking of *absolute* eminence. The strife for that we admit to be noble. That is emulation in the good sense, to which we have referred, and which Paul commended. What we condemn is the selfish spirit of *rivalry.*

But let us allow the best of the case. Suppose the man does not wish to keep his rival back; he only wishes to excel him and get the prize. His rival, however, outstrips him, and the prize is lost. From the nature of the case, he *must* feel unhappy at the result. Precisely as Reid says, "emulation is accompanied with *uneasiness* at being surpassed."

Now what is this uneasiness? If it is *envy*, all agree to condemn it. But why blame the unfortunate man for what he could not prevent? He did as well as he could; and now, as conceded, he cannot avoid this unhappy feeling. If it is mortification, or chagrin, at having failed; this, too, is undeserved, when one has done his best. In every view, the result to the loser is disastrous. It can do him only injury, either to feel envious, or to feel mortified and vexed, for not succeeding, when conscious of having done all in his power to succeed. It cannot incite him to do better next time, for he has done his best already. It can only discourage him, enfeeble his spirit, and sour his temper. Call not this a needful trial of moral discipline. For moral discipline, such as God, and not man provides, is exactly the reverse of this, both in its nature and tendency.

And as to the *winner;* is it certain that the exultation of triumph over his defeated rival, will make *him* any wiser or better? Will it adorn him more profusely with the graces of modesty, meekness, benevolence, which all admire as the brightest of human virtues; or will it send him forth, with a more vigorous and self-sustained energy, on the path to absolute and exalted eminence? Who that struggles thus for a mere adventitious prize, ever rises thereby much above the object of his grovelling ambition?

EMULATION UNNECESSARY.—There are two conclusive reasons why the spirit of rivalry is unnecessary, and these are, of course, reasons for believing that the Creator did not implant it.

1. *We have impulses enough without it.*—Consider the

seven primitive desires which we have enumerated, and the direction in which they all urge; to these add the force of conscience and regard to personal worthiness, and, if Christianity is admitted, the high motives revealed from heaven and constantly reflected by Providence; we shall then no longer doubt that motives all but omnipotent are pressing us to the highest possible attainments. We no longer fear that "life would stagnate, and the discoveries of art and genius would be at a stand," but for the fiery spirit of rivalry to "produce a constant fermentation in society." There are enough less questionable motives to keep life from stagnation, and to conduct art and genius to glory.

2. *In the struggle for absolute eminence there is no need of rivalry, for the prize is ample for all.*—In the struggle of emulation, "they which run in a race, run all, but *one* receiveth the prize." This is the great difficulty in all such contests. They are contests for *comparative* standing, and, of necessity, for few prizes. The unavoidable result is many failures, and with them repining, jealousy, envy. It is idle to say such feelings ought not to exist. Until one "can go upon hot coals and his feet not be burned," we must despair of an effectual divorce between them and the spirit of rivalry.

Now, in place of rivalry, let the primitive desires of knowledge, esteem, possession, power, combine with high moral and Christian motive, to urge one to make the most of his talents and opportunities. He desires the highest possible attainments in virtue, knowledge, lawful possessions, art, power, influence; all that is truly for his welfare as a rational being. If actuated by Christian principle, he desires these attainments not only for himself and for the happiness they afford, but that he may accomplish his mission in glorifying God and conferring blessings upon mankind.

There is here *ample prize for all.* One does not lose, because another wins; *all* may win, and *be rewarded.* Nor is the reward of one man in the least diminished, because another gains a higher. On the contrary, every acquisition, by whomsoever made, is a contribution to the general honor and welfare.

In respect to all truly great and valuable attainments, there is a community of interests. One professor in a college loses nothing, because another professor reaches a higher point than he; on the contrary, that higher attainment reflects a proportionate honor on the institution, and is of advantage to all connected with it. It would be as impolitic as it would be base, for one professor to desire to keep the whole institution in obscurity, that his own little light might appear the brighter.

One pupil in a school is not injured by being excelled by others, provided there is no spirit of rivalry. Their higher attainments exert a happy influence upon the entire school, and upon himself personally as a member. They all help to raise a higher standard, and to keep the motives of true eminence in sight.

One merchant, or mechanic, or farmer, is not injured by another's success, unless something unfair is done; on the contrary, that success gives a spur to business and helps all concerned in it.

If we take a religious view, one member of a Christian community, or church, loses nothing because another excels him in Christian knowledge and character; on the contrary, those superior attainments, by the force of their example, are of great assistance to him and to the entire church. St. Paul in heaven loses nothing because Gabriel is in advance of him. The splendors reflected from that "tall archangel bright," may cheer the heart, enrich the zeal, and quicken the steps, of the sainted apostle, on his way to yet higher attainments.

It may be said, the above principle holds only in the case of *communities*, where there is, of course, a common interest. I reply, there is a community of interests in respect to *all* beings. No being in the universe is isolated. The community is smaller and the mutual interest is closer in the family than in the town, in the school than in the State, in the nation than in the world, in one particular church than in the church at large; still, a community of interests exists, more or less intimate, throughout the universe; so as to make the superior attainments of any one being of more or less advantage to all. If the personal advantage diminishes as the circle enlarges, it is in proportion to the diminution of force from motives of rivalry; so that the one is an offset to the other. If the attainments of a pupil in New York are of small advantage to a pupil in Pekin, equally small are the advantages to be realized from motives of rivalry between them.

Some Men not actuated by Emulation.—There seems to be conclusive proof, that the motive of rivalry is no part of our "primitive and pure nature," in the fact that some men have, through the influence of the Gospel, dispensed with it, and have afforded ample evidence of being as entire and perfect men without it as with it. They have not appeared to be maimed, or crippled, as though they had lost a leg or an arm, or any portion of their *mental* constitution. They have perceived as clearly, reasoned as soundly, struggled to do well as intensely and steadily, loved as sincerely, and risen as rapidly, as those who act from motives of rivalry; and, it is due to them to add, that they have *more frequently succeeded*, and their success has been crowned with *richer and more lasting honors.*

There *are* men who aspire to all that is truly great and good, who are single-eyed, far-reaching, industrious, earnest, to the extent of their ability, who have no fellowship with the motive of rivalry. Their aim is *too high* to be affected by such a motive. The question with them is not, whether they are above or beneath others, but whether they are doing the *best they can* for themselves and for their fellow-beings, in the great battle of life. They do not look upon others as rivals, but as co-workers; and if others can accomplish what they cannot, they rejoice in it. They are content to do *their* best; they are glad when others do better. Is not this more excellent than rivalry?

Such was our illustrious Washington. How would he sink from his high eminence, in the estimation of mankind, if thought to have been actuated by the motive of rivalry? Such was John Howard. Was it the spirit of rivalry, that made his life great and his name immortal? Such was Isaac Newton. Was it by the aid ot rivalry, that he soared among the stars, and made his home above the highest of them? The spirit of rivalry, earthly and sensual, never carried a mortal half so high.

A Single Prize supposed.—It may be said, there are instances in which only *one* object is set before two or more aspirants, as in the case of an office, and that emulation is then unavoidable. Suppose, then, two prominent candidates for the presidency of the United States. What has each to do, but to be faithful to himself and to his country, and thus render himself *worthy* of that office. If already deemed worthy, let him not become otherwise by indulging rivalry. So sure as he manifests that selfish spirit, he will defeat his end, the common voice will condemn him. But if he ought not to *manifest* it, he ought not to *cherish* it. To make the point clear, let the candidates be equally qualified for the office in all respects, save this, that one of them has a sincere regard to the welfare of the nation, and the other is actuated by a spirit of rivalry. The former is seeking the good of his *country;*

the latter is seeking his *own* good. Who can hesitate in deciding which of the two is the right man for the office?

And why not? Because we all see, when a striking case is presented and great interests are involved, that the spirit of rivalry is base, mean, dangerous, compared with that high, noble, benign principle, which ever ought to guide us. But let us suppose the worst. The worthy candidate is rejected; the ambitious aspirant is chosen. Has the rejected man any occasion to regret his course? None. He may say to his countrymen, as a greater did before him, "Weep not for me, but for yourselves and your children." He has *done his duty.* His destiny is not staked upon the office; he is the same excellent man without it that he would be with it; and he is pursuing a course that will secure immortal honor and peace, when the ephemeral triumphs of rivalry are all forgotten. But if the right man is chosen, it is well both for him and for the nation that he never allowed the spirit of rivalry to enter his heart; and we need not stop to show, that it would have been immeasurably better for the defeated man to have done the same.

This looks well in theory, say some, but we are not those noble and magnanimous beings which the case supposes, and which we must be, in order to feel and act thus. Nor are we likely to become such, so long as that morality is sanctioned and is inculcated in our schools, which maintains that the spirit of rivalry is "God's work within us," and should be encouraged; which infers duty from what man *is*, as a fallen being, rather that from what he *was*, as originally created, and, with the grace of Christianity, *is bound to be.*

So long as we take our lessons of duty from heathen philosophers, and from "the bolder animals in their conflicts with one another," instead of Jesus Christ; so long as we are taught that but for the spirit of rivalry "life would stagnate, and the discoveries of art and genius would be at a stand;" so long as teachers and guardians, through all our tender and formative years, inculcate, stimulate, reward it; what ought we to expect, but that we shall grow up and come forth into active life its miserable victims?

Well did one of the most distinguished advocates of the spirit of rivalry say, "Dismal are its effects, when it is not under the direction of reason and virtue. It has often the most malignant influence on men's opinions, on their affections, and on their actions."* But better yet, had he said, that it should never be indulged at all; that it should be utterly and for ever cast out of the soul, root and branch, as an abominable and detestable thing. Then, and not till then, does man know true peace. Then, his eye is single, his countenance serene, his step steady and firm. Then, he feels the inspiration of a new spirit. Then, with a heart that embraces every man's welfare, an object in view which no mortal can let or hinder, and a hope as high as heaven, he begins to feel and to act as becomes a rational and immortal being.

Do we then discard all exhibitions, shows, fairs, whose object is the comparison of works of genius and industry? By no means. Let these comparisons be made, and let genius and industry receive suitable tokens of approval. But how noble is the man who lays his works by the side of those of his fellow-men, and, if he has been enabled to do well, gratefully rejoices in it; and if others have done well, or even better than he, rejoices in that also; compared with the man who is actuated by the selfish spirit of rivalry, rejoicing only in his own success, or realizing

* Reid's Works, vol. IV., p. 112.

"uneasiness at being surpassed." The one is the spirit that has its eye upon a *rival*, and is pained at defeat, or exultant at a petty triumph over him; the other spirit contemplates the highest *absolute* excellence; itself aspiring to it, and rejoicing to see others do the same. This is the motive which true morality and Christianity inculcate, in the place of that whose effects are often so "dismal and malignant."

The truly ingenuous person does not *wish* to receive honors, unless conscious of *deserving* them. If he is a noble youth who desires the highest academic honors, and receives them without pride, no less noble is he who does his best, and yet cordially awards those honors to his successful companion. As his aim was not for the mere honors, but for the substantial prize beyond them, he still presses onward, with a heart as sound, unenvious, and happy as ever, assured that whatever his companion may have gained, he has himself thereby lost nothing.

When academic honors are regarded as objects of rivalrous pursuit, as the *end* for which to strive, they divert pupils from the true aim, and thus frequently injure their intellectual scarcely less than their moral character. The best scholars need no such stimulus. Due regard to their health more frequently makes it necessary to *restrain* them. While they who are slow to learn, but disposed to do the best they can, can realize only harm from appeals to the spirit of rivalry. A prize which they know they *cannot* reach, is, of course, to them no motive to study; and sometimes even serves to dishearten them. They need rather to be *encouraged*, by being assured that the *real* prize is for *them*, as truly as for the more gifted minds. Their feelings are often as keen as those of persons favored with the brightest intellect; and they are usually *more* susceptible than they to sympathy and encouragement, because conscious that they more need them.

Hence the kind and gentle stimulus of patient explanation and assurance of ultimate success avail, where appeals to the spirit of rivalry are utterly impotent; and they often eventually realize, even from those of little early promise, the brightest ornaments and most distinguished benefactors of mankind.

CHAPTER V.

MORALLY RIGHT EMOTION.

MORAL action is usually attended with some *emotion*, which partakes of the moral quality of the act. Thus, when a man, from a sense of duty, chooses to practise self-denial, or to bestow charity, or to encounter perils or hardships, that choice is a good moral act, and the emotion which prompts and attends it is the same morally with the act itself.

Although simple volition is not emotion, nor emotion volition, yet blending together for the same good or evil end, they constitute the same moral act. While the constitutional or natural feelings and volitions are simple, the moral are complex. Hence our only method of analyzing them, is to class them according to the *predominant* or *characteristic element*. Thus, those acts in which the emotional element is predominant, we term *emotional*, or simply *emotions*. Those in which affection predominates, we call *affections;* those in which desires predominate, we call *desires*.

When emotion becomes *intense*, and predominates not only over the other feelings but over reason itself, so that a man is controlled by this impulse, he is in a *passion.* He is apparently *all* emotion; so to speak. His emotion varies in intensity, according to his natural temperament, to circumstances, and to the objects to which it is directed.

He may be in a passion of anger, a passion of love, or a passion of ambition. The passion of *anger* is the most violent, and is of course the soonest spent. This is often little else than mere emotion. The passion of *love* is less violent and often deeper than that of anger, and is therefore more enduring. In this there is a larger infusion of affection and desire. The passion of *ambition* is usually deeper and stronger than either of the preceding, and is of course more steady and persistent. Not like the furious tornado, nor the capricious gale, but like the steady trade-wind, it bears its subject firmly and continuously onward to some distant port. Such was the ambition of Alexander, of Cæsar, of Napoleon.

Their desire of power was not perhaps greater than that of many unknown to fame; but, unlike theirs, it was actuated by a more impassioned and protracted emotion. It was the fire of an *ambitious zeal*, burning in their bones, that made their desires and their wills so mighty and effective. All great orators, revolutionists, and reformers have much of emotion.

CLASSIFICATION OF THE MORAL EMOTIONS.

Let it be remembered, then, that those moral acts in which emotion, even if it does not rise to a passion, is yet *predominant*, are called *moral emotions;* thus taking their name from their most characteristic clement.

These emotions are of two kinds, the morally right and the morally wrong.

Of the former are the emotions of love, of pity, of forgiveness, of gratitude, of penitence, of humility, of confidence, of self-approbation, of hope.

Of the latter, corresponding mostly to the former, are the emotions of hatred, of anger, of revenge, of envy, of obstinacy, of pride, of jealousy, of remorse, and of despair.

In this chapter we are to examine the former class.

Emotion of Love.—Moral love includes, as we have seen, cordial affection and corresponding *emotion*, together with benevolent desire for its object.

In the love of an upright heart towards a good being, all these elements combine; but as a good being cannot contemplate what is morally wrong with complacency, his love for a bad man is mostly that of benevolence.

Whereas, the love which a truly good and genial heart feels towards all truly good beings, varying with their peculiar qualities and their relations to him, is in the highest degree *complacent*, and is enriched with an emotion of vivid *delight* in him. This is *emotional moral love.*

Emotion of Pity.—Emotions of pity and of compassion are nearly the same, but the former has more respect to condition; the latter, to character. We pity the unfortunate, the suffering, the needy; we compassionate the erring and the fallen. Accompanied with benevolent desire and effort, these emotions have moral character.

If they are mere excitements of passive or immanent feeling, in contemplation of the calamities of others; attended with no yearnings of heart towards them, and no endeavors to do them good, they are not only destitute of moral excellence, but they often render the heart colder and more selfish than they found it. Such excitements are often occasioned by the reading of novels, and by attending dramatic exhibitions. The subjects of them are prone to flatter themselves that they possess refined benevolent sensibilities, just because they love to riot in the selfish luxury of excited imagination. Their hearts, the meanwhile, are turning to marble.

But when these emotions lead us to seek the good of their object, as in the case of the good Samaritan mentioned by Christ, and as illustrated in the whole course of his own life, they possess a high order of excellence. We ought all to cultivate them; for there are objects of pity and compassion on every side. Our Maker has set us the example. It is because his compassions fail not, that we are not consumed. And we are clearly taught, that he who withholds pity and compassion from his suffering and erring brethren, should expect them to be withheld from him in the day of his calamity.

Emotion of Sympathy.—This is a fellow-feeling with the sufferings and joys of others. We may pity those with whom we have no fellow-feeling; but we sympathize with those only with whom we are on terms of friendship. We in imagination assume their place, and suffer and enjoy with them.

But our sympathies are mostly with the *afflicted.* If our fellow-beings are enjoying a state of ordinary prosperity, they do not *need* our sympathy. They and we pass along the journey of life together, without intermeddling with each other's affairs. In his Theory of Moral Sentiments, Adam Smith says, "The word sympathy, in its most proper and primitive signification, denotes our fellow-feeling with the *sufferings*, not with the *enjoyments* of others. What can be added to the happiness of the man who is in health, who is out of debt, and has a clear conscience. This situation, however, may very well be called the natural and ordinary state of mankind." The times seem to have degenerated since he wrote.

We sympathize with *individuals.* We hear of a national disaster with sadness; of the misfortunes of an individual, with sympathy. We hear of a battle, or of a shipwreck, in which multitudes have perished, and we are shocked, as though an earthquake had spoken. But it is not until imagination has taken up the individual sufferers, and presented them to us in their personal calamities, that our sympathy is moved. Hence the writer who would excite our sympathy, does not deal in generals; but pictures to our imagination cases of personal suffering. Lively and generous sympathy is an element of character, having great beauty and excellence.

Emotion of Forgiveness.—This is the counterpart to the emotion of revenge. The revengeful heart would render evil for evil; the forgiving heart would overcome evil with good. This does not imply a want of sensibility to the injury received, but a forgiving spirit, rising above and controlling the wounded sensibility, and having the offender's welfare for its object.

Forgiveness, then, is eminently a benevolent emotion. To the selfish heart, revenge is sweet; to the benevolent heart, forgiveness is sweeter. He in whose heart the emotion of forgiveness finds no delightful play, in a world so replete as this with provocations, must be himself a wretched sufferer, and must be an occasion of much suffering to others. Hence morality attaches great importance to this virtue; and Jesus Christ has assigned to it a prominent place in his religion. "*Forgive, and ye shall be forgiven.*"

When a man of forgiving temper sees that justice is cared for, he embraces the repenting offender with the cordiality of a brother. He rejoices that it is not his to punish, but to forgive. If ever he punishes, it is because he must. He forgives, because it is his delight. Such is the spirit of Jehovah; otherwise, we should all be destroyed. "To err, is human; to forgive, *divine.*"

Forgiveness is magnanimous, and there can be no true magnanimity without it. An unforgiving man may be bold, brave, courageous, but magnanimous he cannot be. He may be mighty, for a time; but he cannot be morally great. He may tower in pride, but he is doomed to fall.

Both Alexander and Napoleon boasted that they never forgave. It is hoped that their doings were in this respect better than their professions. He who never forgives, *will never be forgiven!* "If ye forgive not men their trespasses, *neither will your Heavenly Father forgive yours.*" *

EMOTION OF GRATITUDE.—A grateful emotion arises from a sense of obligation for favors received, and is attended with desire to make some suitable return. But whatever return the grateful person may make, it is not like paying a debt. Gold may be too cheap to express his obligation. Whatever return he may make, his emotion of gratitude is as vivid as ever. This is a cardinal virtue; essential alike to individual and to national prosperity.

The combined indignation of both earth and heaven will finally concentrate upon the head of him, who persists in requiting distinguished benefits with base ingratitude. The same is true of communities; of nations. We read of ancient states and republics, which were shamefully ungrateful to their benefactors; and the same pens which have recorded their guilt, have recorded also their ruin.

The Saxon term for grateful is *thankful;* the term employed in the Scriptures. The want of thankfulness, is by them indicated as marking a very deep and desperate stage of depravity. Because men, when they knew God, "glorified him not as God, *neither were thankful,*" they were abandoned to their crimes.

* Jesus Christ, Matt. 6: 14.

Emotion of Penitence.—This emotion, like all others, depends mostly for its definition upon synonims. To be really known, it must be *felt*. It is an emotion of sincere sorrow and contrition for having done wrong. It implies a just conviction of wrong done, a cordial disapprobation of it, together with a sincere desire and purpose to do so no more.

It is not therefore, as is often supposed, a mere ebullition or excitement of feeling, in view of misconduct. However intense and vivid, unless it tends to purify the soul which it agitates, unless it turns the deep current of its desires and purposes from evil to good, unless it renders its subject practically wiser and better, it has no moral worth.

The truly penitential emotion is tender, serious, earnest; it subdues and sweetens the temper; it impresses lasting lessons of humility, as it rolls over the spirit. It renders its subject keen to discern and quick to feel the distinction between right and wrong, and makes him direct his steps cautiously in the narrow path of moral rectitude.

Emotion of Humility.—This is a gem of beauty, unsurpassed in the whole diadem of virtues. It is a grace of great loveliness, peculiarly befitting beings like us. For while we have nothing for which to be proud, we have much for which to be humble.

This emotion is an appropriate feeling of self-abasement, in view of our ignorance, our errors, and our misdeeds. The truly humble man is disposed to take a very low place. He is meek and lowly in heart. At the same time, he does not undervalue his gifts, exaggerate his faults, nor compromise his dignity with his fellow-men. He knows his position and his claims. He is humble, but he is still a man; and the more a man for his humility.

His humility comes of looking upward. He is more humble than his neighbor, not because he has more reason to be so, but because he has a higher standard and a juster sense of his deficiencies. Thus, while pride comes of ignorance, humility comes of knowledge. Sir Isaac Newton was one of the most illustrious of men, both in intellectual and moral greatness, walking as an angel among the stars and reading their sublime lessons, but he was as distinguished for his humility as for his knowledge.

"In this way we are to account for that humility which is so peculiarly a part of the Christian character, as contrasted with the general pride which other systems either recommend or allow. The Christian religion is, indeed, as has been often sarcastically said by those who revile it, the religion of the humble in heart; but it is the religion of the humble, only because it presents to our contemplation a higher excellence than was ever before exhibited to man. The proud look down upon the earth, and see nothing that creeps upon the earth more noble than themselves. The humble look upward to their God." *

Emotion of Confidence.—Emotions of confidence, trust, faith, are much the same, and morally the counterpart to those of suspicion, jealousy, distrust. A man of moral confidence is of a childlike spirit. His disposition is open, frank, genial. His experience of the falsehoods and deceits practised by men, has not destroyed his faith in humanity, nor in the principles of morality, nor in the ultimate triumph of virtue; much less in the truth and promises of God. In all these he still confides, with the simplicity of childhood.

This confidence is characterized with an emotion of

* Brown's Phil., Vol. II., p. 121.

calm and steadfast repose. A sublime virtue in itself, it is also the basis of many others. Without it, "it is impossible to please God;" impossible to fight successfully the great battle of life. It gives courage to encounter danger, and fortitude to endure suffering, in the faithful discharge of duty. It has ever animated the struggles of good men in the cause of virtue and religion. It has supported martyrs at the stake.

Thus important to the cause of morality and religion, in a general view, it is equally essential to the individual relations of man to man. Without it, society could not exist, even in its most limited form. It is the indispensable bond of union in the conjugal relation. Remove it, and all domestic bliss, even the matrimonial covenant itself, is at an end. And he who reposes with no genial and confiding emotion upon his brother man; who contemplates all around him with a cold, calculating distrust; virtually bids adieu to the charms of social life, and spends his days in the gloom of a solitary cell.

Emotion of Self-approbation.—The delightful emotion attending a good conscience may seem to be rather a *reward* of virtue than virtue itself. But the fact that it is the exponent of a good conscience, and utters its sympathies with every right act, in the satisfaction it imparts, proves that it is itself morally excellent. It is scarcely less the duty than the privilege of the good man, to cherish the pleasing emotion that arises in his soul in consideration of having done right. This feeling was divinely intended to nourish his good purposes and nerve him to future duty. The joy of a good conscience is his strength. With this, he can face the frowning world; with this, enter the lion's den.

In vain, then, does the skeptic deride, and the ultra-moralist disown, this grateful emotion. Consciousness is firmly and for ever against them. There *is* substantial joy imparted by an approving conscience, and that joy is itself an element of moral excellence. The man who could derive no other satisfaction from having, under trying circumstances, faithfully discharged his duty, than from having merely obeyed the demands of appetite, would be wanting in one of the most essential elements of a good character. What an evidence of the wisdom and goodness of the Creator, that he has thus identified duty with happiness.

EMOTION OF HOPE.—The animating feeling awakened in the heart of a good man, in anticipation of benefits to be secured to himself and to others by a course of faithful service, is an emotion of *hope*. He prizes moral worthiness, it is true, for its own sake; but the ultimate reward of good endeavor has also a value, which he was made to anticipate with joy. Moses doubtless prized the excellence of self-sacrificing devotion to the welfare of mankind, for its own sake; but he also "had respect to the recompense of reward."

The hope of securing some *future* benefit, to ourselves or to others, as the reward of faithful endeavors, is an indispensable motive to all benevolent enterprise. Without it, little would ever be done to elevate the character, or improve the condition of mankind.

It was this that induced Howard to explore dungeons and "take the gauge and dimensions of human misery;" that nerved Washington to the long and arduous conflict for the freedom of his country; that prompts the true-hearted missionary to forsake home and kindred to extend the blessings of Christianity to benighted nations. The same it was, that made Moses willing to "suffer affliction with the people of God;" and, to pass from these to an example transcendently surpassing all others, it was this that animated the heart of the author and finisher of our faith; "who, *for the joy that was set before him*, endured the cross, despising the shame."

The man who goes forth to sow with no cheering anticipation of a harvest, will sow sparingly and reap also sparingly. For the same reason, the man who attempts to go forth in the great conflict of this life, sustained by no hope reaching to the life that is to come, is more to be pitied than commended. What the heart does not joyfully anticipate, the hand cannot vigorously achieve. Other things equal, those with whom the emotion of hope is most active, are the most successful. "*We are saved by hope.*"

VARIOUS UNCLASSIFIED EMOTIONS.

In addition to the above classes, there is a large variety of emotions indicated by the general terms sorrow, grief, sadness, &c., which may be purely natural or partly moral. The spontaneous gush of sorrow, or outburst of grief, or feeling of sadness, when death or disaster approach us, is as natural as our breath. Not to be thus moved, would be most unnatural. And it is no stinted measure of emotions like these, that is allotted to humanity. This is a world of disappointments and losses, and of groans and tears. Every heart must heave with sorrow, every eye must weep, every spirit must be weighed down with grief.

This might not have been so, were there no sin; but it does not follow that the sorrow which sin has made necessary, is itself wrong. It is wrong in the child to *need* chastisement, but the painful feeling involved in the chastisement, is unavoidable. The moral wrong of *remorse* is, that it is the feeling of a guilty conscience, which might and should find peace in repentance. But no repentance can bring back the lost child to the mother's arms, or the lost husband to the widow's agonized bosom. She may find repose and consolation in the grace of God, but nature must weep still.

Nor let her be severely judged, if she incline to nourish her grief, and to shed unseen many sacred tears over the grave of bereaved affection. It *must* be so. She is not the true mother, or the true wife, if it be otherwise. Then let those smitten with sorrow weep freely and unrebuked. There is sacredness in their sorrow; the unfeeling stranger shall not intermeddle with it; no cold philosophy shall interpose its rebuke; but He who wept at the grave of Lazarus, will mingle his tears with theirs.

The moral quality of all such sorrow, depends upon the direction it takes. If it leads to murmuring, repining, rebellion; if it thus removes the heart farther from God, and hardens it against him; it is decidedly evil. But if it leads to submission, trust, loyalty; if it thus brings the soul nearer to God, and renders his love more precious; it is decidedly good. The end of the chastisement is then gained, and God's own hand will in due time wipe every tear away. "It is *good* for me that I have been afflicted, that I might *learn thy statutes.*"

That we may impart the right character to all our emotions of grief and sorrow, we should ever look up from them to our Heavenly Father and compassionate Saviour; consider that he loves us still, although he chastises, and chastises *because* he loves us; and never cease to remember that, however much we may deserve and feel his rebuke, "like as a *father* pitieth *his children*, so the Lord pitieth them that fear him; *for he knoweth our frame; he remembereth that we are dust.*"

CHAPTER VI.

MORALLY WRONG EMOTION.

The class of emotions now to be examined are the opposite to those of the preceding chapter. While those pertain to affections, desires, purposes, which are morally right, these pertain to such as are morally wrong.

Emotion of Hatred.—As moral love implies complacence towards its object with benevolent desire for his welfare, so hatred implies aversion towards him, with malevolent desire for his injury. From this perverse state of heart arises the *emotion* in question. Sometimes it mounts to a passion, at other times, it is not so much a passion as an emotion of settled and deliberate hate.

Such a feeling, as we have shown in the chapter upon malevolent affection, is never to be justified. If men would injure us or ours, we should defend ourselves by bringing them to justice, but indulge no revengeful temper. Our emotion should be that of abhorrence of their deeds, blended with benevolent compassion towards themselves. Such were the feelings of Jesus Christ towards his enemies. He never manifested a malevolent emotion.

Emotion of Anger.—This is a passionate emotion ex

cited against those who we suppose have intentionally injured us. It may be a mere instinctive emotion, having only self-defence for its object. This is an impulse implanted in our nature for important ends. He who could receive a wanton blow in the face, or hear himself reviled, with no other emotion than he would feel towards an act of courtesy, must be something other than a man.

Nor is it any part of duty to repress the emotion, which simply prompts to self-defence. "Be ye angry, and *sin not.*" But when the emotion springs from a malevolent desire to injure its object, it is never innocent. It is a murderous fiend. "He that *hateth* his brother, is a *murderer.*"

The vice of malicious anger is one of small and selfish minds. He who indulges it, is usually a person of narrow views, fiery spirit, and mean ambition. Restive and impetuous, he would rush madly upon his victim, to deal out to him the retribution which rightful authority has placed in better hands.

Retribution should never be inflicted by a person in anger. It is next to impossible for an angry person to inflict punishment, without doing something to be subsequently regretted. The passionate man is a dangerous citizen. He is a foe to law and to mankind, but especially to his own household and to himself.

EMOTION OF REVENGE.—This emotion is of a more malignant and desperate type than that of anger, being more calculating and protracted. The angry man is soon over the passion; the revengeful man, never. The motive of revenge is the mere gratification of a malicious temper. It contemplates the welfare of neither party; for it often prompts one to inflict evil upon another, when he knows that he thereby inflicts evil upon himself.

It makes its subject more infernal than human. It is

a *furor*, urging him in defiance of all law and equity to inflict injury upon his fellow-being. Reputation, property, life itself, are all in jeopardy by his presence. Falsehood, slander, arson, murder, are all in his service.

In savage tribes, where there is little law and government, the revengeful man is the most terrible and destructive of all possible foes. No wild beast, no raging pestilence, is half so dreadful; for *his* fury is guided and intensified by a human *intellect*, which renders it surer and more effective. Hence civil governments justly set the blackest mark of reprobation upon this fearful vice.

It is equally condemned by Christianity. "Recompense to no man *evil for evil*." "*Avenge not* yourselves." "Vengeance is mine; I will repay, saith the Lord." "Therefore, if thine enemy hunger, feed him; if he thirst, give him drink."

Emotion of Envy.—This is a feeling of discontent at another's prosperity. Like all other malevolent emotions, it is attended with pain. As this pain is peculiar, there being no other like it, it can of course be known only as it is experienced. It respects something relating to another, not to one's self; hence it is unlike regret, and still more unlike remorse.

Cicero remarks that envy is felt towards one that is an equal, or nearly an equal, more than towards one far above or far beneath us. This is doubtless true; and it is owing to the fact that there is more *rivalry* in the one case, than in the other.

For the same reason, it is apt to exist between those of the same aspirations and pursuits. Thus it often exists between fellow-students, who are of nearly the same standing, and in pursuit of the same prize; between ladies of the same company, each of whom aspires to be the belle; between men of the same profession in a town, each of whom covets the patronage; between candidates for an office, who are alike anxious to succeed. Hence, rivalry and envy are usually united.

Still, envy is confined to no rank nor calling. It sometimes forces its dark wing the whole distance from the dunghill to the throne, compelling its wretched subject to seek relief in the calamity of those related to him only as fellow-beings. Its protection is hypocrisy and deceit; its instruments are falsehood and slander; its food, the misfortunes of others; and its end, if allowed long to rule the heart, the ruin of its miserable subject.

He who would escape one of earth's direst curses, must keep all envy out of his heart, and also keep himself at the farthest possible remove from envious persons. "Their *teeth are spears and arrows*, and their *tongue a sharp sword*." Persons of an envious spirit are given to slander. By this we may know them.

Emotion of Obstinacy.—Firmness in resisting evil is always noble. Obstinacy is a sort of counterfeit of this virtue. It is a mulish and dogged feeling, defying reason and argument, and set on having its own way. The obstinate man lacks delicacy and refinement of temper. He is a churl.

The emotion of obstinacy may be no less vivid and active than that of penitence. In the relations of man with man, the two emotions are counterpart to each other. Penitence is yielding; impenitence is obstinate; and there is as much moral activity in resisting conviction of duty, as in yielding to it. The former is, therefore, as truly a vice, as the latter is a virtue.

The child who allows the feeling of aversion to parental authority to rule his heart and sway his conduct; the pupil who allows the same in relation to school authority; will, in later years, find this feeling prompting him to resist the authority of the State, and perhaps to perpetrate those acts of rebellion which will complete his ruin. Hence children should be taught, from their earliest years, to be equally firm in resisting evil, and docile and yielding to every conviction of duty.

Emotion of Pride.—There is a feeling of satisfaction in view of worthy attainments as the fruit of virtuous industry, which is no part of pride, but which some writers have called by this name. There is no virtue in being blind, or even indifferent, to our attainments, whether personal or adventitious. On the contrary, it is our duty to know ourselves, and the extent of our circumstantial advantages. Pride and humility are opposite terms. The one makes a man think *more* highly of himself than he ought to think; the other makes him think *only as* highly of himself as he ought to think. The vice of pride is in the disposition itself; not at all depending upon its object.

Thus, one man is proud of his dog; another, of his horse; another, of his person. One man is proud of his wealth; another, of his family; another, of his intellect. Some of these are much nobler possessions than others; but the vice in question does not lie in being proud of unworthy objects, but in being proud at all. It is a vice of all conditions. It may mingle with the loftiest as well as the meanest pursuits. The same man who, under one kind of training and one set of circumstances, would be proud of his intellectual attainments, or of his post of honor, would, under others, be proud of his coat, or of his moustache, or of his distinction in a street riot.

Although some writers, from associating the disposition itself with the objects and circumstances in relation to which it is exercised, have spoken of a commendable pride, yet, strictly speaking, there can be no such thing. Pure morality condemns it. We might as well speak of a commendable envy. Religion, too, is no less sweeping in her condemnation. All pride is forbidden in the Bible. There is not an instance in which the sacred writers employ the term in any other than a bad sense.

It does indeed betray a most pitiable folly, as well as vice, to be proud of contemptible attainments; and it certainly bespeaks a man in the lowest stages of degeneracy, to be proud of that which he ought to be ashamed of; but all this does not abate the folly and the vice of him, who, having risen to eminence in knowledge and power, spoils the glory of the whole by being proud of it. In point of attainment, he is better off than his less informed and less fortunate neighbors, who are proud of their fine apparel and gorgeous furniture; but in point of *character*, so far as pride is concerned, he is neither wiser nor better than they.

EMOTION OF JEALOUSY.—This is nearly the opposite to confidence. As the latter is an emotion of trust and composure, the former is one of distrust and uneasiness. The term is usually applied to distrust in love. Thus the suitor is jealous of his lady, or the lady of her suitor; the husband of his wife, or the wife of her husband, when either party suspects the fidelity of the other. But the term is not restricted to these relations.

Unlike pride, jealousy may be a just and proper emotion; since there may be real *cause* for it. Although no possible cause can justify us in being proud, there may be causes to justify us in being jealous. Not only morality, but religion, admits of a righteous jealousy. The sacred writers ascribe it to God himself. They never speak of his being proud, but they speak of his being jealous. "I the Lord thy God am a *jealous* God." They ascribe the same to pious men, as a religious emotion. "I am *jealous* over you," said an apostle, "with godly jealousy."

But the term is generally used in a *bad* sense, because a prevailing disposition to jealousy is evil. It is in this respect like anger. Although, under certain provocations, a man may be "angry and sin not," yet, prevailing *proneness* to anger indicates malevolence; so, while circumstances may sometimes justify jealousy, yet proneness to jealousy indicates the want of a loving and generous spirit. Love and generosity are always confiding. Hence jealousy, as a prevailing temper, is selfish and mean.

We look upon a jealous-minded person with distrust and contempt. We are never at ease in his presence. We expect him to scan all our looks, words, and actions, and to construe them to our disadvantage. Jealousy cannot see things in their true light; she is "green-eyed." She is thus a mortal foe to all domestic and social bliss. Under the influence of this direful emotion, men have proceeded from slander, falsehood, abuse, to the desperate acts of murder and suicide. For "jealousy is the *rage* of a man, therefore he *will not spare* in the day of vengeance." "Jealousy is *cruel* as the grave; the coals thereof are coals of fire, which hath a *most vehement heat*."

Emotion of Remorse.—We have already noticed remorse, in connection with conscience. We refer to it in this connection, not to distinguish between remorse itself and its attending emotion, for the distinction is not important, but to notice more particularly its emotional nature. We now particularly refer to the *vivid compunction* of conscience, more or less consequent on misdoing. This is always a painful, and sometimes even an agonizing emotion. It is of every degree of intensity, from the feeblest twinges to the most terrible throbs of anguish.

Conscience gives premonitions, to prevent contemplated crime; but if the person persists in doing it, she often allows him to go on and complete his work, and to become entangled in the snares which he has laid for his own feet, before she again seriously disturbs him. Then, in hours of reflection, when memory recalls the past, and sets his conduct before him in its true light, she resumes her work. She does not inflict upon him her severest pangs at first; her retributions, like his crimes, approach gradually. The more he reflects, the more she rebukes him. For this reason, he often seeks to drown reflection, by plunging into active cares and amusements. But relief thus obtained is temporary, and is usually followed by still severer pangs; for the time at length comes when he *must* reflect, and that continuously.

Sometimes the compunctious emotion is very violent, and even spasmodic; urging its wretched subject to desperation and even to suicide. But at other times it takes the chronic type, embittering his whole life. He cannot again feel as he did in the days of his innocence; something like a canker-worm gnaws perpetually at his heart. In vain he exclaims, "*O that I were as in months past.*" He can never again be as he has been. Sometimes he is fain to say, "O that I had wings like a dove, for then I would *flee away and be at rest.*" Unhappy man! Were he gifted with even morning's bright wings, and could he fly apace as upon a sunbeam to distant climes, and even to distant worlds, he could neither escape himself, nor that unchanging law which binds iniquity and misery indissolubly together.

He may find some relief in a well-formed purpose of amendment, followed by reformation of conduct. If he regains the path of virtue and steadfastly pursues it for a period of years, his pains of conscience may be greatly mitigated; but they can be fully and for ever *removed*, only as he becomes *truly penitent before God for all his sins, and lays hold by faith upon the gracious provisions of the Gospel.*

Emotion of Despair.—This is seldom experienced on earth, and is indeed but little known, except in some of its more obvious effects. When it is of a moral nature, it includes a feeling of remorse, intensified with a new element of malignity by the utter exclusion of hope. Indeed the entire absence of hope gives birth to the characteristic emotion of despair. Could we then imagine the feeling of one suffering the severest stings of conscience, with no hope of ever finding relief from them, we should have some just notion of despair.

Its suffering is so intense, that it cannot be long endured without dethronement of reason. It therefore often prompts to suicide. There are other inducements to this act, found in morbid physical and mental states; so that the act does not always imply guilt. But in cases like those to which we have referred, it *does* imply guilt, and that of the deepest dye. The wretched sufferer, whether he believes or not in a future state, probably concludes, if he reasons at all, that his condition can be no worse, and may possibly be better, by making the fearful plunge. Perhaps, in the absence of all hope of a better state of existence, the thought of annihilation flits as a gleam of light across his distempered brain, and with exulting madness he leaps to embrace the dread reality.

But it is not profitable to dwell upon these appalling retributions of crime. Philosophy has done her duty, when she has pointed them out, and has lifted her warning voice against every approach to them.

CHAPTER VII.

MORALLY RIGHT WILL.

MORAL will is a rational choice or purpose in reference to duty. Morally *right* will is an honest choice or purpose to enlighten and obey conscience; or, which is the same thing, to do what duty requires. Such should be the governing aim of every man, regulating all his appetites, affections, desires, emotions.

RIGHT AGENCY OF WILL OVER THE APPETITES.—There are two ways in which man may control his appetites.

First, he can *avoid temptations*. He can shun the society and the places which unduly excite them. If inclined to inebriation, he should not "look upon the wine when it is red, when it giveth its color in the cup, when it moveth itself aright." Considering that "at the last it biteth like a serpent, and stingeth like an adder," he should wisely avoid the tempter. He should resolutely do the same in regard to *every* temptation, by which virtue is endangered. It is mockery to pray, "Lead us not into temptation," without a determination to shun it.

Secondly, if inadvertently drawn into temptation, he

should firmly *resist* it. If he has allowed the first citadel to be taken, and the tempter to approach him, he must the more manfully resist in the second. Here is no surprise. His eyes are now opened. He sees his danger, he knows his duty, and conscience urges him to do it. Now is the time for him to be valiant, and to say with a brave spirit of other days, "I have *set my face like a flint*, and I know that I *shall not be ashamed.*"

RIGHT AGENCY OF WILL OVER THE AFFECTIONS.—We have previously noticed the distinction between the will and the affections. The question now is, What control may we exert by the former over the latter? Suppose a man to be conscious of a malevolent affection towards a fellow-being. Can he by a direct executive act of will expel it at once from his heart? Experience answers in the negative. The evil spirit is already in his heart; it has obtained a lodgment, and so strengthened itself there, that it does not readily yield.

But he can take effectual means to *mortify* and *subdue* it. He can refrain his lips from the slander which it prompts; he can condemn the spirit itself, and refuse every act to which it urges. And while thus refusing it indulgence, he can seek to cultivate the spirit of forgiveness and kindness. A sincere and firm determination to this end is a morally right choice, and tends to beget the spirit of love. If when he "*would* do good, evil is still present with" him, let him firmly persist in the right purpose, and what he "*would*" be, he eventually *will* be.

A more difficult point remains. Suppose a person to be conscious of not loving God. Can he, by a direct act of will, render to him the affection due? The truth is, in such a case, before the Gospel takes effect, that he does not really *will* to love God. We never sincerely will to love a person whom we have offended and who is justly displeased with us, unless penitent for our misconduct towards him. Sin renders man proud and self-willed, indisposed to repentance and submission. He is willing to be *saved*, but not to *obey*. If through grace he becomes penitent, and is thus sincerely willing to serve God, but is still painfully conscious of unstable or inadequate affection for him, he should, through all mutations and conditions of feeling, firmly maintain his purpose of allegiance to him; promptly submitting to every self-denial and performing every duty enjoined, and ever relying with implicit trust in Him by whom we receive "power to become the sons of God," and who is "able even to subdue *all* things to himself." He will thus succeed at last, and his character, in some future day, will shine in the full-orbed radiance of an entire and perfect devotion to God.

This direction is of course valid only in the case of those who believe the Gospel to be a divine revelation. They who reject Christ must remain, for aught I can see, "without God in the world." Whatever philosophy may achieve in mere social virtue and secular morality, she knows "none other name under heaven given among men, whereby we must be saved."

It has been shown that we are *naturally inclined* to love our families, our friends, and our fellow-beings generally, with whom we associate. Love is the normal state of affection. No direct effort of will is therefore here required, except to cultivate and control the affection, and thus give it moral worth, by a faithful discharge of all the duties to which it prompts.

Right agency of the Will over the Desires.—We should will to cherish those desires which are purely natural, and to seek their ends by lawful means. For instance, the *desire of life* is natural. To cherish this desire, to exert a purposed guardianship over life, to seek to prolong it by means which God has appointed, implies a right exercise of will in this particular. The same is the office of the will in relation to *all* the natural desires.

But some have contended that, although we are guilty for *being* the subjects of wrong desires, when they have gained a certain ascendency they so cripple and enslave the will as to impel its choices in spite of us.

On this point the following remarks are quite to our purpose. "The hypothesis that desires impel the will to act, is inconsistent with observed facts. If this hypothesis were true, the phenomena of volition would be very different from what they are. A man may desire that it should rain, for example; he may have the most intense feeling on this subject imaginable, and there may be no counteracting desire or feeling whatever. Now if desire ever impelled a man to volition, it would induce him, in such a case, to will that it should rain. But no man in his senses ever put forth a volition to make it rain. And why? Just because he is a rational creature, and knows that his volition cannot produce any such effect."

"In the same manner, a man might desire to fly, or to do a thousand other things which are beyond his power; and yet not make the least effort to do so, not because he has no power to put forth such efforts, but because he does not choose to make a fool of himself. This shows that desire, feeling, &c., is merely one of the conditions necessary to volition, and not its procuring cause." *

The plain truth is, no desire can impel a rational being to any executive choice, against which he can see *sufficient reasons*; and as he *can always* see sufficient reasons for not choosing to gratify vicious desires, it is in his power, and is his duty, to deny and master them. Hence that man is

* Bledsoe's Examination.

guilty of a perverse will, who allows any corrupt desire to have dominion over him.

We are sometimes conscious of *conflicting* desires. Can a man actually desire *opposite* things, the right and the wrong, at the same time? The case seems to be like that of divided *attention*. The transitions of attention are often so rapid as to elude our notice, and thus lead us to suppose that the mind is actually directed to two or more objects at the same instant. When a person contemplates the motive to a virtuous course, he is inclined to that; when he contemplates the allurements to a vicious course, he is inclined to that. For some reasons he desires the one, for other reasons he desires the other; and yet he cannot *prefer* both. He balances betwixt conflicting desires.

But he may exercise his rational judgment and will. Self-control does not come of his merely *desiring* but of his *willing*. To deny this, is to deny his consciousness. It is his duty to *will*, in obedience to conscience, and despite of all desires to the contrary, to take the *right* course. The consequence of such a choice, faithfully sustained, will be the eventual subjugation of every wrong desire to its rightful authority.

Right Agency of Will over the Emotions.—When the will maintains rightful ascendency over the affections and desires, it governs all the emotions which pertain to them. The will should govern passionate emotions, and all mental excitements in which the emotional element predominates, precisely as it should the appetites. Most of them arise from causes which we can foresee, and can thus solicit or avoid, according as the prospective emotion is good or bad. If we can reasonably anticipate the cause of a bad emotion, and yet willingly expose ourselves to it, we are as responsible for that emotion as a man is for the flames which consume the building to which he voluntarily applied the torch. A man of hasty temper should be especially guarded at this point.

If his passion is already excited, he should by a firm exertion of will hold himself in a state of silent quiescence, until passion has had time to cool, reason to regain her seat, and he is thus qualified again to act as a rational being. If every passionate person would do thus, violence would soon cease from the earth.

There is not a good emotion which may not be nourished and rendered immortal, and there is not an evil emotion which may not be rebuked and finally overcome, by the firm and persistent determination of an upright will.

Thus was man constituted to exercise a free and willing control over all his appetites, affections, desires, and emotions, and to keep them in due subjection to the law of God.

MORAL CERTAINTY DOES NOT IMPAIR FREEDOM.

It has been asserted, that if men are thus free and sovereign in the exercise of their wills, there can be no moral certainty in regard to their future choices. There *is* moral certainty; and in the divine mind all our future actions must be as well known as the past. It may be morally certain, even to *us*, how a man will choose in a given case; but this does not impair his freedom nor his responsibility in the volition; nay, it rather enhances them.

It may be morally certain, for instance, that a man practised in iniquity will, under certain temptations, accept of a bribe. Still he is as free and responsible in his choice, as though there were no certainty in the case. He acts even *more* unrestrainedly in his choices now, than in the earlier and more hesitating stages of his depravity;

his choice is therefore a more convincing demonstration of confirmed guilt. The worse a man is, the more certain it is that he will do wrong, and the more free and earnest he is in choosing to do so.

And so also the man of whom there can be no doubt that he will choose *right*, in a case of unquestionable *duty*, is a person of higher moral excellence than one of whose choice we have reason to doubt. We know men of whom we no more doubt, beforehand, whether they *will* choose to do right, than we doubt, after the result has transpired, whether they *have* chosen to do so. This is not because their wills are in bondage, and the freedom and virtue of their choice are thus impaired, but because they are persons of such known excellence of character.

Such is moral certainty, and such is its consistency with human freedom; a certainty which must in the divine mind embrace all future as well as all past human choices, and a freedom not at all impaired, but even augmented and confirmed, by the certainty.

TRUE MORAL RECTITUDE.

It follows from the view we have taken, that true moral rectitude is the free and willing subjection of all the appetites, affections, desires, emotions, tastes, to the demands of an enlightened and faithful conscience. This is the standard of natural morality. Such would be our duty, if we had no special revelation from God. So far as one fails in either of these particulars, he comes short of what he ought to be. He may be right in respect to some of them, and faulty in respect to others. He may govern his appetites, he may be strictly temperate and chaste, but fail to govern his affections, desires, or passions; he may be malicious, or covetous, or passionate. He may perhaps hold in check some wrong feeling which he less cares to indulge, that he may give the freer rein to a *favorite* lust. Thus he may be temperate from a motive of avarice, chaste from a motive of ambition, generous from a motive of vanity. Such is not true moral rectitude.

Unlike this is the case of him, whose governing principle is the subjection of *all* his powers and propensities to the rule of right. He may be conscious of coming short in some or even in all particulars, but he is right in the main article. Such a man is neither wilfully perverse, on the one hand, nor perfect, on the other. A constant warfare with all that remains in him of evil must be his, until the victory is won. Such is morally right will.

The conflict which every person aspiring to moral rectitude must maintain with evils within and around him, demands *courage*, *fortitude*, and *firmness*. As these pertain chiefly to the will, we shall notice them here.

Courage.—The principal element of this virtue is a firm and steady *determination*. It implies intrepidity of purpose amidst all dangers that may beset the path of duty. We sometimes speak of the courageousness of a man in doing wrong. This is not courage, but recklessness in crime. The word, both in its etymology and use, indicates whole-heartedness; and this can exist only in reference to what a man believes to be right. If there is any misgiving on this point, the heart cannot be thoroughly sound and strong in the matter.

True courage, then, supposes an honest conviction of being righteously engaged in a righteous cause. It carries with it the conscience, the affections, desires, emotions; in a word, the whole heart. All the impulses of the soul are taken up by the rational will, and concentrated upon its object. It is the honest conviction of duty that thus nerves the good man to the conflict; it renders him fearless of reproach and slander; it is his shield and his sword on the field of battle.

It was true courage that emboldened Paul to contend manfully for the truth, in opposition to the combined hostility of Jews and Gentiles; that made Luther stand erect, in the great struggle for civil and religious freedom. It was this, that more than once delivered Greece from her formidable foes, and that fought the battles of our own national independence. In a world where virtue has so much to contend with, a man without courage is a useless and pitiable object.

FORTITUDE.—While courage is a prominently *active* virtue, fortitude is more *passive*. The former struggles and contends, the latter suffers and endures. Men have usually more courage; women more fortitude.

But these virtues are always to some extent combined. Perseverance in conflict, implies also the spirit of endurance. Daniel and Paul seem to have had as much fortitude in the dens of wild beasts as courage in the courts of wicked tyrants. The fortitude of John Rogers at the stake, of La Fayette in prison, of Washington in trial and disaster, was equalled by their courage to face hostility and death in the conflict for truth and freedom.

True fortitude, like courage, is found only in integrity of heart. It is among the sublimest of virtues. It may not be irreverent to add, that it shone second to none in the constellation of virtues which crowned the life and death of Jesus Christ.

FIRMNESS.—This implies steadfastness of purpose, and is opposed to fickleness. But it is more than steadfastness; for a man may be steadfast in crime. This is obstinacy. True firmness, like courage and fortitude, is based upon honest convictions, and dwells only with integrity of heart.

A man of moral firmness has an iron will; but the iron is tempered with benignity, and glows with love. Enlightened judgment, an active conscience, a supreme regard to duty, guide that will and give to it enduring command.

Such a will no power can break, no temptation bend. Wielded in obedience to the will of heaven, it has omnipotence with it. Men may torment and kill the body, but they cannot subdue the will of a truly firm and righteous man in a righteous cause. Dungeons, scaffolds, fires, racks, have all proved equally powerless with bribes and flatteries, to move him from his lofty purpose. Amidst them all he stands erect, like granite rock, around which ocean waves eternally dash in vain.

CHAPTER VIII.

MORALLY WRONG WILL.

THE mere animal can will only in obedience to *instinct;* man can will from a regard to *duty.* When false to conscience, he sinks in some respects below the brute; for the brute has a larger endowment of instinct than he, which does not allow the self-abasement which he can practise. By acting irrationally he may fall as far *below* brutes, as in the constitution of his being he is *superior* to them.

It is then obvious why he ought to govern his animal nature by his rational, and not his rational nature by his animal. It is because he was *made* to act, not as a mere animal, or something worse, but as a *rational* and *accountable* being. We must not, however, identify his rational *powers* with *himself.* They are not himself, any more than his animal impulses are. The former, as truly as the latter, *belong* to him. The latter qualify him to act as an animal; the former, added to the latter, qualify him to act as a rational being; but neither nor all combined are the identical *person* indicated when he says *I.* It is the *Ego,* that efficiently moves the will, and by it, directly or indirectly, all the mental powers; and, because *endowed* with reason and conscience, is responsible for the volitions.

A man may *exist* with his reason dethroned and his moral powers thus entirely disabled. He is in that state the same *person* which he was at a previous period, when he was rational. The difference is, that he was then accountable for his acts, because he had the *use* of his rational powers, but now he is *not* accountable, because he has *not* the use of them.

In this view the following remarks, which are suggestive and mainly correct, seem to need some modification. "Though each man's desires and affections," says Whewell, "belong especially to himself, while reason is a common faculty in all men, we consider our reason as being *ourselves*, rather than our desires and affections. We speak of desire, love, anger, as mastering *us*, or of *ourselves* as controlling them. If we decide to prefer some remote and abstract good to immediate pleasure; or to conform to a rule which brings us present pain; which decision implies the exercise of reason; we more particularly consider such acts as our *own* acts. Such acts are deemed especially the result, not of the impulse of our desires, but of our own volitions." *

Here we pause to inquire, Can the "impulse of our desires" lead us to any executive acts whatever, excepting as we *will?* And whenever we *do* "decide," is not the choice "our *own* act," and are we not personally responsible for it? This laying the blame of our *bad* conduct upon the "desires and affections," because they *belong* to us, and taking the credit of our *good* conduct, since it is dictated by our "reason as being *ourselves*," too often serves as a quieting panacea to conscience.

Our author continues, "If we ask why we thus identify ourselves with our rational part, rather than with our

* Whewell, Vol. I. p. 58.

desires and affections, we reply, that it is because the reason alone is capable of that reflex act by which we become conscious of ourselves. To have so much thought as to distinguish between ourselves and our springs of action, is to be rational; and the reason which can make this distinction, necessarily places us on one side, and the desires which make no such distinction, on the other. It is by the reason that we are conscious; and hence we place the seat of our consciousness in the reason."

But are not brutes, as well as we, conscious of their pains, pleasures, wants, &c.? If they are hungry, are they not conscious of it? If we tear their flesh, or deprive the mothers of their young, do they not *feel it*, and *know* that they feel it? They are not conscious of *rational* perceptions, nor of *moral* acts, just because they *have* none; but so far as they are the subjects of any thing to be conscious of, they evince as much consciousness as we do. Our reason, then, as related to consciousness, is merely the cause of our being conscious of *more* than they. Hence the argument from consciousness, that would identify ourselves with our reason, proves nothing.

We quote further, "The habit of identifying ourselves with our reason, and not with our desires, is further indicated by the term passion, which is applied to desire and affection when uncontrolled by reason; as if man, in such cases, were passive, and merely acted upon; and as if he were really active, only when he acts in conformity with his reason. Thus we speak of a man's being *in a passion*, meaning an uncontrolled fit of anger; and *having* a passion for an object, meaning an uncontrolled desire."

"Still, it is to be recollected that man, under the influence of such passions, is not really passive. When he acts under such influences, he adopts the suggestions of desire or affection, and rejects the control of reason; but this he does in violation of reasonable rules. Passion does not prevent a man's knowing that there is a rule, and that he is violating it. To say that passion is irresistible, is to annihilate reason, and to exclude the most essential condition of human action."

This is very true and important, but we are at the same time to remember, that whenever a sane man, whether from passion or any other cause, "adopts the suggestions of desire and affection, and rejects the control of reason," however unreasonably he may *act*, he is still a *rational being*, and is himself entirely responsible for his acts. He "adopts" no suggestions, however urgent, but by the free consent of his *will;* and to yield to *any* "suggestions," in opposition to the plain dictates of reason and conscience, is a morally wrong choice. Whenever he does this, conscience has a charge against *him*, and sooner or later *he* must be arraigned at her bar.

EXTREME IMPULSIVE EXCITEMENTS.

That we have a responsible power of control over our *ordinary* impulses, no moralist denies. It is only under intense excitements, that the responsibility is questioned. But who shall decide where the limit of responsibility lies? If responsibility diminishes, as passion increases; if, under one degree of passion, a man is guilty for choosing to commit murder, but under a higher degree the same choice becomes guiltless; we may as well throw up our courts of justice and let all the passions loose.

Let us test the question by supposing an extreme case of each of the natural impulses.

1. An Extreme Case of Appetite.—A man has by indulgence enraged a morbid appetite for strong drink, until it has risen to an agony. In such cases men have been

known to tear their own flesh, that they might avail themselves of the alcohol furnished to dress their wound. Does the intensity of appetite in such a case justify a man in taking the fatal cup?

We firmly answer, no. It was by guilty indulgence that he brought himself into this fearful dilemma; and now his only alternative is, to endure the pangs of self-denial and determined resistance, or to do worse; to add to his guilt, and plunge onward to certain ruin. The first choice may involve the greater present suffering; but it is the pain of a man who submits to the amputation of a limb to save his life.

To say that he *cannot* resist the temptation, is not true; for thousands, in such cases, *have* resisted. Let him see you put a deadly poison in the cup, such as would kill him in five minutes, and he would not touch it.

He *can* refuse, and no amount of suffering from the refusal of this or any morbid craving, can excuse him from acting the part of a rational being. It is his duty to decide, positively and at all hazards, to hold his appetite in perfect subjection to the laws of reason.

2. An Extreme Case of Affection.—Instead of a malevolent affection, which most would admit should not be indulged, let us suppose a *benevolent* one. A man is passionately in love. We will suppose his love to be such as, under ordinary circumstances, it would be right to gratify. But he sees positive and sufficient reasons why he should not choose the loved object for his wife.

What ought he to do? Should he give the preference to affection, or to reason; to passion, or to conscience? He must practise severe self-denial; he must pluck out his right eye and cast it from him, or do worse. Shall he do the painful thing, or the worse thing? To follow the leading of benevolent affection, is the general rule of right; but there *are* cases when it conflicts with the higher law of reason and conscience; and in all such cases the higher law must rule, and the self-denial, however painful, must be endured.

3. An Extreme Case of Desire.—Suppose a man desires a portion of his neighbor's property. His neighbor is rich, and he himself is poor. His neighbor does not need all he has; indeed there is reason to believe that he would be better off with less; for so much property is a burden to him, and tempts his children to idleness and vice. Whereas, if he himself possessed a portion of it, he could thereby provide for the real wants of his family and could educate his children for respectability and usefulness. What would thus be no loss to his neighbor, but great gain to himself and his family, why should he not choose to make his own?

He has only to use his neighbor's name, or employ some person to use it for him, and the paper is good in the market. The desire is urgent, he wills to obey it. He has nourished the desire by plausible arguments, and now he sustains his decision by the same. But if the civil law detects him, it will not regard those arguments: neither will his conscience regard them. They will prove as a spider's web to protect him from even the civil law, and especially from the ever sure retributions of avenging conscience.

And why? Because he was *made* to govern his desire by the law of conscience, and not to govern his conscience by the law of desire. His desire of property was not in itself wrong; but to desire to possess it by unrighteous means, was a wrong desire, and hence the choice to gratify that desire was an unrighteous choice. Here is guilt added to guilt, wrong choice added to wrong desire, hurrying its victim to swift destruction.

4. An Extreme Case of Emotion.—Let us suppose a man in the intensest passion of *anger*. He is not insane; so as to be irresponsible for his acts, but he is in such a temper of passion that he can scarcely refrain from striking the fatal blow. He is in an agony to do it. It would give vent to his passion, and afford him infinite relief. Shall he do it? If he does he is indicted for manslaughter.

Is the law unjust? No. The law is right; because, as we have said, the man *was made* to govern his impulses by his rational powers, and not his rational powers by his impulses. The law is right, not merely because it is prudential, and necessary to society, but because it is in accordance with the constitution of our being, and is therefore founded in essential morality.

Now if we are guilty for not governing by the law of conscience even our most *urgent* natural impulses, under the *most powerful* temptations to yield to them, no one can doubt that we are guilty for not governing, by the same law, those which are less urgent and more easily controlled.

PERMANENT WRONG CHOICE.

We have considered wrong *specific* choices. There is another kind of choice, deep and generic, which may be called *permanent*. A man may have a wrong choice, as well as a right one, as lasting as life. To fix upon a suitable calling for life, and steadfastly pursue it, is right and important. It is the only way to insure success. As a man cannot succeed with divided efforts, he should early give his undivided and persistent choice to the pursuit for which he is best adapted, and, with strict regard to duty, accomplish in it the most he can. It is thus that the greatest and best of men have given their names to immortality.

The permanent *wrong* choice to which we refer is much the same as this, with the single momentous exception that it does not regard the law of conscience. The choice is supreme and absolute, not subordinate and conditional. Thus a man may choose wealth, literary distinction, military glory, office, power, the gratification of vanity, or mere pleasure, as his supreme object of pursuit. To be upright, just, pure; to accomplish a mission of good to his fellow-beings; to do the will of God; is to him a subordinate consideration.

That choice may go with him to the grave and mould his entire character. It is the ruling principle of his life. Suppose it to have grown to full and permanent effectiveness when he is at the age of twenty-five. He lives to the age of seventy-five, and thus maintains his choice fifty years. There is then charged to his account a wrong choice, fifty years old. It is a crime of half a century. It has lived to see his bright eye fade, his fair cheek ploughed with furrows, his black locks frosted and fallen, the marrow dug from his bones, and his once firm step tottering to the grave. His soul has become as withered and sightless as his body. We must leave him to settle his long and dread account with his conscience and his God.

But we should not fail to notice the wrong done to others, as well as to himself, by that guilty choice. We should think of the tender sympathies it has crushed, the sweet charities it has withheld, the cruel games it has played with the necessities and credulities of men; of the envious feelings, slanderous words, and unfair means, to which it has given rise; of its ruthless sacrifice of the peace, comfort, virtue, and hopes of men, whenever they came its way; of the havoc it has made of parental, conjugal, filial, fraternal love, of the love of humanity, and of the homage due to God. Its whole pathway of fifty years is strewed with mischief and crime.

Nearly the opposite to courage, fortitude, and firmness, noticed in the previous chapter, are cowardice, stoicism, and obstinacy. These, too, are qualities with which the will is mostly concerned, and they are as evil as the others are good.

Cowardice.—This is the opposite to courage. It may result in part from a man's feebleness of nervous temperament. So far it is not moral. It is usually due, however, to his want of a well-settled conviction of being in the right, or his consciousness of being in the wrong; or to his want of confidence in the success of the cause; or to his selfish fear to encounter danger; or, worst of all, to his want of cordial and supreme devotion to truth and duty. He takes counsel of selfish prudence, rather than of conscience. He is therefore of a weak and timid heart. His will is effeminate and sickly.

A coward in any responsible position is a miserable poltroon, whose personal safety and selfish aims are to him more important than the cause which he is set to defend. He can therefore never be relied upon. However boastful in the onset, he will prove treacherous in the conflict, whenever he fails to receive bright assurances. To pacify his childish fears and secure his selfish ends, he will in the hour of conflict abandon his most sacred principles and desert his best friends. In a world like this, where so many hard battles for the right against the wrong must be fought, a coward in any responsible position is sadly out of place.

Stoicism.—This is not the *opposite* to fortitude, but a *substitute* for it. Fortitude affects no indifference to suffering, but patiently endures it. Stoicism affects to disregard both pleasure and pain altogether. It is a sullen and desperate *will*, resolved only on caring for nothing.

Its rational basis is the doctrine of fatality. Adopting the necessitarian scheme, and considering our destiny fixed by the stars, the stoic makes a virtue of necessity, and determines to be as much a mere *thing* as possible. Truth does not teach him; Providence does not admonish him; neither mercies nor judgments move him. Having assumed a false position, against which the sensibilities of his nature and the course of Providence are at war, he endures all the pains and penalties of probation without any of its benefits or rewards.

Obstinacy.—As stoicism is a vicious substitute for fortitude, so is obstinacy for firmness. The term obstinacy is sometimes used in a good sense, as when we speak of soldiers fighting obstinately in a righteous cause. It however usually denotes an unreasonable course of conduct. It sets reason and argument at defiance. It yields to no persuasion, and is reckless of consequences. It is thus a blind and sulky stubbornness of will, overmastering the rational powers. It implies narrow views and a mean spirit, and is sustained by an intensely selfish and sensitive jealousy.

An obstinate man is apt to be sullen and revengeful. He is not usually *quick* to revenge, like a person of vivid emotions; but he is surer, more calculating, and more vindictive. Magnanimity and generosity being no part of his character, he finds few congenial friendships, and is therefore usually as miserable as he is mean.

CHAPTER IX.

SOURCE OF THE MORALITY OF ACTIONS.

MEN have been much divided in opinions respecting the source of the morality of actions. Some of the Grecian philosophers referred it to the *emotions*, as urging us to extremes; some of the early Christian fathers referred it to the *appetites;* others, of the transcendental school, have referred it wholly to the *will;* others have considered man a mere *machine*, and God himself the only responsible agent; while more modern writers have supposed that they have found it in a supposed *taste* or *relish*, or in the *affections* and *desires.* *

Now, according to our analysis, the moral *quality* of each elementary mental act or state, is in the act or state *itself*, and is known by being compared with its rule. We determine the quality of an action just as we do that of any thing else, by comparing it with its *standard*, and thus deciding whether it is what it ought to be. What the rules or principles of action *are*, we shall show hereafter.

* The reader is here referred for the above views, severally, to the writings of Plato and Socrates; of Augustine; of Kant and his disciples, including Cudworth and Coleridge; of Spinoza, Swedenborg, and others of the pantheistic and the necessitarian school; of Burton, and other tasters; and of more recent and still living authors, who need not be mentioned.

But when we would find the *source* of the moral quality of actions, we must look to the responsible *agent himself.* If we ask, *what* makes an action wrong, the answer is, its deviation from the rule. If we ask, *who* makes an action wrong, the answer is, the man who makes the action. It is the *man himself*, who craves, loves, desires, wills, and if he does these things wrongly, that is, differently from what the just rules prescribe, *he* is the source of the wrong done, and must account for it.

He must not refer the bad quality of a volition to a bad desire which prompts it, and so pronounce the volition itself characterless; nor the bad quality of an affection to a morbid appetite, and so divest the affection itself of quality. Each has its own peculiar quality of good or evil, and the responsible man must answer for it.

As the opinions upon this subject have now become reduced mainly to three, that which locates all moral quality in the affections and desires, that which places it in the will, and that which makes man merely passive, our remarks will have particular reference to these, while illustrating the general principle that includes them all.

"It hence appears," says Dr. Alexander, in deducing an inference from his argument, "that the true and ultimate source of the morality of actions is not found in the will, but in the desires and affections. The simple act of volition, namely, a determination to do a certain act, is always the same, whatever be the motive. And to ascertain that an action proceeds from an act of will, only determines that it is the act of a particular agent, but gives us no knowledge respecting the true moral quality of the act. This will be found universally true." *

But it would be difficult to prove that if a man has

* Outlines of Moral Science, p. 139.

wrong "desires and affections," his "determination" to gratify them is not wrong also. The excellent author had a specific truth in mind, which he well illustrated; but he does not use the term "will," when speaking of the "source of the morality of actions," in the true philosophical sense. Considered as a mere nervous impulse upon the muscles, physically determining them in a particular way, itself disconnected from all relation to the rational faculties, an act of will is of course destitute of moral quality; as truly so as mere brute volition.

But this is not what philosophers and theologians mean by *will*, when treating of moral action. They mean the will as related to reason and conscience. When they speak of "an act of volition," or "a determination to do a certain act," they indicate the volition or determination of a *man*, knowing his duty, to do or not to do it. When a man, in the exercise of his rational powers, determines to do the will of God, so far as he knows it, his determination is *morally right*. He then makes a good choice; that is, he puts a good moral quality into that act of will. If he chooses to do something else, rather than obey the divine will, he makes a *bad* choice; that is, he puts a bad moral quality into that act of will. In each case, the good or the bad *quality* is in the *choice*, *determination*, or *volition;* the *man himself* is the *source* of it; that is, *he put* it there; and he must answer for it. This seems, indeed, too plain to need to be stated.

And this is certainly the scriptural view of it. The Scriptures call upon men to make a right use of their will, and predicate moral quality of its action. The Israelites were commanded to *choose* whom they would serve. To choose to do otherwise than serve the Lord, was *itself* an act having decided moral quality, and one for which he would not fail to hold them responsible.

This is the generic use of the term, and the same is true of all *specific* acts of will, when the choice or the volition lies between doing right or wrong. To say that a man *chooses* wrong, because he has a wrong *desire*, is just saying that he does *two* wrong things; and that he does the one because he does the other. He *desires* wrong and he *chooses* wrong. If it is wrong to *have* a bad desire, it would take more logic than we have ever yet seen, to prove that it is not *also* wrong to *determine to gratify it.*

EACH ACT HAS ITS OWN QUALITY.

We really make no progress, we get no deeper into the mind, when searching for the source of a moral quality, by referring that of one state or act to another. If a person may will wrong because he has a wrong desire, so he may desire wrong because he has a wrong will. If our desires affect our wills, so our wills affect our desires; and a person may be as much in fault for the one as for the other. Why does the stubborn child desire to have his own way, despite of parental authority? Because he is *wilful?* Do we not justly ascribe moral quality to his wilfulness? He is punished for that state or act of *will*, that he may be induced to give it up and cherish a right one in its place.

The truth is, all the powers of the mind, as well as all the members of the body, have more or less of good or bad effect upon each other, according as they are severally in a sound or a disordered state; and, although several in elements, they blend together and become one in action. A sunbeam is one in action, as it goes forth from its source upon the world; but as painted upon the arch of the rainbow, it is seen in seven distinct colors. These colors proceed alike from the same great source, and were the sun an accountable being, he would be responsible alike for them all.

For the sake of analysis, the philosopher applies his prism and separates the solar light, as we divide the mental action, into its several elements, but he never supposes that the elementary hues owe their quality to each other. Each has its own color; each comes from the same source; and all blend together in one combined action of the sun, as witnessed in a beam of light.

Such is moral action. Considered as a whole, it is never a single element; as our entire examination has shown. It is always composed of several elements, each having its own quality and coming from one and the same responsible source. We have thus the psychological analysis and the moral synthesis.

THE DOCTRINE OF HUMAN PASSIVITY.

As to the view that considers men *passive*, in the sense that virtually absolves them from responsibility, it is settled by answering the question, not whether God has made them *independent* of himself, as the advocates of the view would have it; for nobody pretends this; but whether he has made them *moral agents;* that is, beings endowed with powers which render them *justly responsible* for their conduct.*

The sun is dependent upon its Maker. It is only as sustained by him that it shines. Still it was made to enlighten the world; and it actually does what it was made

* "He who feels himself responsible for the good and evil which proceed from him, or feels a *property* in them, must have previously forgotten that all his life is from God, and have come to find it in himself. This is the reason why, as Swedénborg says, 'he appropriates to himself all evil and falsity, which he would never do were his belief formed according to the real truth in the case.'"—*The Nature of Evil, by* HENRY JAMES, p. 144.

to do. To say that the sun is nothing and God is all, in producing the effect, is just charging God with making the sun in vain. This notion is both unphilosophical and unscriptural. It is one phase of virtual pantheism.

The Scriptures instruct us that "God made two great lights; the greater light to rule the day, and the lesser light to rule the night." The greater light, or source of light, is of course the sun; and it rules the day by shedding its light over the earth. God does not shed the light himself, by the bare exertion of his power; he made the sun to do it, and the sun, as his instrument, does it.

But if he could create and sustain a mass of inanimate matter, and empower it to do so important a service,* he could also create and sustain responsible *beings*, and empower them to do another and far nobler service. Such beings he has made men. Having given them a rational nature, written his law in their conscience, laid his command upon them, made them free to choose the way of obedience, and placed the stupendous motives of his moral government before them, to induce them to do so, he justly holds them accountable for the service for which he made them. They ought to render it. It is a reasonable, right, glorious service; as befitting and blessed to them, as it is honorable to the Being who made them. If the sun by shining reflects the glory of God's creative power, the beings made in his likeness ought to reflect those brighter splendors of his *moral* glory, which the beams of the sun are too feeble to represent.

* All *causality* originates and is sustained by free voluntary beings, divine or human; hence, when we predicate *power*, *cause*, *action*, of inanimate or irrational nature, it is only in the secondary sense of *means* or *instruments*. Thus the molecular action and rate of vibrations on which light seems directly to depend, are as ineffectual to the end as the inert mass of the sun itself, excepting as they are made effectual by the divine will. The agency of the divine will, itself transcendent and known only in and by its effects, is the ultimatum of all science.

But *how* may they do this? Evidently by being, in respect to character, *like* God; holy as he is holy, righteous as he is righteous. Such are the angels in heaven; such were our first parents before they fell. This righteousness consists in right affection, desire, choice, emotion, in reference to all beings and all objects in the universe. It has its seat in the heart, and is always direct and true to its end. It implies the desire of moral excellence, because it *is* excellent; the love of being, because it *is* being; the choice to do right, because it *is* right; and all the attending appropriate emotions.

It is evident that a heart thus disposed, when directed towards such a being as God, will supremely love him. When men "hunger and thirst after righteousness," that is, supremely desire righteousness for its own sake, they will, of course, supremely delight in God; for in him is the living embodiment of all righteousness. And he who thus delights in God, will choose to do his will. Here, then, we have the whole heart going forth to God. Desire embraces his righteousness; love, his being; will, his service; and, in and through all, the emotions vibrate to enrich and enliven the devotion. Such is true religious homage. It is precisely this, the supreme homage of the soul to God, that man lost by the fall.

MORAL RENOVATION.

We thus learn the nature of the change wrought in man by the grace of the Gospel. It is not merely a change of appetite, or of affection, or of desire, or of volition, so that one of these, being itself renovated, may rectify the others; neither is it a change or refining of mere taste, nor a quickening or exaltation of emotion. It extends to and embraces all these, but is restricted to neither. Deeper, more thorough and generic, it is a change of the *man himself*. *He* is "*born again;*"* *he* becomes a "*new man;*"† *he* is a "*new creature*."‡ He is not changed as to personal *identity*, nor as to *natural* powers; he becomes a new *moral* man. And his change is not only moral, but *generic*. He becomes a new man as to his *entire* heart.

The new-born infant, however infirm, feeble, or sickly, is yet *entire*. It has all the *parts* of the full-grown and perfect man. One member is not born into the world alone, that it may beget the other members. Neither is one element of the heart brought alone into newness of life, that it may impart that life to the other elements. On becoming a "new man," the *person himself* devotes *all* the powers of his being a "living sacrifice to God," as his "reasonable service."

But this may still seem too vague. The reader may desire a more definite idea of the *precise seat* of the change in question. I do not know of any one word which better indicates the seat of the change than *disposition;* for this refers equally to *all* the moral powers. When a man is *not* disposed to love, desire, choose, act, as he ought, in his relation to God, he is not a religious man. He is in that state into which the *fall* brought mankind. When he becomes through grace *disposed* to love, desire, choose, act, as he ought, in his relation to God, he *is* a religious man. He is in the renewed state into which the *Gospel* brings mankind. The change in question is thus a radical and generic change of the *moral man*. He *himself* becomes *rightly disposed* in reference to *all duty*.

But while renewing grace thus touches and moves him at once in all the springs of character, it perfects him in none. He neither loves, desires, nor wills, perfectly; he

* John iii. 7. † Col. iii. 10. ‡ 2 Cor. v 17.

has no moral element, and performs no duty, in all respects right. But to be and to do all that he ought, and thus to glorify God in his spirit and in his body, is now his ruling principle of heart and life. Hence, if this change is predicated only of the will, we must understand the will in the largest sense, as involving and ruling the entire heart. "Old things are passed away, behold *all* things are become new." Not in some things, but in *all* things, does the new man become subject to the law of the new life. Even his most virtuous desires and affections receive a new quality of moral excellence, by the divine "image" after which he is "renewed."

The natural sun blends and harmonizes all its elemen tary rays in one glorious beam of dazzling brightness, because it does as it was *made* to do; and so also they who, by receiving Christ, receive "power to become sons of God," blend and harmonize all their elementary impulses in a life of moral excellence, because *they* also now begin to do as they were made to do.

The man thus renewed has become right in principle. He *aims* right. His eye is "single." He therefore sees, more clearly than he did before his renewal, what *is* right. Darkness may be on each side, but he sees the way of duty, right onward before him, as luminous as the path of the sun through the heavens. "*If thine eye be single, thy whole body shall be full of light.*"

Although the "new man" has not any of his powers in perfect subjection to the ruling law of his life, yet since he is faithfully striving to have them so, he is in *principle* upright. His homage is sincere and entire, embracing all his faculties, but it is imperfect. Such has been the character of every righteous man that has lived upon earth since the fall, with the single exception of "the man Christ Jesus."

On the other hand, if a man is *not* under the controlling influence of right principle, whatever may be the states or exercises of his several mental elements, he is *not* a morally upright man. He is not merely *imperfect*, as all are, but he is wanting in the right *aim*. His *eye* is "evil." He is essentially and radically wrong.

And for this reason, he is also full of darkness and doubt. The way of duty is to him uncertain and cheerless, because his eye is not single. Thick and portentous clouds gather along his path, wrapping their gloomy folds eternally about his guilty spirit. "*If thine eye be evil, thy whole body shall be full of darkness.*"

Not the least characteristic qualities of the new man and of the old, are the spirit of humility in the one, and the spirit of pride in the other. The latter, "through the *pride* of his countenance, will not seek after God;" the former has been led in humbleness and contrition of spirit to see him, and in the view, to "abhor" himself, and to "repent in dust and ashes." Thus seeing himself in the light of the divine character, and realizing his entire dependence both upon divine power and grace, he is "clothed with humility;" a garment which, however despised on earth, is as much esteemed in heaven as the shining robes which angels wear.

We thus reach the true *source* of the moral quality of all mental states and actions. Of all *bad* moral quality, it is found in the man himself, the progenitor of the race, and each of his responsible descendants, misusing and perverting his powers as a moral agent. Of all *good* moral quality, the source is found, first of all, in God himself, through the grace of the Gospel begetting and replenishing the "new man;" and, secondarily, in the new man himself, using his powers as he was made to do.

This fundamental distinction in human character is

recognized throughout the Scriptures, in a great variety of forms; it accords with the known laws of mind and of moral action, and must always enter into every sound and thorough system of moral science. Nor has he whose especial calling it is to endeavor to make mankind what they should be, learned well his duty, until he clearly sees this distinction, and with skilful hand lays the axe at the root of the tree.

PART IV.

PRINCIPLES.

I. NATURAL PRINCIPLES OF MORALITY.

CHAPTER I.

THEORIES OF THE LAW OF RIGHT.

THE word *principle* has various applications. It is sometimes used to denote a mental *faculty;* as when we speak of the principle of perception, of imagination, of affection, &c. It is also used to denote a mental *state* or *continuous act*, as when we speak of the principle of envy, of ambition, of revenge, &c. When a man is influenced by one of these motives, we say he is envious, or ambitious, or revengeful, according to the particular principle which rules his conduct.

In the above senses the term is used *subjectively;* that is, it indicates something *within* us, pertaining to the mind itself, or to its character. But we are now to use the term *objectively;* that is, as indicating something presented to the mind from *without*, to be by it *adopted* as a *rule of duty*. In this sense, the term may indicate either the *rule itself*, or the *reason* for it.

ESSENTIAL AND POSITIVE PRINCIPLES.—The *essential* principles of morality have their *perceived reason in themselves.* No extraneous reason can be given *why* they are right, any more than one can be given for the truth of a mathematical axiom. The mind has only to perceive the *rule itself* to perceive its *rightfulness.* The *positive* principles of morality are rules of conduct whose reason, or that which makes them right, is *not* seen in the rules themselves, but exists in some *unperceived* necessity, or some necessity lying *without* them.

NATURAL AND REVEALED PRINCIPLES.—A more important distinction of moral principles is that of *natural* and *revealed.* The former are taught us by the light of *nature*, and are binding on *all* accountable beings. The latter are taught us by a *special revelation* from God, and are made obligatory upon us by his *authority.* They are hence called *revealed* principles of morality.

For instance, the rule of *benevolence*, is *natural.* It is binding on *all* accountable beings, and can never be altered. But the rule for the observance of the *Sabbath*, is *revealed.* It is binding only upon those to whom the revelation is made.

Hence, as we have natural and revealed religion, so we have natural and revealed morality ; and their analogy and unity of design in the all-embracing government of God, are clearly manifest. Both in acting upon the principle of benevolence, and upon the principle of observing the Sabbath, we obey the same government and fulfil the same design of God.

The term *morality*, in the secular sense, indicates the duties of man to man, in distinction from his duties to God.

In this view, he is a *religious* man, who does as he ought in his relation to God; while he is a *moral* man, who does as he ought in his relation to his fellow-beings.

But in the generic and highest sense, morality respects an *universal* ought. It looks in *all* directions, and inquires for the right in every relation. The central law of morality is the law of our *entire duty*, both as it respects ourselves and our relations to all other beings. Our relation to God as well as to men, has its morality.

The word *right*, from the Latin *rectus*, and having corresponding terms to denote the same idea in all languages, indicates the existence of law, by which all rules and actions are to be tried. When conformed to their laws, they are right, just, good; or, in other words, what they *ought* to be.

Where, then, must we look for the *ultimate* law of right? What is it that makes rules themselves, and of course the actions conformed to them, what they *ought* to be? What makes the rules just, and the obedient actions right? Is it something within us, around us, from above us, or from all these sources? Is it absolute and eternal, or conventional and changing; or does it partake of both? We have not space to examine in detail the voluminous speculations upon this subject, but will condense them into a single chapter. They may be comprised in the following theories: the arbitrary, the greatest happiness, the highest good, and the subjective.

THE ARBITRARY THEORY.

This theory refers all moral right to *positive institutions and enactments.* Nothing is right in itself; it is made so by circumstances and the consequent necessary laws. The theory assumes that the powers which be, whether divine or human, have the right to control us as they please; it being theirs to command, ours to obey.

We must not go behind the law to find a *reason* for it; for none is to be found; all right and all wrong being made such by the authority of God, or of his duly constituted magistrates. Hence this is called the doctrine of blind and passive obedience, and is of excellent use in all despotic governments.

This theory is the counterpart of a fanatical error which sets all positive enactments at defiance, on the ground that the law of conscience is sufficient for every man. It was advocated by Hobbe and other loyalists, in opposition to the spirit of misrule which prevailed at the time of the decapitation of Charles I.

It more than deifies human governments; for even God himself does not govern upon arbitrary principles. He calls upon us to consider the reasonableness of his requirements, and to judge if his ways are equal.

This theory arose from mistaking the ground and the limits of positive enactments. These do not supersede the *essential* right; they are founded upon it, and are intended to furnish and to sanction its details.

For instance, benevolence is right, irrespective of all enactment. God's requiring it does not *make* it right; he requires it because it *is* right. Hence his law requiring us to love is not an arbitrary enactment, but is essentially right. It would be just as right as it now is, if it came from any other source. On the other hand, we cannot conceive of a law, by whomsoever enacted, that could make it right for us to be malicious.

"Our notions of right and wrong are so far from owing their authority to positive institutions, that they afford us the chief standard to which we appeal in comparing different positive institutions with each other. Were it not for this test, how could we pronounce one code to be more humane, more liberal, or more equitable than another? Or how could we feel that, in our municipal regulations, some are consonant and others repugnant to the principles of justice?" *

THE GREATEST HAPPINESS THEORY.

Some have supposed that nothing is right *in itself*, but that whatever is right, is so, because it promotes the highest welfare. Virtue is only a means to an end. Our way to learn the divine will respecting an action, is to inquire whether it tends to promote the general happiness.

"We conclude," says Dr. Paley, "that God wills and wishes the happiness of his creatures. And this conclusion being once established, we are at liberty to go on with the rule built upon it, namely, that the method of coming at the will of God concerning any action, by the light of nature, is, to inquire into the *tendency* of that action to promote or diminish the general happiness."

"So, then, actions are to be estimated by their tendency. It is the utility of any moral rule alone, which constitutes the obligation of it. Whatever is expedient is right. But then it must be expedient on the whole, at the long run, in all its effects, collateral and remote, as well as in those which are immediate and direct; as it is obvious, that, in computing consequences, it makes no difference in what way or at what distance they ensue."

In this view, the only difference between an act of prudence and an act of moral and religious duty is this, "that in the one case we consider what we shall gain or

* Stewart, p. 183.

lose in the present world; and in the other case, we consider also what we shall gain or lose in the world to come." *

Morality, then, is prudence embracing our temporal welfare; religion is prudence projected into eternity.

To admit "that God wills and wishes the happiness of his creatures," is only admitting that he is a benevolent being; but it does not follow that there is no such thing as moral virtue, which is a good in itself, and which a wise and righteous benevolence would not fail to regard.

But it is said that virtue "is not an *ultimate* good," that it is good only as a means to the end, happiness. To this I reply, that, so far as we know, all things and events in the phenomenal universe are followed by others, to which they sustain some relation of cause or means, and thus the affairs of the universe move on in endless succession. It is the glory of God to make all present things and events subservient to others, and these again to others; thus for ever augmenting the riches of the universe, by allowing nothing to be unproductive.

But we may in this relation speak of a *chief* end more understandingly; and to that end may be attached various degrees of importance. One man's chief end in going a journey may be *health*, another's *pleasure*. There may be a question as to which is the most valued, but the same man may desire and seek each, both as a good in itself and as a means to the other.

It is manifest that God *does* make our happiness, as well as our suffering, a means of promoting our moral welfare; and also that he makes our morality a means of happiness. He must, therefore, value both character and happiness, each for itself and for the good of which it is the means; whilst, as a benevolent being, he cannot be sup-

* Paley's Moral Phil., B. II. Ch. 3.

posed to put any value whatever upon suffering, which is always in itself an evil, except as it is a means to some good end.

Hence right character and happiness must ever coincide. The truly upright man cannot fail to be on the way to the highest happiness. But while God always sees the relation of the one to the other, we cannot; and hence, if we must decide upon the moral quality of an act *only* by its perceived tendency to happiness, we should often be in a fearful dilemma. There would be a sad defect in the system of moral government.

But no such defect exists; we are in no such dilemma. Uprightness is uprightness; it is right in itself, and may often be distinctly known as such, irrespective of all consequences. Neither is a right act a bargain for happiness; it is prompted by a supreme and direct regard to what is intrinsically good.

At the same time, it is impossible for us not to desire happiness; for this desire, as we have seen, is a part of our nature. If, therefore, while conscience impels us to the right, we were not at the same time assured that uprightness tends to happiness, there would be a strange incongruity in our constitution. The law of a pure instinct and the law of a good conscience would be at war with each other. But no such incongruity exists. The satisfaction imparted by conscience in the performance of duty, even at the greatest sacrifice, is itself an earnest of future good, and our assurance that the path of duty leads to happiness.

"Since happiness is necessarily the supreme object of our desires," says Whewell, "and duty the supreme rule of our actions, there can be no harmony in our being, except our happiness coincide with our duty. That which we contemplate as the ultimate and universal object of desire, must be identical with that which we contemplate as the ultimate and supreme guide of our intentions. As moral beings, our happiness must be found in our moral progress, and in consequence of our moral progress. We must be happy by being virtuous." *

While the cardinal virtues of benevolence, justice, gratitude, &c., may be known as morally excellent, irrespective of consequences, there are others, as we shall hereafter see, whose character we learn either by their perceived tendencies, or by the positive institutions and teachings of Christianity.

THE HIGHEST GOOD THEORY.

The advocates of this theory maintain that the *highest good* is the ultimate rule of right. All else must be made subservient to this. They have only to ascertain what the highest good *is*. With this view they institute a comparison between the relative claims of our lower and our higher faculties.

Our attention is first directed to the demands of *appetite*. These must be regarded; and the means of their gratification is a good in relation to this particular interest.

From this inferior good we ascend to that of rational art, of *sentiment* and *taste*. Here is no craving of appetite to be satiated, but the feelings rest with complacent delight in the contemplation of their object. This is an intrinsic and dignified good.

We next consider the cultivation of *science*. Here the human intellect comes to commune with the divine, in apprehending the laws of nature, and conversing with those primordial ideas which guided the great Architect in constructing the universe. This, again, is a very noble and exalted good.

* Whewell's Elements, Vol. I. p. 385.

But over and above these is still another, the highest good of all; it is *worthiness of spiritual approbation.* Here, then, is found the ultimate rule of right; the law supreme, at whose bidding all other demands must yield. "We may call this the imperative of reason, the constraint of conscience, or the voice of God within him; but by whatever term expressed, the real meaning will be, that every man has consciously the bond upon him *to do that, and that only, which is due to his spiritual excellency.*"—"To be thus worthy of spiritual approbation is the end of all ends."*

This beautiful theory assigns the true relative importance to the several demands of our lower and higher faculties, enthroning the enlightened conscience in supreme authority over them all. But whether the desire of simplification, so characteristic of original, theorizing thinkers, may not have had undue influence in framing it, is perhaps a fair question.

That every man is bound "to do that, and that only, which is due to his spiritual excellency," is a first maxim in morals. But whether we are always to put our minds in the reflex position to find our duty, and to act *with a view* to "worthiness of spiritual approbation," as "the end of all ends," may be reasonably doubted. In our noblest and best acts, and especially in our loftiest religious homage, we are almost wholly objective. We lose sight of ourselves, and of regard to our personal excellency and worthiness of approbation. Our thoughts and desires are outward and right onward to their object, whether it be the welfare of a fellow-being, or the glory of God. That we could not rightfully seek the welfare of men or the glory of God, in a way *inconsistent* with our spiritual ex

* Hickok's Moral Science, pp. 48, 49.

cellency, or even without *promoting* it, is very certain. We glorify God when we reflect his character, and we reflect his character by being and doing good, like him. The difficulty with this theory is the one usually inherent in attempts at great simplification. Such attempts are wont to leave some facts unprovided for.

To make my meaning clear, let us suppose a man to be a believer in God, and in the Bible as his revelation to us. What ought that man to regard as "the end of all ends," or, in other words, the ultimate *object* of his being? Answer. To glorify God and enjoy him for ever. By what *means* can he do this? Answer. By being, in his humble sphere and capacity, like God in character. By what *rules* can he become so? Answer. By those furnished in the Bible. Here we have three distinct things, the man's *object*, his *means* to it, and his *guide*.

I have said above, with the Assembly's Catechism, that man's chief end is to glorify God *and* enjoy him for ever, because the one implies the other. It is impossible to be *like* God in character, without *enjoying* him; and it is impossible to enjoy him, without being like him. When, therefore, we seek to glorify God as our ultimate *moral* end, by becoming in character like him, we at the same time act in accordance with our highest rational *instinct*, which is an aspiration or desire to be for ever happy. It has been previously shown that we ought not to attempt to extinguish or repress our natural desires, but to direct them in obedience to moral law. There is no moral excellence in merely seeking our happiness, but there *is* moral excellence in doing that, namely, glorifying God, in the doing of which our happiness is involved. Hence, our true end of all ends, *morally*, is the glory of God; whilst our end of all ends, *instinctively*, is our highest happiness; and, as our moral and instinctive being was never designed to be separated, *so our duty and happiness must be eternally united.*

But if man ignores his relation to God, the case is materially altered. Two of the above three things are then to him wanting, namely, his objective *object*, which is the glory of God, and his objective *guide*, which is the Bible. There remains to him only *one* of the three things, namely, his *personal worthiness*, which becomes both his object and guide. All is merged into this. It follows, in such a case, that "in personal worthiness, as the end of all action, every claim centres; and in the attainment and preservation of this, all imperatives are satisfied;" also, that the man "is a law to himself, and has both the judge and executioner within him and inseparable from him."*

But we have seen that pure morality embraces *all* intrinsic obligations. If, then, man is aware of the existence of God as revealed in the Bible, he is morally bound to render to him supreme homage. His obligations to God involve as *pure* morality, as his obligations to himself and to his fellow-beings do. He ought to make the glory of God his supreme object, even if no positive authority enjoined it. The bond precedes the command. The command of God does not *make* it right; he commands it because it *is* right. Morality alone as much binds him to glorify God in his spirit and in his body which are his, as it does to pay his just debts to his neighbor. This prior obligation Christianity *assumes*. It is precisely here that morality and religion unite and become one. Morality according with religion, and religion heightening and intensifying morality, they thus present man's *entire* lesson of obligation, both as a moral and religious being.

* Hickok's Moral Science, pp. 48, 65.

In this view, the following position seems to me to be *wrong end first.* "The existence of God being apprehended," &c., "we need only to know our spiritual communication with him, and for our own worthiness' sake there immediately arises the consciousness of moral obligation."* Instead of our obligation's arising "for our own worthiness' sake," we are under prior obligation of spiritual worthiness *for the sake of glorifying God.* Instead of making our own worthiness the *end* of the *means,* we should make it the *means* of the *end.*

It is with much self-distrust that I dissent, in any particular, from the views of so able an author as the one above cited. But it seems to me that we are driven to this dilemma, and must hang upon one or the other of its horns. A man may make *either* the glory of God, *or* self-worthiness, his final object, but he cannot do *both.* If his ultimate object is the former, it is not the latter; and if it is the latter, it is not the former. The one must be means to the other. His aim must be ultimately God-wise, or self-wise.

If it be said that to inculcate the glory of God as man's object, is to travel out of our sphere as mere philosophers, and to teach religion instead of pure morality, I must again say, that what we here teach is morality and religion too; otherwise, pure morality, as an intrinsic obligation, and pure religion, as positively enjoined, are not only in this respect *distinct,* but they are *opposed* to each other.

THE SUBJECTIVE THEORY.

The most objectionable form of this theory was advocated by some of the Grecian sophists, and subsequently by Hume and other skeptical writers. It maintains that

* Hickok's Moral Science, p. 147.

all virtue and all vice are such, only as they are so conceived and regarded by the human mind.

This is the same notion in respect to moral science with that in respect to natural science, which denies the existence of objective beauty or deformity in material objects. In this view a Venus is in herself no more beautiful than a porcupine. We have a certain impression in regard to the one which we have not in regard to the other, and this constitutes the whole of beauty. In like manner this theory maintains, that there is no objective difference between what we call a good and a bad action; all the difference being in our minds.

"The words right and wrong, signify nothing in the *objects themselves* to which they are applied, any more than the words *sweet* and *bitter*, *pleasant* and *painful*, but only *certain effects* in the mind of the spectator. Protagoras and his followers extended it to all truths, physical as well as moral, and maintained that every thing was relative to perception. The following maxims in particular have a wonderful coincidence with Hume's philosophy. "Nothing is true or false, any more than sweet or sour, *in itself*, but relatively to the perceiving mind." "Man is the measure of all things, and every thing is that, and no other, which to every one it *seems* to be, so that there can be nothing true, nothing existent, distinct from the mind's own perceptions." *

"Were I not afraid of appearing too philosophical," continues Stewart, in animadverting upon this theory, "I should remind my reader of the famous doctrine supposed to be fully proved in modern times, that tastes and colors and all other sensible qualities lie not in bodies, but merely in the *senses*. The same is the case with beauty and deformity, virtue and vice." †

* Hume's Essay, Part I. † Stewart, p. 193.

This scheme mistakes the true function of our rational powers. They are not literally to *be* our rule of duty, but to enable us to *learn* it. When we speak understandingly of "the law of conscience," we mean the law which conscience *approves* and *enforces*. But this scheme virtually leaves every man to do what is right in his own eyes, regardless of the teachings and admonitions of both God and man. Man is not, in this view, a learner, but is himself lawgiver and judge.

It is a curious illustration of the remark that extremes sometimes meet, to find the sensational Hume, on the one hand, uniting with the advocate of the infallible moral sense, or inward light; on the other, in dispensing with the necessity of a revelation from God.

A less objectionable view, is that maintained by Jacobi and other German philosophers, and also by Cudworth, and, with some modifications, by Coleridge and his followers. In this view, right and wrong are objective entities, but they are directly apprehended by the eye of reason as abstract truths. The general doctrine of an immediate abstract intuition of first truths, seems also to have been maintained by Kant, and subsequently to have been by him relinquished or modified. For this, Jacobi charges him with inconsistency. "The Critical philosophy," he says, "first out of love to science, theoretically subverts metaphysic; then, when all is about to sink into the yawning abyss of an absolute subjectivity, it again, out of love to metaphysic, subverts science."*

The advocates of this view hold, that from the bright domain of the pure reason, the senses, and all knowledge received by them, stand apart from us, while the clear

* Works, vol. II., p. 44. See also Hamilton's Phil. of Common Sense, p. 136.

eye of intuition directly perceives the eternal principles of right. Their rightfulness is not seen in the concrete, and depends upon no relations and contingencies; it is seen of itself, in pure abstraction, as an essential and absolute entity. The *ought* is thus safely lodged, *a priori*, in the reason of every individual.

Objections to this theory will appear in the subsequent chapter, in which we shall endeavor to view the whole subject in as clear a light as possible, regardless of all theories, and appealing directly to human consciousness.

CHAPTER II.

FIRST PRINCIPLES.

WE have seen that the desire to simplify has induced philosophers to attempt to resolve all the principles of morality into one simple law of right. But when that law is found, or supposed to be found, it is proved to be made up of several elements. Thus the law of *love*, which is all-embracing, is not simple, but complex.

The same attempts at simplification have been made in *natural* science. Men have endeavored to refer all the phenomena of nature to one law; but their law proves to be a compound of several.

The truth is, the Creator seems to have had more than *one idea*, in both the natural and the moral creation; and while the ideas in each are in perfect harmony, we vainly attempt, in either case, to resolve them into a simple unity.

Still all the works of God are characterized by great and even amazing simplicity, when we contemplate their extent; and the wonder is, not that the original ideas in reference to which they are constituted are so many, but that they are so few. It is our present object to ascertain these few elementary ideas, or first principles, as they are found in the moral world. To make my view the clearer, as well as to confirm it by analogy, let us briefly refer to other departments of science.

The science of *mathematics* has its first principles, and erects its entire superstructure upon them. They are familiar to all educated minds. The axioms of geometry are not made what they are by any ordinance, either human or divine; they are the exponents of truths that are essential and everlasting.

The science of *nature* has also its first principles. Until the student of nature begins to apprehend them, he makes no scientific progress. He may observe individual *facts*, but he cannot *interpret* them. Like the printer's types when thrown into *pi*, they lie in confusion around him, until he sees the *principles* which bring order out of chaos.

It is evident that the universe was constructed, so to speak, upon scientific principles; for it is by the use of mathematical truths and calculations that we are enabled to study it, and to calculate its movements. Did matter attract and repel at random, or the heavenly bodies move irrespective of certain first principles, there could be no science of nature.

So also the science of *morals* has its first principles. As in the previous sciences, so in this also, they are the product of no creative power. They are absolute and essential. The mental states and exercises indicated by the terms benevolence, gratitude, justice, &c., are conformity to principles absolutely right. Nothing can make them otherwise. The moral philosopher must apprehend these principles, and build his science upon them.

HOW FIRST PRINCIPLES ARE KNOWN.

All sciences, then, have their first principles, to which the human mind is constitutionally adapted. Thus the whole system of the universe, both natural and moral, was made to be a *study* for rational minds; and the minds are constituted with powers precisely adapted to the study, both in the principles and the systematic completion of every science.* The child has seen that the whole of an apple, or of any thing else, is more than half of it; that

* The simple *fact* of the analogy of the subject and object, that is, of the mind of man and the universe without him, is all that is here asserted. Attempting to go *beyond* the fact, as known only so far as it is affirmed by the actual study of nature, has led to many ingenious and brilliant *a priori* speculations, and sometimes to those which are absurd and mischievous. They have even subverted the first truths of science itself, denied the testimony of consciousness, annihilated the objective universe, and resolved all into a solitary subjectivity.

"Some philosophers (as Anaxagoras, Heraclitus, Alcmæon,) maintained that knowledge implied even a *contrariety* of subject and object. But since the time of Empedocles, no opinion has been more universally admitted, than that the *relation of knowledge* inferred the *analogy of existence.* This analogy may be supposed in two potencies. What knows and what is known, are either, 1st, *similar*, or, 2d, the *same:* and if the general principle be true, the latter is the more philosophical. This principle it was, which immediately determined the whole doctrine of a representative perception. Its lower potence is seen in the *intentional species* of the schools, and in the *ideas* of Malebranche and Berkeley; its higher, in the gnostic reasons of the Platonists, in the *pre-existing species* of Avicenna and the Arabians, in the *ideas* of Descartes and Leibnitz, in the phenomena of Kant, and in the external states of Dr. Brown. It mediately determines the *hierarchical gradation of faculties or souls* of the Aristotelians; the *vehicular media* of the Platonists; the theories of a *common intellect* of Alexander, Themistius, Averroes, Cajetanus, and Zabarella; the *vision in the Deity* of Malebranche; and the Cartesian and Leibnitzian doctrines of *assistance* and *predetermined harmony.* To no other origin is to be ascribed the *refusal of the fact of consciousness in its primitive duality;* and the unitarian systems of *identity*, *materialism*, *idealism*, are the result."—*Hamilton's Phil. of Perception*, p. 189.

the two halves put together are equal to the whole; that halves of the same or equal things are equal to each other; that what is round cannot coincide with what is square, and so on. Thus, long before he begins to study mathematics as a *science*, he comes into possession of its primary truths.

You have then only to embody these truths in distinct statements, or axioms, and his mind at once admits them. He now perceives them, not merely in the individual facts which he has witnessed, but as indicating *absolute and universal* truths. He thus comes to a clear and unquestioning recognition of those abstract principles of mathematics, which are equally applicable in all places and for ever.

We proceed to *natural* science. It was by the observation of *individual facts*, that its *principles* became known. It was by observing the descent of an apple from the tree to the ground, by measuring the accelerated speed of a falling body, by observing and computing the movements of a revolving sphere, and so on, that those *universal* truths were apprehended upon which the science of nature rests. The universality of these truths is learned by induction, but, like the principles of mathematics, they come of the observation of facts. They are all first learned in the concrete.

We advance next to *moral* science. The child has no intuition of the abstract principles of right and wrong, until he witnesses an *act* of kindness, or of fidelity, or of gratitude; he then instantly perceives and feels that what he witnesses is a *good* act. He witnesses an act of unkindness, of treachery, of ingratitude; he instantly perceives and feels that what he witnesses is a *bad* act. He does not need to stop and reason upon these acts, or to survey their consequences, before he decides upon them; he knows *at once*, that the former are right and the latter wrong. Here, then, is an intuitive perception and a feeling of conscience, by which a rational moral judgment is passed upon those acts.*

Nor is it needful that these acts be directed towards the child himself. This might heighten his emotions and thus intensify his moral judgment, but it would not change its nature.

In this way, long before the child comes to study moral science, he becomes possessed of its elements. What then remains to be done? He has only to exercise that power of generalization, with which rational beings are endowed, and, in the right and the wrong of the particular acts which he has witnessed, he recognizes the *principles*, which stamp the same character upon *all* similar acts.

Consequently, when, in after life, he enters upon the study of moral science, he only needs to have its first principles clearly *stated* to him, and he as readily assents to them as to the axioms of geometry. Proof is no more required in the one case than in the other. To go behind

* This, it seems to me, is all that Descartes and other intelligent advocates of innate ideas could have really intended. The first principles of every science are *innate*, or *native* to the mind, only in the sense that such is its *nature*, that it directly *intuits* them, a priori, as *necessary* and *absolute* truths, independently of the affirmations of sense, experience, or any discursive proof.

The confusion and misapprehension here between authors seem to arise, mostly, from their not distinguishing between the *perception* and the *proof* of the principles in question. The principles are first *perceived* in the *concrete;* and therefore we are dependent upon the senses for being put in relation to them; but their *proof* is in *themselves*, being intuitively perceived by the mind the moment it apprehends them. These principles are the elements of all our systematic knowledge, in every department of science.

"Such elements, however, are obtained only by a process of sundering and abstraction. In actual or concrete thinking, there is given nothing pure; the native and foreign, the a priori and a posteriori, are there presented in mutual fusion."—*Hamilton's Phil. Com. Sense.*

the simple *statement* of the principles, with a view to establishing their truth, is just throwing arguments away in an attempt to prove what is proved already.

To speculate upon their beauty, their fitness, their utility, their relation to the highest happiness or the highest good, or their innate existence in the mind, in order to prove their truth and importance, is like lighting candles at blazing noon to help the sun. The mind was *made* for them. It was made to perceive, feel, *know* them, with a clearness and certainty that put all argument at defiance, and laugh all speculations to scorn.

If there is *any* thing that man knows beyond all possible question, it is, that benevolence is good and malice evil, that justice and gratitude are right, and ingratitude and injustice wrong, and other such moral truths; and he knows them to be *universally* and *unalterably* so. The place for the man who does not know this is not in the lecture-room, nor in rational society, but in the mad-house.

PRINCIPLES AND MORAL VIRTUES.

Principles, then, considered as reasons and rules of conduct, are *objective;* moral virtues are *subjective.* We perceive and adopt principles; we approve and practise virtues. First principles in morals are universal rules of conduct, having their reason or authority in themselves; actions conformed to them are cardinal virtues. The principles are essentially and perfectly reasonable and just, under all possible circumstancces; actions are more or less what they should be, according to their degree of conformity with the principles.

Moral virtues are related to their objective principles, as the diagrams upon the blackboard are to the mathematical principles which they represent. The diagrams are made by man; the principles are eternal. The lines, circles, angles, are themselves imperfect; but they represent perfect ideas. All human virtues are imperfect; the principles of morality are perfect. All human virtues have degrees; the principles of morality have no degrees. The ultimate principles of moral right, are the primary and essential elements of God's comprehensive and everlasting law.

Some men have been able to carry on extensive mathematical calculations, without the aid of figures and diagrams. From this it has been inferred, that the mind apprehends its first truths in the abstract. Such were the views of Jacobi, Cudworth, Coleridge, and other transcendentalists. But the men supposed, did not carry on the calculations in question, until they had learned the first principles in the concrete.

Every child takes his first lesson in morals, when he intelligently sees the first right or wrong *action;* but he does not study morality as a *science*, until he begins to make a systematic and universal application of its principles.

GROUNDS IN WHICH PRINCIPLES ARE APPREHENDED.

Let us begin with the lower demands of our nature, the cravings of *appetite.* These demands must be met in some way, and there is a right way and a wrong one, between which we must choose.

We first notice the appetite for *food* and *drink.* Every person readily sees that its leading object is his healthful nourishment. Whatever pleasure there may be in its gratification, is obviously designed to be subservient to this object. To sacrifice this object to a mere lust of pleasure, is morally wrong; but to rule the appetite with faithful reference to the end for which it was given, is morally right. Man *knows* this, as well as he knows the truth of an axiom. He thus knows the *principle* by which he ought to govern this appetite. Obedience to it is the virtue of *Temperance.*

Men may differ respecting the kind, quality, and amount of nourishment best for them. These things are not learned by intuitive perception; they depend upon circumstances, and must be learned by experience. But this does not affect the principle, nor the obligation to obey it.

Instance next the *appetite of the sex.* This appetite was manifestly designed to be ever subordinate to the healthful continuance and welfare of the race. And the more effectually to guard this end, the Creator has implanted a sort of higher instinct, a feeling of *modesty*, which all have by nature, and which only vicious influences can resist. Here again the right *principle* is obvious. Obedience to it is the virtue of *Chastity.*

We come next to the feelings of *affection*, *desire*, and *emotion.* The demands of these are scarcely less imperious than those of appetite. We were made to love and to desire, as truly as to eat and drink. The former is as needful to the soul as the latter is to the body. And all may see that we ought to *control* our affections and desires, as well as our appetites. Also the *emotions* attending them, however valuable when in due subjection, become terribly disastrous when unrestrained. All men know that it is wrong to allow their passions to master them.

Now we have seen that there are two opposite kinds of moral affection, that of love, kindness, good will to all men, and that of hatred, selfishness, envy. Every man knows the former to be right, and the latter to be wrong. He needs no argument to prove it; the truth flashes upon his mind by intuition, like the truth of an axiom. He has only to think upon them, and the knowledge is his;

the rule of duty is present to his mind. He is thus furnished with the *principle.* Obedience to it is the virtue of *Benevolence.* This virtue is in the Scriptures termed *love* and *charity.* These terms are there used in the most comprehensive sense, including our obligations to God as well as man.

Every man sees that others have claims to be regarded as well as he. Even the child has his *own* things. What these are, whether they are his character, his person, his possessions, or how he came by them, is not material. It is enough that they are *his.* The fact that they are his, gives him a right to them which no other person has.

He perceives that others, too, have *their* own things; and that for the same reason why he has a right to *his,* they have a right to *theirs.* Along with this perception, he has also a *feeling,* that he *ought* to regard the rights of others as well as his own. Such is the *principle* which his conscience enjoins. Obedience to it is the virtue of *justice.*

He listens at one time to what he knows to be intentional *truth;* at another to what he knows to be intentional *falsehood.* He perceives the difference between them, and his conscience admonishes him that the former is right and the latter wrong. He does not decide upon the rightfulness of truth from its perceived *utility;* for long before he reflects upon its advantages to society, and perhaps even while perceiving some immediate personal advantage from it, his conscience decides that it is *right in itself.* Thus conscience furnishes him with the *principle* of duty. Obedience to it is the virtue of *Veracity.*

He becomes early acquainted with *promises.* He gives and receives them. The parent makes promises to his child; the child makes them to the parent. They are often exchanged between the child and his companions.

He understands their meaning, and he knows that he ought to keep them. Questions as to how they may be affected by circumstances, as in case of being extorted by force, do not affect the obligation to be faithful to every free and reasonable promise. Conscience informs him that he *ought* to do as he has *agreed* to do. Such is the *principle.* Obedience to it is the virtue of *Faithfulness.*

Every man witnesses the reception of *favors.* Children receive support from their parents, and instruction from their teachers. In sickness and affliction, we receive the sympathy and attentions of our friends. In want and in danger we have been relieved by those upon whom we had no legal claim. All men know that such favors impose obligation. It may not be in our power to return favor for favor; but we can exercise and manifest an appropriate feeling. This we are bound to do. Such is the *principle* of obligation universally admitted. Obedience to it is the virtue of *Gratitude.*

He who practises all the above virtues, escapes the censure of the civil law, and passes for a good moral man. He fulfils his duties to himself and to his fellow-men, as related to this world. But the question of his relation to the Being who made him, and to another world, is also to be considered. He has also some higher endowments to be regarded, for the use of which he is responsible.

He has a class of feelings which realize their end in the pleasing *contemplation* of their objects. These feelings are termed *sentiment.* In fulfilling their demands, he both seeks for the pleasing objects actually existing in nature, and also forms *ideal* ones in his mind. He also seeks to embody his ideal forms in works of *art;* and both by copying nature, and by furnishing the additional adornments of genius and fancy, to enhance the means of enjoyment.

Hence painting, sculpture, architecture, ornamental gardening; also the embellishments of furniture, dress, equipage; all those pleasing arts which give elegance to civilized life. Such works are related to the sentiment of *taste;* and are as truly adapted to meet a demand of our *rational* nature, as food and drink are to meet a demand of the body, or as the *moral* affections are to meet a demand of our *social* nature.

This sentiment, duly exercised, tends to elevate man above the gross pleasures of the mere animal. Not only in the drawing-room, the picture-gallery, the garden, but even at the festive board, it subjects the grossness of mere sensual indulgence to the more delicate and refined banquet of the soul. But the fact that it elevates and refines, does not exonerate it from the necessity of being subject to moral rule. Rightly ruled, it becomes auxiliary to the highest virtues of morality and religion; not thus ruled, it becomes as subservient to vice as any other feeling. The fine arts, refining and ennobling as they are, have yet often been prostituted to base purposes.

We have also the thirst for *knowledge* to be regarded. It is well to gratify this craving. He is scarcely worthy to be called man, who never aspires after knowledge for its own sake. To feel the conscious ability to master difficulties in the pursuits of literature and science, to realize the satisfaction of comprehending the sublime laws of nature, and the dignity of holding communion with those eternal truths to which they relate, is a privilege and an honor worthy of a rational mind.

But is this the *end* of intellectual pursuits? Is this *all* that intellect was given us for? Was man made intellectual *only* to please himself in gratifying his thirst for knowledge? No more than he was made animal, only to please himself in gratifying the desires of appetite. The former gratification may be more *dignified* than the latter, but it may be also none the freer from the vice of selfishness. Every man *knows* this, or may know it. He knows that his intellect was given, to teach him what he is to believe and to do, as an *accountable* being; to solve the problem of his obligations and destinies. He may pervert and abuse the gift of intellect, as truly as any other. He is therefore bound by his conscience to be ever searching after truth, to be open to conviction, and to be faithful in the performance of every known duty.

All of the above virtues are binding upon the *atheist*, as well as upon the theist. The question now is, Is the atheist bound to believe in the existence of God, and to do him homage? He may have no intuitive perception of the divine existence. But God has revealed himself so clearly in his works, that man has only to contemplate them, with a *mind open to conviction*, to see the *evidence* of "his eternal power and Godhead;" so that he is "without excuse" for not admitting his existence. Moreover, the feeling of *moral obligation*, and the conscious reaching of the soul after its object, forbids all repose until that object is recognized and admitted. Thus the evidence furnished in the constitution of the soul itself, unites with that furnished by objective nature, to prove that there is and must be a God of infinite natural and moral perfections.

Hence, if men are "without God in the world," it is because "they *do not like to retain him* in their knowledge." Although "the fool hath said in his heart, No God," his conscience, enlightened by a single flash from the glorious face of creation, declares loudly against him. When he thus perceives the evidence of the existence and perfections of God, his conscience exalts and intensifies this perception, and unfailingly admonishes him to render to that glorious and Supreme Being his sacred and supreme homage.

The evidence for the divine existence being so obvious, and so closely related to the first acts of conscience, all pagan nations have, *in fact*, ideas of God; and, the more virtuous the people are, the nearer they approach to just views of his character. However men may differ in opinions respecting the mode of his existence, or the form of service most acceptable to him, they cannot innocently fail to know, that they ought to render to him their supreme homage; that they are bound to rule not only their appetites and affections, but all their tastes, sentiments, and intellectual aspirations, with a supreme regard to his pleasure. Such is the *principle* enjoined by conscience; obedience to it is *Religion*. This is *natural* religion, or the religion of *pure morality*.

We thus see that piety to God is both a moral and a religious duty. To withhold from him our homage is, in the mere light of nature, a *moral* wrong, as truly as it is to withhold an act of justice or of gratitude due to a fellow-being.

THE ABOVE OBLIGATIONS UNIVERSAL.

We have thus specified the first principles of virtue and morality, and have shown how the mind comes to the knowledge of them. The duties they enjoin are temperance, chastity, benevolence, justice, veracity, faithfulness, gratitude, piety. The list of terms might be extended to include such as charity, forbearance, kindness, &c.; but their meaning is all comprised in the above. The duties which we have considered cover the entire field of morality, as surveyed by reason and conscience unaided by experience and by revelation.

They are binding upon all men, Pagans, Mahometans,

Jews, as well as Christians. For Christianity did not create the human mind, nor endow it with reason and conscience; neither did it originate the first principles of morality. It recognizes, sanctions, and enforces the principles taught by nature; it also enriches them with other and higher principles and motives; thus augmenting the responsibility of those to whom it is given, without diminishing the responsibility of those who are without it.

If we have correctly stated the first principles of morality, and the way by which they may be known, *all men can know them*, and, knowing them, *ought to obey them.* They are "written in their hearts," approved by their "consciences," and are the rules which righteous judgment must eternally approve. *

* The critical student or curious reader, who is desirous of consulting authors respecting the first principles of knowledge, and of duty, is referred to the following works, most of which are in the Astor Library, New York. Plato, Œuvres complêtes, traduite par V. Cousin; also Eng. Lond. Ed. especially Vol. I. Crito and Phædo. Malebranche, Recherche de la Verité, and Traité de Moral. Descartes, Lux Naturæ. Leibnitz, Nouveaux Essais. Buffier, Traité des Premiers Vérites. Wollaston, Religion of Nature Delineated, p. 25. D'Alembert, who says that teaching first principles is only reminding one of what he previously knew. Beattie, Essay on Truth, p. 25. Kant, Critique of Pure Reason, and Jacobi's strictures upon it, and exposition of the distinction between Sense, as teaching us corporeal and conditioned existences, and Reason (Vernunft), as teaching us supersensible truths. These last he terms revelations, intuitions, &c. Bishop R. D. Hampden, Lectures on Moral Phil., p. 40. Hartley, Theory of the Human Mind. Mackintosh, Ethical Phil. George Moore, M. D., Man and his Motives; also, Power of the Soul and Use of the Body, p. 40. Sydney Smith, Elementary Sketches of Moral Phil. Cudworth, Intel. System. V. Cousin, especially his translation of Descartes' Discour de la Methode pour bien conduire la Raison. G. W. F. Hegel, Werke Vollständigt Ausgabe. Schelling, Philosophische Schriften; especially his System des Transcendentalen Idealismus. J. Mill, Phenomena of the Human Mind. Lord Herbert, De Veritate. Sir William Hamilton, Phil. of Common Sense, p. 19. Locke, Essay, b. I., p. 20. Other authors upon the same subject, to whom I have referred elsewhere, are in most libraries, and are familiar to the general student.

The point to which I would invite particular attention, is the remarkable

GENERAL INDEX TO OUR VIEWS.

He who is temperate, chaste, honest, well-behaved, from mere *prudential* considerations, or any others not involving regard to *duty*, or what is *morally right*, is, in the vulgar sense, a *virtuous* man.

He who is *conscientious* in his conduct, acting upon principles of social honor and integrity as involved in *duty*, but only as the duty respects himself and his fellow-beings, is, in the same sense as above, a *moral* man.

He who is conscientious in his conduct, acting upon principles of *all* honor and integrity as involved in duty, not merely as the duty respects himself and his fellow-beings, but, over and above all, *his* God, is a *religious* man.

The antithetic terms are: *virtue* and *vice; morality* and *crime; piety* and *sin*. And as the so called virtues, in the vulgar sense, may be merely *prudential*, we sometimes designate those which are practised from regard to *duty*, as *moral* virtues.

We thus have the following: constitution, virtue, morality, religion; each and all of the *preceding* being included in the *succeeding*. Instinct is minor to virtue, virtue to morality, and morality to religion. A person cannot be virtuous without instinct, nor moral without virtue, nor religious without morality. He may have the

agreement among all these authors, as to the *existence*, the *nature*, and the *claims* of these first principles. The main difference between the authors has respect to the *number* and *extent* of the principles, and to the *way by which the mind comes to the knowledge of them.* All ontological speculations respecting principles supposed to be known otherwise than through the observation and study of the *phenomenal* universe, will have more or less value with different minds, according to constitutional tendency and to education. Such speculations carry us at once into those transcendent nebulous realms, where words grow tall and bright, but thoughts become dwarfish and murky.

less without the greater, but he cannot have the greater without all the less. Religion is major to all; it is the all-embracing excellence, which includes, perfects, and adorns every other, and devotes it to the GLORY OF GOD as the END OF ALL ENDS.

We thus see in what essentially consists the *depravity* predicated of man in the Scriptures. It is not the loss of all amiable instincts, nor of all secular virtue and morality, but it is *apostasy from God.* It is being *practically* "*without God* in the world." And as the fall of man was a fall *from* God, so the change wrought in him, by the grace of the Gospel, is a restoration *to* God. His restoration to God quickens, exalts, and guides all his instincts, virtues and moralities, leading him to devote them all, in newness of life, to the divine service.

As the absence of piety *imperils* all moralities, and *tends to their utter undoing;* so true piety *protects* them all, and *tends to their ultimate perfection.* But this is always a *gradual* work. The *evil begins* in *departure* from God; the *good begins* in *return* to him. From these beginnings the good and the evil gradually increase. No man becomes eminently good, and no man becomes a reckless villain, *at once.* No man ascends to angelic excellence, and no man sinks to infernal wickedness, by a single leap.

CHAPTER III.

MORALITY TAUGHT BY EXPERIENCE.

EXPERIENCE reaffirms all that reason and conscience assert, and besides this, furnishes *additional* rules of duty. It was divinely intended to teach us what we *ought* to do, as well as what is *expedient* for us.

We refer to the experience of mankind at large; not merely to that which is personal. We are bound to take lessons of duty from authentic history, from natural science, from the admonitions of wise and good men, as well as from our individual experience.

We learn duty from experience on the principle assumed by Paley, that "as God wills and wishes the happiness of his creatures," the moral quality of an action may be known by its "tendency to promote or hinder the general welfare." This is the method of ascertaining duty only where the other fails.

Paley does not consider an action right, on the mere ground that it promotes happiness. He is not so boldly utilitarian. He considers it right, on the ground that, *because* it promotes happiness, it is *manifestly according to the will of God.* He supposes that God "wills and wishes" our happiness, and hence that whatever promotes it must be according to his will, and *therefore* right.

His error lies in taking what seems to be the *tendency* of actions, as always indicating the divine will, instead of directly apprehending the first principles of morality as right in themselves, irrespective of all consequences. Hence Stewart has well remarked, "If we could take into due account the whole value of right principle, and the whole happiness produced by virtuous feelings, we could commit no practical error in making the advantageous consequences of actions the measure of their morality. But this can happen only by considering moral good as a primary good, valuable for its own sake; not by supposing that virtue is aimed at as subservient to some other purpose of more genuine utility; and no sagacity or fairness of estimating useful consequences can stand as a substitute for the love of right itself. It is true that honesty is the best policy; but he who is honest only out of policy, does not come up even to the vulgar notion of a virtuous man. If a man were tempted by the opportunity of gaining a large estate, through a safe but fraudulent proceeding, the utilitarian scheme would seem to recommend him to weigh both sides well, though it would direct him in conclusion to decide in favor of probity; but the common judgment of mankind would hardly deem him honest, if he hesitated at all."*

But if Paley erred on the one side, by positing the entire cause of morality upon the utilitarian or greatest happiness scheme, some have also erred on the other side, by throwing the tendency of actions entirely out of the account, and falling wholly back upon the supposed infallible decisions of what they call the moral sense. If the

* Active and Moral Powers, p. 409.

former error makes men too calculating and prudent, the latter renders them self-willed and fanatical.

At any rate, too much forethought, and too prudent regard to the consequences of our conduct, are not vices of which the Bible loudly complains, nor for the prevalence of which we have any special cause of alarm at the present time.

*Fiat justitia, ruat cœlum,** is a maxim of undoubted soundness, but there are more ways than one, by which we are to determine what the "justitia" *is*.

THE QUALITY OF ACTIONS LEARNED BY EXPERIENCE.

The pain attending injuries inflicted upon our persons is an indication that it is wrong to inflict them, and an admonition to us not to do it. To cut, burn, or bruise the flesh; to contract or distort the figure, for the gratification of vanity; needless exposure to sickness, perils, or undue severities; all violations of natural laws, as related to health and vigor; are clearly contrary to the will of God, because they tend to produce pain and death, where he designed happiness and life. It is sufficient to condemn them, that they are violations of natural law; but it is by their *tendencies* that we know they *are* such violations.

Needlessly to extract a tooth or amputate a limb, is a violation of natural law; but if the member is so diseased that general experience has proved its removal promotive of health and comfort, the act of removing it ceases to be any such violation, and becomes morally right.

In the same way we are to decide respecting the use of intoxicating drinks or of opium. We have no instinct to guide us, as the brute is guided, in determining whether

* Let right be done, be the consequences what they may.

the temperate use of these things is injurious; nor does reason afford us any clear light, nor conscience any sure admonition, upon the subject. The immediate effect of them is usually pleasing, and hence offers strong inducements to use them. The only way, therefore, to determine whether the temperate use of them is morally right, is by observing their ultimate tendencies. If they are proved to impair health, entail suffering, and shorten life, the use of them is as immoral as it is imprudent.

In the same way we are to decide whether indulgence of *any* kind is *immoderate*. Appetite is not an infallible monitor. Indeed it can seldom be fully indulged without harm, for it is seldom in a strictly normal condition. Every person is therefore bound to consult *experience*, and to restrain his appetites within the limit which it proves to be most conducive to health. To fail in this, is to fail of the cardinal virtue of *temperance*.

FASHION AND DRESS.

The Chinese adopt the fashion of compressing the feet of their female children of high birth into small wooden shoes, to prevent their growing to a natural size. They thus render such children cripples for life. Some western nations, instead of compressing the feet, attack the more dangerous part, and compress the waist; thus inducing feebleness, diseases of the spine and lungs, and inviting premature death.

In both cases the motive is the same; namely, to remove the subject from the appearance of vulgar labor, and impart to her an air of refinement and beauty. A small foot to the eye of the fashionable Chinese, is what a slender waist is to the eye of a fashionable American. To each it is beautiful.

But while it is beautiful to the eye of one person, it is quite the reverse to the eye of another. Nor is this because the one is cultivated and the other rude; for persons of the highest culture differ upon this point. We cannot then determine by any *æsthetical* rule which fashion is right.

Nor can we decide this by adopting the principle, that we ought not to divert the body from its natural growth; for all nature is made subject to our pruning and culture. If we do not attend to the development and growth of the body, it becomes deformed. Who shall decide how far this culture should be carried? We submit while young to painful dental operations, to secure the future beauty of the teeth; why not do the same for the feet, the waist, the head?

There is but one answer: whatever *experience* proves to be most conducive to health, vigor, the full and free use of our faculties, and length of life, is certainly according to the divine intent. The wearing of the hair long or short, the tonsuring of the beard or allowing it to vegetate in full, the cultivation of the moustache or the imperial, &c., &c., about which grave questions of morality and religion have been raised, are mere matters of taste and convenience. But to follow any fashion that wars against health and life, is as immoral as it is unwise. We may call it only an innocent foible, but offended law, both natural and moral, will punish it as a *crime*.

CONFLICT OF TASTE WITH UTILITY.

What gratifies the sentiment of *taste*, sometimes conflicts with apparent *utility*. In this case, as in all others, the most important demand must rule. But who shall decide which *is* the most important?

A farmer has upon his grounds near his dwelling a fine grove of trees. He has little taste for the ornamental; his thoughts are for the profitable. The wood might be sold for much, and the land made to yield an annual harvest. Nor need we suppose him miserly. He may be a conscientious and benevolent man. He has children to educate, and is disposed to contribute generously to worthy objects. He therefore thinks it his *duty*, to sacrifice the grove to a useful purpose.

His neighbor, being of a different taste and culture, pronounces the direst anathema upon his head. The most sacred sentiments of his heart have been outraged. Had he been owner of the ground, he would have subsisted upon one meal a day, and even have curtailed the education of his children, rather than perpetrate so savage a deed. To mar the beauties of nature thus, is an offence for which he has no forgiveness.

Which of these men is right? Each may be right, in his way. Each must view the subject with his own eyes; and until they can exchange the use of them, they should agree to differ. The one man is *utilitarian;* the other is *æsthetical;* but they may be equally conscientious. It was divinely intended that men should thus differ; for from differences like this spring the various pursuits which are the bond of harmony, and which furnish the "spice of life."

In all such cases, we should allow every man to follow the dictates of his own conscience, and be sure that we offend not our own. "Why is my liberty judged of another man's conscience?" "Happy is he that condemneth not himself in the thing which he alloweth." If one man is captivated with the *grandeur* of Niagara Falls, and another sees in them nothing to admire, but thinks only of the *useful* purpose they might subserve, in driving machinery, we have only to smile at the difference between them, and devoutly wish that each may be true to his mission.

THE RIGHT OF PROHIBITORY LAWS.

No human laws are designed to *make* men righteous. Their object is to *restrain* immoralities within limits essential to the general welfare. The righteous do not *need* law; it is made for the vicious. "The law is not made for a *righteous* man, but for the lawless and disobedient." Such are the persons for whom the State must enact prohibitory laws, and establish courts and prisons. But while restraining these, they should place the least possible bond upon human liberty. They should respect the privileges of the virtuous, while restraining the misdeeds of the vicious. They should be just to all, and never attempt to rule the conscience.

How, then, are we to judge of the rightfulness of a prohibitory law? Suppose one, for instance, restraining the sale and use of intoxicating liquors. That such a law is not needful for the temperate, all admit. The man whose conduct is ruled by the cardinal principles of virtue, needs no such artificial rule as this. But is it needful for the *intemperate?* That is the question; and it must be settled by experience.

That it imposes undue restraint upon any man's *conscience*, would not be pretended. The restraint is wholly upon the demands of the *appetite* or of the *purse*. Hence we have only to inquire whether its *tendency* is favorable to the general and individual welfare. If it is found to prevent vice, to protect virtue, to encourage industry and thrift; to carry peace and abundance to the domestic hearth; to empty jails, prisons, poorhouses, and asylums for the insane, and to replenish shops, manufactories, farms, and schools of learning, with useful talent and wise endeavor; if it thus helps to redeem men from debasing bondage, and to raise them to the dignity and happiness for which they were made; then such law is clearly just and good, and every man ought to sustain it.

But should *any* privilege of the temperate be curtailed, for the sake of removing temptation from the intemperate? What privilege is curtailed? The former no more need the unrestrained use of intoxicating drink than the latter. If its presence is no temptation to them, restraint is no loss. Indeed, it is not the strictly virtuous who usually complain of such prohibitions.

I offer no special pleading in behalf of any particular law. I only assert that *any* prohibitory law not forbidden by conscience nor the Bible, which has been proved to be beneficial to the general welfare, and which curtails no *virtuous* privilege, is morally right. In all civilized communities many such laws are enacted, to prevent crime, to encourage industry, to promote education; and they are as binding upon our consciences as the first principles of morality. Indeed, these principles themselves require us to do what we can to procure the enactment of such laws, to obey them, and to enforce their observance.

THE PRINCIPLE OF EXPEDIENCY.

But he who merely conforms to the letter of law, does not reach his duty. A man is bound to do what is *expedient*, as well as lawful. "All things are *lawful* unto me; but all things are *not expedient*." The law may allow things which expediency forbids, and which are *therefore* wrong.

For example, the law may allow a man to take intoxicating drink at the festive board. To take it might do *him* no harm, and might afford him pleasure. But circumstances may make it inexpedient. He might, by indulgence, encourage others to do the same, whom it *would* injure. They may be reclaimed inebriates, or persons of ill-governed appetite, whom the least indulgence might entice to ruin.

He might also weaken the cause of temperance, and put arguments into the lips of every inebriate about him. Shall he do what is *lawful*, or what is *expedient?* Shall he avail himself of the *law*, to protect his indulgence, or shall he practise *self-denial*, if such it be, for the general welfare? A good conscience could not hesitate as to duty.

Nor is there here any ground for the stale charge of pretension and hypocrisy. In obeying his conscience, the man does exactly as he pretends. He does not claim a higher morality than he practises. He does not pretend, that the use of wine is in itself and under all circumstances wrong; but that, when it is unnecessary, and tends to evil, it is his duty to refrain from using it. His example says to those inclining to intemperance, that he refrains for *their* sake, not his own. It is an act of self-denial for their good.

Not only so, it is an act of kind regard to the strictly temperate. He might by indulgence offend their consciences, or embolden them to do what their consciences condemn. To practise self-denial, from such motives, is to act upon the principle which induced Paul to refrain from meat that had been offered to idols. He knew and averred that there was nothing wrong in the use of the meat, considered in itself; but he said, "When ye sin so against the brethren, and wound their weak consciences, ye sin against Christ. Wherefore, if meat make my brother to offend, I will eat no flesh while the world standeth, lest I make my brother to offend."*

* 1 Cor. viii. 13.

MORALITY OF AMUSEMENTS.

Intemperate and cruel amusements are condemned by the first principles of virtue and benevolence. But there are many amusements not necessarily of this kind. Among these we may enumerate fashionable assemblies, balls, theatres, horse-racing, gaming; in short, all those recreations whose direct object is pleasure.

Pleasure is a good, and may be sought by right means; but whether these means are right, can be judged only by their effects. We have no intuitions, and there are no positive precepts, which directly determine their quality; and there are plausible arguments both for and against them.

If they are proved to be, under certain restrictions, means of virtue as well as pleasure; if they contribute to the health, thrift, cheerfulness, and morality of the community; especially, if they are strictly subservient to our spiritual duties and interests; they are so far forth lawful and right. To what extent they *are* so, if at all, it is left with our judgment and observation to determine. Hence, different men will decide somewhat differently.

But wherein these things are proved to be of an opposite tendency; to induce indolence, waste, intemperance, and other vices; to displace the fear of God and the duties of religion; they are unquestionably wrong, and will be condemned by every enlightened judgment.

The responsibility is therefore laid upon all men, subjects as well as magistrates, to have an eye to the *tendencies* of popular amusements, and to countenance such, and only such, as are conducive to the general welfare. Enough amusements are at command, which are strictly harmless, without adventuring upon any which are of a dangerous or even doubtful tendency.

CHAPTER IV.

II.—REVEALED PRINCIPLES OF MORALITY.

MORALITY OF CHRISTIANITY.

We are next to consider the *revealed* principles of morality. We find these in the Christian religion; and it is our present purpose to examine their *ethical claims.* Our task here is not with the external *evidences* for Christianity, furnished by history, miracles, and prophecies, but with its *rightfulness*, as related to our moral nature. Let us then glance at its relations to our several faculties.

Relation of Christianity to the Appetites.—We have seen that morality requires us to restrain indulgence of the appetites within the limits most conducive to the health and welfare of our race. To do thus, is to practise the virtues of temperance and chastity, and is precisely what Christianity enjoins. She enforces these virtues, not only by the motives of prudence and morality, but by the higher motives of religion.

She announces the most terrible judgments upon the vices of unrestrained appetite; drunkenness, gluttony, fornication, and self-pollution; and admonishes us that "every man that striveth for the mastery is *temperate* in *all* things." To "keep under the body and bring it into subjection" to the law of spiritual life, she inculcates as an indispensable condition of both our temporal and spiritual welfare.

At the same time, she enjoins no *austerities;* she is kind and generous to all the bodily wants; she invites a free and full expansion of all its powers; she says to every one, in respect to body as well as soul, "*Do thyself no harm.*" And facts have proved, that they who best regard her admonitions, take the surest way to health, happiness, and length of days.

Relation of Christianity to the Affections.—We have seen that morality condemns every malignant affection, and requires of us benevolence towards all men, even our enemies. So does Christianity. She says: "Love is the fulfilling of the law." "Love your enemies, pray for them that curse you and despitefully use you, that ye may be the children of your Father which is in heaven."

She provides for all the natural affections, and demands their due exercise. She gives full and harmonious play to the parental, filial, fraternal, conjugal, and social affections; and employs them all in her service, in a way to render us prompt and happy in discharging our various relative duties.

But while she calls for these affections, she does not allow our love to take a narrow and selfish form. It must be all-embracing. She enjoins an impartial philanthropy. She teaches us that every man is our brother, and that we ought to regard his temporal and eternal welfare. Her command is ever upon us, "*Love all men.*"

Relation of Christianity to the Desires.—The first of these in our enumeration is the *desire of life.* Christianity nourishes and animates this desire; augments the value of life, by considerations of infinite moment; teaches

14*

us how to prolong it; presides as a guardian angel over it; and finally teaches us to project the desire for it beyond the grave, and to live here in view of living for ever hereafter.

Next is the *desire of happiness.* Christianity encourages this desire, and makes earnest appeals to it. She teaches us to live in view of the highest happiness; never taking one pleasure from us, but for the sake of giving us a better. She forbids no pleasures but such as tend to misery. She thus guides, tranquillizes, and strengthens the desire itself, while proffering to it the highest possible means of gratification. We have only to heed her admonitions, and for every hurtful indulgence renounced, we receive "joy unspeakable and full of glory;" for "the pleasures of sin for a season," we receive full draughts of endless blessedness from the "pure river of water of life, clear as crystal, proceeding out of the throne of God and of the Lamb."

The *desire of society*, or the social feeling, is another element in the mental constitution; and for this, too, Christianity fully provides. She always regards us as social beings, destined to find much of our happiness in each other; and many of her precepts respect our mutual relations as members of the same community. The public worship of God she has made social; the Christian Church is social; the Christian heaven is social. And Christianity teaches us so to cultivate the social affection and live together upon earth, that we may live together in blessedness for ever in heaven.

We have the *desire of knowledge.* No desire is more constant and active; and for none does Christianity more generously provide. She places at our disposal all the treasures of science, all the operations of nature, all languages and all arts. She invites us to study the heavens as the work of God's hands, the moon and the stars which he has ordained; to take lessons from the fowls of the air, the lilies of the valley, the grass that clothes the field.

She provides also for that deeper thirst of knowledge, which pertains to our *spiritual* nature. She reveals a portion of the wonders of the invisible world. She makes known to us some of the "things" which "the angels desire to look into." In view of her disclosures we are sometimes constrained to exclaim, "O the depth of the riches, both of the wisdom and the knowledge of God!" And at every step of our way, she cheers us with the assurance, that if true to her teachings, we shall never cease to grow in knowledge.

We have the *desire of esteem.* Nor does Christianity disregard this. She discountenances vanity, and other errors to which the desire often leads, but she cherishes the desire itself, and seeks to gratify it in the highest degree. She would first of all render us *worthy* of the esteem we desire, and then put us in possession of it. She teaches us to discriminate between that esteem which is valuable and that which is worthless, to seek the former and despise the latter; to conduct so as to win the esteem of the wise, and secure "the honor that cometh from God only." Jesus Christ said, "If any man serve me, *him will my Father honor;*" thus appealing to our desire of esteem, and telling us how to obtain for it the highest possible satisfaction.

We desire to sustain the relation to beings and to things, by which we can claim them as our *own.* And this craving Christianity would gratify, in the truest and fullest sense. It is only the *covetous* desire, that she condemns. She would not only protect us in the enjoyment of what we have, but put us in relation to *new* friends and possessions, to be sacredly ours for ever.

She so enlarges our inheritance, if we obey her, as to make it include *all* that can be desired, both in this life and in that which is to come. "Therefore, let no man glory in men, for *all things are yours;* whether Paul, or Apollos, or Cephas, or the world, or life, or death, or things present, or things to come, *all are yours;* and ye are Christ's, and Christ is God's." It is the exalted privilege of the Christian, that the friendship and riches of Christ's kingdom are his *own;* that even the God of heaven is his *own* God.

Finally, we have the *desire of power.* No instinct of the human mind does Christianity more cautiously guard than this, and more vigilantly guide to the realization of its true object. While she condemns, in no measured terms, all selfish ambition, she teaches us to aspire to the sublimest of all power, the "power to become the sons of God;" and, by becoming such, to obtain power to rule our own spirit; power over temptation; power to tread the world under our feet; and, by a life of supreme devotion to the great end for which we were made, to wield a benign moral inflence over the character and destinies of mankind. No other power is so worthy of our supreme desire and untiring pursuit.

And more than this, Christianity teaches us to anticipate thrones of power and influence *in the world to come.* "To him that overcometh, will I grant *to sit with me on my throne,* even as I also overcame, and am set down with my Father on his throne."

Relation of Christianity to the Emotions.—Christianity allows the boundless exercise of all the purely natural emotions, and furnishes motives to excite them Emotions of the beautiful, the grand, the sublime, the terrible, the awful, are addressed by no appeals more vivid and stirring than those furnished in the life, teachings, sufferings, and death of Jesus Christ; and especially in the disclosures made by him and his disciples relating to the end of time, the general judgment, and the retributions of eternity.

Moral science recognizes another class of emotions, as morally right or wrong. It condemns hatred, anger, revenge, envy, pride, every form of malignant passion; and holds remorse and despair to be the fruit of evil doing. Christianity, in like manner, condemns them; and also presents motives to restrain them, drawn from the forgiving love of God in Christ.

"*Avenge not* yourselves," she says, "but rather give place unto wrath." "Let all bitterness, and wrath, and anger, and clamor, and evil speaking, be put away from you, with all malice; and be ye kind one to another, tender-hearted, forgiving one another; even as God for Christ's sake hath forgiven you."

Condemning all emotions which morality disowns, she also utters her divine approval of those which morality allows. Thus emotions of love, pity, sympathy, forgiveness, gratitude, penitence, humility, faith, and hope, are by her regarded as the fruits of divine grace in the heart, and evidences of a regenerate spirit. "The fruit of the Spirit," she says, "is love, joy, peace, long-suffering, gentleness, goodness, faith, meekness, temperance; against such there is no law." "Godly sorrow worketh repentance to salvation, not to be repented of." Thus the best and happiest emotions that ever beat in the human heart, are due to the Christian religion.

Relation of Christianity to Taste and Sentiment.—Christianity condemns all false taste and sickly sentimentalism. But there is a taste true to nature, which refines and elevates the soul; and there is a sentiment which finds delightful repose in whatever is pure and lovely. These Christianity protects and fosters. There are no forms of true beauty and sublimity, whether actual or ideal, to which she is a stranger. No conceptions of imagination are richer, bolder, more original, or more vivid, than those to which she gives rise.

The *effect* of Christianity, wherever she has prevailed, has always been to correct and exalt the taste. A friend to the fine arts, she guards them with an ever vigilant eye from perversion and abuse. Hers is a religion of meditation, as well as of action; not only affording to us the luxury of doing good, but of feasting our minds with ennobling thoughts, cheering hopes, and charming sentiments. By studying her lessons and imbibing her spirit, we realize the finest sentiments and most brilliant conceptions of which the mind is capable.

Relation of Christianity to the Will.—We have had previous occasion to refer to this, with reference to a particular point. We have now another in view. It has been supposed that some of the doctrines of Christianity are at variance with the entire *freedom* of the human will. They are so, only as viewed through the mists of false philosophy. Whatever may be the nature of the gracious influence by which the mind is renewed, we cannot suppose, without denying the teachings of Christ, that it is at variance with our responsible power of will; for to that he appeals. Men do as they will in religion, not less than in other matters.

The influence which Christ by his Spirit exerts upon the human will, to induce a right choice, is not that of mechanical force. He operates upon mind, not by the laws of matter, but by the laws of *mental* operation. His method of approach to us, when he would gain our consent to be his, is on this wise: "*Behold, I stand at the door and knock.*"

By his providential dealings, by his teaching and example, and especially by the influences of the Holy Spirit, he presents himself to us as a friend, knocking at our door to gain admission. He comes to save us from sin, reclaim us to God, and give us foretastes and hopes of eternal life. He does not knock once or twice, and then, if unanswered, turn away. His attempts to gain admission are so repeated, that he is said to "*stand* at the door."

"If any man *hear* my voice, and *open* unto me." We must *attend* to his teachings; we must *hearken* to his call. *We* must also "*open*" the door to him. The act implied in opening the door, is, *our free consent to receive him.* We must be cordially *willing* to have him enter, to abide with us as our indwelling and informing Word, and to be our only and our sufficient Saviour.

To every one who shall thus receive him, he graciously promises, "I will come in to him, and will sup with him and he with me." The cordial consent gained, Christ enters, mutual friendship is declared, and the royal banquet commences.

We hence see that Christianity respects the natural laws of the will, as truly as she does those of the other mental powers. She treats us as voluntary, not less than as susceptible and as intelligent beings. She aims to move the will and the whole heart through the intellect, and to induce us heartily to *choose* "the good part that shall never be taken away from us." And if all history and observation are not false, by thus yielding our hearts to Christ and following him, we are sure to reach the highest moral excellence attainable upon earth.

RELATION OF CHRISTIANITY TO REASON AND CONSCIENCE. —It has been objected to Christianity that she does not appeal to our *reason*, but to our *faith*. It is said that she does not address us as rational beings, but as confiding, trusting beings, who, sensible of our ignorance and feebleness, and awed by the majesty of her miracles, have only to prostrate our reason at her feet, and follow her commands with a blind and submissive credulity.

Christianity does, indeed, make demands upon our faith; nor could she otherwise be true to our necessities. We have seen that faith is itself a sublime virtue, and is parent to many others. She also regards us as feeble and ignorant, nor could she truly regard us otherwise. She moreover commends herself to our homage, by stupendous miracles of power and grace, such as God only could perform; and this is what we ought to expect from such a Being, when putting his seal upon so important a message from his throne.

There is nothing unreasonable in all this; and if she teaches us things which unaided reason could never have known, this again is what we ought to expect; for why should she come to teach us only what we knew before, or could as well learn without her? It is enough that she teaches nothing *contrary* to reason; that she sanctions and confirms all that reason could learn without her; and then, taking the human mind in charge, conducts it straight upward in the same path, upon which it has by the light of reason entered, to the full blaze of eternal light and glory.

We have seen that the essential principles of morality are perceived in the concrete, by the intuitions of reason, and that actions conformed to them are cardinal virtues. These, conscientiously practised, are the only true basis of morality, and they lie also at the foundation of Christianity. She is thus an eminently *reasonable* religion. She rests her claims upon the decisions of enlightened conscience, and commands us to judge and to act, not less in religion than in other matters, as rational beings. Hence, to deny the fundamental principles of Christianity, is to subvert morality; to be false to our own nature, and to act irrationally in the highest degree.

In the chapter upon Conscience we have seen that this faculty, in the large and Scriptural sense, includes the reason and understanding. All of its admonitions, appeals, rebukes, all the pangs and all the joys it imparts, depend upon the intellective powers. In its legitimate exercise, it never admonishes us to act unreasonably. It never inflicts upon us a pang, for doing what we believe to be a truly reasonable act; it has no joys for us, in reward for an unreasonable one. A man justly reproaches himself, only when he sees that his feelings and conduct are unworthy of himself as a rational being. Christianity without and conscience within unite in one voice, commanding us to devote *all* our powers of body, of feeling, and of will, to the noblest and most "reasonable service." Thus she enthrones herself in our rational nature, and employs all the force of conscience within, and all the machinery of government without to make us faithful to its high demands. The truest Christian is the best of moralists and the most reasonable of men.

CHAPTER V.

REVEALED FACTS OF CHRISTIANITY.

THE most important of the revealed *facts*, from which are deduced the principles of Christian morality, are the following:

1. THE EXISTENCE AND PERFECTIONS OF THE TRUE GOD.—None of the heathen nations seem to have arrived at any certainty upon the question, whether there are several gods or only one. Even the wisest of the Grecian and Roman philosophers were in doubt upon this subject.

Christianity has settled it. She reveals one only living and true God, and condemns all other claims to divinity.

Pagan nations have also been ever in doubt respecting the *moral perfections* of God. They have usually invested their deities with some malignant passions. But Christianity has taught us that "*God is love;*" thus divesting him of every malignant temper, and revealing him as a Being of infinite moral excellence. Perhaps no cause has operated more disastrously upon the morality of heathen nations, than their imparting to their deities gross and selfish feelings.

2. The Creation of Man.—Revelation apart, mankind have never been able to come to any tolerable conjecture respecting their origin. Speculations upon this point have been endless, and all equally unsatisfactory. Christianity has taught us, re-uttering the language of the Hebrew Scriptures, that "in the beginning God *created* man male and female;" and that the human race have sprung, by natural descent, from this divinely created pair.

3. The Primitive Purity of Man.—Whether man has ever been in a state of perfect *purity*, has also been questioned. Poets have sung of a golden age, a purer state, from which we have degenerated; but even this conception seems to have been remotely due to revelation. Christianity reveals the primitive purity of man; and by thus holding distinctly before us the state for which we were designed; what we have been, may be, ought to be, and, if we embrace the gospel, *will* be, is at once a guide and incentive to moral excellence.

4. The Origin and Extent of Human Sinfulness.—All agree that mankind are sinful, but how they came to be so, none have been able to tell us. Christianity instructs us, that our first parents became sinners by transgressing the divine command; and that the transgression, thus commenced, has been perpetuated by their descendants. Our first parents fell from their allegiance, became indisposed to obey God; and their posterity have the disposition which their progenitors had after they fell.

Christianity enlightens us also respecting the *extent* of human sinfulness; teaching us that it is *universal*. "*All* have gone out of the way." "There is *none* that doeth good, *no*, *not one*." This fact is of great importance, in a moral as well as religious view. We are *all* in fault. We cannot glory over one another; boasting is excluded.

Humility and repentance are cardinal moral virtues, equally binding upon all mankind.

5. The Dispensation of Grace.—Whether there is help for human sinfulness, or whether men must impotently submit to its dominion and inevitably pay the penalty incurred by sin, it seems to have been impossible for unaided reason fully to determine. Christianity has revealed a dispensation of *grace.* "God so loved the world that he gave his only begotten Son, that whosoever believeth in him might not perish, but have eternal life." He has thus revealed himself a *redeeming* God. A sun of *righteousness* has thus risen upon the world, "with *healing* in his wings." There is *hope* for man, fallen and guilty though he be.

A healing and restoring process is going on all around us; should it pass by the human soul? This gracious dispensation is the most effective of all means to promote morality, causing the main difference between the morals of Christian and those of pagan nations. Upon the redeeming grace of God in Christ, the world's morality, as well as its religion, ultimately depends.

6. The Certainty of Future Existence and Retribution.—That we shall exist, in some mode, beyond the grave, has been imagined, hoped, and even expected, by pagan philosophers. But the *certainty* of this, it remained for Christianity to reveal. "Life and immortality are *brought to light in the Gospel.*"

Christianity assures us that we shall exist as conscious and accountable beings beyond the grave; that we shall be righteously judged; and that we shall receive according to the deeds done in the body. "For we must all appear before the judgment-seat of Christ, that every one may receive the things done in his body, whether they be good or bad." This revealed fact is of the highest practical importance to the cause of morality. Indeed, the validity of an oath, and the main supports of civil and religious freedom, depend in great measure upon it.

7. The Resurrection of the Body.—Arguments for the resurrection of the body have been drawn from the analogies of nature, especially from the seeming resurrection of the vegetable and lower animal creations. But these are *mere* analogies, after all; they positively prove nothing. For the *proof* of this doctrine, we are entirely dependent upon Christianity. She informs us that our immortal spirits will hereafter be invested with immortal bodies. They will not be, like these, gross, sensual, earthy; they will be spiritual, refined, angelic. Yet they will sustain to these some unrevealed important relation of identity. "So, also, is the resurrection of the dead. It is sown in corruption, it is raised in incorruption; it is sown in dishonor, it is raised in glory; it is sown in weakness, it is raised in power; it is sown a natural body, it is raised a spiritual body."

As this is a doctrine entirely *above* the reach of unaided reason, but not contrary to it, it is the province of reason to receive it by faith as a learner; not doubting that God is able to teach us, by revelation, what we could not otherwise have known. If the claims of Christianity as a revelation from God are well established, the resurrection of the dead is a fact in the future as certain as our death. The same Omnipotence that lays the body in the dust, can rob the grave of its treasure, and from the ruin and waste of ages clothe every redeemed spirit with a glorious immortal form.

As to the *moral tendency* of the doctrine, we cannot fail to see, that if we are to be raised incorruptible, and an important relation is to be for ever realized between our mortal and our immortal bodies, we are under powerful inducements not to yield our "members as instruments of unrighteousness unto sin," but "as instruments of righteousness unto God."

PRINCIPLES OF DUTY DEDUCED FROM CHRISTIANITY.

These, then, are the leading *facts*, for the knowledge of which we are mostly indebted to revelation: the existence and perfections of the true God; the creation of man; the primitive purity of man; the origin and extent of human sinfulness; the dispensation of grace; the certainty of future existence and retribution; and the resurrection of the dead.

If Christianity is true, these revealed facts impose obligations upon us *additional* to those imposed by the light of nature. Where much is given much also is required. Thus, although Christianity does not *make* us accountable beings, it greatly *enhances* our accountability.

From the first of the above revealed facts, we clearly and fully learn the duty, already partially taught by the light of nature, *to render supreme religious homage to one only living and true God.*

From the second, we learn the direct claim of God upon us, as *the Maker of our frames and the Father of our spirits*, and our general duty to all mankind, as *children with us of a common Father.*

From the third, we see in man's original character, which God pronounced "very good," the *moral and spiritual excellence for which we were made, and to which we should aspire.*

From the fourth, we deduce the rule of duty, binding alike upon all men, *to be penitent and humble before God for our sins;* the penalty of neglecting it being announced in the weighty words of Christ himself, "*Except ye repent, ye shall all likewise perish.*"

From the fifth, it becomes our manifest duty, not only to be penitent for our sins, but also to *trust the proffered grace of God for pardon and salvation;* accepting the generous provisions of his Gospel, and reposing in the assurance that "*he who believeth shall be saved.*"

From the sixth, we learn the rule of duty *always to conduct in view of the righteous retributions of eternity.*

From the seventh, we learn that we ought to rise above the servile fear of death and the grave, *and so to consecrate* "*our bodies a living sacrifice unto God,*" *that we may hope to live and shine with them before his throne for ever, in new and glorious forms.*

If Christianity is true, we are all bound to adopt the above principles and to act habitually upon them. Such is Christian morality. It conducts us quite up to the borders of purely spiritual philosophy, upon which the limit of our present subject does not permit us to enter.

Along with the revelation of these momentous *facts*, and her bright and shining array of precepts and warnings attending them, Christianity has also enjoined upon us certain *Institutions*, which are of the highest importance, both to our temporal and eternal welfare. She did not *originate* them all, but she has put her seal upon them, and has placed mankind under a bond sacredly to regard them. These are the Sabbath, Marriage, Public Worship, the Church and its ordinances, and Civil Government.

CHAPTER VI.

INSTITUTIONS OF CHRISTIANITY.

THE SABBATH.

A HEBDOMADAL period of rest and devotion is rendered necessary by the physical, the intellectual, the moral, and the religious wants of the human race.

The *physical* wants of both man and beast demand it. All laboring men, and all domesticated animals subjected to service, need one day in seven for repose. This has been proved by careful induction of facts. Those communities which most faithfully observe the Sabbath as a day of rest, enjoy the most vigorous and prolonged health. The French nation, at the period of the great revolution, *decimated* the time, allowing only one day in *ten* for rest; but this was found insufficient, and they were obliged to return to the observance of one day in seven.

The *intellect*, as well as the body, requires the same rest. Clergymen, whose vocation calls for special mental activity upon the Sabbath, find it necessary to rest upon the following day. Those who fail to allow their minds an amount of repose tantamount to one day in seven, are not long able to endure the labors of their profession.

Mental rest is found in *change*. It is not so much in doing *less*, as in doing something *else*, that the mind recovers its exhausted vigor. The laboring man who spends the Sabbath as he ought, gives his mind more activity, perhaps, upon that day than upon others; but it is a kind of activity that relieves it of the burden which it has borne through the week, and prepares it to resume that burden with renewed vigor for the week to come. While the merchant, the politician, the professional man, finds in the calm and elevated devotions of the Sabbath the only adequate repose from the bustle and vexations of secular time.

More especially is the Sabbath needful to man as a *moral* and *religious* being. No elevated state of morals has ever been sustained without it. Mere intellectual culture, however severe and refined, cannot supply its place. The morals of the Greeks and Romans, even under the most rigorous discipline, became so debased as to subvert their civil institutions. Without the Sabbath, no nation has ever been able to establish and perpetuate free institutions.

By turning our minds to our moral and religious responsibilities, by leading us to thoughtful reflections upon the past and anticipations of the future, by enlightening and quickening our consciences, the Sabbath becomes an essential means of improving our character. Those communities which best observe the Sabbath, are the most intelligent, virtuous, and pious. The habitual violators of it, even in the best communities, usually become debauched in morals, and frequently end their lives in disgrace.

Perceiving thus a *necessity* for the Sabbath, we reasonably presume that God has instituted one. Let us then briefly inquire whether a hebdomadal Sabbath, that is, the observance of one day in seven as a time of rest, has been divinely appointed. Our examination covers three distinct periods; the first, from the creation to Moses; the second, from Moses to Christ; the third, from Christ till the present time. We have thus the Primitive, the Mosaic, and the Christian Sabbath.

THE PRIMITIVE SABBATH.

In the book of Genesis, the second chapter, we find that as soon as God had created the world he instituted a Sabbath. "Thus the heavens and the earth were finished, and all the host of them; and on the seventh day God ended his work which he had made; and he *rested* on the seventh day from all his work which he had made. And God *blessed the seventh day, and sanctified it;* because that in it he had rested from all his work which God created and made."

We are here taught the following facts:

1. As his crowning act at the completion of creation, God ordained a *Sabbath.* It was "made for *man*," as Christ has taught us; made for him in his infancy, that he might, under its benign influence, be trained up in virtue and piety. As it was given to our progenitors, it was of course given to the *race* whom they represented. It is an institution coeval with creation, and enduring as the human family.

2. He not only ordained a Sabbath, but set us the example of *observing* it. He himself "*rested* on the seventh day." And we are expressly taught in the twentieth chapter of Exodus, that his rest was divinely intended to be an example for us to follow.

3. He also "*blessed*" the day. He put the seal of his special favor upon it, as the day above all others fraught with his richest gifts to man.

4. He "*sanctified*" it. That is, he set it apart, or consecrated it, from secular to sacred purposes. Thus by his positive act, it was set apart from the other days of the week expressly for religious purposes.

In the brief history of the race furnished in the Septuagint, from the creation to the time of Moses, we find distinct reference to this Sabbath. Noah was commanded to enter the ark, with his family and the numerous creatures committed to him, "seven days" before the flood. This command seems to have provided against his trespassing upon the Sabbath; as the gathering of so many creatures together with all his effects into the ark, would occupy several days. For a similar reason, he waited seven days between the times of sending forth the dove.

We find explicit reference to this Sabbath in the sixteenth chapter of Exodus. The Israelites are there expressly commanded to provide manna beforehand for this day. "This is that which the Lord hath said, To-morrow is the *rest of the Holy Sabbath* unto the Lord." When some of the people violated the injunction, they were sternly rebuked, "How long refuse ye to keep my commandments and my law? See, for that the Lord *hath given you the Sabbath*, therefore he giveth you on the sixth day the bread of two days; abide ye every man in his place, let no man go out of his place on the seventh day. *So the people rested on the seventh day.*"

Thus it appears that the Sabbath was instituted, observed, and blessed by God, and was also made obligatory upon men, *previous to the Mosaic law given on Sinai.* The earliest Grecian and Roman classics, also, refer to the hebdomadal division of time.

THE MOSAIC SABBATH.

This is the same as the Sabbath of creation, reaffirmed by the voice of God on Sinai. But as the command to observe it was incorporated in the civil and religious code furnished by Moses, it is hence called the *Mosaic Sabbath.* Three particulars must here be noticed.

1. The government of the Israelites was a *Theocracy;* that is, a government administered by God, having both a civil and religious end. Hence some of the laws given to them through Moses were of a national character, binding only on this particular people; while others were of a strictly moral and religious character, equally obligatory upon all men.

2. Of the latter is the *command to keep the Sabbath.* It is found in the law of the Ten Commandments, which is always referred to in the Scriptures as containing the sum of the moral code given by God to man. Jesus Christ and his apostles, who made a distinction between what was moral and religious, and what was ceremonial and national, always referred to the *Sabbath* as an institution of *permanent* and *universal* obligation. "The Sabbath," said Christ, "was made for *man;*" that is, for man in general, for the *human race.* It is an institution which all men equally need, and are equally bound to observe.

3. The Sabbath was set apart not only as a day of *rest* from secular pursuits, but of *religious worship.* While the most solemn denunciations were uttered against those who desecrated it to secular purposes, most animating promises of favor were made to those who kept it holy unto the Lord. "If thou turn away thy foot from the Sabbath, from doing thy pleasure on my holy day, and call the Sabbath a delight, the holy of the Lord, honor-

able; and shalt honor him, not doing thine own ways, nor finding thine own pleasures, nor speaking thine own words; then shalt thou delight thyself in the Lord, and I will cause thee to ride upon the high places of the earth, and feed thee with the heritage of Jacob thy father; for the mouth of the Lord hath spoken it." "From one Sabbath to another, shall all flesh come to *worship* before me, saith the Lord." The Sabbath was sacredly observed by the Jews as a day of solemn convocation and of preaching.*

THE CHRISTIAN SABBATH.

The Christian Sabbath is a continuation of the Mosaic. The only material question here respects the *change of the time* from the seventh to the first day of the week. The solution of the question is found in the following particulars:—

1. Although the necessity for the Sabbath exists in nature, this necessity does not indicate *any one day in preference to another.* It is one seventh portion of time that is needed for rest and devotion; and, considered merely in this view, it is not material which day is taken.

2. The wisdom of God, which frequently secures subordinate ends along with the main one, at the creation of the world chose the *last* day of the seven for the Sabbath, because it fitly commemorated the great work which he had then completed. This was the reason assigned by him why he *then* preferred the seventh day to any other.

3. But he regarded the work of *redemption greater* than the original work of creation. "Behold," he says, "I create a *new* heaven and a *new* earth: and the former *shall not be remembered*, nor come into mind." This new

* See Neh. 13: 15–21. Isaiah 58: 13. Lev. 23: 3. Isaiah 66: 23. Acts 15: 21.

creation is evidently the work of redemption by Jesus Christ. As it transcends in a moral and religious view the first creation, the same reason which designated the *seventh* day for the Sabbath under the *old* dispensation, designated the *first* day under the *new*. Each alike immediately follow the completion of the great work which it commemorates.

Such, then, are the *reasons* for the change. Let us now see whether the change was actually made by divine authority.

1. The first day of the week commemorates *the completion of the work of redemption.* On the morning of this day the Lord arose from the dead, and thus turned the thoughts of his disciples upon *this* as henceforth the *great day* of his church. It was from this time called the *Lord's day.*

2. On the next Lord's day, *one week from his resurrection*, he appeared to his apostles.* It was then that he conversed with Thomas. The disciples were assembled within a house, evidently for worship. Thus early did Christians commence observing this day.

3. From that time they *continued* to assemble for worship on the first day of the week, and in so doing acted by the authority of God, and with his signal blessing. Their great Pentecostal season; their stated meetings to celebrate the Lord's supper; their contributions for benevolent objects; the spiritual raptures of John in Patmos; were all upon this day.†

4. What was thus commenced by the inspired Apostles, *was continued by their immediate successors.* The early Fathers speak of this day as the one set apart for religious worship, because it commemorates the resurrec-

* John 20: 26.

† See 1 Cor. 11: 14. 1 Cor. 16: 1, 2. Acts 20: 6. Rev. 1: 10.

tion of the Lord. The celebrated letter of Pliny to Trajan, in which he speaks of the stated meetings of Christians for worship, is to the same effect. All the earliest ecclesiastical historians testify, that Christians observed the Lord's day as holy time.

Should any still object to the change, we may add that the universal observance of the first day by Christians renders it extremely inconvenient, if not quite impracticable, for a few individuals strictly to observe any other; and that the example of inspired Apostles, with the seal of God's approbation, ought to suffice with every reasonable conscience to establish the divine authority of the Christian Sabbath.

WHEN THE SABBATH BEGINS.

The Jewish Sabbath commenced on the *eve* of the day; that is, on the evening *preceding* the Sabbath day. Many have inferred from this, that the Christian Sabbath should commence at the same time. But a leading idea of the Jewish Sabbath was *rest*, which naturally commences at the *close* of the day; while a leading idea of the Christian Sabbath is *resurrection*, *rising*, which naturally occurs in the *morning*. It was then that Christ arose.

It is also generally admitted, for good reasons, that we should commence the Sabbath at the same time we commence other days. If, however, any still prefer to commence their Sabbath on Saturday evening, they have the example of our excellent Puritan ancestors, and usually, also, the advantage of keeping two evenings as holy time instead of one.

CHAPTER VII.

INSTITUTIONS OF CHRISTIANITY CONTINUED.

MARRIAGE.

THE conjugal relation was instituted by God in paradise before the fall. It is not, then, like some institutions, a mere expedient of a fallen state; it belongs to man in innocence. It originated in the fact that our race was made male and female, each having peculiarities of constitution, temperament, and disposition, which could find their appropriate object only in the other sex. Hence God said, "It is not good that man should be alone."

The institution remains unchanged.—It survived the fall, and subsequently the great deluge, which swept all but one family from the earth. The Abrahamic covenant ratified and confirmed it; the revolutions of the Jewish state and polity did not change it; Messiah's advent gave it new confirmation; and, at the calling of the Gentiles, it was passed over to them with all its original sanctions. Thus launched in the beginning upon the stream of ages, it has passed through all its breaks and rapids, has outrode every storm, and has descended in its primitive integrity to these latter ages. It will thus endure until the end of time.

The conjugal union is both a religious and civil contract, formed by the mutual choice of the parties. They are united as husband and wife, agreeably to the design of the Creator, as indicated by the constitution of the sexes and by his word. It has ever been found an indispensable means of promoting industry, intelligence, morals, and religion.

Wherever it has been disregarded, the people have descended to all the abominations of pagan licentiousness. All that is dear in natural affection, lovely in virtue, and glorious in religion, has there been sacrificed. No marvel that an institution so important should have been ordained by God, under most solemn sanctions, and that the nations most highly civilized and moral are precisely those who have enjoyed its benign influence.

It thus appears that *polygamy is not of divine origin.* The parties originally united in the conjugal relation were *one man with one woman.* God gave to Adam but *one* wife. Polygamy was introduced by the wickedness of mankind. God never approved of it, although for a time he "*endured*" it, as he often has other evils, to avoid those which, under the circumstances, might be greater. "For the hardness of your heart," said Christ, "Moses wrote you this precept, *but from the beginning of the creation* God made them male and female. For this cause a man shall leave father and mother, and cleave to his wife, and they *twain* shall be one flesh. What, therefore, God hath joined together, let not man put asunder."

The marriage covenant is binding *during the natural life of both the parties.* Nothing but death, or the infidelity of one of the parties, can annul it. "What, therefore, God hath joined together," said Christ, "*let not man put asunder.*" "Whosoever *shall put away his wife*, except it be for fornication, and shall marry another, committeth adultery."

This covenant is subject to the will of God, and can involve no promise, or duty, at variance with morality and religion. The command, "Wives, submit yourselves unto your own husbands, as unto the Lord, has sometimes been supposed to imply *absolute* submission. But it evidently would not be a submission as *unto the Lord*, if it involved the violation of any religious obligation. The same principle applies to each of the sexes. Neither can have a right to require of the other what conscience does not approve. They may enlighten and convince each other; but if light and argument fail, they must agree to differ.

The covenant presupposes these points settled. It is ordinarily inexpedient, to say the least, for parties to unite in marriage who are not of the same religious faith. "How can two walk together *except they be agreed?*" The evils resulting from want of union on this vital subject, are often lasting as life, and they seriously affect the destinies of the children.

It has been thought unreasonable that the relation of each party to the other should be restricted for life to a single individual. But when we consider, that the equality of the sexes in number is the same now as it was at the beginning, when God "made them male and female," and thus by his creative act constituted them to unite in *pairs;* and when we consider, further, that the laws of both body and mind, and the united voices of all human experience, affirm that the benign purposes of the institution can be fully secured in no other way, the entire reasonableness of the restriction is put for ever at rest.

PUBLIC WORSHIP.

The public worship of God was an institution of the Mosaic religion, and was modified and adopted by Christianity. All pagan nations have some forms of public worship, and the more cultivated of them, as the Greeks and Romans, erected for this purpose temples and altars. Sometimes they erected temples even to "unknown gods;" so urgent is the feeling in man that he ought to worship.

But in the Christian religion, the public worship of "the only living and true God" is instituted with a simplicity and a distinctness beautifully appropriate to its sublime object. We are there taught to worship God "*in spirit and in truth.*" While Christ was upon earth, he worshipped thus with his disciples; and after his death, they were accustomed to assemble for the same worship upon the Christian Sabbath; thus transmitting to us, by their example as well as teaching, not only the institution itself, but the nature of the service enjoined.

This public worship of God was not designed to supersede private devotion, nor any personal and relative duties whatever, but to provide for the social religious principle of our nature; to afford us opportunity to pay our united homage to our common Lord and Saviour, and thus to anticipate upon earth the eternal worship above.

THE CHURCH.

A covenant existed between the people of God under the ancient dispensation, which has been modified and perpetuated in the form of the Christian church. The church was instituted by the apostles, under the immediate guidance of heaven; it was by them planted in numerous places, and great numbers were added to it under their ministry.

In Palestine, in Asia-Minor, in Macedonia, in Greece, in Rome, the apostles preached the Gospel with success, and established churches. These churches were visibly separate bodies, having local interests; but they were spiritually one and the same church of their common Lord and Saviour. They were all one in Christ.

The institution of the Christian church has descended to us, with all its divine sanctions. It is as obligatory upon us, as it was upon Christians of the first century. The same reasons still exist, why Christians should publicly espouse the cause of their Master, acknowledge their faith in him, and covenant with each other in sacred fellowship. Man is still the same being, and Christianity is still the same religion. And experience has abundantly proved, that the Christian church, in its pure state, is an advocate and support of every virtue and morality, and a "pillar and ground of the truth."

The Christian church has *two ordinances*, Baptism, and the Lord's Supper.

BAPTISM.—The ordinance of *baptism* seems to have been observed, in some form, before the advent of Christ. John the Baptist, his forerunner, administered it, and Christ himself was baptized by him on entering upon his great mission. Although Christ did not himself baptize, he commanded his disciples to do so. In obedience to his instruction, wherever they preached the Gospel successfully they also baptized.

And that the ordinance might not be restricted to that particular age or people, Christ gave to his disciples as his last command, after his resurrection, "Go ye, therefore, and teach *all nations*, *baptizing them* in the name of the Father, and of the Son, and of the Holy Ghost;

and lo I am with you *always, even unto the end of the world.*" Thus authorized, the ordinance is to descend to the end of time.

Baptism seems to have been appropriated by Christianity as a badge or seal of discipleship, and an emblem of purification. As an ordinance of the Christian church, it indicates the purity required of those who become members of it, and serves to perpetuate its identity, distinctness, and organic power.

THE LORD'S SUPPER.—This ordinance was enjoined by Christ, a short time before his death. Its design is clearly indicated by his own words. "Jesus took bread, and blessed, and brake it, and gave to them, and said, Take, eat; this is my body. And he took the cup, and when he had given thanks, he gave it to them; and they all drank of it. And he said unto them, This is my blood of the New Testament, which is shed for many." This ordinance is then designed to commemorate the death of Christ. With this view it was transmitted, by his authority, to Christians of all ages.

"For I have received of the Lord," an apostle informs us, "that which also I delivered unto you, that the Lord Jesus, the same night in which he was betrayed, took bread; and when he had given thanks, he brake it, and said, This is my body, which is broken for you; this do in remembrance of me. After the same manner also he took the cup, when he had supped, saying, This cup is the New Testament in my blood, this do ye, as oft as ye drink it, in remembrance of me. For as often as ye eat this bread and drink this cup, ye do show the Lord's death till he come."*

That there should be a special ordinance to commem-

* Matt. 26: 26. 1 Cor. 11:

orate so important an event as the death of Christ, is in the highest degree reasonable; while the severe and repeated self-inspection enjoined as a prerequisite to its observance, must, if faithfully performed, be greatly conducive to purity of heart and life. "Let a man *examine* himself; and so let him eat."

CIVIL GOVERNMENT.

Civil Government, like the preceding institutions, is not a mere conventional arrangement of men. It is a *divine* institution. It was formally sanctioned, and duties respecting it were enjoined, in both the Old and the New dispensations from heaven. To fulfil their destiny, men must live *in society;* and it was not the will of God, that they should dwell together in a state of anarchy. Accordingly we find civil government existing, by his appointment, under guidance of the Patriarchs, and subsequently under the leadership of Moses; and obedience to its laws was by him enforced with severe penalties.

When Christ came, he did not annul the institution, but inculcated the duty of sustaining it. He distinguished between temporal and spiritual governments, and required due regard to both. He enjoined obedience to all civil laws, so far as they are consistent with the laws of God.

SUMMARY.

We have thus briefly noticed the leading *doctrines* and *institutions* of Christianity. The reader will see that by this religion we understand the entire revelation made to us in the Bible, of which Christianity is the consummation. The rules of conduct which it prescribes are called *revealed* principles, in distinction from those which are purely *natural*. The latter are also *essential*, having their reason and authority in themselves, while the former are *positive*, resting their claim upon the authority of divine revelation.

But Christianity enjoins also the natural principles of morality as well as those which she reveals. She would have us not fail to be true to nature, as well as to herself; she therefore teaches us that we can be dutiful to her, only as we are so to nature also. She embraces in her wide domain the entire ground of both natural and revealed morality. She holds it to be as immoral in us to violate a principle of the one as of the other. Arraigned at her bar, an act of injustice to a fellow-being is as truly an immorality as the profanation of the Sabbath; and the worship of God is as binding upon every individual as the duty of temperance.

We have considered the *evidences* for Christianity only so far as they are involved in a purely *moral* view. Our single inquiry has been, What is *right?* What *ought* to be? We have seen that the requirements of Christianity, so far as they are viewed in the light of morality taught by nature and approved by conscience, are wholly reasonable and just, and that we cannot disown the morality of Christianity without disowning that of nature also. But there are also positive external evidences of her divine mission, which no man has ever been able to refute. They have become established historical *facts*, as truly so as those relating to Grecian and Roman history. The examination of these does not come within the design of the present work.

But the thoughtful reader will not fail to see that even the purely moral claims of Christianity, which are only a part of its internal evidences, are convincing proof of its divine origin, while the flood of clear light which it pours upon the feeble teachings of nature, and its revelation of new and momentous truths rising high above them, impose upon us peculiar and most weighty obligations. For in a strictly moral view, our obligations are in proportion to what we receive. Where much is given, much is also justly required; hence no moral system can be entire which leaves the claims of Christianity out of view.

Christianity, as I have before said, does not make us accountable beings; nor is she responsible for the helpless and miserable condition in which she finds us. She finds us as we are; she had no agency in making us so. Her entire mission to us is one of mercy and redemption. Nor was her mission uncalled for by our condition. There was no other eye to pity, no other arm to save. Without her aid, despite of all his science and philosophy, man is in deep darkness respecting the most important of all subjects. He is an awful mystery to himself. He stands trembling, with one foot in the grave, on the verge of an unknown eternity, with a burden of guilt upon his conscience and of sorrow in his heart. He and the world must soon part for ever, and what then remains to him? A conscious existence? And if so, must he bear that guilt and that sorrow for ever? May he never look up and behold a smiling God, and bright heavens above and around him? Must the last throb of expiring nature, for aught he can see, separate him for ever from all that renders his existence desirable? Is there any name given under heaven amongst men, whereby he can be saved from sin, from sorrow, from the fear of death, from the grave itself, and be made to realize the lofty aspirations of his rational and immortal being?

In vain does he invoke the heathen oracles, in vain summon all the philosophers of the olden and the modern times, in vain importune science, in its profoundest researches, to answer these inquiries. All human tongues, all science, and all nature, are here silent. Even the shining orbs of heaven, that hymn so eloquently their Maker's praise, and which inspired the sublimest strains of the royal minstrel, are voiceless here. It is in this our deep and fearful necessity, that Christianity comes to our rescue. By embracing her friendly hand and following her guidance, myriads have already overcome sin, temptation, and the fear of death, and have left behind them a shining path, through which they ascended into the heavens. She has the same triumphs for myriads more; for us and for all who will receive her. Does she not, then, impose upon us a special obligation? Is it not a fearful wrong, a vast and terrible immorality, to neglect this great salvation?

Unless all history and experience are false, in rejecting Christianity we reject the *only* means adequate to the salvation we need. This faith, ruling the heart and life, is the only victory that overcomes the world. Without this, there *is no* overcoming; life is all *under*coming, from the beginning to the end of it. The mark is ever low, the vision short and dim, the arm feeble; and even the bravest and most successful man, in the very act of reaching forth to grasp his wretched all, stumbles into his grave, and is soon forgotten! The winds sigh for a little time around his grave, and the storms of a few winters sweep over it, but finally even the winds forget where his dust was laid, and know not where to sing his requiem.

"Oh, what *is* this world," says an excellent author, in language whose beauty and force are equalled only by its severe and exact truthfulness, "when we have turned away from the cross of Christ, and from the instruction which God has given us in his word? Man is seen upon the earth a strange being, playing a strange part, and encircled by mysteries. He has been created he knows not by whom, or when, or for what end. He begins to sin as soon as he begins to act, but he knows not why. He finds himself prone to evil by some mysterious law for which there is no explanation. He suffers, he knows not why; he lives, he knows not for what end; and when he dies, he goes into another world, he knows not whither or why. He can do nothing to stay the progress of the plague which sweeps away the race, and he can only stand and weep over the grave which he digs for his pale brother, and which he himself must soon enter. He stretches out his hands to heaven, *as if* there might be help there, but none appears."

"His eye poureth out tears" as it is lifted towards the skies; it gazes intensely for light, but not a ray is seen. His nature pants to live for ever, but no response is given to the aspirings of his soul; nothing tells him that he *may* live. He is a poor, ignorant, degraded, and dying being, seeking for a guide and panting for a system of religion that will meet the wants of his nature and raise him up to God. Revealed religion comes and tells him who made him, and why; explains the way in which the race sank into this melancholy condition, and how it may be recovered; proposes promises adapted to him as an immortal being; reveals a brighter world, and explains to him how it may be his own." *

Our references to Christianity have thus far been with a view to showing its coincidence with the natural principles of morality, its adaptation to our constitution and necessities, the intrinsic reasonableness and justice of its claims, and, along with these, the positive obligations it imposes upon us, on the supposition that its divine authority is admitted.

* "The Way of Salvation," by Albert Barnes, p. 57.

If any of my readers demand other and more positive demonstrations of its divine authority, I must refer them to authors especially devoted to that service. In expounding the code of moral duties, I shall assume that the divine claims of Christianity *are* admitted. Pure morality enjoins, as we have seen, supreme regard to the will of God. That will is made known to us in the *essential* principles of duty addressed to every man's conscience by the light of nature, and in the *revealed* principles of duty furnished us by the Bible. These, united, are God's COMPREHENSIVE LAW, our supreme and ultimate RULE OF RIGHT, in obedience to which we are to secure the true end for which we were made.

PART V.

THE CODE OF DUTIES.

CHAPTER I.

RELIGIOUS DUTIES.

We are now prepared to expound the code of duties. Having examined their grounds and principles, we are next to explain and enforce them, presenting them in connection as constituting a complete system of practical morality. We begin with religious duties, or our duties to God.

In the highest sense we owe *all* our duties to God, as the subjects of his supreme authority ; duties to ourselves and our fellow-creatures being demanded by his law. But we are now to consider those duties which we owe to God directly and exclusively. We are morally bound to be religious. We owe duties supremely to God, as well as subordinately to our fellow-beings. "*Will a man rob God?*" If a man is guilty who robs his fellow, much more is he who robs his Maker. Let us then proceed to consider our strictly religious duties, as demanded by the principle of moral obligation.

THE DUTY OF OBEDIENCE TO GOD.

Why is it our duty to obey the will of God? The an swer to this question will appear in the following facts:

1. His perfections render him WORTHY of our obedience. He is a being of infinite power, wisdom, justice, and benevolence. All those attributes which we were *made* to reverence and obey, exist in him in the highest possible degree. They shine forth in all his works like the sun in the firmament. We cannot open our eyes without beholding them; and we see them all engaged in sustaining and blessing the universe which he has made.

2. He is our CREATOR. To him we owe our existence. But for his sovereign pleasure, we should have had no part nor lot in the universe. Yonder sun might have walked the skies as brightly as he now does; the morning stars might have sung together as sweetly; the heavenly choirs might have rolled up as loud and harmonious anthems of praise; Jehovah might have been as great and glorious in all his works, though our existence had been no part of his purpose. It is then of his generosity alone that we exist, and are put in relation to the wealth of the universe.

3. He is our PRESERVER. Our obligation to his preserving care is as constant as the moments of our lives. Should he withhold his sustaining power, we must instantly perish. "Thou hidest thy face, they are troubled; thou takest away their breath, they die and return to the dust." This was said of the brute creation, and is equally true of us. Whether we are asleep or awake, we depend

upon his guardian care, to deal out to us one breath after another, and send the warm currents of life through our veins.

4. He is our BENEFACTOR. All the blessings we enjoy come of his hand. "The eyes of all wait upon thee, and thou givest them their meat in due season. Thou openest thine hand, and satisfiest the desire of every living thing." Every moment comes to us laden with the fruits of his bounty. Through all our senses, through all our powers of thought and feeling, he ministers to our enjoyment. By day and by night, at home and abroad, in health and in sickness, amid all the vicissitudes of life, from the cradle to the grave, we are the constant recipients of his gifts.

5. He is our RIGHTFUL RULER. He has made us capable of knowing his will, and of perceiving our obligations to obey it. He reigns over the universe to uphold its laws and promote its welfare, through the willing and obedient service of his accountable subjects. If we disregard his pleasure and refuse to serve him, if we thus set our wills in opposition to his, we are both false to him and to the interests of the moral kingdom over which he reigns.

6. He is our REDEEMER. We have rebelled against him, and have thus rendered ourselves obnoxious to his justice. But instead of inflicting its demands upon us, he has graciously provided for our redemption. He "so *loved* the world, that he gave his only begotten Son, that whosoever believeth on him should not perish, but have eternal life." "*For ye are not your own, but ye are bought with a price; wherefore glorify God in your spirit and in your bodies, which are his.*"

NATURE OF THE SERVICE DUE.

Thus the claim of God to our service is predicated upon his intrinsic worthiness, and his relation to us as our Creator, Preserver, Benefactor, Ruler, and Redeemer. This service should be *cordial*, *supreme*, *reverential*, *constant.*

It should be *cordial.* Our whole heart should go with it. It should be our *meat* and *drink* to do the will of God. "I *delight* to do thy will, O my God; yea, thy law is *within my heart.*" Such should be our feelings in relation to the service of God.

It should be *supreme.* All other demands should give place to those of God. To do his will, should be the ruling motive of our lives. We have only to know what he would have us do, and the path of duty is bright as a sunbeam. To know his will is the highest study; to do it, the highest morality.

It should be *reverential.* We should consider the *majesty* of Him whom we attempt to serve. He is "THE GREAT AND DREADFUL GOD." At his presence "the pillars of heaven tremble, and are astonished." If we would acceptably serve a mere earthly potentate, we must do it with profound respect. How much more should we revere the "KING of kings." "Serve the Lord *with fear.*" "Let all the earth *fear* the Lord; let all the inhabitants of the world *stand in awe* of him."

It should be *constant.* The obedience required is not that of individual and disconnected acts; it is a deep and steady *principle.* It is like that mysterious power which holds the planets in steady allegiance to the sun. In some parts of their orbits they are nearer the sun and move faster than at others, but their hold upon the glorious object of their devotion is never relaxed for a moment.*

DUTY IN REFERENCE TO THE WORD OF GOD.

We have in our hands a Book of very ancient writings, claiming to be of divine authority, and hence called the Word of God. Of all the books ever written, this has exerted immeasurably the most power over the character and destinies of mankind. Under its influence, we see men reclaimed from vice to lives of virtue and benevolence; we see even whole nations redeemed from sottish idolatry to the rational and pure worship of the only living and true God. The most enlightened, virtuous, enterprising, and efficient people in the world, are precisely those most under the influence of this wonderful Book.

What then is our duty in respect to it? Evidently, to "*search*" it, with great care; and, if we have any doubt of its divine authority, to examine its credentials. The subject is too important to be neglected. A book claiming to contain a revelation from God, and attended with so many wonderful demonstrations of its divine origin and power, cannot be innocently disregarded.

If any one upon due examination professes to believe the book false, we must leave the strange person to his own thoughts, while we consider the duties implied in a rational conviction of its truth.

Receiving the Bible as from God, we ought to hold it in great *reverence*. To trifle with it; to quote from it with a view to pleasantry and jest; to question its veracity, or impugn its authority; in short, to treat it as we would a book of mere human origin, is immoral and profane. We are ever to consider that this book has the

* The nature of the *affection* due to God has been considered in a previous chapter. See page 169.

seal of God upon it; and if he will not hold him guiltless who taketh his *name* in vain, no more will he hold him guiltless who taketh his *word* in vain.

Still the Bible is a *rational* book, given in the language of men; and it is to be examined, interpreted, and applied, by the same rules which we apply to other books. We should read and study it, with the sincerity and earnestness becoming such a book, and with a prayerful desire to know its meaning. We should regard it as dutiful children would daily letters of instruction from a revered and beloved parent. We should thus keep our consciences enlightened in respect to duty.

We should faithfully *follow its instructions.* Every truth taught in the Bible we should eagerly embrace; every duty inculcated we should promptly obey. It is only as we thus honor it that we may hope to understand it, and thus become wiser and better by its teachings. "If any man will *do* his will, he shall *know of the doctrine.*" If there are portions of the Bible which we do not at first understand, this is the way to understand them. "Thy word is a light to my feet and a lamp to my path." "I have more understanding than all my teachers, *because I keep thy testimonies.*" "Search the Scriptures, for in them ye think ye have eternal life; and these are they which testify of me."

Better to be without all other books in the world, than to be without the Bible; better to neglect all other books, than to neglect this. "Young man," said Benjamin Franklin, when near his end, "my advice to you is, that you cultivate an acquaintance with and form a belief in the Holy Scriptures." "Attend," said Dr. Samuel Johnson, "to the voice of one who has possessed a certain degree of fame in the world, and who will shortly appear before his Maker. Read the Bible every day of your life." The great philosopher, John Locke, gives his advice thus: "Study the Holy Scriptures, especially the New Testament. Here are contained words of eternal life. It has God for its Author, salvation for its end, and truth, without any mixture of error, for its matter."

THE DUTY OF REPENTANCE AND FAITH.

We are not only dependent and accountable, but *sinful.* This is true of us all. "*All have sinned.*" This fact makes it *the duty of all to repent.* "God commandeth all men, every where, to repent." "Except ye repent, ye shall all likewise perish."

An offence against a fellow-being, is a *fault* or *crime;* an offence against God is a *sin.* Hence David said to God, "Against *thee, thee only,* have I *sinned.*" He had committed *crime* against man, but *sin* against God. Hence an offence against a fellow-being calls for *confession* and *amendment;* while an offence against God calls also for *repentance.* The reason is that repentance is a deep *spiritual* work, and God has to do with the heart.

Repentance of sin is not, as is often imagined, a mere painful excitement of the sensibilities, through fear of the divine displeasure; nor a feeling of mere regret for sin, in view of its natural consequences; nor the feeling termed remorse, inflicted by an offended conscience; nor a mere sentimental emotion, produced in view of sin by an excited imagination; it is *sincere contrition and cordial aversion for all sin, as an offence against God.*

It is always attended with earnest desires for purity of heart and life, and with vigorous endeavors after it; with a disposition to confess every sin to God, and to forsake it; with a feeling of dependence upon divine grace; with a sweetening of the social temper, and, so far as is needed, with reformation of conduct.

Religious *faith* is a hearty *trust* or *confidence* in God. Although the terms belief and faith are often used in the Scriptures synonymously, yet faith is more than mere belief. Belief may be only an act of the *intellect;* faith always includes also an act of the *heart.* "For with the *heart* man believeth unto righteousness." As God is infinitely worthy of our confidence, to withhold from him our faith is a great sin, and the source of *all other* sins. On the other hand, faith in God is the crowning act of obedience, and the mainspring of *all* obedience. "Without faith, it is impossible to please him."

As God has graciously offered us pardon and salvation through the Gospel, saving faith has a special reference to this overture. This is sometimes called *evangelical* faith, because it refers particularly to the gospel. It cordially welcomes the proclamation made by the Gospel, and places implicit reliance upon its proffered grace. Such faith works by love, imparts a filial spirit, transforms the character, and gives victory over sin and death.

THE DUTY OF PRAYER AND PRAISE.

The duty of prayer and praise, or what is usually called *worship*, has been ever recognized, in some form, by all religions. Christian prayer is the language of the human heart, addressed to God through Christ. It speaks to him of sins, fears, trials, wants; it supplicates his pardon, and seeks his favor. It is humble, earnest, believing, submissive.

It is *humble.* It is the offering of a contrite spirit. "The sacrifices of God are a *broken spirit*, a *broken and a contrite heart*, O God, thou wilt not despise." One of the most acceptable prayers ever offered, was in these words, "*God be merciful to me a sinner.*"

It is *earnest.* Realizing his pressing necessity, the suppliant pleads as for his life. We read of one, "who in the days of his flesh, when he had offered up prayers and supplications, *with strong crying and tears*, unto him that was able to save him from death, was heard in that he feared." Multitudes have successfully followed his example. Our Saviour has set us the same. He sometimes continued all night in prayer; and on one occasion the agony of his soul was such that he "prayed the *more earnestly*, and his sweat was, as it were, great drops of blood falling down to the ground." "The effectual *fervent* prayer of the righteous man *availeth much.*" There is not a promise in the Bible to a cold and heartless prayer.

It is *believing.* "He that cometh to God must *believe* that he is, and that he is a *rewarder* of those that diligently seek him." Christ said, "What things soever ye desire, when ye pray, *believe* that ye receive them, and ye *shall receive* them." It is an insult to God, to ask him to fulfil his promises, without believing that he will do so. As unbelief is the parent sin, and faith the parent grace, it is only as we pray in faith that we can pray aright, and thus avail with God.

It is *submissive.* The grace of the Holy Spirit is the only gift *absolutely* promised to prayer. For this only may we pray with invincible importunity and an assurance of receiving precisely what we ask. "How much more shall your Heavenly Father give the *Holy Spirit* to them that ask him." We should ask for mere earthly blessings, with a deep conviction of our incapacity to know what is best for us, and with submission to the ultimate decisions of divine wisdom. However earnestly we may desire what we seek, we should say, as Christ did, "*Nevertheless not as I will, but as thou wilt.*"

Such is the spirit of Christian prayer. We add, that it may be *private*, *social*, or *public*.

Private prayer is the offering of an *individual heart alone* to God. This is the spring of all true devotion; since none but those who pray in secret, can pray acceptably to God in public. Christ uttered the severest rebukes upon those who pray to be seen of men. "And when thou prayest, thou shalt not be as the hypocrites are; for they love to pray standing in the synagogues, and in the corners of the streets, that they may be seen of men. Verily I say unto you, they have their reward. But thou, when thou prayest, *enter into thy closet*, and when thou hast shut thy door, pray to thy Father which is in secret, and thy Father which seeth in secret shall reward thee openly." In the closet the heart opens all its wants, freely confesses its sins, and pours out its desires for personal good and for blessings upon others, with a freedom enjoyed only in secret. Jesus Christ was much alone in prayer.

Social prayer is the united offering of several hearts at once, in a small social gathering. Of this kind is *family* prayer. Even the heathens have their household gods and their family offerings. The mutual relations of husband and wife, of parents and children, and of children of the same family, are so intimate and peculiar, that their social recognition of dependence upon God, and their united supplication of his favor, is a most natural and important duty. Children can scarcely enjoy a greater earthly blessing, than that of being daily conducted by Christian parents to the throne of grace at the family altar. Long after their parents have become silent in the grave, they will remember their prayers with gratitude and joy. On the contrary, the divine malediction will fall alike upon heathen and upon prayerless families.

"Pour out thy fury upon the heathen that know thee not, and *upon the families that call not upon thy name.*"

Public prayer is the united offering of the hearts of God's people, when assembled in his house of worship. The devotional parts of the Old Testament are replete with public prayers; and the example and teachings of Christ and of his apostles, admonish us that public acts of devotion are a part of religious duty. The most beautiful and comprehensive model of public prayer is furnished in the words of Christ himself. In this form, called the Lord's Prayer, are embraced most of the essential ideas which usually enter into the public petitions of Christians.

Religious Praise is an expression of gratitude, adoration, and joyful homage to God, in view of his glorious perfections, and of blessings which he has bestowed upon us. It is as truly a duty as prayer, and is as earnestly enjoined in the Scriptures. It is, like prayer, private, social, and public. It is a pleasing consideration, that this part of religious devotion will not cease at death. We have no reason to suppose that there will be *prayer* in heaven, but we are assured that *praise* will enter largely into the employments of the heavenly state.

The question is often asked, why prayer and praise are *enjoined*, since they cannot benefit God? Knowing our wants before we ask, as well as after, why does he wait to be requested? and why demand our praise, which can add nothing to his glory? The answer is briefly this. The affairs of the world move on, for obvious reasons, in an established order of sequence. Each event is preceded by another preparatory to it. No blessing comes to us without its appropriate antecedent. If the grass is to grow, there must be rain; if there is to be rain, there must be clouds; and if clouds, the causes which form them. The same law of antecedence obtains in the kingdom of mind. It is as unphilosophical to say that prayer, the divinely appointed antecedent to the gift of the Holy Spirit, has no agency in securing the desired blessing, as to say that the cloud has no agency in producing rain. God could doubtless give us rain without clouds, and so he could give us the Holy Spirit without prayer, but that is not his way.

But as in the natural world so also in the spiritual, we can see some *reasons* for this arrangement. The devout homage of prayer and praise *prepares* the mind for the favors sought. The mind is thus turned to God as the source of all blessings. Feelings of dependence and gratitude are enkindled. The very act of *looking* to God in prayer and praise, implies the work of the Spirit already commenced; and the answer to the prayer prepares the soul to receive yet larger gifts of the Spirit, and with them all other blessings.

THE DUTY OF OBSERVING THE SABBATH.

How are we required to keep the Sabbath?

1. *As a day of rest from secular labor.* The command is, "*Thou shalt do no work.*" But we are to give a reasonable interpretation to this command as well as to all others. The law of God, in reference to which all commands are to be interpreted, is a law of *love* and *kindness.* Hence to do such things upon the Sabbath as attending upon the sick, burying the dead, taking care of our beasts, serving our needful food, preventing the destruction of property, as in the case of fire, is sanctioned by the example of Christ, and the obvious principles of humanity. These are usually called "works of necessity and mercy." The Jews, who had mistaken the spirit of the

command, rebuked Christ for doing such things upon the Sabbath. He replied, that "the Sabbath was made for man and not man for the Sabbath." By which he meant, that the Sabbath was made to *bless* man, not to bring him into bondage.

The command to observe it embraces children, servants, beasts, guests, "all that is within thy gates." We are thus required not only to rest ourselves, but to cause all under our control to rest with us.

2. *As a day of abstinence from the pursuits of pleasure.* "If thou turn," &c. "*from doing thine own pleasure;*"—"*not doing thine own ways, nor finding thine own pleasure, nor speaking thine own words*, then shalt thou delight thyself in the Lord," &c.* We may *hence* violate the Sabbath by so indulging the pleasures of the table as to produce dulness of mind, by taking excursions for amusement; by secular reading and conversation, by social visiting and recreation, in a word, by any employment whose direct object is *worldly pleasure.*

3. *As a day of religious devotion.* It is a day consecrated to religious reading, meditation, and prayer. On this day, therefore, we ought to spend more *time* than we can usually afford upon other days, in reading the Scriptures and other religious books, in self-examination, and in private devotions.

The day is consecrated also to the *public* worship of God. His express command, and the example of his people in all ages, admonish us to assemble together upon the Sabbath, to engage in united acts of public devotion. Those who neglect the worship of God in the sanctuary, on pretence of offering more acceptable service in private, or amidst the works of nature, usually give feeble evidence

* Isaiah 58 : 13.

of possessing any of the true spirit of piety, and frequently sink at last into avowed infidelity.

OTHER DUTIES CONNECTED WITH THE SABBATH.

The other religious duties connected with the Sabbath are, a public profession of religion, observance of the sacraments of Baptism and the Lord's Supper, sustaining the preaching of the gospel, and contributing to the extension of Christianity over the earth. Indeed, the Sabbath is so related to all religious duties, that a faithful observance of it goes very far towards securing them all.

He who is truly religious upon the Sabbath, is a religious man through the week. It can never be justly said of him, as unhappily it may of some, that although he seems to have excellent gifts of prayer in the house of God, he has other gifts less desirable in the place of business. His Sabbath consecrates the entire week to truth, justice, purity; to the fear and service of God. He is as conscientious in the shop as in the prayer-meeting; in the exchange as in the church. The precept is written upon his heart, never to be erased, "*Whether therefore ye eat or drink, or whatsoever ye do, do all to the glory of God.*"

Such is the truly religious man. His is the religion of sound morality, and the morality of true religion. His spirituality is strictly moral, and his morality has the strength, grandeur, and glory which only spiritual mindedness can impart. Although his present sphere of action is upon earth, his motives are drawn from eternity. His choicest treasures are all safely garnered up where moth and rust doth not corrupt, and with calm assurance he awaits his everlasting rest in the bosom of God.

CHAPTER II.

PERSONAL DUTIES.

Next to the duties which every accountable being owes to his God, are those which he owes to himself. These last are what we term *personal* duties. There are certain very essential things which every person can and must do for himself, or they must remain for ever undone; as no other being can do them for him. He is morally bound to do them. The doing of them is directly due to himself, and also indirectly due to others; for he owes it to others, as well as to himself, to pursue the course which best promotes his own welfare. The duties in question are self-respect, self-control, self-defence, self-purity, self-providing, self-culture, and self-salvation.

SELF-RESPECT.

There is an important distinction between self-respect and self-esteem. The latter partakes of vanity; the former implies that we do not dishonor ourselves, nor allow others to do so. "Let no man despise thee," is an injunction binding upon all men. But no man can secure the respect of others, unless he respects himself.

No sooner does a person cease to respect himself than the nerve of his virtue is broken; his moral resolution and his manliness are gone; he cannot stand erect and look his fellow-man in the face. A consciousness of being despised naturally leads to low, servile, despicable acts, and thus gradually displaces whatever remains of virtue.

But if it is a man's duty to respect himself, it is of course his duty, under all circumstances, in secret as well as openly, to do nothing which will *diminish* his self-respect. Many are anxious to secure the approbation of others, even at the expense of their own. However desirable the good opinion of others, conscious integrity is much more so.

We may be blind to our faults, and thus judge ourselves too favorably. This is a common error. But even this is not so fatal to character as to perpetrate secret acts of dishonesty, meanness, malice, or impurity, and realize the withering consciousness of self-degradation which they inevitably inflict.

Self-respect is also essential to a due *self-reliance*, without which character has no firmness nor efficiency. No man was ever truly great without it.

SELF-CONTROL.

This implies the due government of the *temper*, and that restraint of other active propensities which we denominate *temperance*.

"He that is slow to anger is better than the mighty; and he that *ruleth his spirit*, than he that taketh a city." Alexander conquered the world, but he never conquered himself. Many a hero has encountered armies, stormed citadels, and subdued kingdoms, who never mastered his own temper.

A man of hasty temper is his own worst enemy. He betrays himself to the mercy of his antagonist. Many have thus not only lost their character and influence, but even their lives. In a fit of passion they have done that which, in all after life, they have been condemned to weep over with unavailing tears.

Anger is not always wrong, but *uncontrolled* anger is both wrong and dangerous. Even the best friend is not safe in its presence. It breaks covenants, betrays trusts, alienates friendship, and deals mortal blows upon the head of innocence. It is a frenzied wild beast let loose. It perpetrates crimes in a moment, which the agony of a lifetime cannot atone for.

It should, therefore, be among the first endeavors of the child, to govern his temper. As he advances in years, he should accustom himself, when angry, to pause and reflect before acting. A man of hasty temper learned to control himself by pausing to count a hundred, when he was angry, before he spoke or acted. The only cure of a hasty spirit is *time.*

But self-control, in the broad sense, includes the cardinal virtue of *temperance.* There is a limit to healthful endurance and action, to transcend which is intemperance. That limit is indicated by the point at which effort and pleasure cease to invigorate, and are followed by permanent loss of energy. It may be difficult to determine always this precise point; but careful observation will soon teach us how far it is wise to indulge.

Despite of prudence, however, we are sometimes liable to err; and there is provision for this in our constitution. An occasional slight excess, if followed by abstinence and caution, usually results in no obvious permanent injury. This elasticity of constitution was necessary to freedom of action. Without it, all our labors and pleasures would need to be measured by so exact a rule, and inspected with so severe vigilance, as to render them mechanical.

A truly temperate man acts unconstrainedly. Nature is in a great measure his guide. If he incidentally toils or indulges too much at any time, nature suggests to him the alternative of corresponding rest and abstinence. Thus, within reasonable limits, nature holds the balance and adjusts the weights for him, that he may act the freeman and not the slave.

But the *habitual* transgressor will not go unpunished. He who habitually overtaxes the mind, precipitates himself into mental imbecility, and sometimes into insanity. He who habitually overworks the body, induces debility and shortens life.

But such are slight offences, in a moral view, compared with the undue indulgence of the *appetites*. A person may overtax both body and mind in a good cause, and from benevolent motives. But it is quite different with the indulgence of the *appetites*. Men do not indulge these to excess from any benevolent motive, but always from a grovelling lust of pleasure.

In this indulgence, however, they soon defeat their own end. For a few momentary gratifications, they barter away their liberty, their manhood, their souls; and become the wretched slaves of exorbitant and tormenting desires. "A man so enslaved by his animal appetites, exhibits humanity in one of its most miserable and contemptible forms. As an additional proof of the misery of such a state, it is of great importance to remark, that, while habit strengthens all our *active* determinations, it diminishes the liveliness of our passive *impressions;* a remarkable instance of which occurs in the effects produced by an immoderate use of strong liquors, which, at the same time that it confirms the active habit of intemperance, deadens and destroys the sensibility of the palate. In consequence of this law of our nature, the evils of excessive indulgence are doubled; inasmuch as our sensibility to pleasure decays in proportion as the cravings of appetite increase. In general, it will be found, that whenever we attempt to enlarge the sphere of enjoyment beyond the limits prescribed by nature, we frustrate our own purpose." *

A habit of strict and uniform self-control, in all particulars, early formed and maintained through life, is among the greatest of earthly blessings. It is at the basis of all other virtues, and the most important element of success in every calling. Health, cheerfulness, vigor of mind, purity of desire, efficiency, long and useful life, are its natural attendants. "He that striveth for the mastery is *temperate in all things.*"

SELF-DEFENCE.

Some ultra-moralists have pushed the doctrine of forbearance to the extreme of non-resistance. The precept of Christ, "Whosoever shall smite thee on thy right cheek, turn to him the other also," which was obviously designed to inculcate a meek and forbearing *spirit*, they have interpreted by the *letter;* so as to deny even the right of personal self-defence.

We are admonished that the "letter *killeth*, but the spirit giveth life." That it was not the intention of Christ to deny the right in question, and that it is not only a right but a *duty*, is manifest from the following facts:

* Stewart, Active and Moral Powers, p. 11.

1. Our Saviour himself and his disciples have set us the *example* of self-defence. They defended themselves not only by fleeing from danger, by rebutting malicious attacks upon their character, and by prudently thwarting the designs of their enemies, but by actually *arming* themselves with deadly weapons, having reference to any emergency in which self-protection might require them.*

2. Self-defence is dictated by an *instinct* of our nature. All of our constitutional impulses have designs, which we have no right to frustrate. That one which respects personal safety and welfare, is as clearly marked and certain as any principle of our nature.

3. Every person is the constituted *guardian of himself.* His life and happiness are more important to him than to any other being; for this reason they are placed primarily in his own hands. No fellow-being can do for him what he can do for himself. Every person is a distinct centre of thought and power, whose first object naturally is his personal safety and happiness.

It is a man's duty to defend his *person*, his *property*, and his *reputation.*

In case of a surprise, as when met by an assassin or robber, he must take his protection, at once, into his own hands. He must defend himself, if need be, at the risk of the aggressor's life. If either is to be put to death, it should evidently be the one who *deserves* it. He who shrinks from self-defence, in such an emergency, is a coward, and must suffer a coward's deserts. Such cowardice is self-desertion; and, if universal, would leave no adequate protection to human life.

In all cases admitting the intervention of law, resort

* See Matth. 2: 13. John 8: 40–59. Luke 22: 36.

should be had to it. For such cases the law was made. He who does the duties of a good citizen, and pays his tax to support government, is entitled to the law's protection. But if he snatches from the hands of law what government has placed in them, he becomes himself a culprit. The man who, impatient of revenge, takes the life of a murderer under trial, is *himself* a murderer; and the law justly holds him guilty.

What we have said of the defence of life, is equally applicable to the defence of *property*. Robbery and theft may sometimes call for personal and direct resistance; but fraud, deception, forgery, &c., should be met by a legal process.

When *reputation* is attacked by falsehood that cannot be exposed without resort to law, the injured party *may himself expose it*. He is under no obligation to incur the expense of a court, nor to allow his reputation to suffer for a single day, to await the slow process of law. To expose falsehood, deceit, or any kind of crime, where personal protection or the public welfare demands it, is morally right.

But when the attack is of a nature to be more successfully repelled by a *legal* process, such a process should be had. Attacks upon personal and professional reputation involve so many particulars, and such various kinds of evidence, as to render defence impracticable, except by a severe legal investigation.

In *what cases* an injured man should resort to law, it is the business of a candid counsellor to decide. Personal feelings and comparative ignorance of law, usually render men incompetent judges in their own cause. He who goes into court against wise counsel, for the benefit of his good name, usually comes out with his name little if any improved.

A barbarous method of self-defence is that of *duelling*. Its folly is manifest in the fact, that it does nothing towards determining which party was originally in the wrong. It adduces no evidence; it settles no question; it passes no judgment.

Can we believe that the God of heaven interposes a *miracle* to settle a question of innocence or guilt in this way? It was once supposed that he does; and hence the origin of duels. They were a bold appeal to God. But that profane notion has passed away; the light of Christianity condemns it. All enlightened minds have discarded the belief that Providence teaches us truth and duty thus.

The result of a duel decides only, which of the parties could hold the firmest hand and aim the deadliest blow; while the acceptance of a challenge only proves, that all the folly and guilt were not confined to one side. It is to be hoped, for the honor of humanity, that this stupid method of self-defence will soon be among the monstrous things that *have been*.

SELF-PURITY.

This includes the cardinal virtue of chastity, and is itself involved in the duty of self-control. But it implies purity of imagination and feeling, as well as the control of appetite. It is to the former that I now particularly refer. No virtue is more essential to personal welfare. When once the desires to which a vile imagination gives rise have become a mental habit, a dark prospect opens to the unhappy victim.

1. His *body* suffers. Insidious nervous affections invade it, tending to debility and early death. This connection between the vice and its effects may not be immediate and perceptible, but it is sure.

2. His *intellect* suffers. The calamity usually falls more heavily upon the intellect than upon the body. The fine prospects of many youths at school have thus been blighted, by causes eluding the most vigilant guardianship. Listlessness, aversion to mental effort, feebleness of memory, the want of resolution and perseverance, are among the most significant attendants of the vice in question. Parents and teachers labor in vain to ennoble the intellect that is debased by lust.

3. The *heart* suffers. The amiable affections, which render husbands and wives, parents and children, neighbors and associates, happy in their mutual relations and duties, are vitiated and impaired. Lust and love, although they seem often to approach each other, and almost to unite, are yet mutual enemies. Their antagonism increases as they approximate. When the one is habitually harbored, the other is habitually excluded. The one is benevolent, the other is selfish ; the one is from above, the other from beneath.

4. *Reason herself* is sometimes dethroned. A large portion of the victims of lunacy and idiocy, in the asylums of both continents, have been brought there, as statistics prove, by the vices in question. But where one person passes to the extremity and becomes a public example, hundreds suffer and perish on the way. Their vices live and die mostly in their own bosoms. Multitudes enfeeble their health, impair their mental vigor, curtail their usefulness, diminish their substantial enjoyments, and shorten their lives, by vices which only the light of eternity will reveal.

The Scriptures are very explicit in condemnation of all impurity. No judgments are heavier, no penalties more severe, than those which they pronounce against this vice. *

* See Prov. 5 : 3–29. 7 : 5–26. Gal. 5 : 19–25. Matth. 5 : 27–32. Lev. 10 : 22. Col. 5 : 6.

The following are the rules by which to preserve self-purity:

1. Never allow the imagination to form impure images, or to dwell upon scenes calculated to excite the sensual passions.

2. Never frequent those kinds of theatrical or other amusements, which tend to defile the imagination and inflame the lust of pleasure.

3. Avoid all those books whose chief attraction is that they excite and please the mind, at the expense of enfeebling and debauching it.

4. Discard all such pictures, however beautiful and fascinating, as tend to enkindle impure feelings. There are enough in the great world of fine arts, without them.

5. Lend no ear to conversation or songs of an impure character. Every person who would protect his purity, must guard the avenues to his mind through the ear as well as the eye.

6. Never associate with lewd company. A person is not only *known* by the company he keeps, but he is morally *made* by it. The young person who associates with vile company, will surely be drawn into the vortex, and go with them to destruction.

7. Most important of all, *be ever interested and engaged in some worthy occupation.* This is the most successful antagonism to vice of every kind. He who has on hand enough good work to do, and is intent on doing it, has no time to foster and gratify a wanton imagination. His tastes and pleasures are too elevated and inspiring to assort with grovelling and vicious desires.

Such are rules for keeping the *mind* pure. Nor let it be thought trifling with our subject, if, in the same connection, we speak of purity of *body.* Cleanliness is more than mere decency; it is a virtue. The want of it is more than vulgarity; it is a vice. God enjoined upon a people under his special care, the strictest observances with reference to their cleanliness. There is an intimate connection between purity of body and purity of mind, which induced Addison to say, that cleanliness is next to Godliness. For this reason, the cleansing of the body was by the Jews regarded as a part of their needful preparation to worship God in his temple.

Not less important is this virtue to *bodily health.* Many of the most loathsome and fatal diseases come of the want of cleanliness. Allowing the insensible perspiration to be checked, and the free egress of the bodily wastes to be prevented by impurities upon the skin, tends to vitiate the secretions, injure the blood, impede the circulation, and thus impair digestion and invite disease.

He who would be cleanly, must ordinarily wash his entire person daily, at least during the warm seasons; must cleanse his mouth and teeth, after meals and just before retiring; must use the comb and brush sufficiently to keep the head and hair clean; must wear clean apparel, at least next to his person, so far as his employment allows; must keep the atmosphere about him as pure as possible, by day and by night; and must abstain from all grossness in eating and drinking. He will then have a clean person, sweet breath, a pure and wholesome appearance, and will usually enjoy good health. He will at least enjoy all the better health for his cleanliness, and will be protected against infectious diseases.

SELF-PROVIDING.

It is the duty of every person, so far as he can, to *provide for his temporal wants.* This requires *industry* and *frugality.*

Industry.—That industry which is prompted by instinct in brutes, is dictated by forethought in man. The whole irrational creation, down to the humble ant, teaches us the lesson of industry. "Go to the ant, thou sluggard, *consider her ways and be wise;* which, having no guide, overseer, or ruler, provideth her meat in the summer, and gathereth her food in the harvest." "Seest thou a man *diligent* in business? He shall stand before kings." "The hand of the *diligent* maketh rich."

We are commanded to be "*not slothful in business.*" Let the habits of industry be early formed, so that labor itself becomes a delight, and the foundation is laid for success in any calling.

Frugality.—Benjamin Franklin, by his lessons and example of frugality, did much to make the people of this rising republic what they have been in enterprise, thrift, and wealth. But his lessons seem to have become a dead letter. A greater benefit could scarcely be conferred upon us than to revive them. The "hard times," of which he wrote and furnished the cure, are perpetually recurring, and the same remedy is ever demanded. To the industrious and frugal man, all times are easy. His wants are few, his resources abundant, his cup always full.

Wealth and independence are terms indicating not the quantity *possessed*, but the quantity *needed.* Were all children and youth, especially all persons setting forth upon the responsibilities of business and family connections, accustomed to habits of reasonable frugality, those disasters termed "failures" would be very few. Broken fortunes, broken hearts, want, despair, would be almost unknown.

All young families who have their fortunes to make, should adopt the rule of reserving a margin of at least one fourth of their earnings, to accumulate for future increased wants. If their earnings are eight hundred dollars a year, they should reserve two hundred to be on interest; if their earnings are two thousand, they should reserve five hundred. They will then never fail; and will be able to educate their children. The same frugality will enable them to contribute to benevolent objects. Frugality, not luxury, is the parent of beneficence.

Prevailing frugality among a people is one of the strongest pillars of national safety. So long as men enjoy the abundance which frugality imparts, they are content with their government, and combine to uphold it. But when luxury begins to produce enervation, want, impatient lust, and daring recklessness, the foundations of government tremble. The early period of a nation is the one in which the people are frugal and thrifty, and of course patriotic; the middle is the one in which the children, inheriting abundance, are less frugal and more self-indulgent; the final period is that of prevailing luxury, effeminacy, and bankruptcy, in which law and judgment are swept from the land by the surges of anarchy.

The remedy for all this is to be found only in the conscientious distribution of wealth to the various benevolent objects suggested by Christian benevolence, and in the perpetual inculcation and practice of the stern virtues of industry and frugality.

SELF-CULTURE.

When a man duly respects, controls, and defends himself, when he keeps himself pure, and provides for his wants, he thus far does well. But if he stops here, he leaves the most important duties to himself undone. He ought to *cultivate his mind.* There is a mine of wealth *within* him to be developed. He will be mentally great or small, poor or rich, according to the culture which he bestows upon himself.

It is a great practical error of this age, that mental culture is so much sought with reference only to *business* and *gain*. These are subordinate aims, and the culture which respects only these, is low and vulgar. Men of only this culture have no inward resources. As soon as they retire from business with a competency they become unhappy. Having reached the condition most favorable to repose, dignity, intellectual pursuits, rational greatness, and influence, they expose a wretched poverty of intellect by their incapacity for enjoyment.

Mental culture is not necessarily restricted to professional men. Eminent attainments have been made by men of various callings. Benjamin Franklin was a printer; George Washington was a farmer; Hugh R. Miller was a mason. Let a young person firmly resolve on self-culture, and a systematic and persevering application of his leisure time will insure the result.

He must be *systematic*. Talents of a very humble order, systematically employed, have achieved wonders. A methodical and exact distribution of time and duties, can scarcely fail of splendid results. A man of thorough system is seldom in a hurry, because he has a time for all things. He rises early, and keeps time and duties ever before him.

Few men, in the tug of life, can secure any other portions of time for self-culture than mornings and evenings. Of these, the morning is usually the brightest and best. With many it is the *only* time of which they can be sure. By rising early, they can usually appropriate two hours in the morning to languages, science, history, philosophy, and other severe studies, which discipline the mind and give it command and reach of thought. The evenings may then be devoted to lighter studies and amusements, and to the entertainment of friends.

Men distinguished for self-culture have been usually very systematic in the use of time, and have been early risers. Such were Plato, Socrates, Julius Cæsar, Martin Luther, Newton, Milton, La Place, Napoleon, Franklin, Webster, and many others scarcely less renowned.

But there must be withal *perseverance*. It is not the effort of a month, or of a year, that will suffice. Nothing truly great and valuable comes but of steady and prolonged labor. We are in a world of conflict. The avenue to every object worth seeking is beset with difficulties. Every man should lay his account with these, and nerve his spirit to press valiantly through them. Perseverance will succeed at last; and when the result is realized, it will be the more valuable for the conflict.

Let a young man pursue this course, and twenty years will show an amazing difference between him and the man who has neglected it. If then favored with a competency, and disposed to retire from active business, he will be at no loss how to dispose of his time, or where to find enjoyment. His own mind and his library will be to him a source of unfailing pleasure. He will also be able to command and to honor posts of public office and general usefulness, by which he can confer distinguished and lasting benefits upon mankind.

SELF-SALVATION.

Man has more than body and intellect to care for. He has also more than a merely moral nature. He has a *spiritual* nature, a *soul;* to provide for the eternal well-being of which, is transcendently the most important of all self-duties. So far as duty to *himself* is concerned, this is first, midst, and last; it absorbs and controls all others. If the object of this duty is lost, *all* is lost. "For what shall it profit a man, if he *shall gain the whole world and lose his own soul; or what shall a man give in exchange for his soul?*"

We were not placed here to provide merely for these few moments of time, but for everlasting ages. We were made to look forward, *indefinitely* forward; to provide for the future, the *eternal* future. The man who restricts his vision of the future, and aims at providing for only a limited period, is false to his rational nature. Nor does it answer for him to say, that he will provide for himself up to a given point, to the point where his sensuous vision terminates, and risk what lies beyond. This is precisely what God has commanded him *not* to do, on peril of being in the end denounced as "a fool."* He is to look after the *interests* of the soul, with the *eye of the soul;* and that eye *looks beyond time*, ETERNALLY ONWARD.

The brute, having only an animal and corruptible nature, heeds only the present state; but man, having a rational and immortal nature, does and must think of eternity. Eternity is the appropriate centre of his thoughts, the home of his spirit; *there, and there only, may he lay up his treasures.*

The *means* of securing his eternal salvation are revealed in the Scriptures, and a full consideration of them belongs to *religious* teaching. Moral philosophy conducts us to this point, and here leaves us; with the obligation resting upon every individual, as his first and highest *self-duty*, to secure his spiritual worthiness and his everlasting bliss in heaven.

* Luke 12: 20.

CHAPTER III.

CONJUGAL DUTIES.

THE conjugal relation is indicated by Christ in the following words: "Have ye not read that he which made them in the beginning made them male and female, and said, For this cause a man shall *leave father and mother, and shall cleave to his wife;* and they twain shall be *one flesh. Wherefore they are no more twain, but one flesh.*" This is then the most intimate and endearing of all earthly relations. It even transcends that of the parent and child. There is no other relation which makes the parties so emphatically "*one flesh.*" The duties of this relation require,

1. *Union of affection.*—Unless the parties are united in affection before they become so in law, they act in opposition to the spirit of the institution. To marry from motives of distinction, pride, wealth, or mere sensual pleasure, is to perpetrate a flagrant moral wrong. Few crimes receive more severe and protracted recompense than false-hearted marriage vows.

When the parties are married, they proclaim to the world that they love each other more than they love any other human being. The necessity for this affection is obvious. They cannot be happy in each other without it.

Nothing else can be substituted. They may acquire wealth and distinction; they may build and furnish fine houses, and plant beautiful gardens; they may ride in elegant coaches, and give and receive luxurious entertainments; but all this, without true conjugal affection, is splendid wretchedness. The parties have frustrated the benevolent design of the marriage covenant, they have solemnly proclaimed to God and to the world an awful lie, and they must through life reap their reward in bitter and unavailing regret.

2. *Union of interest and reputation.*—For purposes of convenience, civil laws often make some distinction between the property of the wife and that of the husband; but this is with reference to their children, or to the surviving party. So long as they *both live*, whatever is possessed by either, should be equally enjoyed by both. Their interests are one. The less there is of *mine* and *thine* between them, the more do they act upon the spirit and enjoy the blessings of the marriage covenant. They have also a common inheritance of *reputation*. Any blot upon the character of the one, dishonors also the other.

The prosperity or adversity, glory or shame, weal or woe, of either the husband or the wife, is peculiarly and intensely shared in common between them. This fact is forcibly taught in the following declaration: "And the rib which the Lord God had taken from the man he made a woman, and brought her to the man. And Adam said, This is now *bone of my bone, and flesh of my flesh.*" Hence any good or evil befalling the one, befalls also the other.

3. *Union of parental affection.*—This can be secured by no other means than the marriage covenant. United in the same relation to the same offspring, their affections are to flow through the same channels to the same objects.

Thus parental love serves to strengthen conjugal love, and *vice versa.* The mutual love of husband and wife is usually increased or diminished, in the degree that the one sees the other affectionately devoted to the welfare of their common offspring.

4. *Union of regard for each other's relatives and friends.*—Being now made one, the parties sustain the same relation to each other's kinsmen and associates. The parents, brothers, sisters, cousins, and companions of the one, become those of the other. Upon these their affections must now unite. The wife could scarcely offend the husband more, than to disregard his relatives and friends; and the husband could scarcely injure the sensibilities of the wife more, than to be indifferent to hers. Serious alienations and jealousies have sometimes arisen between married parties, from want of due consideration in this particular.

5. *Union of domestic responsibility.*—Although every one must give an account for himself, and there is an individual responsibility which can never be divided with another, yet the conjugal union involves a most weighty one, which must be borne in common by both the parties. Neither can say, This is *my* duty, and that is *yours.* The duty is common to both. They are mutually and equally pledged to do all in their power to secure the prudent management of their secular interests, the order and peace of their households, the right training of their offspring, and all those temporal and everlasting benefits, for which the domestic constitution was established. One party may never attempt to put exclusively upon the other any portion of this responsibility. They mutually assume it, and are equally pledged to sustain it.

6. *Mutual chastity and fidelity.*—The parties are equally pledged to abstinence from sexual intercourse with

any other person, and to the observance of strict chastity. A violation of this pledge is the crime of adultery, and is a gross trespass upon a natural as well as revealed principle of morality. No crime is more loudly condemned by the voice of nature and by the Word of God, and upon none are inflicted more terrible retributions.*

RELATIVE POSITION OF THE PARTIES.

The following Scripture has been often cited to prove that the rights are mostly the husband's, and the duties the wife's: "For the man is not of the woman; but the woman of the man. Neither was the man created for the woman; but the woman for the man."

But the context makes it evident that the precedence of natural and social *position*, not of *right*, is here predicated of the man. The man is the natural and constituted head of the wife, and of the entire household; but the relation between them is not that of master and slave. It is as much the husband's duty to love, cherish, and honor the wife, as it is the wife's duty to love, cherish, and honor the husband. They are to be one in counsel, deliberation, judgment, feeling, interest, while the husband is the constituted exponent and executor of their united wisdom. "Neither is the man without the woman, neither the woman without the man, in the Lord. For as the woman is of the man, even so is the man also of the woman." In other words, they are equally important to each other; while their blended and harmonious agency should be represented in the appointed head.

But they are by no means to merge their respective *identities*. Their distinct individuality remains unimpaired. Each of them becomes much more, but neither

* See Heb. 13: 4. Rev. 21: 8. Lev. 20: 10. Matth. 5: 7.

of them any the less, for the union. Neither is the wife to refer the decision of all matters in *her* appropriate sphere to the husband, any more than the husband is to refer the decision of all matters in *his* appropriate sphere to the wife. Each, so far as is practicable, should be supreme in his or her appointed sphere, in order to lighten the burden of the other.

Still, questions are sometimes to be decided respecting which both have the same concern, and on which they are liable to differ. They are questions which practically respect the business, the safety, the happiness, of both alike, and yet they cannot unite in opinion upon them. What then? As to mere *opinion*, they should "agree to differ;" but as to *action*, the husband must finally decide.

Yet the wife should never be urged into circumstances of danger, or compelled to resist her fears, unless there is obviously greater danger in any other course. She may, through fear, refuse to leave the sinking ship and take the life-boat, and the husband may see this to be the only escape for her; in that case he must not regard her fears, but her safety. In all ordinary cases, however, the fears of "the weaker vessel" should be sacredly regarded. The dashing steed that just delights the iron nerves of man, is often a terror to the gentler sex; and the sensitive nerves, so instinctive of danger, usually suggest the safer and wiser course.

In all cases, if a truly conjugal spirit rules, the point will seldom be reached at which the husband's "authority" will be demanded. Long before arriving at that issue, the wife will give the preference to the opinions and wishes of the husband; while the gentle expression of her own, even in matters of the greatest moment, will not fail to be by him gratefully received, and perhaps adopted. To decide, at last, is his; but to guide, assist, and sustain the decision, is hers. Their duties and privileges are thus equal, although modified to their respective sexes and positions.

DUTIES OF THE HUSBAND TO THE WIFE.

1. He is bound *to provide for her.* He has no right to marry without some reasonable prospect of having a comfortable home for his wife. For him she leaves father and mother. He takes her from the home of her childhood, to possess a home of his own procuring. And the home which he provides should have some reference to that which she leaves. It may not be as elegant; for those setting out in life must not ordinarily expect what years of toil procure; but it should be adapted to her previous habits and culture. If through indolence or improvidence he neglects to provide her a suitable home and support, he is false to his vow, and forfeits claim to her affection. "If any provide not for his own, and especially for those of his own household, he hath denied the faith, and is worse than an infidel." *

2. He should *protect her person.* He should watch over her health, comfort, and safety. He should never require her to live in situations to which her constitution is not adapted. He should impose upon her no cares, and subject her to no avoidable burdens and anxieties, which tend to impair her vigor or shorten her days. He should cherish and protect her as the prudent man would his own life, always placing himself between her and harm.

Even if disposed himself to encounter dangers, he has no right needlessly to subject his wife to them. She has a personal right to her own safety, which the marriage

* 1 Tim. 5 : 8.

vow does not impair; and hence, if her fears prevail, he is bound to regard them. The rash husband, by disregarding the prudent fears of his wife, has sometimes been the unmeaning cause of her death.

3. He should treat her with *delicacy and respect.* It is said that "familiarity breeds contempt." And so it certainly does, unless strict delicacy is observed. Hence the husband should endeavor always to practise the same delicacy of conduct towards his wife which he did before they were married. The same delicate courtesy that won her affections and esteem, should retain them. Familiarity may contribute to ease and freedom between them, but must never be allowed to degenerate to rudeness.

4. He should also treat her *kindly* and *affectionately.* He should never wound her feelings by unkind remarks, or ill-natured rebukes; especially he should avoid speaking of her faults in the presence of others. He should relieve her anxieties respecting servants, table, wardrobe, and other domestic matters, and render them all easy to bear, by his manifested satisfaction. He should be slow to complain and quick to commend.

He should consider her temperament, education, and early life, and make due allowances for them. He should never interfere with the proper development of her natural or acquired gifts. If she has genius, taste, or skill, qualifying her to succeed in any department of literature or of art, he should generously encourage it. He should endeavor to anticipate all her reasonable wants, and to animate all her just endeavors.

He should not bestow upon her grudgingly, or compel her to come to him begging for money, but consider that her purse has a right to be filled as well as his. She may not wish to tell him all her wants, any more than he may wish to tell her his. She may desire to surprise her hus-

17*

band by appearing in a new dress, or by making him a beautiful present; or she may have charitable objects in view. It is not for him to inquire *why* she needs the money, but to see that she *has* it. His attention to her should never be ostentatious, nor more marked in public than in private. This will disgust a sensible wife, as well as others who witness it. His devotion should be ever the same hearty, noiseless, self-sacrificing endeavor to secure her highest welfare and happiness.

"*Husbands, love your wives, and be not bitter against them.*" "*Love your wives, even as Christ also loved the Church, and gave himself for it.*" * As Christ loves the Church, and tenderly protects her as the apple of his eye, so ought the husband to love and cherish his wife.

5. He should be *especially attentive to her in sickness.* When suffering with pain, disease, languor, she naturally looks to her dearest earthly friend for sympathy and relief. She should never look in vain. She may be nervous, impatient, unreasonable; but he must bear with these infirmities, and sympathize with her imagined as well as real sicknesses. Most of them are *real*, and severer than the husband has ever supposed. To complain of her sufferings is not the usual way of woman. To suffer on in silence, to bear with uncomplaining submission, is her common habit.

The brightest examples of conjugal fidelity have sometimes been furnished by men of the highest standing in their professions, who have resigned honorable stations and lucrative business to bestow all their time and attentions upon their suffering wives. Disease had laid its hand upon the objects dearer to them than fame or wealth. For anxious weeks and months they travelled

* Col. 3 : 19. Eph. 5 : 25.

with them and watched over them, leaving no means untried to heal or mitigate their diseases, until the final mandate came. At no time does the conjugal affection appear more beautiful than in seasons of sickness.

6. He should sacredly regard *her spiritual welfare.* If he loves her with a true affection, he will desire and seek the welfare of her soul. His views may differ from hers, but he is bound to respect hers as sacredly as he does his own. He may seek to enlighten her conscience, if he thinks her in error; this he is bound to do; but he must never attempt to *control* it. She is personally responsible as well as he. He should, if possible, provide for her the place of worship which she most approves, allow her to make such a profession of religion as accords with her sense of duty, and always treat her religious sentiments with tenderness and respect.

This much, at least, the marriage covenant binds him to do. But if a believer in Christianity and moved by its spirit, he will do more. He will make her the subject of his daily prayers, and will labor to cause all the events of joy and of sorrow through which they may be called to pass, the means of leading her spirit to God and securing its eternal rest and glory in heaven. "*What knowest thou, O husband, whether thou shalt save thy wife?*"

DUTIES OF THE WIFE TO THE HUSBAND.

The duties of the wife are correlative to those of the husband, being modified by the difference of her sphere. If he is the leading head of the family, she is to be the "help meet for him."

1. She should *assist him in providing.* If it is the duty of the husband to provide for the wife, it is no less her duty to coöperate with him, and thus do all in her

power to relieve his task. It was never intended that the husband should bear *alone* the burden of supporting the household. The wife is morally bound to help him. Failure in this duty will bring its appropriate punishment. "Many a man has failed to succeed in life," says a blunt but truthful writer, "because his wife, instead of being a help *meet*, was only a help *eat*." If there are particular duties in providing for the family appropriate to *his* sphere, so there are others appropriate to *hers;* and the neglect of either may prove equally fatal to their common interest.

2. She should *adapt herself to his circumstances and calling.* Her wants must be graduated by his means. An ambitious wife and a poor husband make an unhappy match. She must consider this beforehand, and resolve on contentment. She did not wed a house, or a garden, or a luxurious table, or a fine dress; she wedded a *husband.* And if his means are humble, she should cheerfully conform to them. She has probably heard of "love in a cottage;" she now has a chance to taste its sweets.

The wife of a poor husband should practise industry, frugality, and economy, with untiring vigilance; but if her husband is rich, she may have more regard to adornment. To render home elegant and attractive, to make it an abode of hospitality, and to abound in deeds of personal kindness and charity to the poor, will then enter more largely into the sphere of her duties. The wives of rich men may thus impart true value to wealth, and make it an ornament to their possessors and a blessing to the world.

3. *She should look well to the ways of her household.* She should anticipate the wants of her husband, and see that all things pertaining to his wardrobe, apartments, and home-comforts, are duly arranged. She should have

the same eye of vigilance to the wants of the family, and to the comfort and happiness of guests. She should seek to prevent waste, to have every thing in its right time and place, and to diffuse an air of grace and comfort over the house. She should be prompt to every emergency; ready to rise early, sit up late, or make unusual efforts, when demanded by special calls upon her husband's time. Presiding thus with generous heart and queenly grace over the household, she will make home what heaven designed it to be, the paradise of earth.

"Teach the young women to be sober, *to love their husbands, to love their children; to be discreet, chaste, keepers at home, good, obedient to their own husbands;* that the word of God be not blasphemed."* "Who can find a virtuous woman? for her price is far above rubies. The heart of her husband doth safely trust in her, so that she shall have no need of spoil. She will do him good and not evil all the days of her life. She seeketh wool and flax, and worketh diligently with her hands. She is like the merchant's ships; she bringeth her food from afar. She riseth while it is yet night, and giveth meat to her household, and a portion to her maidens.—She stretcheth out her hand to the poor; yea, she stretcheth out her hands to the needy. She looketh well to the ways of her household, and eateth not the bread of idleness. Her children arise up and call her blessed; her husband also, and he praiseth her. Many daughters have done virtuously, but thou excellest them all."

4. She should endeavor to retain and increase *his satisfaction in her personal attractions.* To this end, she should always continue to be as neat and tasteful in dress, as modest, dignified, and graceful in manners, as when

* Tit. ii: 4, 5.

she first won his affection. She should furnish him no ground for disappointment. If she cannot continue to command the charms of personal beauty, she can exhibit what is more valuable, the graces of an amiable temper, and of a pure and benevolent heart.

If she would not disgust her husband, and prove herself unworthy of his affection and unable to retain it, she must never indulge *jealousy.* She must be generous and confiding. She must rejoice to have others share with her all proper attentions from him, and to have him enjoy their society as well as hers. Few things are more offensive even to the casual observer, than that exclusive devotion of the married pair to each other, which proclaims their affection to be narrow, sensual, and selfish.

She must be *submissive.* "Wives, *submit yourselves unto your own husbands, as is fit in the Lord.*" This is not a servile submission, but such as is "fit," that is, *becoming.* It should be the cheerful and graceful submission of a confiding heart. She should understand his disposition, and be indulgent to his infirmities. If superior to him in talent or culture, she should guard against appearing conscious of it. If he is sometimes petulant or ill-natured, she should not reproach him, but leave him to reproach himself in silence. A spirited and high-minded husband cannot be safely rebuked by his wife. Indeed she would soon despise him if he allowed it. There is a mingling of chivalrous pride in his affection for her, which may be turned into hate and bitterness by indiscreet rebukes.

5. *She should be especially devoted to him in trouble and in sickness.* Reverses of fortune may overtake him. He may lose his property, or his business; or his reputation may be assailed; but so long as his wife stands by his side, cheerful, resolute, hopeful, he can still act the

man. He has the "help *meet* for him." In some instances men have felt more than compensated for the severest losses by the noble character thus developed in their wives.

That the husband may be under no temptation to seek comfort abroad, and to drown his anxieties amidst scenes of dissipation, his wife should be as an angel of light and love about him. She should seek to make her own society the most agreeable to him, her own table the most inviting, her home the most attractive, her fireside entertainments the most satisfying, of all on earth. If the husband of such a wife breaks down under trials, or resorts to vicious practices, the fault will not be hers. Ordinarily he will not. Her endeavors will be crowned with success. Had the wife of Job been such, she would not have spoken "as one of the foolish women speaketh," and he would not probably have been left to murmur.

The same principle which should guide the conduct of the husband, in the sickness of the wife, should also guide hers in the sickness of the husband. Indeed the balance of duty here is rather on her side. No other person can do for her husband in sickness what she can do. The affectionate and devoted wife is then physician, nurse, friend, comforter; the ever present angel of love and mercy about his pillow. Her presence, sympathy, and care, are more precious and important to him than those of all the world besides.

6. She should *earnestly seek his spiritual welfare.* No other person can exert the religious influence upon him which she can. If a consistent Christian and devoted wife, she may confidently hope that her faithful and persevering instrumentality will be blest to his salvation. This hope is expressly encouraged by the highest authority. "For what knowest thou, O wife, *whether thou shalt save thy husband?*"

God has committed his spiritual destiny, in an eminent degree, to her charge. He is immersed in business. "The cares of this world, and the deceitfulness of riches, and the lusts of other things," press him on all sides. She is more withdrawn from the world, and her thoughts and sensibilities naturally commune more with religion. Hence husbands usually look to their wives for religious example, guidance, and encouragement. Even if sceptical and irreligious themselves, they usually prefer to have their wives pious.

Unless Christianity is a fable, the wife is morally bound to make the salvation of her husband, next to her own, the most important object of her life. An excellent woman, living in the enjoyment of great wealth and luxury, was asked what she would give to see her husband a Christian. "I appreciate these temporal blessings," was her reply, "and hope I am thankful for them, but have often thought that I would gladly exchange them all and live in the humblest poverty, for that greatest desire and prayer of my heart." She was put to the test. He failed in business, and after living two years in an obscure cottage, in great poverty, he died. But in the mean time he found treasures in heaven, and of this gave the brightest evidence. She has often remarked, that those two last years were the happiest period of her life. None who know her can doubt the truth of this; and there are many others, we are sure, who have the same spirit. Such are *true wives*, in the true sense; they are to their husbands the *helps* "*meet*" for them, in the most important of all interests.

CONCLUDING REMARKS.

All of the above duties are deduced from one and the same *principle*, which is involved in the marriage covenant. The parties are pledged to promote their highest united and individual welfare. Whatever contributes to this, each of the parties is bound to do.

Let this principle be universally adopted and obeyed, and there would be an end to all divorces, and to all occasions for them; an end to all jealousies and contentions between husband and wife; and an end, doubtless, to three-fourths of the misery that afflicts mankind. All families would become nurseries of every thing pure, sweet, genial, and the heavenly influences going forth of them would, in a great measure, restore the bliss of Eden lost by the fall.

Nor let it be said that we have set the standard too high, and cannot approach it. Christian morality has set it where it is, and it cannot be altered. Not a duty have we indicated, which both natural and revealed morality do not conspire to enjoin. Nor is this all. Many have proved by their lives that it *can be* approached. There are at this moment thousands of illustrations of the blessedness of the conjugal union, in which the principle of the bond is faithfully regarded, as has been indicated above; nor let us despair of that brighter day, when all the families of the earth will become illustrations of the same.

CHAPTER IV.

PARENTAL DUTIES.

Next to the conjugal relation the parental is most important. On the right discharge of its duties mainly depends the welfare of the state and of the church. The family is both of these in embryo.

The duties now to be considered result directly from the parental relation. The father and mother are *parents* to their child; that is, as the word imports, the authors under God of his existence. Had it not been for them he would never have had a being. They hence sustain to him the most vital of all relations, and one which no other person, in the fullest sense, *can* sustain.

PARENTAL AFFECTION.

Along with the birth of the child there is also born in the hearts of his parents a peculiar *affection* for him. This affection is strictly the work of God, and always exists where nature is not grossly abused. It prompts them to do whatever is in their power for his safety and welfare.

Following the indication of nature, it is plainly their duty to cultivate and direct this impulse. They should put it in school to conscience, and thus make their happiness and their duty one, in paying the precious debt they owe to their beloved offspring.

They should always cherish such an affection for him, that the neglect of any duty, however self-sacrificing, to promote his welfare, would be to them a greater trial than its performance. This is not an affection that idolizes its object, and expends itself in fondling and caressing him, or in displaying vanity in his dress and appearance; it moves the heart, the lips, the hands, in the faithful use of all the appointed means for securing his highest temporal and everlasting well-being. Such is true parental love. It is perhaps usually found in higher perfection in the heart of the mother than of the father, making there greater sacrifices and enduring more abuse. It is a union of all the elements of moral love animated by the peculiar parental feeling.

PARENTAL GUARDIANSHIP.

As parents have some practical knowledge of nature's laws, of the ways in which they are violated, and the dangers to which their violation exposes us, and as the child has not this knowledge, parental guardianship is one of their first duties. They must watch over his health, and guard him from exposure to disease, and from all malformations of the limbs and organs. They must attend to his diet, clothing, exercise, recreation, and all the means of the symmetrical and perfect development and growth of his physical system.

The child is as ignorant and as heedless of his moral as of his physical dangers, and hence parental guardianship is not less important in the one case than in the other.

The germs of a virtuous or of a vicious character, are planted at a period when he is too young to anticipate their consequences. His parents must therefore anticipate them for him. They must keep him from vicious companions, from the corrupting influence of profanity, obscenity, falsehood, deceit, and all base passions, as they would from pestilence and death. The child who acquires evil habits through their neglect, will be a speedy and fearful witness against them.

PARENTAL GOVERNMENT.

Parents are bound to *govern* their child. All rational beings are made to be subjects of government, and the first natural lawgivers and rulers of the child are his parents. They are to form in him those habits of obedience to rightful authority, which are subsequently to be exercised with reference to the State and to the higher government of God. There is nothing which they can substitute for these. They may give him all the advantages of wealth, learning, art, society, travel, and refined manners; but if they have not withal taught him to "*obey his parents in the Lord*," they will probably live to see their brightest hopes of him blasted.

Parents should govern their child for the same end that God governs us. All their requirements and prohibitions, rewards and penalties, should be with a view to his welfare. When the apostle says, "we have had fathers of our flesh which corrected us, *after their own pleasure*," he tells us what some fathers *have* done, rather than what they *ought* to have done. Their *duty* is written thus: "And ye fathers, *provoke not your children to wrath, but bring them up in the nurture and admonition of the Lord*." "Provoke not your children to anger lest they be discouraged."

Parental government should therefore be *reasonable and enlightened.* It should never be swayed by blind impulse. It should take into view the child's substantial welfare, rather than his present indulgence. As it should prohibit only where prohibition is necessary, so it should indulge only where indulgence is safe. It should also study the child's peculiarities of temperament, and aim so to touch his hidden springs of action, as to secure the most perfect obedience with the least possible resistance.

It should also be patient and forbearing. Like the government of God, who "maketh his sun to rise on the evil and on the good, and sendeth rain on the just and on the unjust," it should endure "with much long suffering," the waywardness and folly of childhood. It seems to have been divinely intended that parents should willingly endure more from their own children than they would from others; because they have more to do with their faults. But patience must never degenerate to weak indulgence, nor forbearance to pusillanimity.

It should be *uniform.* No parent can well govern his child, who does not govern himself. He who is severe one day and indulgent the next, chastising and caressing according to the caprices of passion, fails to secure either obedience or respect. As the Almighty bears forward the laws of his government with the same steady hand under all provocations from his rebellious children, so should earthly parents do, that their children may always know assuredly what to expect. Passionate and capricious government is an inevitable failure.

It should be *efficient.* It must maintain its position and secure its object. Assuming that filial obedience *must* be secured, or the child will be ruined, it must be, like the government of God, firm and persistent unto the end. It must take no denial. The child must be made to submit, *at all events*. It is, however, often expedient to allow *time* for his temper to cool and his reason and conscience to operate. The object is thus often wisely gained by delay. But ultimately gained it must surely be. The child's waywardness must be thoroughly subdued; he must be made to realize that his parent is entirely in the right, and to yield to him cordial obedience.

If no other means are effectual, the rod must be used. But it should be used with the due mingling of goodness and severity, and yet always with a firmness of decision effectual to its end. "He that *spareth his rod* hateth his son; but he that loveth him *chastiseth him betimes*."

MAINTENANCE.

Parents are bound to provide *maintenance* for their children. This is evident from the following considerations: First, children cannot provide for themselves. Secondly, the natural provision in the person of the mother and her instinctive desire to nourish her offspring, indicate the divine will in this particular. Thirdly, the natural affection of both the parents prompts them to provide for their offspring. Fourthly, it is manifestly unjust for them to impose upon others the task of supporting children, for whose existence they are themselves responsible. Finally, the Scriptures expressly assert: "If any *provide not* for his own, and especially for those of *his own house*, he hath denied the faith, and is worse than an infidel."

Of the *nature and extent* of the maintenance, parents are ordinarily the proper judges. The rich parent ought to provide for his children more liberally than the poor can. He is bound to give them advantages, according as God has given him means. As to food and dress, he should do for his children as he does for himself. To live in luxury himself, and subject his children to coarse and hard fare, is unparental and unjust. Their fare should be simple, perhaps more so than his own, but it should be to them what his is to him.

On the other hand, he is bound to guard against enervating his children by indulgence. If he has passed through early years of hardship, and reached a period demanding more repose and indulgence than are best for them, he should give them the advantage of his experience. The parent, however wealthy, who brings up his children in indolence and pleasure, inflicts an irreparable wrong upon them and upon society.

The age of the child, at which the responsibility of the parent to provide and of the child to serve ceases, is in this country fixed by law at twenty-one. But the law justly provides that the parties may enter into a contract at any earlier period, after the child has become capable of providing for himself, by which their mutual obligations are formally cancelled. The law also provides that the parent may give or apprentice his child to another, under circumstances favorable to the child's welfare, and thus transfer the legal obligation to support him.

But the *moral* obligation of the parent does not cease then, nor after the child becomes of age. Their interests become then distinct in law, but duty demands of the parent, through life, a peculiar regard to his offspring. At his death, our law divides his property equally among them, abating the widow's portion; but other relatives and objects frequently have demands, for which the law cannot specifically provide, thus occasioning the necessity for a will. In that case the parent, making due provision for other claims, should divide equally with his children, unless some defect of intellect or character should justify a distinction. A just portion should then be so left in trust as to guard against both personal want and a public burden.

PHYSICAL EDUCATION.

The infant is a feeble and helpless object. Every member and every muscle needs to be expanded and strengthened. Nature has in a measure provided for this, in the ceaseless activity which she prompts. But there is also demanded unwearied parental care. Children left to themselves will come to an early end, or grow up deformed, feeble, and sickly.

It is the duty of parents to see that their children have wholesome and nourishing food, in suitable quantities; that they have regular and appropriate hours of sleep; that they have pure air and regular alternations of exercise and repose; that they are inured to labor, and even, with due caution, to hardships; in a word, to see that they are so trained as to enjoy, if possible, symmetrical, vigorous, enduring bodies. The blessings of good health through life depend much upon the parental care of childhood.

Hence parents who bring up their offspring delicately and indolently, with systems frail and feeble through want of due exercise, who pamper their appetites, thus engendering unnatural desires and incipient diseases; and parents who, on the other hand, impose crushing burdens or unsuitable tasks upon them, or confine them in bad air, or give them unwholesome food; inflict an injury upon them, beyond the power of gold or of tears to recall. A large portion of the deaths among children, and many of the diseases which follow those through life who survive, are due to the want of right physical training.

INTELLECTUAL EDUCATION.

The infant brings with him into the world the embryo powers of acquisition, but no innate ideas. All that he ever knows must be *learned.* His powers of acquisition were given him to be used; in other words, he was designed to be educated. Education is as needful for his mind, as food and clothing are for his body; and the duty of providing for both devolves upon the parents.

The only question here has respect to the *extent* of parental responsibility. The general principle is this: The parent is bound to do what he can for the intellectual culture of his children, consistently with his other duties. Some can do much more than others; all can do something. Nothing can justify parental neglect in this important matter. He who thinks to substitute wealth for education, or who, from motives of avarice, indolence, or pleasure, allows his children to grow up in ignorance, perpetrates a wrong for which there is no redemption.

The following rules are here obligatory upon parents:

1. They should make the education of their children a *prominent* object. They should have an eye to it in choosing their employment, selecting their place of residence, regulating their expenses, and disposing of their time. The question whether they shall live in town or country, whether they shall acquire more property or less, whether their house and furniture shall be elegant or plain, whether their table shall be abundant or simple, is of small moment, compared with the question whether their children shall be well or badly educated.

2. They should endeavor to provide for them the *best teachers.* Some parents are prompted by avarice to employ the *cheapest* teachers; others, by pride, to employ the *dearest;* others, by a grovelling ambition, to send their children to a *fashionable* school. Verily they have their reward. But better is the reward of those who, moved by a wise conviction of duty, seek for their children those teachers who will give them the most thorough and efficient mental culture. As nothing can repair the loss occasioned by superficial and unfaithful teaching, so scarcely any price is too great to reward that teaching which is what it should be.

3. They should, as far as possible, have a *personal* eye to the education of their children. So far as their time and qualifications allow, they should themselves teach them. All parents of ordinary attainments can do this to some extent. They thus encourage their children to learn by leading the way. They inspirit them by their example, as the successful husbandman does his workmen by putting his own hand to the plough. Whatever deeply interests parents is wont to interest their children. But when the child sees his parents attaching no practical value to his hard and dry lessons, and devoting all their evenings to light reading and amusements, he naturally imbibes their spirit and follows their example.

Let parents gather at evening with their children around the table, let them enter into their difficulties and their triumphs, let them thus show that they attach real importance to their studies, and the effect upon their endeavors will be most happy. They will also thus become acquainted with their several aptitudes, and learn how to direct their course in life.

4. They should *adapt the education of their children to their various talents.* Up to a certain period, the edu-

cation of all children must be nearly the same. But beyond the common rudiments, a wide field opens, in which the course should be directed by a wise regard to natural genius and bent of inclination. Parents should seek to ascertain in what calling their children are most likely to excel, and to direct their education accordingly. The child who is sent to college, or into the army, or placed in a store, or even upon a farm, against his prevailing inclination, is almost sure to encounter failure. Happy is the child who learns in season what calling he was made for, and happy are the parents who guide his steps into it.

MORAL AND RELIGIOUS EDUCATION.

Some have argued that parents ought not to mould the character and faith of their child, maintaining that he should be left to do it for himself on his own responsibility. It might as reasonably be argued that they should neglect the care of his body and his intellect. Is a deformed limb or a feeble memory more to be dreaded than a bad character? A wise man said: "Train up a child in the way he *should* go, and when he is old he *will not depart* from it." Another has added, with scarcely less of truth: "Train up a child in the way he *would* go, and when he is old he *will probably be hanged.*"

But it is said that parents may be themselves in error, and may thus mislead their children. So they may mistake respecting their physical and intellectual training. But is this a good reason for neglecting it? No. God has laid upon parents the obligation to *train up* their children in the way they should go. If it is their duty to attend to their physical and intellectual culture, it is no less their duty to "bring them up in the nurture and admonition of the Lord."

The following rules indicate the duties of parents to their children in this particular.

1. They should inculcate upon them *their own* convictions of truth and duty. They should also see to it, that those to whom they commit their instruction do not teach them otherwise. Parents are responsible not only for what they themselves teach their children, but for what they allow others to teach them. The parent who believes intoxication injurious to the body, or frivolous reading injurious to the intellect, and yet permits an instructor to teach his children otherwise, is no less guilty of parental neglect than he who believes the profanation of the Sabbath to be injurious to morals and religion, and yet allows their instructor to teach them to profane it.

But there is a limit to this authority. The law presumes children to be, after the age of twenty-one, as capable of directing their moral and spiritual as their secular interests. Before this period, the authority of parents may be exercised; after this, only the influence of their *counsel* and *love*. But their authority should never be sharp, severe, imperious, so as to leave no play for the personal judgment and conscience of their children. And as children advance towards seniority, parents should gradually relax their authority over them, and thus by degrees place them upon their own responsibility. In this way there will be no sudden break or jar in their course, but they will pass imperceptibly upward from the dependence of childhood to the independence of manhood.

2. Parents should give to their children *the benefit of their example.* No other teaching is so explicit and effective as this. Their children may not apprehend the force of their reasoning, but they will feel the power of their example. Although parents teach and pray like saints, they

will avail little without consistent lives. On the other hand, a few words of judicious instruction, attended with the influence of a pure and bright example, will fall into the balances of their children like pounds of shining gold.

When children see the law of love and of justice reigning in the hearts of their parents; when they see in them benignity and gentleness blending with firmness and decision; when they see them strictly truthful in all they say, and faithful to all their engagements; when they hear from their lips no unchaste, or profane, or slanderous words; they have before them a constant lesson of excellence which they cannot fail to understand.

And when they see their parents temperate in eating and drinking; prudent in their habits and economical in their expenses, yet given to hospitality, and abundant in noiseless benefactions to worthy objects; when they see them "recompense to no man evil, but overcome evil with good;" in a word, when they see them "do justly, love mercy, and walk humbly with God;" they see in their example, as clearly as with the flash of an angel's eye, *their own duty.* It is as if a voice from some bright shekinah said to them, "*Go and do likewise.*"

3. Parents should *check the first appearance of evil dispositions in their children.* Anger, petulance, revenge, envy, cruelty, pride, vanity, obstinacy, and every other wrong temper, they should rebuke, by placing them in the clear light of God's holy law, by showing his just abhorrence of them, and by exhibiting the moral beauty and grandeur of the virtues which they displace. The disposition to *lie* is perhaps one of the most common. Nearly all parents are pained at detecting some indications of it in their children. It usually first appears in the mild form of equivocation. But it soon passes, unless checked, to the bolder crime of downright falsehood. No

disposition is harder to correct, and none is more fatal. Anger, petulance, vanity, the child may outgrow; but lying, unless speedily rebuked, will soon outgrow him. It is a cancer, eating into the vitals of the soul. Parents must therefore use their most earnest endeavors to correct it.

They should settle this point with their children, under the solemnities of eternity, that they *must cease entirely and for ever from the disposition to lie*, or be doomed to remediless ruin. They should hold the words of God himself continually before them, "*All liars shall have their part in the lake which burneth with fire and brimstone, which is the second death.*"

They should aim to remove from them all *temptations* to lie. They should also endeavor to make them feel, so far as they consistently can, that they place entire confidence in their word. One of the most essential means of inducing children to be always truthful, is, to let them see that we presume they always *are* so. Frequently accuse a child of lying, and he will usually first be grieved, then indignant, and then begin to lie.

4. Parents should *keep their children from all vicious habits.* Left to themselves, children will frequently contract habits whose disastrous consequences are lasting as life. Impure practices, indulgence in pernicious stimulants, profanity, vulgarity, obscenity, often commence before parents suspect them. That bright and lovely son, that beautiful and charming daughter, too young to be yet capable of vicious practices, may be exposed to influences leading directly to them.

These corrupting influences often come from servants, or inmates, or from persons in the neighborhood, with whom their children associate. Many a child has been taught vicious habits by domestics in the absence of parents. There are also, in most neighborhoods, evil-minded and evil practised boys, older than others in years and in the arts of vice, who take pleasure in corrupting the young and unwary.

The means of protecting children from such dangers, are mainly the following:

First, they must be duly *warned* against them. Parents must not affect to ignore them, but assume that they actually exist. Delicately but plainly they should point them out, expose their guilt and consequences, and with the combined earnestness of all their parental love and authority, warn their children against them.

Secondly, they should have an eye to the character of the *indwellers* in their house. It may not be in their power always to command religious inmates and servants, but nothing can justify their employing those who are immoral. The place for such is certainly not where they can corrupt and ruin children. Parents vainly hope to protect their children from the influence of harbored vice. They must follow the example of him who said, "I will set no wicked thing before mine eyes. I hate the work of them that turn aside; it shall not cleave to me. A froward heart shall depart from me; I will not know a wicked person. Mine eyes shall be upon the faithful of the land, that they may dwell with me. *He that walketh in a perfect way, he shall serve me.*" Parents should also, as before intimated, guard their children against all bad influence without, keeping them from such companions and such places of resort as might lead to vicious habits.

Thirdly, they should provide suitable *amusements* for them. Children must have amusements of some kind. Their natures are adapted to them, and without them cannot be fully developed. They are social; they must have companions. They are ingenious; they must have their little arts. They are curious and imaginative; they must have some books of interesting stories. They are restless and active; they must have abundance of play. They must have their fireside recreations and their out-of-door sports. All of these may be either such as to elevate and refine, or to debase and corrupt. It depends mostly upon the parents to determine which they shall be.

5. They should most of all seek their children's *spiritual* welfare. It is not enough that they restrain them from vices, and train them to habits of secular morality; they are bound to regard them also in their relations to God. There is a higher life than that of the flesh, and there are more precious and enduring interests than those of time, which parents are bound to seek for their children. If they aim no higher than to see them well conditioned in the world, they aim immeasurably below their mark.

If they ought to teach them benevolence and justice towards their fellow-beings, much more should they teach them to love and serve their Maker. If they ought to teach them to "provide things honest in the sight of all men" needful to the perishing body, much more should they teach them to treasure up the needful riches of the soul. They will soon be compelled to see that all the honors and riches of the world are dust and dross, compared with treasures in heaven. Anticipating this from the beginning, they should lift up their eyes to "the everlasting hills," and seek for their children "*an inheritance that fadeth not away.*"

CHAPTER V.

FILIAL DUTIES.

Filial duty is the counterpart to parental. Parental affection, authority, government, instruction, example, and kindness, should be responded to with corresponding love, reverence, obedience, docility and gratitude, on the part of the children. Thus all the parental and filial duties are reciprocal, and equally binding upon the respective parties.

But the failure of the parent to do *his* duty, does not exonerate the child from doing his. The obligations of children are greatly augmented by their being favored with loving and faithful parents; but the bond of filial duty is ever upon them, although more or less modified, under every possible development of parental character.

FILIAL LOVE.

It has been previously shown that children have a peculiar natural affection for their parents. It is an affection which nothing but crime on the child's part can destroy. The parent may wound it; he may be severe, unkind, capricious, cruel; he may indulge in degrading vices; still, so long as the child is himself what he ought to be, his heart will yearn towards the unnatural parent.

All children should sacredly *cherish* this affection as a *duty*. To allow it to die out of the heart, or to be displaced by other affections, is to squander one of the most precious of heaven's gifts, and to incur a fearful penalty. "Cursed is he that *setteth light by his father or mother*, and all the people shall say, Amen."

The absence of filial affection, or failure suitably to manifest it, is condemned by the general consent of mankind. A child "without natural affection" towards his parents, is a monster which the world seems unwilling to own. Every child, then, as he values the favor of both God and man, should cherish a deep, abiding, controlling affection for his parents. There is but one earthly affection that may *transcend* this; and even that should not *displace* it. When the son or daughter leaves father and mother to be joined to another in marriage, it is not that he or she may love parents less, but wife or husband more.

FILIAL REVERENCE.

Children have naturally a feeling of peculiar *reverence* for their parents. To them, under God, they owe their existence; and hence they are *bound* to regard them with a kind of reverential homage, which is due to no other human being. This feeling blends with that of filial love, and is the basis of true obedience. Children who suitably love and revere their parents, are sure to obey them, and to obey from the right motives.

Hence to honor and to obey, as indicating filial duty, are in the Scriptures synonymous. "*Honor* thy father and thy mother, that thy days may be long upon the land which the Lord thy God giveth thee." Referring to this command, the apostle says, "Children, *obey* your parents in the Lord, for this is right. *Honor* thy father and mother; which is the first commandment with promise."

The child who properly reveres his parents, will always be gentle and respectful towards them, will treat them with marked attention, will delicately regard their feelings and consult their wishes, will speak of them with affectionate respect, and will never allow them to be spoken against in his presence.

FILIAL OBEDIENCE.

As it is the parent's duty to *govern*, so it is the child's duty to *obey*. Upon fewer duties do the Scriptures insist more earnestly. "My son, *hear the instruction of thy father, and forsake not the law of thy mother;* they shall be an ornament of grace unto thine head, and chains about thy neck. *Keep thy father's commandments, and forsake not the law of thy mother.* A wise son heareth his father's instruction; a foolish son despiseth his mother."

"Honor thy father and thy mother, which is the first commandment with promise, that it may be well with thee, and that thou mayest live long on the earth." "The eye that *mocketh at his father*, and *despiseth to obey his mother*, the ravens of the valley shall pick it out, and the young eagles shall eat it." "If a man have a stubborn and rebellious son, that will not obey the voice of his father, or the voice of his mother, all the men of the city shall stone him with stones that he die." * Thus persistent disobedience in a child was, under the Mosaic economy, punished with death. Obey he *must*, or he should not live.

Filial obedience should always be *cordial* and *prompt*.

* Prov. 1: 8. 10: 7. Ex. 20: 12. Prov. 30: 7. Deut. 21: 18.

Its quality of moral excellence depends wholly upon this. If it is grudged, unwilling, extorted by threat or punishment, it is not *moral* obedience. It is essential to the very nature of true obedience, that it be hearty, willing, cheerful. When Christ said, "I *delight* to do thy will, O my God; yea, thy law is within my *heart*," he expressed to his Heavenly Father the spirit of obedience, which children should exercise towards their earthly parents.

But filial obedience is subject to some *limitation.* Parental government has a striking resemblance to the divine, but differs from it in one capital respect. While the latter never errs, the former may err. Hence cases may occur in which filial obedience should be withheld. These are of two kinds.

First, parents may require their children to do *wrong;* as to lie, steal, cheat, swear, violate the Sabbath, or practise impurities. In such cases the child, ought not to obey; for a higher than parental authority forbids him. To obey his parents, in such cases, would be to disobey God. The command is, "Obey your parents *in the Lord.*"

Secondly, children may have *religious scruples* at variance with parental commands. In such cases duty is determined with less readiness. The child, while yet a minor, may be of a different *faith* from his parent, may wish to unite with a church which the parent disapproves; or may consider himself bound by some religious obligation, of which his parent does not feel the force, and to which he will not give his consent.

In this case the child should consider the sacredness of the filial relation, and remember that nothing but the clearest will of God can justify him in disobedience. He should also consider his own youth and inexperience, and the possibility of his viewing things differently at a future time; he should seek the consent of his parents, with a manifest desire to please them; and finally, he should consider, if he cannot obtain their consent, that the period of his minority will soon terminate, and that present submission to their authority may be a more truly religious act than any mere formal connection with religious ordinances.

Such considerations will serve to keep conscience void of offence; while at the same time they will render the necessity for resisting parental authority, from religious scruples, of very rare occurrence.

FILIAL DOCILITY.

If it is the parent's duty to *teach* and to set the *example*, it is no less the child's duty to *learn*. Docility, or a disposition to learn, is one of the first and most characteristic duties of all childhood. Coming into the world entirely ignorant, all children alike have every thing to learn. Genius, however brilliant, makes no exceptions. Indeed genius and docility are almost synonymous terms. And as the parent is the first and most responsible teacher, so to the parent, before all others, should the child submit himself to be taught.

A propensity to this is implanted by nature. The infant child looks up to its parent earnestly, confidingly, submissively, for knowledge. It believes and accepts all. It hangs upon its parent's lips and eyes as oracles. It eagerly watches every action and emotion, to learn its destiny and duty. So marked and important is this propensity, that Christ refers to it as indicating the spirit with which we must receive his gospel. "Except ye *become as little children*, ye shall in no wise enter into the kingdom of God."

This docility of spirit all children should cherish as a *duty.* It is indispensable to their progress in knowledge and virtue. It is both their ornament and security. Nothing is more offensive to God and man, nothing more surely indicates the future ruin of a child, than that spirit of arrogance and conceit which contemns parental instruction. This spirit is one of the greatest dangers of the present generation.

Many of the children of "Young America," where youth is in the ascendant, and childhood asserts the honors hitherto accorded only to gray hairs, are becoming fascinated with the conceit that the law of nature has changed; that the time has come for age to keep silence and the lips of infancy to speak; and that they are to make their first demonstrations of superiority by assuming to be wiser than their parents. But the law of nature has not changed; it is the same now as when the command to hearken to parental instruction was first written by the finger of God; and they who disregard it, will eventually be taught their error in lessons of bitter experience. Thousands of ruined men are at this moment lamenting in vain their youthful folly, in not listening to the instructions of their parents; and what *they* now suffer, they will also leave for those youths to suffer in their turn, who follow in their footsteps.

Children blessed with good parents should also *imitate their example.* The principle of imitation is in no respect more active and important, than as inducing children to follow the example of their parents. It lays the responsibility with great emphasis upon parents to set a good example; while it also fastens the duty upon their children to follow it. In this way parents become, in the most practical sense, the moulders of their children's character.

The children of good parents have their lesson ever before them, not in the form of mere abstract principles and precepts, but of living example. It is a picture they need only to copy. They have but to imitate the justice and benevolence, the courage and meekness, the industry and self-sacrifice, the fidelity and truthfulness, the conscientious regard to duty, exhibited in the daily conduct of their parents, and their own character is securely formed. It is by this means, preëminently, that parents are to train up their children in the way they should go.

But let the child entertain the false notion, that the example of his parents, however good, has no binding force upon him; that it even bespeaks a noble independence to depart from it; let him listen to the voice which says, "Walk in the ways of thine heart, and in the sight of thine eyes;" let him thus "break their bands in sunder, and cast away their cords from him;" and he is self-doomed to ruin. Thousands of children, instigated by bad companions and evil dispositions, are continually destroying themselves in this manner. The temperance, the sobriety, the observance of the Sabbath, the industry, the frugality, which have made their parents successful and independent, they discard as old-fashioned and puritanic, in favor of those freer and more self-indulgent habits whose end is ruin and sorrow.

FILIAL GRATITUDE.

The affectionate and self-sacrificing attentions bestowed by parents upon their children, demand corresponding returns of *gratitude*. The principle of gratitude is innate. It is often marred and sometimes perhaps quite displaced by wickedness, but every person true to his nature is grateful for benefits. He who is never grateful for favors is not only below humanity, but even below the brutes.

But if the Creator thus designed that we should be grateful to *all* who do us good, he obviously meant that we should be *especially* so to our parents, who are our greatest earthly benefactors. The anxiety and pain, the care and thought, the watchfulness and toil, the generous sacrifice of ease and health and sometimes of even life itself, to which they cheerfully submit for the sake of their children, can never be by the children fully appreciated, until they have themselves become parents and experience the same. It was thus divinely intended that filial gratitude, so far from ceasing with the age of minority, should continue to increase through life.

A good child manifests a grateful disposition towards his parents, as soon as he is old enough to appreciate their favors. As every day renews their favors, it increases his feeling of obligation. Nor is the feeling a passive sentiment; it is active and efficient. It makes him prompt to obey them, and to do all in his power to relieve their cares and contribute to their happiness. Knowing that they are anxious for his welfare, he strives to be worthy of their benefactions. As he sees them toiling to educate and train him for honor and usefulness, he himself toils for the same end. He thus throws himself into their plans and wishes, sympathizes with their feelings, and makes common cause with them in his personal welfare.

Some may call this a selfish gratitude; but by whatever name called, its prevalence is greatly to be desired. If all children favored with good parents were under its controlling influence, the world would be rapidly redeemed from its crimes and its miseries. The gratitude of children thus expressed would infallibly conduct them to lives of virtue and honor, and would thus realize to parents the promise, "Instead of thy fathers *shall be thy children*, whom thou mayest make *princes in all the earth.*"

But true filial gratitude by no means exhausts itself in this direction. It looks towards the personal welfare and happiness of the *parents.* It seeks to relieve their cares, lighten their burdens, anticipate their wants, and augment their means of comfort.

After the grateful child has passed the years of his minority, and he sees the infirmity of years pressing upon his parents, his endeavors for their comfort are characterized by that delicacy which never allows them to feel that the care of them is a burden. The attentions which they have from his infancy bestowed upon him, he now returns in unceasing attentions to them. If they are called first to "walk through the valley of the shadow of death," his prayers and blessings will follow them all the way, until they finally disappear from the scenes of earth; and, as long as he lives, his tears of grateful remembrance will not cease to fall upon their graves.

CHAPTER VI.

FRATERNAL DUTIES.

Next to the relation of husband and wife, and of parents and children, is that of the children of the same family to each other. Born of the same parents, subject to the same government, trained under the same culture, heirs to the same inheritance, and having a common interest in the weal or woe of the family, their relation is very intimate, and involves some special duties. We shall notice these in the most natural order.

And first of all, they should tenderly *love* each other. The fraternal affection originates, as we have seen, in nature. Children of the same family are naturally inclined to love one another. This is in part owing to their being brought up together, but the peculiar affection to which we refer, is mostly due to their regarding each other as children of the same parents.

This affection was implanted for an important purpose, and should be sacredly cherished. In order to this, every child has these two duties to perform.

First, he should so conduct towards his brothers and sisters as to render himself *lovely* to them. He will thus deserve their affection. By forbearance towards their provocations, by acts of kindness and generosity towards them, by sympathy with their wants and trials, in short, by exhibiting towards them the true fraternal spirit, he may render it an easy and delightful task for them to love him. He may thus bind their hearts to him with cords that can never be broken.

Secondly, while binding their hearts to him, he should also bind *his own heart to them.* He should tenderly regard them as children with himself of the same parents; he should appreciate all their kindnesses, and be ever quick to see in them whatever is deserving of his approbation. He must be to them not the mere guardian and benefactor, but the affectionate brother. The fraternal affection is not a mere patronizing feeling on the one side, nor a mere grateful one on the other; it is mutual and unselfish love, in view of sustaining the endearing relation of children of the same parents.

This reciprocity of fraternal affection *should continue through life.* It should not be allowed to languish, after the children leave the parental roof. Having so conducted towards each other while together as to give it deep root in their hearts, they should carefully avoid any cause, whether in the distribution of property or subsequent pursuits, that might tend to alienation. The affection begun in childhood, should grow and bear fruit through all their lives.

If Providence casts their lot near each other, it will contribute in various ways to their mutual advantage and happiness. It will dispose them to bear each other's burdens, and to heighten each other's joys. It will render sweet and delightful the social intercourse of their families, and thus greatly augment the pleasures of daily life within their enchanted circle. Brothers, sisters, and the numerous host of cousins, are thus made happy in each other. The delightful intimacies of families thus related, have a benign influence upon the moral and religious culture of the young, and upon the stability and general welfare of the state.

If their lots are cast far apart, they should cherish the mutual affection by correspondence. True fraternal love is superior to time and distance. Rolling prairies, towering mountains, wide oceans, cannot destroy it. And however widely separated, brothers and sisters feel the power of each other's love, strengthening, cheering, blessing them, in the great battle of life. How angel-like is the voice of a dear brother or sister coming from a distant land, telling us of the heart that still loves us, of the lips that still pray for us; reminding us of the "sweet home" that we once enjoyed together, and pointing us to our eternal home in heaven, where we hope to meet again.

In a world so cold and selfish as this, fraternal love, deeply rooted in childhood and nurtured through life, is of unspeakable worth. No amount of parental estate, for which children too often contend, can compare in value with it. Better that the largest fortune be sunk in the sea, than that it should become an occasion of alienation between them. "Behold, how *good* and how *pleasant* it is for *brethren to dwell together in unity.*"

MUTUAL INFLUENCE.

Children of the same family are so intimately related in their daily intercourse as to have a most decisive influence upon each other. One bad child may, by the contagion of his words and his example, spread pestilence through the household. If he resists parental authority, example, instruction; if he uses vulgar or profane language; if he indulges in vicious practices; he both teaches and emboldens the other children to do the same. If he is selfish, morose, fretful, he infuses the same unhappy spirit into those around him. If he is idle, foppish, vain, his influence will tend to make the others like himself. If he is wasteful, extravagant, reckless, he may by his example become the means of ruin to the whole household. "A little leaven leaveneth the whole lump."

On the other hand, like an angel from the skies hovering around the family and showering blessings upon it from his golden wings, such is a truly loving and faithful elder brother to the younger children of the household. He is of more value to them than mines of wealth. His conduct wins their confidence and affection, and the influence thus secured he exerts for their present and future welfare. They will remember him, with gratitude which words are too feeble to express, in all after time. The same may be true of an elder sister.

Children should consider this before it is too late. Here is a duty to be done during the brief period in which they are *together* under the parental roof; a period soon to be passed, and never to return.

PARTICULAR DUTY OF BROTHERS TO SISTERS.

A brother may confer many favors upon his sisters, which no other person can. Their physical delicacy and the customs of society render them peculiarly dependent upon the other sex. They cannot go out of evenings alone or unprotected; they must not thrust themselves forward into society; they have need of peculiar caution in making acquaintances; prudence forbids them to speak in their own behalf; and they often endure neglect, slander, insult, rather than be bold in their own defence.

In all these particulars a kind and judicious brother may render them essential service. He may favor them with his company and attentions; he may assist them in forming suitable acquaintances; he may protect them from slander and insult; he may often be the means of so bringing them forward in their education, and introducing them into society, as to place them in desirable positions for life.

All this should be done, not with the grudging of a patronizing spirit, but with the cheerful, unselfish, chivalrous spirit of the *loving brother*. By these delicate and generous attentions, he will deeply embalm himself in their affections; for who ever knew the sister that did not love such a brother? And more than this, he will realize an unspeakable reward in their greatly augmented welfare and happiness.

PARTICULAR DUTY OF SISTERS TO BROTHERS.

A sister may also be of peculiar service to her brothers. She can do for them what none but a sister can do, at least so well.

Boys are inclined to be rough and boisterous in their manners; to be selfish and impatient in their demands; to be fond of being absent of evenings, amidst dissipating excitements; and, in various ways, to disregard the duties of home, and the restraints of parental authority. The peculiar faults of boys often arise mostly from the excess of animalism, and the rude impatience to which it impels.

A sister may do much towards correcting all this. By her gentleness and delicacy, she may refine their manners. By her kind sympathy with their trials, devotion to their wants, and endeavors to promote their happiness, she may obtain such hold on their affections as to have a magic sway over them. A loving and kind sister is her brother's intercessor with their father, and seldom fails of success. If they are sick, no attentions are more soothing than hers. She beguiles the long winter evenings with music, reading, and agreeable and instructive conversation, and thus makes home attractive.

The home of cultivated, amiable, loving sisters, faithful to their vocation, is the most charming spot upon earth. Seldom is a brother so wayward as to resist its influence. Its power over him is very great, while he is present; it is scarcely less, when he is absent. If exposed to the temptations of a great city, if a sailor upon the ocean, if a stranger in foreign lands, he remembers that dear home, those precious sisters, the smiles and tears caught from them by his last parting look, and by all the love he bears them, feels constrained to do nothing which they would not approve. By the hope of again enjoying their society, he summons a brave heart to the conflicts and duties before him.

Thus the character, the happiness, the success of young men depends, in a great measure, upon their sisters. Their influence is next to that of parents, and sometimes even transcends it.

DUTIES OF THE ELDER TO THE YOUNGER CHILDREN.

The elder children owe some special duties to the younger. Once the eldest child was the *only* one. He enjoyed the undivided parental affection, and all the toys, rights and privileges of the nursery, were under his exclusive control. But another has come to share with him, and now his position is materially changed. It is his first duty to welcome the little stranger, and cheerfully to relinquish a due portion of the blessings which he has hitherto possessed alone. Unselfish and unenvious, he must adopt the welfare of the little brother or sister, and seek it as heartily as his own.

Nor is this all. The elder children should assist in *taking care* of the younger, and thus relieve their parents. Otherwise the care of parents, as their families increase, would often be insupportable. They cannot usually afford to keep servants enough to take the entire care of each child, and even if they could, servants cannot fill the place of brothers and sisters. Of these duties the children cannot so well judge as their parents, and should therefore ever be, in these as in all others, subject to their control.

While the elder children assist their parents in protecting and teaching the younger, they must not usurp *authority* over them. They must act the loving and faithful brother or sister, but not the parent. They may instruct, admonish, persuade, but never command and punish. They may, however, greatly *assist* parental government. If they are themselves respectful and obedient, their admonition and example will usually be followed. Thus the filial piety, and even the entire character and destiny of the younger children, often turn upon the conduct of the eldest brother or sister.

SUSPICION OF PARTIALITY TO BE AVOIDED.

A selfish child is prone to suspect his parents of *partiality*. If they do not always espouse *his* interest and gratify *his* wishes, he accuses them of doing better by his brothers and sisters than by himself. He forgets that others have claims as well as he. He sees with the eyes of a selfish individual, while his parents see with the eyes of a guardianship embracing alike the rights of all. They may see reasons for treating their children in some respects differently, while they have the welfare of all equally at heart.

As children are adapted to different situations and callings, the wise parent will have due regard to this adaptation. Those children are unjust to a brother or sister, who would deprive him or her of an advantage, just because they are themselves incompetent to enjoy it. One may have the capacity to excel as a student, which the others do not possess. They must not envy that one the privilege of a liberal education, nor accuse the parents of partiality in affording it. If at the same time *their* capacities are consulted, and the best possible advantages afforded them, no partiality is exercised.

While no sight is more pleasing than that of a family of children uniting in each other's welfare, rejoicing in each other's success, bearing each other's burdens, and never admitting jealousy or strife within their happy circle, nothing on the other hand is more odious than a family feud. Heart-burnings and contentions between children of the same family, whether before or after their legal interests are divided, are so unnatural, so monstrous, that both earth and heaven abhor them.

MUTUAL OBLIGATIONS IN AFTER LIFE.

After children have become of age and have established separate pecuniary interests, they should still do what they can, consistently with duty to their own families, to assist each other. Next to his own family, a man should regard his brothers and sisters. Natural affection suggests this. He acts an unnatural part, who sees the children of his own parents want, when it is in his power to relieve them. If he is prospered, he may often provide favorable situations for his brothers, assist to educate

19

his sisters, and thus be the means of placing them all in eligible circumstances.

Sometimes there is an *unfortunate* child, maimed, cripple, idiotic, or through some idiosyncrasy incapable of self-maintenance. It is the duty of the other children, after the decease of the parents, to provide for him. Nor should they do it grudgingly. They should gratefully consider their own advantages, and gladly do all in their power to compensate the peculiar trials of him less favored. Their regard to family reputation should unite with fraternal affection in forbidding public charity to support him, so long as they are able to do it.

They should not only support him while they live, but make suitable provision for him by will, in case he survives them. Their benefactions of this nature, as well as all others, should be regulated by a suitable regard to other objects. Brothers and sisters, next to their own families, have the first but not the sole claim upon them. There are other objects, educational, social, religious, which demand voluntary aid. It cannot therefore be one's duty to provide so largely for his relatives as to exonerate them from all necessity of effort, and bestow nothing upon these important objects. He has a *legal* right to dispose of his property as he pleases, however narrow and selfish his views; but there is a *moral* demand upon him, that is not so summarily cancelled. On the other hand, he who bestows *all* his remaining property, after providing for his family, upon public objects, disregarding the wants of a needy brother or sister, may obtain praise of man as a public benefactor, but a more righteous tribunal will not hold him guiltless. "*These ought ye to have done, and not to leave the other undone.*"

CHAPTER VII.

CIVIL DUTIES.

MUCH talent and learning have been expended upon the subjects of civil freedom and political economy. Beautiful theories of government have been framed, which have promised a millennium of liberty and of wealth to the nations. But their expectations have not been realized; nor will they ever be. Redemption to the enthralled people does not so come. The difficulty lies deeper than most theorists have looked; it is not primarily in governments, but in the depravity of men. Were all the angels in heaven to combine their wisdom to form a political system and impose it upon the nations, it would not of itself avail to make them contented and happy.

The best possible government, placed over an ignorant and vicious people, would be by them deemed tyrannical and oppressive; and, if submitted to their management, would be by them spoiled within a single year. A fortune might as well be bestowed upon profligate children with the expectation of its doing them good. The troubles of nations are not so much of their governments as of themselves. Both may be bad; but if even God himself failed in *his* government to bless the people, as he would fain have done, because they were "stiff-necked and rebellious," it can hardly be expected that political theorists will hit upon a plan that will prove successful, until the people themselves become wiser and better.

The world is not to be saved by governments. Redemption must come to the nations by other means. Civil government is an *effect* rather than a cause; an exponent of what the people *are*, rather than a power effective to make them what they *should* be. This is especially true of all constitutional governments; and, in fact, of all governments having in them any of the elements of civil liberty.

Intelligence and virtue must go in advance and prepare the way. The people must be taught. Many must run to and fro, and knowledge must be increased. The public conscience must be enlightened and quickened. The principles of sound morality, and their practical bearings upon the individual and general welfare, must be inculcated. The people must be touched and magnetized with the true spirit of liberty. They must be made to see their duties, their capabilities, and their exalted privileges.

Above all, the regenerating power of the Gospel must be put forth upon the people, and "the leaves of the tree for the healing of the nations," must be scattered broadcast over the world. Then "there shall be no more curse;" nations and governments will be what they *ought* to be. Each government will then as naturally assume the form and operation best suited to its people, as the human body naturally assumes the finest symmetry and movement, when its informing dynamic forces are in healthy and harmonious action.

To theorize upon the best form of government is therefore no part of our present object. We have to do with general principles, applicable alike to all governments. We are to take mankind and governments as they are, and to indicate the principles of civil duty under all circumstances.

CIVIL DUTIES DEFINED.

Civil duties are those which relate to the state. But what is the state? It is not a mere voluntary compact, as some have supposed, but an institution of God. People living together in the same country constitute a state, just as parents and children living under the same roof constitute a family.

Let a company of strangers be cast upon a hitherto uninhabited island, and they will there have of necessity certain interests in common. They become, by their position, mutually dependent for protection and liberty, and are thus a state. They may not as yet have adopted any regulations, nor enacted any laws; still the state is a state, just as the family is a family, prior to all its rules. Government is the *instrument*, which the state or the family employs to secure its ends.

The state, then, is created by God; government is established and administered by men. Yet both civil and family governments are *authorized* by God, and are thus sacredly binding upon us. But as the form and administration of governments are of men, and partake of human imperfections, the state may sit in judgment upon them, and annul or alter them, as the interests of the people demand.

Let us then define our several positions.

The entire body of people living together in a condition of mutual dependence for protection and liberty, are the *state*.

The rules and methods which the state employs to secure its ends, are *civil government.*

The persons employed to administer the government, are *magistrates.*

The subjects of government, in their direct relations to it as such, are *citizens.*

There are, then, three general relations, in which men may act in the discharge of civil duties. They may act as the *state*, engaged in instituting government; or as *magistrates*, engaged in executing the will of the state; or as *citizens*, engaged in obeying its laws. In a monarchy, the first two are monopolized by the sovereign.

In constitutional or free governments, they may be shared by the entire people. Human imperfection is thus in a great measure obviated; since the legislator, the judge, and the executor, operate as salutary checks upon each other. If the legislator errs, self-partiality is not allowed to confirm his errors in judgment, but another must judge him. And if the judge errs, he may not confirm his errors by executing his own decrees, but a discretionary power is lodged with the chief executive magistrate. Such is the beautiful arrangement of constitutional government.

Following the above analysis, we shall consider civil duties under three heads; the duties of the state, the duties of magistrates, and the duties of citizens.

I. DUTIES OF THE STATE.

1. The state should *adapt her government to the qualifications of the people.* If the people are capable of sustaining freer institutions than she allows, she keeps herself and her subjects in guilty and degrading bondage. But if she strikes for a freer government than the people can

sustain, she perils the liberty already enjoyed. She ought, then, losing nothing by delay, and yet perilling nothing by haste, to press her government closely along with the qualifications of her subjects, towards the highest practicable liberty. Any attempt to effect a sudden and entire change of government with a view to greater liberty, is seldom safe. Indeed, history seems to prove that it is *never* so, excepting in the case of people geographically separated from the parent state, and able to govern and protect themselves.

2. The state should *place in office the best qualified men.* In a monarchical government, this duty rests with the sovereign; but in a republic it devolves upon all voters. Both they who refrain from voting, and they who vote from mere party or selfish motives, are false to their responsible trust. If all refrain from voting, there can be no organized government, and of course anarchy is the alternative. If all vote from mere party spirit, regardless of the qualifications of their candidates, incompetent rulers will be chosen, and thus government will be badly administered.

The true friend to his country will then be true at the polls. As a part of the state, he will consider it his duty to do his part towards the election of suitable men to office; as much as it is, in the relation of subject, to obey its laws.

3. The state should *provide the means for her prosperity and defence.* She should provide armies, navies, fortifications, and all other things needful for defence; she she should also improve her harbors, facilitate the navigation of her rivers; construct and support light-houses; and do all other public works demanded by the national welfare. These things cannot be done by individuals. They are national. Individual citizens have neither the

ability nor the right to do them. The man who, on his own responsibility, erects a light-house, does as morally wrong an act, and may occasion as much damage, as he who destroys one which the state has erected. The state must do public works; citizens must let them alone.

To provide the means in question, the state should husband to best advantage her natural resources, as from the sale of her lands, &c., and if these are not sufficient, she must levy equitable taxes and imposts. These should bear equally and justly upon all trades, all kinds of property, and all classes of citizens. Where the state can, in justice to all, so levy them as to encourage desirable kinds of industry, and thus enhance the national wealth, she is bound to do so. She thus secures her two great ends, the *protection* and the *industry* of her subjects.

4. The state should *employ the sanctions of religion.* She ought to be tolerant to all her subjects, never attempting to coerce the faith of any; but she must regard the man of *no* faith as an anomaly, a *thing* by itself, and hence no legitimate part of the state. All men in the normal condition have some religious belief and some conscience; they have a sense of accountability to a superior power. This faith the state must protect, and she must *make use* of it for the support of government. No state can institute and enforce laws without it. She cannot without it even administer the civil oath.

But when the state adopts any specific form of religious faith to the exclusion of all others, making it the favorite and the tool of government, she is false to herself and unjust to the people. For the state is not a part, nor a majority, but the *whole* of the responsible people, and hence the whole of that people must be respected in their religion. Be it but one man, and he the humblest in the nation, he is still an integral part of the state, as truly so as a finger or a toe is an integral part of the body. Neither of them should be cut off, merely for being a small and feeble member. The question in morals is never one of *might*, but always a question of *right*. The feeblest man is still a man; his conscience and faith, whatever they may be, are sacredly his own, and the state may never take them from him. He is for these responsible only to God.

5. The state should *employ judicial oaths with strict regard to the religious faith of the people.* No man can conscientiously swear upon a creed which he does not believe. Whenever a man does swear upon such a creed, his oath is of no avail. If a man acknowledges *no* religious responsibility, his oath is a nullity. He is not, as we have said, a legitimate part of the state. As he disowns a rational and accountable nature, and thus takes the position of an animal, the state must treat him as it does other animals.

Oaths are administered in cases of testimony, as when a man is a witness and swears to the truth of what he asserts; and also in cases of engagement, as when a man enters into covenant and swears to abide by it. The former impose fidelity in recalling and stating facts; the latter in discharging official duties and responsible trusts. Hence oaths are naturally divided into two kinds, those of *testimony*, and those of *engagement*.

The modified form of oath called *affirmation*, preferred by the quakers, is equally valid with the usual form. And even an oath on the Koran, or the sacred books of India or China, if the subject is a religious believer in them, must be accepted by the state; the right being reserved of attaching the due relative importance to his testimony or promise. In a Mahometan country, testimony or promise confirmed by an oath on the Koran would naturally pass at par value; in a Christian country, it might pass for less. If a man is a true and consistent believer in future retributions, his oath will pass with considerate persons for much more than if his views were less serious.

As an oath is an appeal to God, a prayer for his assistance and an imprecation of his vengeance, it is a very solemn religious act. On this account, the taking of oaths on common occasions, or what is called *profane* swearing, is immoral and wicked. It is both sinful and vulgar, condemned alike by Christianity and the rules of good breeding. "Swear not at all; neither by heaven, for it is God's throne, neither by the earth, for it is his footstool; neither by Jerusalem, for it is the city of the great king. Neither shalt thou swear by thy head, because thou canst not make one hair white or black. But let your communications be yea, yea; nay, nay: for whatsoever is more than these cometh of evil." * All profane oaths tend to weaken rather than strengthen the affirmation, while they also fix the brand of impiety and vulgarity upon their subject.

But this is no more reason why judicial oaths should be discarded, than the fact that mock worship is often offered to God, is a reason why we should not worship him "in spirit and in truth." The state *needs* the solemn sanctions of religion thus applied, and in availing herself of them, acts under the express authority of God.† Indeed he has himself set us the example.‡ These facts prove at once the immorality and impiety of *profane* oaths, and the entire rightfulness of judicial oaths, when strictly demanded.

* Matth. 5: 35–37.

† See Rom. 1: 9. II. Cor. 1: 23. I. Thess. 2: 5.

‡ See Isaiah 45: 23. Jer. 49: 13. Amos 6: 8.

But even judicial oaths should be as infrequent as possible. Their object is to quicken and elevate the conscience by a solemn appeal to God, and this appeal is the more effective the less frequently it is made. When judicial oaths are administered on trivial occasions, and thus become common and familiar, they degenerate to a vulgar formality. Thoughtlessly administered and received, they partake of the moral quality of profane swearing.

6. The state *should have the control of all property.* A man's property is his *own*, only upon the condition of its being always subject to God and the state. God is the sovereign owner of all property; the state is the second; and the citizen is the third. The right of the citizen to control his own property, is opposed to all rights and attempts of other citizens to control it, but never to the higher rights of God and of the state. Thus every man's property is his own, only as the state makes and keeps it so.

And this the state is always bound to do, reserving the right so to control it as best to promote the welfare of the people, without loss to the individual. The state should encourage industry and promote thrift, by securing to each citizen the proceeds of his own labor, while at the same time it must not allow public and private interests to collide.

The state has the right to impose taxes upon individual property, for general purposes. Education, roads, bridges, public buildings, legislation, courts, penalties, are objects to be provided for by taxes upon the property of citizens.

The state has also the right to appropriate private lands to needful public uses. She may not only *tax* the soil, but *take* it, if the public good requires, and appropriate it to her own use, or to that of an incorporated company, always allowing the owner a fair compensation. Thus if the interests of the people demand a highway, a railroad, a bridge, a ferry, a park, it is not left for the citizen owning the required land to say whether the state shall use it for that purpose, but the state may take it and use it at discretion, allowing for it a reasonable compensation.

7. The state *should not allow unfair monopolies.* She must not herself monopolize, nor must she allow any citizens to do so. She must to some extent hold property, and she must buy and sell. Otherwise she could not have forts, navy-yards, fleets, armies, and the other means of public defence. But she should hold the exclusive possession of property only so far as the general good demands. All wealth, so far as practicable, should be in the hands of the citizens. Scarcely a greater calamity can befall a town than to have the state hold an exclusive control of a large part of it.

Much less may the state embark in *speculation.* As her resources are mostly from the citizens, she can speculate only at their risk. Especially odious is her conduct when, for the sake of augmenting her income, she forestalls the market and monopolizes the sale of an article needful for the sustenance of the citizens, and compels them to pay a forced price for it. This has been done in Great Britain and in some other states, to the great detriment of all parties.

Neither may the state allow her *citizens* to monopolize. She should encourage enterprise in individuals, and she should encourage the same in corpôrate bodies; but the interests of individuals and those of companies must not be allowed to conflict with each other. One of the nicest and most difficult duties of the state is here demanded.

She should not only prevent these interests from colliding, but should make them mutually advantageous. A manufacturing corporation may be so constituted as to diffuse individual industry and thrift on every side, or it may be empowered to produce the very opposite result.

The state must charter banks, factories, railroads, bridges, &c., because the general welfare demands them; but she should never grant a charter conferring a monopoly or any extraordinary advantages upon the grantees, to the detriment of the public. In a word, as the state is bound to consult impartially the interests of the *whole* people, she cannot afford to be generous to a *part* of them. If she is generous to some, she is unjust to others.

8. The state should *foster education*. It is as important that she provide for the *education* of the people, as for their health, wealth, and defence. Indeed, education is an essential means to all these. Public freedom, the first object of the state, cannot be sustained without a general diffusion of knowledge. She is therefore bound to provide for the education of the people, and to exercise her legislative authority in establishing and sustaining literary institutions.

But her duties lie rather in providing the *means* of education, than in directing the specific *course* of it. She is bound to see that nothing *immoral* or *seditious* is taught; but further than this, her duties to literary institutions are general. She may do too much, as well as too little. She should leave it for the citizens of each town or district, to select their teachers, locate their schools, and supervise them; while the teachers should be usually regarded as the most competent to select the books, direct the studies, and secure the discipline. Even the higher institutions, academies, colleges, universities, are usually better directed by their teachers and overseers than by the state.

9. The state should *foster religion.* She is dependent upon it for the support of government. No good government ever did or can exist without it. As well might a palace rest suspended in the air, or the Andes repose on the bosom of the Atlantic, as civil government be sustained without religion.

It is only as the state plants her authority and builds her government upon the fact that man is amenable to his Maker, and will be by him brought into judgment, that her authority has any force, her oaths any meaning, or her government any foundation. She is bound, therefore, to respect the religious as well as intellectual culture of her subjects; to foster religion not less than education.

But here again, as in the case of education, she may do too much. She should bind no man's conscience, but she must assume that all men *have* conscience, and are responsible to God for their conduct.

First, she should *protect religious worship.* She must not undertake to decide for the citizens the particular form of their worship, but allow every man to decide that for himself. She may also leave it to them to defray the expense of their worship, since some choose to expend upon it more than others. Those who prefer the more expensive church and ministrations should pay for them. But the state should impartially charter and protect the societies of every religious creed not subversive of her institutions; she should throw her guardian wing over them all alike, and sacredly regard both their worship and their property.

Secondly, she should enjoin *the sacred observance of her Sabbath.* All states have their sabbaths; for all people have their special religious days. The holy day of all Christian people is of course the Christian Sabbath. Every Christian state is bound to protect it as sacred to her citizens, and as a means of sustaining just authority over them. She needs it to enlighten and quicken their consciences, to form and protect their morals, to regulate their domestic and social habits, and thus to render them enlightened and loyal subjects of her government. If any man's faith requires him to observe the seventh day as sacred, she should allow him to do so; but she must not allow him to disturb the worship nor the sacredness of her own Sabbath.

Thirdly, she should *prohihit all blasphemy and profane swearing.* No man can plead the dictates of conscience, as a reason for being released from such a prohibition. No man's right is invaded by not being allowed to profane and blaspheme God, for no man ever had any such right. On the other hand, the state has very serious rights and duties in the matter. Such immoralities tend to destroy all reverence for God, to annihilate the validity of judicial oaths, and to sap the foundations of civil government.

Fourthly, she should *encourage the free circulation of the Bible.* All states have their sacred books or oracles; that of a Christian state is the Bible. Her laws are founded upon its principles and sustained by its authority. The more the people read and understand it, the greater will be the amount of liberty which the state can give them. She can give them thoroughly free institutions, only as they read and adopt the teachings of that book which is the charter of their liberty. Just in the degree that they become enlightened in its truths and obedient to its principles, they become capable of understanding and sustaining free government.

10. The state should *prohibit all treasonable and im-*

moral conduct. She must do so, not because such conduct is displeasing to God; for she has nothing to do with that consideration; but because it is *injurious to herself.* For this reason she must have prohibitory laws with suitable penalties, and magistrates to enforce them. Thus she must have laws against treason, murder, adultery, perjury, arson, fraud, lying, seduction, uncleanness, theft, cruelty, slander, and other such immoralities; and she should graduate their penalties, not with reference to the offence against God, but against herself. It is her duty to legislate, judge, and punish, for herself, not for God.

Her law is not needed to keep the *righteous* in order; they are controlled by allegiance to the higher law of God. But it *is* needed to keep the *unrighteous* in order, that they may not injure the state and invade the liberties of the virtuous. "The law is not made for a *righteous* man, but for the lawless and disobedient, for the ungodly and sinners, for unholy and profane; for murderers of fathers and murderers of mothers, for manslayers, for whoremongers, for them that defile themselves with mankind; for men-stealers, for liars, for perjured persons; and if there be any other thing contrary to sound doctrine." *

* 1 Tim. 1: 9.

CHAPTER VIII.

CIVIL DUTIES CONTINUED.

II. DUTIES OF MAGISTRATES.

All persons appointed to office by the state, whether in the legislative, judicial, or executive departments, are called *magistrates*. We proceed to notice their respective duties.

Duties of Legislators.—The legislators are men chosen by the people to *enact their laws*. The question arises, whether they are to be bound by the will of their constituents. Ought they to enact such laws as the people desire, or such as their own judgment approves?

They are usually appointed with the knowledge of their constituents' wishes. In such cases they are in honor bound to decline appointment, unless their own views coincide with theirs. But their own views, may change after their appointment, while those of their constituents may remain unchanged. What then? If they cannot execute the known judgment of their constituents without doing violence to their own, they should resign their office.

The only exceptions to this rule are found in those sudden emergencies, in which there is not *time* for them to resign, and to have their place supplied by another, before action is demanded. The legislator must then act upon his own judgment, assuming the responsibility of doing what he honestly believes to be best for the interests which he represents. The state may subsequently view the matter as he does; he will then have saved both his conscience and his honor. Otherwise he has at least saved his conscience, and only lost a re-election to an office, which, as an honest man, he could not wish to hold.

Duties of Judges.—The judges are men appointed to *expound and apply* the law. They are not ordinarily to decide what the law *ought* to be, but what it *is*. The former question has been already settled. They must faithfully educe the exact import and design of the law, and apply it impartially to the cases on hand.

But suppose circumstances are such as to render the law in a particular case, at least in the letter of it, manifestly wrong. The duty of the judge is then one of peculiar responsibility. He is then bound to show, in a clear and convincing light, not merely what the law is, but what it ought to be. This brings up two questions, that of its morality, and that of its constitutionality. As such cases involve the highest and most responsible function of the judiciary, they are usually reserved for the highest tribunals.

The leading qualification of a judge is sound judgment, his leading duty, impartiality.

Duties of Executive Officers.—The executive officers are the men who *enforce* the laws. They include the highest functionaries of state. Autocrats, emperors, kings, presidents, governors, as well as the subordinate executive officers, are of this class. Their power to enforce law is more or less absolute, according to the nature of the government. The autocrat concentrates all the departments of government in himself. He enacts, judges, and enforces the law, according to his sovereign pleasure. But in a constitutional government, the power of the executive is more or less limited by the constitution. In a republic, the chief magistrate has no voice in enacting and judging the laws, and no power to veto their going into effect against a vote of two-thirds of the legislative houses.

But as he *recommends* the measures to be pursued and the laws which he will favor, and as any law enacted by legislators may be by him destroyed, unless it is sustained by a vote of two-thirds of their entire body, an immense power for good or for evil is lodged in his hands. All the national defences, the general improvements, the public revenues, the sources of national and individual wealth, the provisions for education and religion, even the health and life of the people, are in a great measure subject to his control. His moral responsibility is proportionably great.

In addition to the duty of recommending, in all his regular and special proclamations, the best and wisest measures, he has also most responsible duties relating to the distribution of offices, and to the vetoing and the pardoning powers.

1. *Rule of the distribution of offices.*—It is very natural that the chief magistrate should prefer to have in office his political, and, so far as practicable, his personal friends. It is very right, too, that he should duly consider those who have promoted his election. But he is bound by his oath, and by the pure principles of morality, to allow no political nor personal considerations to weigh against the great public interest, of which he is the responsible guardian. He should therefore never displace a faithful servant from office and substitute an unfaithful or less competent one in his place. While favoring his friends and

rewarding his benefactors, so far as he consistently can, he must never forget that the public welfare has the first and highest demand upon him.

2. *Rule of the vetoing power.*—It is only in extreme cases, that the executive can be justified in vetoing a law fairly enacted by both branches of the legislature. The theory of a republic is that the majority shall rule. As a member of the republic, the president or governor is but one man, and his wish should be no more regarded than that of any other man. But as a chief magistrate, having the welfare of the entire state in his eye, be may see reasons for defeating a law, which are not obvious to men in other positions.

If he is thoroughly convinced, after mature and careful deliberation, that the true welfare of the state demands the vetoing of a law submitted to his decision, he is morally bound to veto it, and abide the consequences. This is one of the few instances in a republic, in which the interests of the many are necessarily devolved upon the decision of one person. If his decision is sound, public sentiment will eventually sustain him. If it is unsound, he has at least *meant* to do right, and the public only suffer the consequences of their own doing, in appointing an incompetent ruler They must submit with good grace, and endeavor to act more wisely in future.

3. *Rule of the pardoning power.*—The chief magistrate has also the power of arresting the final *execution* of law. He may pardon or reprieve the criminal, or commute the penalty. The vetoing power goes *before* the judge, and nullifies the law itself; the pardoning power comes *after* the judge, and arrests the execution of judgment. This is a power to take from the hands of declared justice the criminal upon the scaffold, to postpone his execution, or to substitute for it some other punishment, or to pardon

him outright. It is a power to do the same in less criminal cases.

This is of course a most delicate and responsible trust. Its design is to provide for any new development of evidence or of palliating circumstances since the trial, affecting the character and deserts of the criminal. It is intended to prolong the possibility of mercy till the last moment. It has also one other design. The criminal may have rendered to the state some signal service, to which consideration is due. The proper person to remunerate this is the chief magistrate.

When he sees, in the above grounds, clear and satisfactory reasons for arresting the course of law, it is his duty to interpose mercy. But if he pardons or reprieves without such reasons, he is guilty of a breach of trust. If he allows himself to be governed by mere sympathy, or party spirit, or partiality for the criminal, or if he is influenced by a bribe to turn aside the course of justice as proclaimed and enforced by the state, he is a corrupt and treasonable magistrate. It is easy to see that when pardons and reprieves are capriciously or frequently granted, the law loses its power, justice ceases to be feared, civil courts become a mockery, and the flood-gates of crime are widely opened.

But while the executive officer should be firm and decided, he should also be kind and affectionate. He should act the *man* as well as the officer. The sheriff, during all the time in which he has the criminal in charge, and even while executing his dread final task upon the scaffold, should do all in his power for the relief and comfort of the unhappy person. This is the most effectual means to subdue his heart and bring him to repentance. It is said that General Washington sealed the death warrant of Major Andre with his tears.

III. DUTIES OF CITIZENS.

Citizens are the *subjects* of government. Men acting simply in this relation, are not to make, to judge, or to execute the laws, but to *obey* them. They may be summoned and empowered by the authorities, in special emergencies, to assist them in enforcing law, but their duty, acting as mere citizens, is obedience.

Obedience, however, *is not always a duty*. When a man believes a law to be clearly at variance with the law of God, he is not ethically bound to obey it; for his obligation to God is paramount. It is his duty in such a case to flee the country, or to abide the consequences of obeying God where he is.

If a law, for instance, should require him to worship idols, or to abjure his faith in Christ, he could not as a Christian obey it. He must, like many of the early disciples of Jesus, rather suffer martyrdom. But in all cases where the law of the land does not conflict with his conscience, he is bound to obey it. He may think it unwise and unjust; he may regard it as especially prejudicial to his own interests; and he may suppose that the majority of the people agree with him in opinion; still, so long as it remains the *law*, his duty is to obey it. On no other principle can constitutional government be sustained. It is simply a question of law or no law, of rule or anarchy; of a state of things in which life and property are protected, or a state in which they are at the mercy of a mob or a tyrant.

We are thus brought to the question respecting reform and reformation. It is asked, Must the people patiently endure the wrongs of government, and do nothing to obtain relief? No. The means of relief are mostly in their own keeping, and it is both their right and their duty to employ them. They may act either as citizens, or as the state. As citizens, they may reform; it is only as the state, that they may revolutionize.

The form of government must naturally vary according to the intelligence and virtue of the people. If, then, any citizens would influence the government, if they would render it more mild and liberal, they must seek to enlighten and reform the great body of the people. The state, adapting its government to the qualifications of the people, will be constrained to give them liberty according as they are prepared to receive it.

Revolution with a view to more liberty, must prove an inevitable failure, unless the people are *qualified* for freedom. The struggle for independence, if it results in the overthrow of government, is followed by a brief reign of anarchy, which is finally quelled by a military despotism, and succeeded by a government more despotic than the preceding. The unwise citizens who engage in the struggle, lose their labor, and perhaps also their blood, and make things worse than they were when they began to agitate.

Their way to higher liberty, then, is not in direct revolutionary measures, but in laboring to exalt the people to higher capabilities. They may thus secure from the state an increasingly liberal government, as the people are able to appreciate and sustain it, until they attain to all the essential advantages of republican institutions. Such has been the course of the subjects of the British government.

They have thus induced it gradually to extend the privileges of the people, until they have become nearly as great as are enjoyed in a republic. The opposite course has been pursued in continental states, and their governments are still as despotic as ever.

But here is a serious difficulty. The state cannot sustain free institutions without an intelligent and virtuous people, and how can the people become intelligent and virtuous without free institutions?

It is granted that without *some* advantages, no people could rise from a state of abject bondage. But none are deprived of *all* means of self-improvement. Even under the most oppressive governments, the people can do *something* towards it. This they have often done. And as their qualifications for liberty rise, it becomes the duty of the state, as I have said, to grant it to them. Whether the state politic is vested in a despot, a king, an oligarchy, or any privileged body, her duty is the same, to conform to the capabilities of the people. She is *morally bound* to give them all the liberty they are able to bear.

She should grant this, even without being requested. But if she does not, then the people should solicit it. If their request is respectful, earnest, unanimous, no state can long resist it. She may reluctate at a change, she may be unwilling to give the people a free constitution, or a freer one than they enjoy at present, but she cannot long resist the general wish of her intelligent and well-behaved subjects. In all countries the people actually rule, directly or indirectly, according to the measure of their intellectual and moral ability to do so. This is the course of nature; it is in vain for states to contend against it. It is right. The people have a natural claim to all the liberty that is best for them; that is, to all they can appreciate and protect. And this they will eventually have. State authorities may do much towards keeping the people in ignorance; but they may as well attempt to restrain the central fires of the globe, as the spirit of liberty in an intelligent and virtuous people.

Revolution may thus be usually effected by prudence

and moderation, without loss of blood. There may be desperate cases demanding desperate remedies; but there is always danger lest the people, having risen to a degree of power and obtained some privileges from the state, will become impatient, and demand more than they are qualified to sustain, and will thus defeat their end.

Moderation in such cases is usually the only safe course for the people, and therefore usually the right one. If the state does much towards making the people what they are, the people can do more towards making the state what it should be. If citizens wisely use whatever means they enjoy to rise in intellectual and moral power, they will eventually become, what all citizens should aspire to be, an essentially free, sovereign, independent people.

The course indicated above has the sanction of Jesus Christ and his disciples. They never countenanced insubordination. The institutions under which they lived and planted Christianity, were many of them very oppressive. But they nevertheless inculcated submission in all cases not conflicting with the commands of God. They abjured the sword, excepting for self-defence; teaching that "all they who take the sword shall perish by the sword;" while they pressed upon every man's conscience the duty of *immediate personal repentance and righteousness.* They have thus taught the enthralled world a lesson, to which it owes whatever of true freedom it enjoys, and which will ultimately be responded to by a jubilant pean of liberty, going up to heaven from all nations. "*If the Son make you free, ye shall be free indeed.*"

If Christianity thus discountenances insubordination and revolution by the sword, as the way to freedom, it may be said that she condemns the action of the American colonies in demanding as they did their independence of Great Britain. Not at all. They had become, in the course of Providence, a people *capable* of taking care of themselves. They were as children grown to manhood, and no longer of right subject to their father. They were virtually a state, and so the parent state should have acknowledged them.

It was then not so much a revolution as a declaration of *right*, of right insisted upon and maintained, that established the American independence. It was not a *civil war*, but a struggle in *self-defence*, by a people who were, and of right *ought* to be, a free and independent nation.

On the same general principle, we determine the nature and extent of the citizen's right to the free use of his *personal will*. We have said that every citizen has an inalienable right to the free use of his own conscience, and that it is his duty to obey its dictates. As to all other volitions, his right to exercise them turns upon the question, whether they are injurious to the state; and this the state must decide. The object of civil government is the liberty and protection of the people; but not the liberty of each person to will and to act as he pleases, nor his protection in selfish plans and gains, to the detriment of the general welfare. Such a state of things is *anarchy;* and is really the most oppressive of all tyranny.

The choices of the individual citizen must then be restrained within the limits demanded by the *general* welfare. But there are thousands of choices which every man may exercise, without molesting the rights of others. These the state should allow and protect. Thus every citizen may exercise his choice in regard to his profession or trade, his house, living, equipage, place of residence, wife, society, social and domestic habits, &c., &c.; and so long as he does not interfere with the rights of others, the state must allow and protect him in such choices.

But if he chooses to fence in the highway, or obstruct a railroad, or take his neighbor's property, or marry another's wife, or place a nuisance in the neighborhood, or vend poisons in a way to endanger life, &c., the state must forbid him. The liberty and welfare of the people demand this restraint upon the individual, and every citizen should cheerfully submit to it.

The citizen is justly bound to loyalty, not only of conduct, but of *intention*. The same act, performed by the same muscles and instruments, would be *murder* when prompted by one intention, and *benevolence* when prompted by another. The assassin, who intentionally kills, and the surgeon who kindly intends to prolong life, may each be the occasion of death. The one is a humane person, and the other a murderer, purely because of their different intentions.

Hence, in the eye of the state, as well as in the eye of God, a man is to be judged with reference to his *intention*. But there is an important difference between the cases in the following respects. First, the methods are different of ascertaining what the intention *is*. The state must judge of it by *evidence;* but "God looketh on the *heart*." Secondly, the state may never inquire whether the intention is prompted by prudence, or conscience, or loyalty to God; whether it is merely virtuous, or moral, or also religious; but simply whether it is *true to her*. With the question whether a man is conscientious and religious the state has nothing to do, but with this very question the divine government has *every thing* to do.

Civil government is too clumsy an instrument to touch all the secret springs of action, nor has the state eyes to see them. She must not, therefore, attempt to enforce moral rectitude as judged by God; she must not go behind the intentions of man, as they relate to her own interests. All she may demand is, that the conduct of her subjects indicate loyalty of purpose towards *her*, leaving their duties to the divine government to a higher tribunal.

Every good citizen, whatever may be his particular moral and religious views, will thus readily see what the state justly requires of him, and will render cheerful obedience to its demands.

CHAPTER IX.

SOCIAL DUTIES.

We have, in a previous part of the volume, distinguished between prudential and moral virtue, the former springing from mere regard to interest, the latter from conscientious regard to duty. Thus President Edwards, adopting the law epitomized by Christ as the rule of duty, defines it as *love to being in general.* This singular definition of universal benevolence is designed to include our obligation to God, to ourselves, and to all other beings, modified by the nature and circumstances of each being, and our particular relation to him.

We have seen that this law is not an arbitrary enactment, but an embodiment of the essential elements of moral right. Its finality, righteousness, and benevolence, are found in the finality, righteousness, and harmonious blending of its elements, and its consequent tendency to promote the highest moral excellence and blessedness of the universe. A beam of light from the sun is perfectly white, because it has the due blending of all the elementary rays. Remove one or more of them, and it ceases to be perfectly white; it assumes a fiery, lurid, or sickly hue, according as one or another ray is wanting. So the law of God is benevolent, in a strictly moral view, only because it has the due blending of all the elements of moral virtue. Remove from it justice, or veracity, or any of its elements, and it ceases to be righteous; and in ceasing to be righteous, it of necessity ceases to be morally benevolent. Did not the law require us to be just, truthful, &c., as well as merciful, it would not be a law of true moral benevolence, for it would not tend to the highest *welfare* of the moral universe.

Thus the justice of God, in a moral view, is as benevolent as his mercy. "GOD IS LOVE." His moral attributes are the elements of essential excellence harmoniously blended, as proclaimed in his law of perfect and boundless moral benevolence. Now what he is in his sphere, we ought to be in ours. Some things are proper to him which are not so to us, and some things are proper to us which are not so to him, but both he and we are all morally bound by the same law of universal love.

The duties of *all* relations are in some sense social, but as those which we have examined have specific names, those of the more general relations now to be noticed, we conveniently designate by the general term *social duties.* They are the relations of master and servant, of teacher and pupil, of neighbors, of fellow-citizens, and of fellow-men. These are all subject to the same law of benevolence which rules the others. "Thou shalt love thy *neighbor* as thyself;" not merely thy wife, husband, child, parent, cousin, but thy fellow-being in every possible relation. Let us first examine the several dispositions or modifications of benevolence enjoined by this law in the relations which remain to be noticed, and then the particular duties which they suggest.

COURTESY.—This is a disposition to treat others with

due respect. Some respect is due to all, for all partake of our common humanity. No rank nor dignity exonerates a person from the duty of being courteous to those beneath him. The respect shown should be appropriate to its object, but always cordial and sincere. This tends to prevent the envy and scorn which are apt to arise between the different classes of society. It teaches every person to know his place, and to respect himself in it, while it teaches him also to know the place of others, and to regard them with the same consideration that he claims for himself.

It is related of Washington, that when a man asked him why he returned a bow to a negro, his reply was, "Do you think I would be outdone in courtesy by a negro?" It is characteristic of great minds to be considerate of those in the humbler walks. This virtue, so indispensable in courts and all popular assemblies, is scarcely less so in ordinary intercourse. A discourteous person, whether in the family, the drawing-room, the shop, the street, the school, the exchange, or in legislative bodies, is scarcely less an enemy to himself than a plague and torment to others. "*Be courteous.*"

KINDNESS.—This is an advance on courtesy. Courtesy *respects;* kindness *benefits.* The word indicates a regard to the welfare of human *kind.* We ought to be kind to *all*, even to the evil and unthankful. We thus become "children of our Father which is in heaven; for he maketh his sun to rise on the evil and on the good, and sendeth rain on the just and on the unjust." To be kind to those only who do us good, is no virtue; it answers no demand of the moral law.

True kindness is also *self-sacrificing.* That man has no claim to this virtue who submits to no inconvenience and self-denial for the sake of doing a favor to others. It is moreover *impartial.* Benefits conferred upon favorites, merely because they are favorites, do not proceed from pure kindness, but from a lower motive.

Forbearance.—This is nearly the same as long-suffering. It is endurance of others' faults. We are ever exposed to provocation from the unfaithfulness, the stupidity, and the passions of men. Hence forbearance is a virtue that should be ever on hand. A hasty spirit is irrational and foolish. "Be not hasty in thy spirit to be angry; for anger resteth in the bosom of fools."

The forbearance of God is a lesson to us. We continually offend him, yet he forbears. Were he quick to requite, we should be suddenly consumed. But days, months, years roll along; we continue to offend him, and still he forbears. There is doubtless a limit beyond which forbearance ceases to be a virtue, but that limit is not reached until the resources of kindness have failed. If the "riches of kindness and forbearance" are fatally despised, retribution must follow. But it should be with us a retribution mingled with compassion, not with revenge.

"Avenge not yourselves, but rather give place unto wrath; for it is written, Vengeance is mine, I will repay, saith the Lord. Therefore, if thine enemy hunger, feed him; if he thirst, give him drink; for in so doing thou shalt heap coals of fire on his head. Be not overcome of evil, but overcome evil with good." Leaving "vengeance" to a higher power, it is ours to pity and compassionate, even when compelled to punish.

Charity.—This is good will to all men. It is a generic, all-pervading grace. It is the "greatest;" that is, the most comprehensive of all. It disposes us to put a favorable construction upon the conduct of others, and never to slander them. It rejoices in their prosperity, magnifies their virtues, and apologizes for their faults. It gives no indulgence to evil reports against a neighbor; and if compelled by resistless evidence to believe them, makes the least of them possible. It disposes one to be as tender of another's good name as of his own. It "suffereth long and is kind, envieth not, vaunteth not itself, is not puffed up, doth not behave itself unseemly. Charity seeketh not her own, is not easily provoked, thinketh no evil; rejoiceth not in iniquity, but rejoiceth in the truth; believeth all things, hopeth all things, and never faileth." The universal prevalence of this "greatest" of virtues would turn back the tide of human woes, and go far towards restoring paradise.

Hospitality.—This is a disposition to open the home and spread the table to our fellow-beings. It is to be exercised with discretion, but never with stint or grudge. Few virtues more enliven the affections and bless the intercourse of social life than this. They who are "given to hospitality" and who "use hospitality one to another, without grudging," seldom fail to secure friends and to contribute to human happiness.

Hospitality is often more sincere and abundant in new countries, or those thinly inhabited, than in more crowded districts. This may be because there is more demand for it. Under such circumstances, people are more dependent upon each other, and hence they more highly appreciate attentions. In large towns hospitality often degenerates to cold formality, and sometimes quite disappears. But mankind are still essentially the same under all circumstances; and this virtue is really as needful in town as in country, to awaken social and kindly affections, and make neighbors happy in each other.

Generosity.—This is a disposition to give liberally to worthy objects. Indiscriminate and thoughtless giving is not a virtue. It is prodigality. But a truly discriminating generosity is a noble, a divine virtue. It is our duty to be just before we are generous; it is no less our duty to be generous after we have been just.

The state can never afford to be generous; for she is a public steward, and, therefore, if generous to some must be unjust to others. But it is not so with individuals. Of the state *all* is due to justice. What are sometimes called acts of state generosity, are only acts of justice to deserving persons. But individuals may pay all their debts, and yet have remaining the means with which to be generous. What we call public spirit, is generosity directed to public objects. The man of generous public spirit is a benefactor to the neighborhood, the town, the nation. Improvements, reforms, schools, churches, all the means and appliances of human culture and happiness, feel the benign influence of his benefactions and example.

FAITHFULNESS.—This is a disposition *faithfully to fulfil promises.* A promise may be mutual and equally binding on both sides. A failure on one side then absolves the obligation on the other. This is true of the marriage covenant, and of most business engagements. If the husband or wife is proved to have been unfaithful, the other party is absolved from the covenant. If one of the parties in a business transaction is found guilty of fraud, or of a serious violation of promise, connected with the transaction, the other party is released from his obligation.

But there are *unconditional* promises, or promises only on one side, on which questions of duty are raised. Should all such promises be kept? The question is not whether it was right to *make* the promise, but whether, having made it, the party is bound to keep it.

The following are cases in which the spirit of faithfulness does not make the literal promise obligatory:

1. A promise to do a *wrong act*, is not obligatory. A man under a bad impulse, may promise to do a wrong action, and may repent of it before the time for the action arrives. His duty is plain.

2. An unfair promise extorted by *threat*, is not binding. When a person, for instance, is forced to an unreasonable promise by a threat to take his life or property, or to inflict any serious damage upon himself or his family, he does not promise freely, and is not bound by his promise.

But this does not imply that *all* promises made under constraint may be disregarded. Promises of *amendment* may be obtained from the guilty by threat and punishment, and are as binding as those made with the highest freedom of choice. For they are promises to do what *ought* to be done, whether the promises are unconstrained or forced, or whether the guilty persons do not promise at all. Such are the promises made under just punishments and threatenings inflicted by magistrates, parents, and teachers.

3. Promises obtained *deceitfully*, are not binding. If a man purchases a horse, or farm, or any article of merchandise, under false representations, promising to pay for the same, on discovering the deception he is released from his promise. The purchased property reverts to the seller.

4. General promises unexpectedly and wickedly *applied*, are not binding. Such was the promise of Herod to the daughter of Herodias.

During the first war with England, some of the Stockbridge Indians obtained a solemn promise from a woman of a white settlement, that she would not reveal a secret of which they were about to put her in possession. The secret was, that on a certain night they were coming to murder all the families in the settlement, and as she had shown them some favors, they wished her to leave the place before that time to save her own life. Believing it to be her duty to keep her promise, she left the settlement without revealing the secret. The Indians came on the proposed night, as they had purposed, and tomahawked the families while asleep in their beds. The woman kept her promise, but did not do her duty. It was right to obey her conscience, but wrong not to have better enlightened it. In keeping such a promise she was *conscientiously unreasonable.*

The law of faithfulness demands, then, that the greatest caution and integrity of purpose be exercised in *making* promises, and that all promises justly made for lawful ends be *faithfully fulfilled.*

Having thus indicated the most important moral virtues or dispositions to be exercised in social life, I proceed to notice the particular duties which they enjoin in the various social relations.

DUTIES OF MASTER AND SERVANT.

The relation of master and servant, in some form, has existed from a very early period, and their respective duties are enjoined in the Bible. The rightfulness of the relation, or whether it ought to exist, depends upon circumstances. No objection can be raised against voluntary servitude; as when a sailor places himself under a ship-master. The question respects only *involuntary* servitude. That it is right for a man to bring unoffending fellow-beings, who are under no obligations to him, into a state of bondage, can never be pretended.

Still there are circumstances which make it right to exact involuntary service. When a man has, by the violation of law, forfeited claim to liberty, the state may take it from him and compel him to labor, as in her prisons, in compensation for the expense to which he subjects her. But no person has a just right to the involuntary service of another, unless he has a fair demand upon him which can be met in no other way. The right is then limited by the demand. Sustaining the relation of master is not *per se* immoral, but it is immoral to sustain it for the mere benefit of the master and to the injury of the servant. The crime does not lie in the master's power or authority, but in his abuse of it. There are limits within which the authority of the master may be as lawful as that of the parent. Nor are these limits doubtful. Lawful authority is power over those who are in circumstances of dependence, is limited by the demands of their condition, and is to be exercised with as much regard to their welfare as to that of the person in authority. It is only as the man in authority observes this rule, that he loves his dependent fellow-being as himself.

Our limits forbid an extensive discussion of this important subject; I would therefore submit the following summary of what seems to be most essential, in a purely ethical view.

1. To bring into bondage unoffending fellow-beings under no obligations to us, is a crime condemned by every principle of justice and humanity. Hence the criminality of the slave-trade.

2. Laws conferring authority upon masters with reference to their benefit, which do not equally regard the benefit of the slave, are to be held in the same light of criminality with the slave-trade itself.

3. No blame attaches to those who, placed in the relation of masters by causes over which they had no control, or by motives benevolent on their part, regulate the relation by the demands of justice and humanity.

4. As the relation is that of power over feebleness and of authority over dependence, those with whom the responsible power and authority are intrusted, should be especially careful to take no advantage of the feebleness and dependence submitted to their guardianship.

5. As liberty is a most precious boon to all qualified to appreciate and use it, those in possession of it should do what they consistently can to secure the final and complete emancipation of all that are in bondage.

The rules of duty between master and servant are obvious and general, applying mostly to all the relations of this nature, whether the service be voluntary or involuntary.

DUTIES OF MASTERS.—The duties of masters are comprehensively the following:

1. They should be *kind and forbearing* to their servants. They should be careful not to abuse their power over them. They should make due allowance for their ignorance, their infirmities, the peculiar trials of their condition, and thus do for them as they themselves should wish to be done by in like circumstances.

2. They should *treat them as rational and accountable beings.* In this view they should, when practicable, explain their duty, expostulate with them, and secure their obedience by reasonable motives. They should allow them entire freedom of conscience, and opportunity for religious worship and edification.

3. They should *give them a just reward for their service.* They should take no advantage of their power to exact more than is due. If the master has a claim upon the servant, he should have the amount fairly adjusted, allow the servant opportunity to cancel it, and be as conscientiously exact and just in his dealings with him, as he ought to be with any other person. It is as wrong to deprive the *servant* of his due, as to "oppress the *hireling*

in his wages," or to "turn aside the *stranger* from his rights." "Masters, give unto your *servants* that which is *just* and *equal*, knowing that ye also have a master in heaven."

DUTIES OF SERVANTS.—The duties of servants are briefly these:

1. They should *espouse the interest of their masters.* They should regard it as they would their own. Whether they traffic, labor, build, cook, wait, or in any other way serve, they should husband his resources, allow no waste, do their work faithfully, and ever act with hearty reference to his welfare. "It is required in a steward, that a man be found *faithful.*"

2. They should *never require the vigilance of their master's eye.* A higher motive should always actuate them, a regard to the eye of God. They should be as faithful in the absence as in the presence of their master; for his presence imposes no new obligation. "Not with *eye-service*, as men-pleasers, but in singleness of heart, fearing God. And whatsoever ye do, do it heartily, *as to the Lord, and not to man.*"

3. They should *obey their masters.* They must not demand a reason, nor take it upon themselves to decide what ought to be done. The ruling mind may often see reasons which they cannot see. It may be sometimes the master's duty to explain, but it is their duty to obey, whether he explains or not, unless he requires them to disobey God.

"Servants, *obey in all things* your masters according to the flesh." "Be obedient to them that are your masters according to the flesh, with fear and trembling, in singleness of your heart as unto Christ. With good will doing service, as to the Lord, and not to man, knowing that whatsoever good thing any man doeth, the same shall he receive of the Lord, *whether he be bond or free.*" "Exhort servants to be *obedient* to their own masters, and to please them well in all things, not *answering again*, not purloining, but showing *all good fidelity;* that they may adorn the doctrine of God our Saviour in all things."

DUTIES OF TEACHERS AND PUPILS.

Few relations are more delicate and responsible than that of teacher and pupil. The most precious of all human interests are intrusted to it. The teacher's employers are engaged in absorbing pursuits; he must therefore be himself mostly his own judge of both his duty and fidelity. He should, then, exercise the most severe and exacting conscientiousness in the discharge of his trust; while the pupil, on the other hand, is equally bound to do all in his power to accomplish the important object of this relation.

DUTIES OF TEACHERS.—The duties of a teacher are chiefly the following:

1. He should thoroughly *qualify* himself for his task. It is not enough to satisfy his committee or employers. A more important satisfaction is due to his own conscience. In bringing his mind to bear upon those of his pupils, he realizes defects which no other person can see. His education may be incomplete, or there may have been recent discoveries or improvements demanding his constant study. He should never come before his class but with his mind well prepared for his work.

2. He should maintain *uniform and impartial discipline.* In order to this, he must control his own temper. His government should be uniform, like that of Him who rolls the planets and rules the day in the same steady course, that all may know what to expect. It should be

impartial and parental, adopting the true welfare of every pupil, and blending in itself both the paternal and the maternal government. If resort must be had to the rod, it should be with the reluctance of a parent's heart. But if imperiously demanded, no false tenderness, no mawkish kindness, may withhold it. "Foolishness is bound in the heart of a child, but the *rod of correction* will drive it far from him." "*Chasten thy son* while there is hope, and let not thy soul spare for his crying."

3. His *instruction should be thorough.* From the first rudiments upward, this rule should never be relaxed. There is often great temptation to relax it, but it cannot be done but by a positive moral wrong to both child and parent. Superficial habits of study, early or late acquired, influence the entire character, and enter into the whole field of subsequent life. Many a man's success in life has been defeated by wrong culture at school. Education should duly respect the physical, intellectual, and moral culture, adapting itself to the age, health, capacity, and circumstances of the pupil, so as to make the most of the means enjoyed to develope a healthy, symmetrical, and happy manhood.

Duties of Pupils.—The pupil has his duties as well as the teacher. He ought to consider the expense and self-sacrifice of his parents, and the labor and anxiety of teachers, for his education, and gratefully to respond to them with his corresponding endeavors. He should also consider that the golden days which are to decide his destiny will soon pass away, and that if he neglects to improve them he will have to reflect upon his folly, as long as he lives, with bitter and unavailing regret.

1. He should render *cordial and prompt obedience* to his teachers. The school or college is a state, whose government is vested in its teachers; and when the pupil

enters it, he is morally bound by its rules, as truly as the citizen is bound by the laws of his country. Hence in both cases alike, obedience is right and honorable, and disobedience is immoral and base.

The pupil, like the good citizen, should not only himself obey, but he should diffuse the spirit of obedience. If he thinks a rule unreasonable, he may take suitable means to have it altered or repealed, but so long as it remains, he must obey it. Discipline can be maintained on no other principle. The pupil who disregards it, however confident at the time of being in the right, is sure to find in the event painful evidence that he was in the wrong.

2. He should *industriously apply himself to his studies.* Unless he does so, the most earnest endeavors of his teachers will be in vain. No genius can supply the demand for effort. The pupil who relies upon the inspiration of genius, while neglecting mental discipline, is doomed to ultimate failure. The vain conceit of such an inspiration is an *ignis fatuus*, that has lured many a victim from the path of industry and honor into the way of indolence and disgrace.

No man ever attained to real greatness without severe and protracted industry. This is especially true of *intellectual* greatness. Genius may do much, but application must do more, or the pupil will never rise to eminence. Acting with this view, he will make a modest estimate of his talents and attainments ; he will be docile to learn and earnest to apply himself ; and the higher he rises, the brighter he will shine in the grace of humility, the crowning glory of all excellence.

3. He should be *courteous and kind to his fellow-students.* The happiness and prosperity of any literary institution depend much upon the mutual feeling and inter-

course among its members. If the spirit of fraternal courtesy prevails, government is easy and teaching delightful. The mind does not thrive amidst a tempest of evil passions, but where the feelings are composed and kind.

And nowhere are ill-will and discourtesy more out of place than in a literary institution, where the chafings and frauds of business, the clamor of politics, the noisy and vulgar strifes for gain, cannot enter; where chosen and favored youth, retired from the world, and gathered around the same altar, are unitedly engaged in the calm, holy, and ennobling pursuit of knowledge. Such a place should be eminently a school of good manners; of kind, generous, chivalrous feelings; of all the social virtues. Every pupil is morally bound to do his part towards making it such.

DUTIES OF NEIGHBORS.

A large portion of the happiness of individuals and of families depends upon their doing the duties of good neighborhood. To be a good *neighbor* is no mean virtue. Many a man has attained to honorable fame abroad, who is not so well spoken of at home. Even the rulers and judges of the land are most in honor, only as they are embalmed in the affectionate esteem of their neighbors. To be a good neighbor, is really a higher honor than to bear the highest office or the proudest title.

The duties to which I refer involve all the cardinal virtues, but the leading ones here demanded are kindness, charity, and courtesy. Where neighbors are mutually *kind*, sympathizing in each other's trials, and ministering to each other's wants; where they exercise that *charity* which "beareth all things," "thinketh no evil," and silences the tongue of slander; and where they mutually practise that *courtesy* which softens, sweetens, and refines social intercourse, *there* is good neighborhood.

DUTIES OF FELLOW-CITIZENS.

The love of fellow-citizens is to some extent a natural affection. For the same reason that we have a peculiar affection for the members of our own family, we have one for the members of our own state. We are not conscious of it, perhaps, while dwelling among them; neither are we fully so of the family affection, while remaining at home; but let us be called away to foreign lands, and dwell among those of a "strange speech," and with what conscious satisfaction do we greet a fellow-countryman.

As this feeling exists in nature, and must have been implanted for some wise end, we infer that fellow-citizens, as such, owe certain peculiar *duties* to each other.

1. They should cherish a *fellow-affection as members of the same state.* They should love each other as children of the same country, as heirs of the same national inheritance, as bound together in a great common cause, and animated by a great common hope. They should regard each other as compatriots. Their safety, their repose, their prosperity, and even their national existence, are their common interest, and, unless they are mutually faithful in protecting it, will be inevitably lost.

The story of the Scythian king and the rods is as applicable to nations as to families. Those animating words, *fellow-citizens!* which have so often thrilled the hearts of compatriots in their united struggles for defence and liberty, should never lose their power over them.

2. They should *befriend and protect each other when abroad.* Members of the same state, they should every where cherish the national feeling. This is sometimes

even more important abroad than at home, for they are there more dependent upon each other, because few in number and among a strange people.

But they may never clan together for the purpose of resisting the laws of the state in which they travel or reside. While enjoying the protection of a state they are bound to obey its laws, and to encourage others to do the same. Neither may they, after becoming permanent members of another state, so retain their national partialities as to sympathize together in concerted efforts for a change of institutions. Such conduct is disorderly and treasonable.

They are bound to merge their sympathies into the adopted state, and to become in good faith part and parcel of it. They should not at first lead, but follow; they should not dictate, but obey; as all other good citizens do. Such should be the conduct of emigrants to this country, and of Americans who become the subjects of foreign states. If foreigners do not like the state which they have chosen to adopt, they should leave it, or passively endure what they do not like and cannot lawfully alter.

3. They should usually *marry with each other in preference to foreign alliances.* A union of parties from different nations not widely different, after becoming one in state, is not always objectionable; but beyond this it becomes a "strange" alliance, and seldom results happily. There is usually more of romance and sorrow than of love and bliss in such unnatural marriages. Similarity of person, of education, of habit, of taste, and of religious faith, are important to a rational and permanent union of the wedded parties.

All the above rules were sacredly enjoined by God upon the Hebrew nation, as means of its prosperity; and although some reasons for them may have then existed which are not now in full force, the general reasons are still much the same. Mankind, nations, and the means of national and individual prosperity, are essentially the same in all ages.

DUTIES OF FELLOW-MEN.

These are the duties we owe to every individual of the human race, *because he is our fellow-being.* He is a partaker with us in a common humanity; he has the same rational and accountable nature, has similar hopes and trials, is amenable at the same ultimate tribunal, has been redeemed by the same blood, and is passing on with us to the same grave and the same eternity. These facts bring him near to us, rendering him what the Scriptures call our "neighbor." With the same view they also call him our "brother." What are the duties we owe him as such?

Wherever we meet him, at home or abroad, we ought to do by him as we would have others do by us in like circumstances. We should respect his interests, defend his rights, seek his happiness, and do him all the good in our power, consistently with justice to ourselves and to those immediately dependent upon us. "*All things whatsoever ye would that men should do to you, do ye even so to them, for this is the law and the prophets.*"

Nor is it merely those whom we meet, to whom we owe this debt of humanity. Our "neighbor" may not be as the man going to Jericho, so kindly relieved by the good Samaritan, who, "*as he journeyed, came where he was.*" Millions to whom we owe this debt we shall never see. We shall not journey where they are, nor will they come to us. Still every man of them is our *neighbor*, our *brother*, and we must pay him a neighbor's and a brother's debt. For this end, by the sacred love we bear, or ought to bear, to our race, we are bound to do what we can, not only for the welfare of those immediately about us, but also to diffuse the blessings of education, of free institutions, of Christianity, of temporal welfare and immortal hope, over the whole world.

CONCLUSION.

SUCH, then, are the duties of man; for these he was made. And he should never forget, that, as he is the subject of a righteous moral government, all his duties are also privileges. His being in a fallen state, and thus disinclined to them, does not absolve his obligation, nor, if he will accept the proffered grace of the Gospel, his ability to perform them. To recover his spiritual lapse, by accepting this grace; to repent of his departure from God, and to return to his love and service; to trust in Christ alone for "redemption through his blood, the forgiveness of sins;" and thus to go forth, "in newness of spirit," to the duties which we have considered; is to fulfil his obligation as a rational being, and thus pursue the narrow way to eternal life. It is a way of self-denial, of conflict with temptation, of "patient continuance in well-doing," against the enticements of "the lust of the flesh, and the lust of the eye, and the pride of life;" but it is not all self-denial, conflict, and patience: incipient rewards, more valuable than mines of gold, succeed every good endeavor, and are finally consummated in "a far more exceeding and eternal weight of glory."

And there is no other way, however pleasant and inviting its beginning, that does not lead to disappointment and ruin. So sure as man exists, he is undone by refusing this for any other course. For the principles which we have examined are taught, as we have seen, both by nature and revelation; they challenge the severest scrutiny; they are as true and abiding as the throne of God. To know and obey them is the highest good.

To shine in wealth, to dwell in palaces, to fare sumptuously every day; to have honors and titles, or to command the world's admiration for illustrious genius or intellectual attainments, is all earthly and fleeting. These are for a day, and all is gone! "For all that is in the world, the lust of the flesh, and the lust of the eyes, and the pride of life, is not of the Father, but is of the world. And the world passeth away, and the lust thereof; *but he that doeth the will of God abideth for ever.*"

The struggles and the pride of wealth, the lusts of pleasure, the triumphs of ambition, the pursuits of knowledge, will soon be over. Time sweeps along, and bears them all with it into everlasting oblivion. But a character formed upon the principles which we have examined, reposing firmly in the provisions of the Gospel, and rising heavenward in a life of supreme and unwearying devotion to life's great end, will abide and shine, amidst the splendors of eternity, when the universe is reduced to ashes.

All passeth away, but God liveth aye,
And changeth in naught; eternal His thought,
His Word and His Will are steadfast and sure;
His Truth and His Love will never decay,
They heal the sad heart of its deadliest smart,
And give it the life that will ever endure.

THE END.

www.ingramcontent.com/pod-product-compliance
Lightning Source LLC
LaVergne TN
LVHW020923110826
845150LV00004B/748

* 9 7 8 1 4 2 5 5 5 3 8 7 6 *